Principles of

Data Structures

Using C and C++

Principles of
Data Structures
Using C and C++

Vinu V Das
M.E.S. College of Engineering
Kuttippuram, Kerala, India.

PUBLISHING FOR ONE WORLD

NEW AGE INTERNATIONAL (P) LIMITED, PUBLISHERS
New Delhi • Bangalore • Chennai • Cochin • Guwahati • Hyderabad
Jalandhar • Kolkata • Lucknow • Mumbai • Ranchi
Visit us at **www.newagepublishers.com**

Published by New Age International (P) Ltd., Publishers
First Edition: 2006
Reprint: 2016

GLOBAL OFFICES

- **New Delhi** **NEW AGE INTERNATIONAL (P) LIMITED, PUBLISHERS**
  7/30 A, Daryaganj, New Delhi-110002, (INDIA)
  Tel.: (011) 23253771, 23253472, **Telefax:** 23267437, 43551305
  E-mail: contactus@newagepublishers.com • Visit us at www.newagepublishers.com
- **London** **NEW AGE INTERNATIONAL (UK) LTD.**
  27 Old Gloucester Street, London, WC1N 3AX, UK
  E-mail: info@newacademicscience.co.uk • Visit us at www.newacademicscience.co.uk
- **Nairobi** **NEW AGE GOLDEN (EAST AFRICA) LTD.**
  Ground Floor, Westlands Arcade, Chiromo Road (Next to Naivas Supermarket), Westlands, Nairobi, KENYA
  Tel.: 00-254-713848772, 00-254-725700286
  E-mail: kenya@newagepublishers.com

BRANCHES

- **Bangalore** 37/10, 8th Cross (Near Hanuman Temple), Azad Nagar, Chamarajpet, Bangalore- 560 018
  Tel.: (080) 26756823, **Telefax:** 26756820, **E-mail: bangalore@newagepublishers.com**
- **Chennai** 26, Damodaran Street, T. Nagar, Chennai-600 017, **Tel.:** (044) 24353401, **Telefax:** 24351463
  E-mail: chennai@newagepublishers.com
- **Cochin** CC-39/1016, Carrier Station Road, Ernakulam South, Cochin-682 016, **Tel.:** (0484) 2377303, **Telefax:** 4051304
  E-mail: cochin@newagepublishers.com
- **Guwahati** Hemsen Complex, Mohd. Shah Road, Paltan Bazar, Near Starline Hotel, Guwahati-781 008,
  Tel.: (0361) 2513881**, Telefax:** 2543669, **E-mail: guwahati@newagepublishers.com**
- **Hyderabad** 105, 1st Floor, Madhiray Kaveri Tower, 3-2-19, Azam Jahi Road, Near Kumar Theater, Nimboliadda Kachiguda, Hyderabad-500 027, **Tel.:** (040) 24652456, **Telefax:** 24652457
  E-mail: hyderabad@newagepublishers.com
- **Kolkata** RDB Chambers (Formerly Lotus Cinema) 106A, 1st Floor, S N Banerjee Road, Kolkata-700 014
  Tel.: (033) 22273773, **Telefax:** 22275247, **E-mail: kolkata@newagepublishers.com**
- **Lucknow** 16-A, Jopling Road, Lucknow-226 001, **Tel.:** (0522) 2209578, 4045297, **Telefax:** 2204098
  E-mail: lucknow@newagepublishers.com
- **Mumbai** 142C, Victor House, Ground Floor, N.M. Joshi Marg, Lower Parel, Mumbai-400 013
  Tel.: (022) 24927869, **Telefax:** 24915415, **E-mail: mumbai@newagepublishers.com**
- **New Delhi** 22, Golden House, Daryaganj, New Delhi-110 002, **Tel.:** (011) 23262368, 23262370, **Telefax:** 43551305
  E-mail: sales@newagepublishers.com

ISBN: 978-81-224-1858-3
₹ 375.00
C-16-07-9541

Printed in India at Kanishik Printing Press, Delhi.
Typeset at Monu Printers, Delhi.

NEW AGE INTERNATIONAL (P) LIMITED, PUBLISHERS
7/30 A, Daryaganj, New Delhi-110002
Visit us at **www.newagepublishers.com**
(CIN: U74899DL1966PTC004618)

To my father, G. Valsala Das,
and mother, S. Usha Kumari

PREFACE

It gives me immense pleasure in presenting the first edition of the book-Principles of DATA STRUCTURES Using C and C++ which is a unique text valuable for professionals that covers both theoretical and practical aspects of the data structures.

The study of data structures is an essential subject of every under graduate and graduate programs related to computer science. A thorough understanding of the basics of this subject is inevitable for efficient programming. This book covers all the fundamental topics to give a better understanding about the subject. This book is written in accordance with the revised syllabus for BTech/BE (both Computer Science and Electronics branches) and MCA students of Kerala University, MG University, Calicut University, CUSAT Cochin (deemed) University, NIT Calicut (deemed) University, Anna University, UP Technical University, Amritha Viswa (deemed) Vidyapeeth, Karunya (deemed) University, Pune University, Bangalore University and Rajasthan Vidyapeeth (deemed) University. Moreover this book covers almost all the topics of the other Indian and International Universities where this subject is there in their under graduate and graduate programs.

While writing the book, I have always considered the examination requirements of the students and various difficulties and troubles, which they face, while studying the subject.

All effort is made to cover the topics in the simplest possible way without loosing its qualities. Almost five hundred questions from various university question papers have been included in this book. In short, I earnestly hope that the book will earn the appreciation of the teachers and students alike.

Although I have tried to check mistakes and misprints, yet it is difficult to claim perfection. Any suggestions for the improvement of any topics, when brought to my notice, will be thankfully acknowledged and will be incorporated in the next edition.

Vinu V Das

ACKNOWLEDGEMENT

I praise and give thanks to the Almighty Living Holy God, without His grace nothing is possible for any one.

I take this opportunity to thank everyone, especially my friends and students who have inspired me to write and complete this book. I am indebted to the many published works available on the subject, which have helped me in the preparation of the manuscript.

I express my sincere thanks to Mr. Sreelal, Mr. Rajesh, Mr. Ajith and others for digitalizing the manuscript.

I am also thankful to the following Indian Universities and examination bodies, whose examination papers have been included in the text as self-review questions. Moreover, their syllabus has been kept in view while writing this treatise.

Kerala University
Calicut University
NIT, Calicut
UP Technical University
Karunya University
Pune University
Anna University
Mahatma Gandhi University
CUSAT, Kochi
Amritha Viswa Vidyapeeth
Rajasthan Vidyapeeth
Bangalore University

Vinu V Das

CONTENTS

1 Programming Methodologies

Programming methodologies deal with different methods of designing programs. This will teach you how to program efficiently. This book restricts itself to the basics of programming in C and C++, by assuming that you are familiar with the syntax of C and C++ and can write, debug and run programs in C and C++. Discussions in this chapter outline the importance of structuring the programs, not only the data pertaining to the solution of a problem but also the programs that operates on the data.

Data is the basic entity or fact that is used in calculation or manipulation process. There are two types of data such as numerical and alphanumerical data. Integer and floating-point numbers are of numerical data type and strings are of alphanumeric data type. Data may be single or a set of values, and it is to be organized in a particular fashion. This organization or structuring of data will have profound impact on the efficiency of the program.

1.1. AN INTRODUCTION TO DATA STRUCTURE

Data structure is the structural representation of logical relationships between elements of data. In other words a data structure is a way of organizing data items by considering its relationship to each other.

Data structure mainly specifies the structured organization of data, by providing accessing methods with correct degree of associativity. Data structure affects the design of both the structural and functional aspects of a program.

Algorithm + Data Structure = Program

Data structures are the building blocks of a program; here the selection of a particular data structure will help the programmer to design more efficient programs as the complexity and volume of the problems solved by the computer is steadily increasing day by day. The programmers have to strive hard to solve these problems. If the problem is analyzed and divided into sub problems, the task will be much easier *i.e.*, divide, conquer and combine.

A complex problem usually cannot be divided and programmed by set of modules unless its solution is structured or organized. This is because when we divide the big problems into sub problems, these sub problems will be programmed by different programmers or group of programmers. But all the programmers should follow a standard structural method so as to make easy and efficient integration of these modules. Such type of hierarchical structuring of program modules and sub modules should not only reduce the complexity and control the flow of program statements but also promote the proper structuring of information. By choosing a particular structure (or data structure) for the data items, certain data items become friends while others loses its relations.

The representation of a particular data structure in the memory of a computer is called a storage structure. That is, a data structure should be represented in such a way that it utilizes maximum efficiency. The data structure can be represented in both main and auxiliary memory of the computer. A storage structure representation in auxiliary memory is often called a file structure.

It is clear from the above discussion that the data structure and the operations on organized data items can integrally solve the problem using a computer

Data structure = Organized data + Operations

1.2. ALGORITHM

Algorithm is a step-by-step finite sequence of instruction, to solve a well-defined computational problem.

That is, in practice to solve any complex real life problems; first we have to define the problems. Second step is to design the algorithm to solve that problem.

Writing and executing programs and then optimizing them may be effective for small programs. Optimization of a program is directly concerned with algorithm design. But for a large program, each part of the program must be well organized before writing the program. There are few steps of refinement involved when a problem is converted to program; this method is called *stepwise refinement method.* There are two approaches for algorithm design; they are *top-down* and *bottom-up* algorithm design.

1.3. STEPWISE REFINEMENT TECHNIQUES

We can write an informal algorithm, if we have an appropriate mathematical model for a problem. The initial version of the algorithm will contain general statements, *i.e.*,; informal instructions. Then we convert this informal algorithm to formal algorithm, that is, more definite instructions by applying any programming language syntax and semantics partially. Finally a program can be developed by converting the formal algorithm by a programming language manual.

From the above discussion we have understood that there are several steps to reach a program from a mathematical model. In every step there is a refinement (or conversion). That is to convert an informal algorithm to a program, we must go through several stages of formalization until we arrive at a program — whose meaning is formally defined by a programming language manual — is called stepwise refinement techniques.

There are three steps in refinement process, which is illustrated in Fig. 1.1.

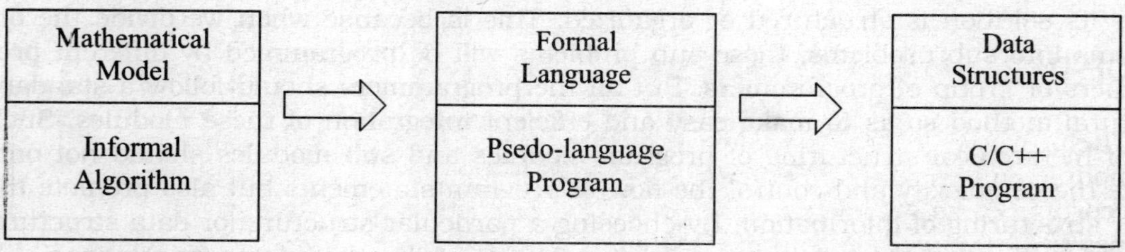

Fig. 1.1

1. In the first stage, modeling, we try to represent the problem using an appropriate mathematical model such as a graph, tree etc. At this stage, the solution to the problem is an algorithm expressed very informally.
2. At the next stage, the algorithm is written in pseudo-language (or formal algorithm) that is, a mixture of any programming language constructs and less formal English statements. The operations to be performed on the various types of data become fixed.
3. In the final stage we choose an implementation for each abstract data type and write the procedures for the various operations on that type. The remaining informal statements in the pseudo-language algorithm are replaced by (or any programming language) C/C++ code.

Following sections will discuss different programming methodologies to design a program.

1.4. MODULAR PROGRAMMING

Modular Programming is heavily procedural. The focus is entirely on writing code (functions). Data is passive in Modular Programming. Any code may access the contents of any data structure passed to it. (There is no concept of encapsulation.) Modular Programming is the act of designing and writing programs as functions, that each one performs a single well-defined function, and which have minimal interaction between them. That is, the content of each function is cohesive, and there is low coupling between functions.

Modular Programming discourages the use of control variables and flags in parameters; their presence tends to indicate that the caller needs to know too much about how the function is implemented. It encourages splitting of functionality into two types: "Master" functions controls the program flow and primarily contain calls to "Slave" functions that handle low-level details, like moving data between structures.

Two methods may be used for modular programming. They are known as top-down and bottom-up, which we have discussed in the above section. Regardless of whether the top-down or bottom-up method is used, the end result is a modular program. This end result is important, because not all errors may be detected at the time of the initial testing. It is possible that there are still bugs in the program. If an error is discovered after the program supposedly has been fully tested, then the modules concerned can be isolated and retested by them.

Regardless of the design method used, if a program has been written in modular form, it is easier to detect the source of the error and to test it in isolation, than if the program were written as one function.

1.5. TOP-DOWN ALGORITHM DESIGN

The principles of top-down design dictates that a program should be divided into a main module and its related modules. Each module should also be divided into sub modules according to software engineering and programming style. The division of modules processes until the module consists only of elementary process that are intrinsically understood and cannot be further subdivided.

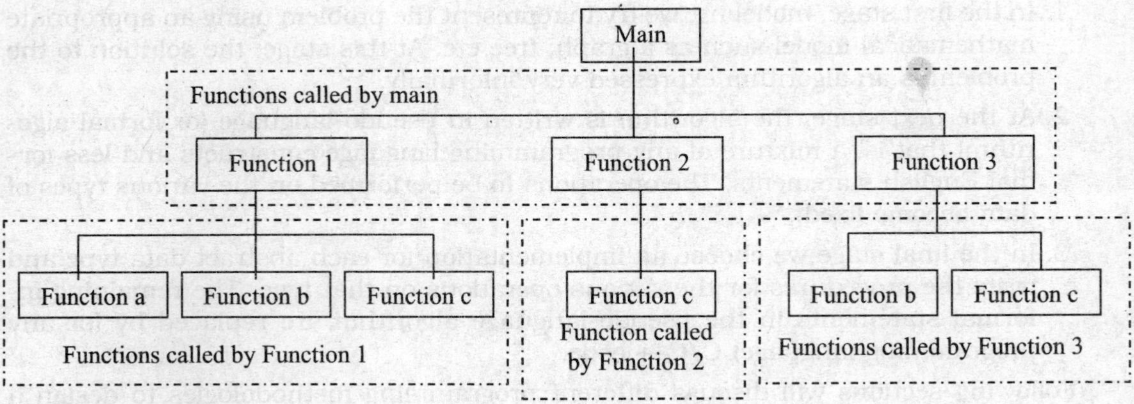

Fig. 1.2

Top-down algorithm design is a technique for organizing and coding programs in which a hierarchy of modules is used, and breaking the specification down into simpler and simpler pieces, each having a single entry and a single exit point, and in which control is passed downward through the structure without unconditional branches to higher levels of the structure. That is top-down programming tends to generate modules that are based on functionality, usually in the form of functions or procedures or methods.

In C, the idea of top-down design is done using functions. A C program is made of one or more functions, one and only one of which must be named *main*. The execution of the program always starts and ends with *main*, but it can call other functions to do special tasks.

1.6. BOTTOM-UP ALGORITHM DESIGN

Bottom-up algorithm design is the opposite of top-down design. It refers to a style of programming where an application is constructed starting with existing primitives of the programming language, and constructing gradually more and more complicated features, until the all of the application has been written. That is, starting the design with specific modules and build them into more complex structures, ending at the top.

The bottom-up method is widely used for testing, because each of the lowest-level functions is written and tested first. This testing is done by special test functions that call the low-level functions, providing them with different parameters and examining the results for correctness. Once lowest-level functions have been tested and verified to be correct, the next level of functions may be tested. Since the lowest-level functions already have been tested, any detected errors are probably due to the higher-level functions. This process continues, moving up the levels, until finally the *main* function is tested.

1.7. STRUCTURED PROGRAMMING

It is a programming style; and this style of programming is known by several names: Procedural decomposition, Structured programming, etc. Structured programming is not programming with structures but by using following types of code structures to write programs:

1. Sequence of sequentially executed statements
2. Conditional execution of statements (*i.e.*, "if" statements)
3. Looping or iteration (*i.e.*, "for, do...while, and while" statements)
4. Structured subroutine calls (*i.e.*, functions)

In particular, the following language usage is forbidden:

- "GoTo" statements
- "Break" or "continue" out of the middle of loops
- Multiple exit points to a function/procedure/subroutine (*i.e.*, multiple "return" statements)
- Multiple entry points to a function/procedure/subroutine/method

In this style of programming there is a great risk that implementation details of many data structures have to be shared between functions, and thus globally exposed. This in turn tempts other functions to use these implementation details; thereby creating unwanted dependencies between different parts of the program.

The main disadvantage is that all decisions made from the start of the project depends directly or indirectly on the high-level specification of the application. It is a well-known fact that this specification tends to change over a time. When that happens, there is a great risk that large parts of the application need to be rewritten.

1.8. ANALYSIS OF ALGORITHM

After designing an algorithm, it has to be checked and its correctness needs to be predicted; this is done by analyzing the algorithm. The algorithm can be analyzed by tracing all step-by-step instructions, reading the algorithm for logical correctness, and testing it on some data using mathematical techniques to prove it correct. Another type of analysis is to analyze the simplicity of the algorithm. That is, design the algorithm in a simple way so that it becomes easier to be implemented. However, the simplest and most straightforward way of solving a problem may not be sometimes the best one. Moreover there may be more than one algorithm to solve a problem. The choice of a particular algorithm depends on following performance analysis and measurements :

1. Space complexity
2. Time complexity

1.8.1. SPACE COMPLEXITY

Analysis of space complexity of an algorithm or program is the amount of memory it needs to run to completion.

Some of the reasons for studying space complexity are:

1. If the program is to run on multi user system, it may be required to specify the amount of memory to be allocated to the program.
2. We may be interested to know in advance that whether sufficient memory is available to run the program.
3. There may be several possible solutions with different space requirements.
4. Can be used to estimate the size of the largest problem that a program can solve.

The space needed by a program consists of following components.

- *Instruction space* : Space needed to store the executable version of the program and it is fixed.
- *Data space* : Space needed to store all constants, variable values and has further two components :
  - (*a*) Space needed by constants and simple variables. This space is fixed.
  - (*b*) Space needed by fixed sized structural variables, such as arrays and structures.
  - (*c*) Dynamically allocated space. This space usually varies.
- *Environment stack space:* This space is needed to store the information to resume the suspended (partially completed) functions. Each time a function is invoked the following data is saved on the environment stack :
  - (*a*) Return address : *i.e.*, from where it has to resume after completion of the called function.
  - (*b*) Values of all lead variables and the values of formal parameters in the function being invoked .

The amount of space needed by recursive function is called the recursion stack space. For each recursive function, this space depends on the space needed by the local variables and the formal parameter. In addition, this space depends on the maximum depth of the recursion *i.e.*, maximum number of nested recursive calls.

1.8.2. TIME COMPLEXITY

The time complexity of an algorithm or a program is the amount of time it needs to run to completion. The exact time will depend on the implementation of the algorithm, programming language, optimizing the capabilities of the compiler used, the CPU speed, other hardware characteristics/specifications and so on. To measure the time complexity accurately, we have to count all sorts of operations performed in an algorithm. If we know the time for each one of the primitive operations performed in a given computer, we can easily compute the time taken by an algorithm to complete its execution. This time will vary from machine to machine. By analyzing an algorithm, it is hard to come out with an exact time required. To find out exact time complexity, we need to know the exact instructions executed by the hardware and the time required for the instruction. The time complexity also depends on the amount of data inputted to an algorithm. But we can calculate the order of magnitude for the time required.

That is, our intention is to estimate the execution time of an algorithm irrespective of the computer machine on which it will be used. Here, the more sophisticated method is to identify the key operations and count such operations performed till the program completes its execution. A key operation in our algorithm is an operation that takes maximum time among all possible operations in the algorithm. Such an abstract, theoretical approach is not only useful for discussing and comparing algorithms, but also it is useful to improve solutions to practical problems. The time complexity can now be expressed as function of number of key operations performed. Before we go ahead with our discussions, it is important to understand the rate growth analysis of an algorithm, as shown in Fig. 1.3.

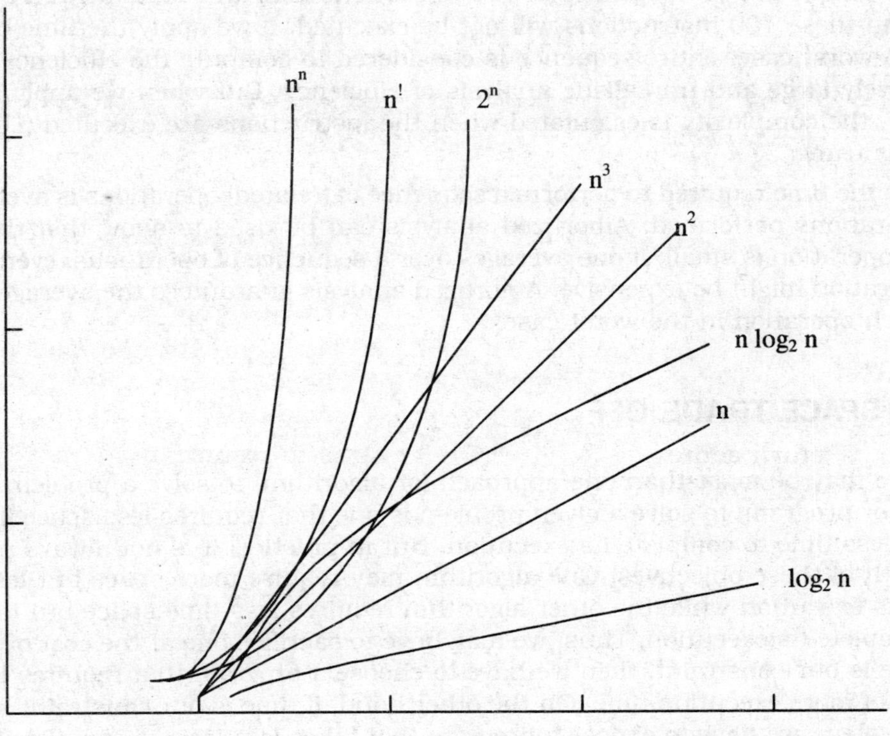

Fig. 1.3

The function that involves 'n' as an exponent, *i.e.*, 2^n, n^n, $n\,!$ are called exponential functions, which is too slow except for small size input function where growth is less than or equal to n^c,(where 'c' is a constant) *i.e.*; n^3, n^2, $n \log_2 n$, n, $\log_2 n$ are said to be polynomial. Algorithms with polynomial time can solve reasonable sized problems if the constant in the exponent is small.

When we analyze an algorithm it depends on the input data, there are three cases :

1. Best case
2. Average case
3. Worst case

In the best case, the amount of time a program might be expected to take on best possible input data.

In the average case, the amount of time a program might be expected to take on typical (or average) input data.

In the worst case, the amount of time a program would take on the worst possible input configuration.

1.8.3. AMSTRONG COMPLEXITY

In many situations, data structures are subjected to a sequence of instructions rather than one set of instruction. In this sequence, one instruction may perform certain modifications that have an impact on other instructions in the sequence at the run time itself. For example in a *for* loop there are 100 instructions in an *if* statement. If *if* condition is false then these 100 instructions will not be executed. If we apply the time complexity analysis in worst case, entire sequence is considered to compute the efficiency, which is an excessively large and unrealistic analysis of efficiency. But when we apply amortized complexity, the complexity is calculated when the instructions are executed (*i.e.*, when *if* condition is true)

Here the time required to perform a sequence of (related) operations is averaged over all the operations performed. Amortized analysis can be used to show that the average cost of an operation is small, if one averages over a sequence of operations, even though a simple operation might be expensive. Amortized analysis guarantees the average performance of each operation in the worst case.

1.9. TIME-SPACE TRADE OFF

There may be more than one approach (or algorithm) to solve a problem. The best algorithm (or program) to solve a given problem is one that requires less space in memory and takes less time to complete its execution. But in practice, it is not always possible to achieve both of these objectives. One algorithm may require more space but less time to complete its execution while the other algorithm requires less time space but takes more time to complete its execution. Thus, we may have to sacrifice one at the cost of the other. If the space is our constraint, then we have to choose a program that requires less space at the cost of more execution time. On the other hand, if time is our constraint such as in real time system, we have to choose a program that takes less time to complete its execution at the cost of more space.

1.10. BIG "OH" NOTATION

Big Oh is a characteristic scheme that measures properties of algorithm complexity performance and/or memory requirements. The algorithm complexity can be determined by eliminating constant factors in the analysis of the algorithm. Clearly, the complexity function $f(n)$ of an algorithm increases as 'n' increases.

Let us find out the algorithm complexity by analyzing the sequential searching algorithm. In the sequential search algorithm we simply try to match the target value against each value in the memory. This process will continue until we find a match or finish scanning the whole elements in the array. If the array contains 'n' elements, the maximum possible number of comparisons with the target value will be 'n' *i.e.*, the worst case. That is the target value will be found at the nth position of the array.

$$f(n) = n$$

i.e., the worst case is when an algorithm requires a maximum number of iterations or steps to search and find out the target value in the array.

The best case is when the number of steps is less as possible. If the target value is found in a sequential search array of the first position (*i.e.*, we need to compare the target value with only one element from the array)—we have found the element by executing only one iteration (or by least possible statements)

$$f(n) = 1$$

Average case falls between these two extremes (*i.e.*, best and worst). If the target value is found at the $n/2$nd position, on an average we need to compare the target value with only half of the elements in the array, so

$$f(n) = n/2$$

The complexity function f(n) of an algorithm increases as 'n' increases. The function $f(n) = O(n)$ can be read as "f of n is big Oh of n" or as "$f(n)$ is of the order of n". The total running time (or time complexity) includes the initializations and several other iterative statements through the loop.

The generalized form of the theorem is

$$f(n) = c_k n^k + c_{k-1} n^{k-1} + c_{k-2} n^{k-2} + \ldots\ldots + c_2 n^2 + c_1 n^1 + c_0 n^0$$

Where the constant $c_k > 0$

Then, $f(n) = O(n^k)$

Based on the time complexity representation of the big Oh notation, the algorithm can be categorized as :

1. Constant time O(1)
2. Logarithmic time O$\log(n)$
3. Linear time $O(n)$
4. Polynomial time $O(n^c)$
5. Exponential time $O(c^n)$

} Where $c > 1$

1.11. LIMITATION OF BIG "OH" NOTATION

Big Oh Notation has following two basic limitations :

1. It contains no effort to improve the programming methodology. Big Oh Notation does not discuss the way and means to improve the efficiency of the program, but it helps to analyze and calculate the efficiency (by finding time complexity) of the program.
2. It does not exhibit the potential of the constants. For example, one algorithm is taking $1000n^2$ time to execute and the other n^3 time. The first algorithm is $O(n^2)$, which implies that it will take less time than the other algorithm which is $O(n^3)$. However in actual execution the second algorithm will be faster for $n < 1000$.

We will analyze and design the problems in data structure. As we have discussed to develop a program of an algorithm, we should select an appropriate data structure for that algorithm.

1.12. CLASSIFICATION OF DATA STRUCTURE

Data structures are broadly divided into two :

1. *Primitive data structures* : These are the basic data structures and are directly operated upon by the machine instructions, which is in a primitive level. They are integers, floating point numbers, characters, string constants, pointers etc. These primitive data structures are the basis for the discussion of more sophisticated (non-primitive) data structures in this book.

2. *Non-primitive data structures* : It is a more sophisticated data structure emphasizing on structuring of a group of homogeneous (same type) or heterogeneous (different type) data items. Array, list, files, linked list, trees and graphs fall in this category.

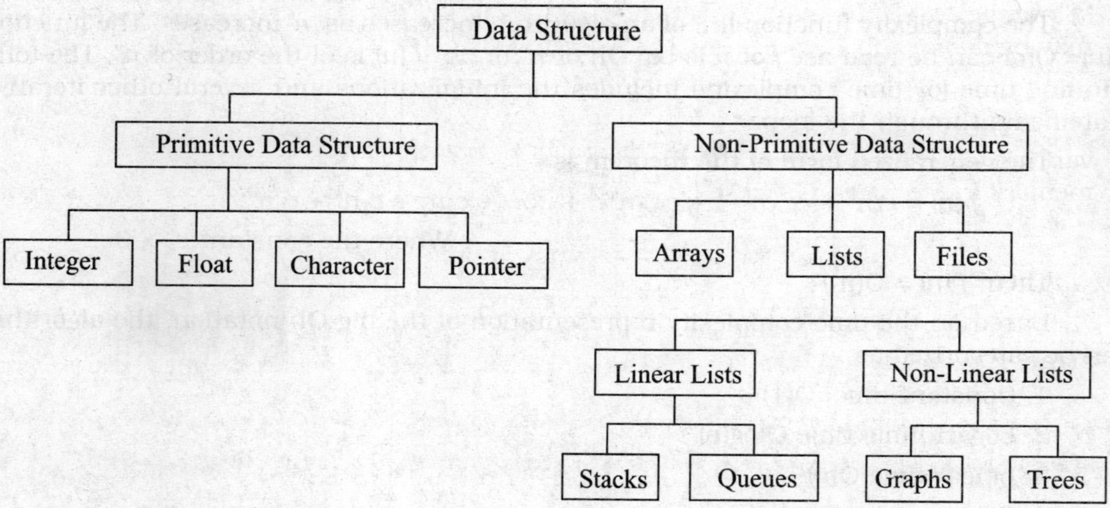

Fig. 1.4. Classifications of data structures

The Fig. 1.4 will briefly explain other classifications of data structures. Basic operations on data structure are to create a (non-primitive) data structure; which is considered to be the first step of writing a program. For example, in Pascal, C and C++, variables are created by using declaration statements.

int Int_Variable;

In C/C++, memory space is allocated for the variable "*Int_Variable*" when the above declaration statement executes. That is a data structure is created. Discussions on primitive data structures are beyond the scope of this book. Let us consider non-primitive data structures.

1.13. ARRAYS

Arrays are most frequently used in programming. Mathematical problems like matrix, algebra and etc can be easily handled by arrays. An array is a collection of homogeneous data elements described by a single name. Each element of an array is referenced by a subscripted variable or value, called subscript or index enclosed in parenthesis. If an element of an array is referenced by single subscript, then the array is known as one dimensional array or linear array and if two subscripts are required to reference an element, the array is known as two dimensional array and so on. Analogously the arrays whose elements are referenced by two or more subscripts are called multi dimensional arrays.

1.13.1. ONE DIMENSIONAL ARRAY

One-dimensional array (or linear array) is a set of '*n*' finite numbers of homogenous data elements such as :

1. The elements of the array are referenced respectively by an index set consisting of '*n*' consecutive numbers.
2. The elements of the array are stored respectively in successive memory locations.

'*n*' number of elements is called the length or size of an array. The elements of an array 'A' may be denoted in C as

A[0], A[1], A[2], ... A[*n* –1].

The number '*n*' in A[*n*] is called a subscript or an index and A[n] is called a subscripted variable. If '*n*' is 10, then the array elements A[0], A[1]......A[9] are stored in sequential memory locations as follows :

A[0]	A[1]	A[2]	......	A[9]

In C, array can always be read or written through loop. To read a one-dimensional array, it requires one loop for reading and writing the array, for example:

For reading an array of '*n*' elements

```
for (i = 0; i < n; i ++)
scanf ("%d",&a[i]);
```

For writing an array

```
for (i = 0; i < n; i ++)
printf ("%d", &a[i]);
```

1.13.2. MULTI DIMENSIONAL ARRAY

If we are reading or writing two-dimensional array, two loops are required. Similarly the array of '*n*' dimensions would require '*n*' loops. The structure of the two dimensional array is illustrated in the following figure :

int A[10][10];

A_{00}	A_{01}	A_{02}						A_{08}	A_{09}
A_{10}	A_{11}								A_{19}
A_{20}									
A_{30}									
									A_{69}
A_{70}								A_{78}	A_{79}
A_{80}	A_{81}						A_{87}	A_{88}	A_{89}
A_{90}	A_{91}	A_{92}				A_{96}	A_{97}	A_{98}	A_{99}

1.13.3. SPARSE ARRAYS

Sparse array is an important application of arrays. A sparse array is an array where nearly all of the elements have the same value (usually zero) and this value is a constant. One-dimensional sparse array is called sparse vectors and two-dimensional sparse arrays are called sparse matrix.

The main objective of using arrays is to minimize the memory space requirement and to improve the execution speed of a program. This can be achieved by allocating memory space for only non-zero elements.

For example a sparse array can be viewed as

$$\begin{matrix} 0 & 0 & 8 & 0 & 0 & 0 & 0 \\ 0 & 1 & 0 & 0 & 0 & 9 & 0 \\ 0 & 0 & 0 & 3 & 0 & 0 & 0 \\ 0 & 31 & 0 & 0 & 0 & 4 & 0 \\ 0 & 0 & 0 & 0 & 7 & 0 & 0 \end{matrix}$$

Fig. 1.5. Sparse array

We will store only non-zero elements in the above sparse matrix because storing all the elements of the sparse array will be consisting of memory sparse. The non-zero elements are stored in an array of the form.

A[0......*n*][1......3]

Where '*n*' is the number of non-zero elements in the array. In the above Fig. 1.4 '*n* = 7'. The space array given in Fig. 1.4 may be represented in the array A[0......7][1.....3].

A[0][1] A[0][2]

	1	**2**	**3**
0	5	7	7
1	1	3	8
2	2	2	1
3	2	6	9
4	3	4	3
5	4	2	31
6	4	6	4
7	5	5	7

Fig. 1.6. Sparse array representation

The element A[0][1] and A[0][2] contain the number of rows and columns of the sparse array. A[0][3] contains the total number of nonzero elements in the sparse array.

A[1][1] contains the number of the row where the first nonzero element is present in the sparse array. A[1][2] contains the number of the column of the corresponding nonzero element. A[1][3] contains the value of the nonzero element. In the Fig. 1.4, the first nonzero element can be found at 1st row in 3rd column.

1.14. VECTORS

A vector is a one-dimensional ordered collection of numbers. Normally, a number of contiguous memory locations are sequentially allocated to the vector. A vector size is fixed and, therefore, requires a fixed number of memory locations. A vector can be a column vector which represents a '*n*' by 1 ordered collections, or a row vector which represents a 1 by '*n*' ordered collections.

The column vector appears symbolically as follows :

$$A = \begin{pmatrix} A_1 \\ A_2 \\ A_3 \\ \vdots \\ A_n \end{pmatrix}$$

A row vector appears symbolically as follows :

$$A = (A_1, A_2, A_3, \ldots\ldots A_n)$$

Vectors can contain either real or complex numbers. When they contain real numbers, they are sometime called real vectors. When they contain complex numbers, they are called complex vectors.

1.15. LISTS

As we have discussed, an array is an ordered set, which consist of a fixed number of elements. No deletion or insertion operations are performed on arrays. Another main disadvantage is its fixed length; we cannot add elements to the array. Lists overcome all the above limitations. A list is an ordered set consisting of a varying number of elements to which insertion and deletion can be made. A list represented by displaying the relationship between the adjacent elements is said to be a linear list. Any other list is said to be non linear. List can be implemented by using pointers. Each element is referred to as nodes; therefore a list can be defined as a collection of nodes as shown below :

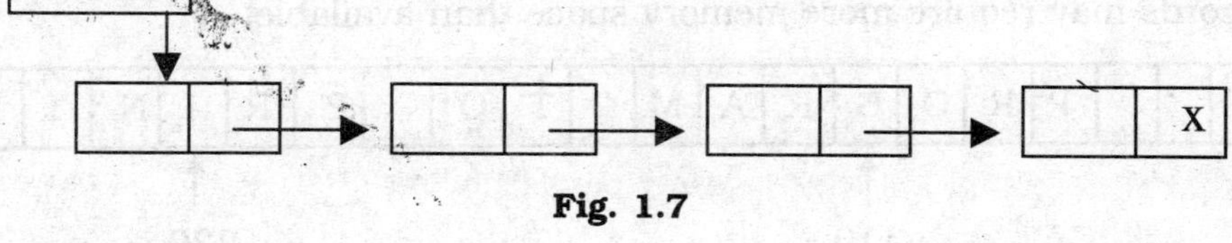

Fig. 1.7

1.16. FILES AND RECORDS

A file is typically a large list that is stored in the external memory (*e.g.*, a magnetic disk) of a computer.

A record is a collection of information (or data items) about a particular entity. More specifically, a record is a collection of related data items, each of which is called a filed or attribute and a file is a collection of similar records.

Although a record is a collection of data items, it differs from a linear array in the following ways:

(*a*) A record may be a collection of non-homogeneous data; *i.e.*, the data items in a record may have different data types.

(*b*) The data items in a record are indexed by attribute names, so there may not be a natural ordering of its elements.

1.17. CHARACTERISTICS OF STRINGS

In computer terminology the term 'string' refers to a sequence of characters. A finite set of sequence (alphabets, digits or special characters) of zero or more characters is called a string. The number of characters in a string is called the length of the string. If the length of the string is zero then it is called the empty string or null string.

1.17.1. STRING REPRESENTATION

Strings are stored or represented in memory by using following three types of structures :

- Fixed length structures
- Variable length structures with fixed maximum
- Linear structures

FIXED LENGTH REPRESENTATION. In fixed length storage each line is viewed as a record, where all records have the same length. That is each record accommodates maximum of same number of characters.

The main advantage of representing the string in the above way is :

1. To access data from any given record easily.
2. It is easy to update the data in any given record.

The main disadvantages are :

1. Entire record will be read even if most of the storage consists of inessential blank space. Time is wasted in reading these blank spaces.
2. The length of certain records will be more than the fixed length. That is certain records may require more memory space than available.

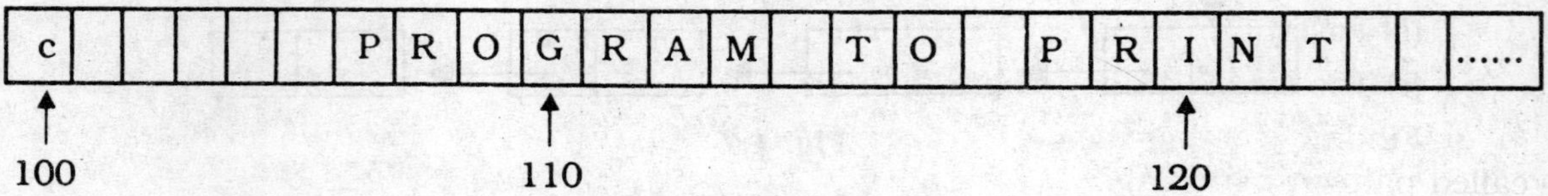

Fig. 1.8. Input data

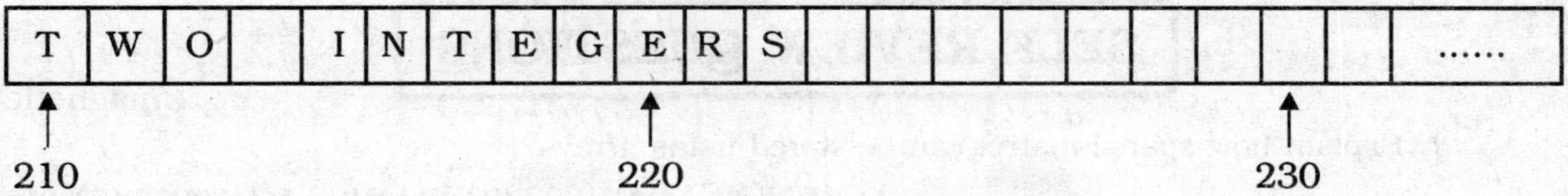

Fig. 1.9. Fixed length representation

Fig. 1.9 is a representation of input data (which is in Fig. 1.8) in a fixed length (records) storage media in a computer.

Variable Length Representation: In variable length representation, strings are stored in a fixed length storage medium. This is done in two ways.

1. One can use a marker, (any special characters) such as two-dollar sign ($$), to signal the end of the string.
2. Listing the length of the string at the first place is another way of representing strings in this method.

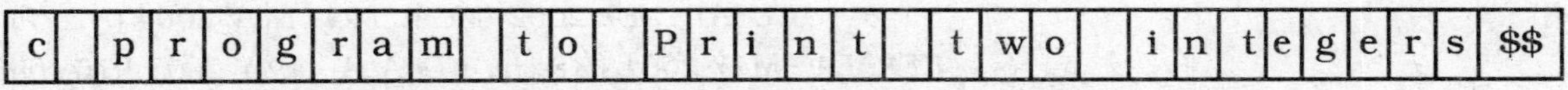

Fig. 1.10. String representation using marker

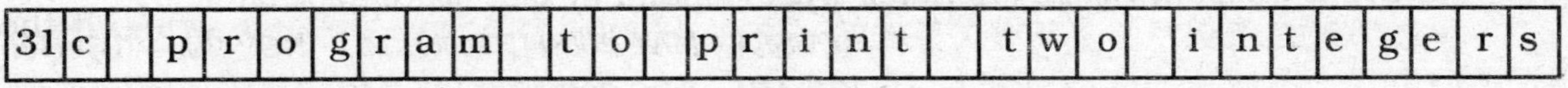

Fig. 1.11. String representation by listing the length

Linked List Representations: In linked list representations each characters in a string are sequentially arranged in memory cells, called nodes, where each node contain an item and link, which points to the next node in the list (*i.e.*, link contain the address of the next node).

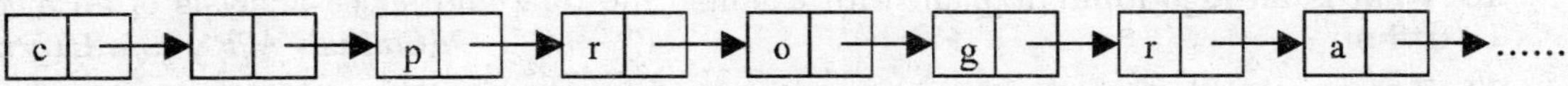

Fig. 1.12. One character per node

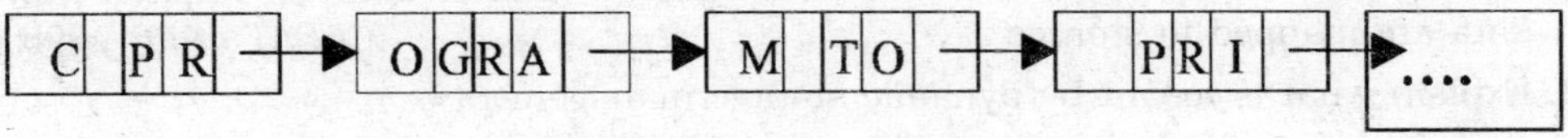

Fig. 1.13. Four character per node

We will discuss the implementation issues of linked list in chapter 5.

1.17.2. SUB STRING

Group of consecutive elements or characters in a string (or sentence) is called sub string. This group of consecutive elements may not have any special meaning. To access a sub string from the given string we need following information :

(*a*) Name of the string

(*b*) Position of the first character of the sub string in the given string

(*c*) The length of the sub string

Finding whether the sub string is available in a string by matching its characters is called pattern matching.

SELF REVIEW QUESTIONS

1. Explain how sparse matrix can be stored using arrays?
[*Calicut - APR 1997 (BTech), MG - MAY 2002 (BTech)
KERALA - MAY 2002 (BTech)*]
2. Distinguish between time and space complexity?
[*ANNA - MAY 2004 (MCA), MG - MAY 2004 (BTech)*]
3. Discuss the performance analysis and evaluation methods of algorithm?
[*KERALA - DEC 2004 (BTech), MG - MAY 2004 (BTech)*]
4. Define and explain Big O notation?
[*MG - NOV 2004 (BTech), MG - NOV 2003 (BTech)*]
5. What are sparse matrixes? Give an example?
[*CUSAT - NOV 2002 (BTech), Calicut - APR 1995 (BTech),
CUSAT - JUL 2002 (MCA), MG - NOV 2004 (BTech)
KERALA - MAY 2001 (BTech), KERALA - MAY 2003 (BTech)*]
6. Explain the schemes of data representations for strings? [*MG - NOV 2004 (BTech)*]
7. Define complexity of an algorithm. What is meant by time-space trade off ?
[*CUSAT - MAY 2000 (BTech), MG - NOV 2004 (BTech),
KERALA - DEC 2002 (BTech), MG - MAY 2000 (BTech)*]
8. Discuss the different steps in the development of an algorithm?
[*MG - NOV 2004 (BTech)*]
9. Discuss the advantages and disadvantages of Modular Programming.
[*Calicut - APR 1995 (BTech)*]
10. What is an Algorithm? Explain with example the time and space analysis of an algorithm. [*Calicut - APR 1995 (BTech)*]
11. Pattern matching in strings. [*Calicut - APR 1997 (BTech)*]
12. Distinguish between primitive and non-primitive data structures. Explain how integer data are mapped to storage. [*CUSAT - APR 1998 (BTech)*]
13. Explain what is meant by dynamic storage management?
[*ANNA - DEC 2004 (BE), CUSAT - MAY 2000 (BTech)*]
14. Explain in detail about *top-down* approach and *bottom-up* approach with suitable programming examples. [*ANNA - MAY 2003 (BE), ANNA - DEC 2003 (BE)*]
15. What do you mean by stepwise refinement?
[*KERALA - DEC 2004 (BTech), ANNA - DEC 2003 (BE)
KERALA - DEC 2003 (BTech), KERALA - JUN 2004 (BTech)
KERALA - MAY 2003 (BTech)*]
16. What are the features of structured programming methodologies? Explain.
[*ANNA - MAY 2003 (BE), ANNA - DEC 2004 (BE)*]
17. Differentiate linear and non-linear data structures.
[*ANNA - MAY 2004 (BE), ANNA - MAY 2004 (MCA)*]
18. What are the primitive functions in a string handling system? [*ANNA - DEC 2004 (BE)*]
19. What is meant by unstructured program? [*ANNA - MAY 2004 (BE)*]

20. What is meant by algorithm ? What are its measures? [*ANNA - MAY 2004 (BE)*]
21. What are primitive data types ? [*ANNA - MAY 2003 (BE)*]
22. Explain (*i*) Array vs. record. (*ii*) Time complexity [*KERALA - MAY 2001 (BTech), KERALA - JUN 2004 (BTech)*]
23. Explain Programming methodology. [*KERALA - DEC 2003 (BTech)*]
24. Explain about analysis of algorithms. [*KERALA - MAY 2003 (BTech), KERALA - DEC 2003 (BTech)*]
25. What is structured programming ? Explain. [*KERALA - MAY 2001 (BTech)*]
26. Distinguish between a program and an algorithm. [*KERALA - MAY 2002 (BTech)*]
27. Explain the advantages and disadvantage of list structure over array structure. [*KERALA - MAY 2002 (BTech)*]
28. Explain the term "data structure". [*KERALA - NOV 2001 (BTech)*]
29. What do you understand by best, worst and average case analysis of an algorithm ? [*KERALA - NOV 2001 (BTech)*]
30. What are the uses of an array ? What is an ordered array ? [*KERALA - NOV 2001 (BTech)*]
31. How will you specify the time complexity of an algorithm ? [*CUSAT - OCT 2000 (BTech)*]

2 Memory Management

A memory or store is required in a computer to store programs (or information or data). Data used by the variables in a program is also loaded into memory for fast access. A memory is made up of a large number of cells, where each cell is capable of storing one bit. The cells may be organized as a set of addressable words, each word storing a sequence of bits. These addressable memory cells should be managed effectively to increase its utilization. That is memory management is to handle request for storage (that is new memory allocations for a variable or data) and release of storage (or freeing the memory) in most effective manner. While designing a program the programmer should concentrate on to allocate memory when it is required and to deallocate once its use is over.

In other words, dynamic data structure provides flexibility in adding, deleting or rearranging data item at run-time. Dynamic memory management techniques permit us to allocate additional memory space or to release unwanted space at run-time, thus optimizing the use of storage space. Next topic will give you a brief introduction about the storage management, static as well as dynamic functions available in C.

2.1. MEMORY ALLOCATION IN C

There are two types of memory allocations in C:

1. Static memory allocation or Compile time
2. Dynamic memory allocation or Run time

In *static or compile time memory allocations*, the required memory is allocated to the variables at the beginning of the program. Here the memory to be allocated is fixed and is determined by the compiler at the compile time itself. For example

```
int i, j;          //Two bytes per (total 2) integer variables
float a[5], f;     //Four bytes per (total 6) floating point variables
```

When the first statement is compiled, two bytes for both the variable '*i*' and '*j*' will be allocated. Second statement will allocate 20 bytes to the array A [5 elements of floating point type, *i.e.*, 5 × 4] and four bytes for the variable '*f*'. But static memory allocation has following drawbacks.

If you try to read 15 elements, of an array whose size is declared as 10, then first 10 values and other five consecutive unknown random memory values will be read. Again if you try to assign values to 15 elements of an array whose size is declared as 10, then first 10 elements can be assigned and the other 5 elements cannot be assigned/accessed.

The second problem with static memory allocation is that if you store less number of elements than the number of elements for which you have declared memory, and then the rest of the memory will be wasted. That is the unused memory cells are not made available to other applications (or process which is running parallel to the program) and its status is set as allocated and not free. This leads to the inefficient use of memory.

The *dynamic or run time memory allocation* helps us to overcome this problem. It makes efficient use of memory by allocating the required amount of memory whenever is needed. In most of the real time problems, we cannot predict the memory requirements. Dynamic memory allocation does the job at run time.

C provides the following dynamic allocation and de-allocation functions :

(*i*) malloc( ) (*ii*) calloc( )

(*iii*) realloc( ) (*iv*) free( )

2.1.1. ALLOCATING A BLOCK OF MEMORY

The malloc( ) function is used to allocate a block of memory in bytes. The malloc function returns a pointer of any specified data type after allocating a block of memory of specified size. It is of the form

ptr = (int_type *) malloc (block_size)

'ptr' is a pointer of any type 'int_type' byte size is the allocated area of memory block. For example

ptr = (int *) malloc (10 * sizeof (int));

On execution of this statement, 10 times memory space equivalent to size of an 'int' byte is allocated and the address of the first byte is assigned to the pointer variable 'ptr' of type 'int'.

Remember the malloc() function allocates a block of contiguous bytes. The allocation can fail if the space in the heap is not sufficient to satisfy the request. If it fails, it returns a NULL pointer. So it is always better to check whether the memory allocation is successful or not before we use the newly allocated memory pointer. Next program will illustrate the same.

PROGRAM 2.1

```
//THIS IS A PROGRAM TO FIND THE SUM OF n ELEMENTS USING
//DYNAMIC MEMORY ALLOCATION

#include<stdio.h>
#include<conio.h>
#include<process.h>

//Defining the NULL pointer as zero
#define     NULL     0

void main()

        int i,n,sum;
        //Allocate memory space for two-integer pointer variable
        int *ptr,*ele;
```

```
    clrscr();    //Clear the screen
    printf("\nEnter the number of the element(s) to be added = ");
    scanf("%d",&n); //Enter the number of elements

    //Allocating memory space for n integers of int type to *ptr
    ptr=(int *)malloc(n*sizeof(int));
    //Checking whether the memory is allocated successfully
    if(ptr == NULL)
    {
        printf("\n\nMemory allocation is failed");
        exit(0);
    }

    //Reading the elements to the pointer variable *ele
    for(ele=ptr,i=1;ele<(ptr+n);ele++,i++)
    {
        printf("Enter the %d element = ",i);
        scanf("%d",ele);
    }

    //Finding the sum of n elements
    for(ele=ptr,sum=0;ele<(ptr+n);ele++)
        sum=sum+(*ele);

    printf("\n\nThe SUM of no(s) is = %d",sum);
    getch();
}
```

Similarly, memory can be allocated to structure variables. For example

```
struct Employee
{
int Emp_Code;
char Emp_Name[50];
float Emp_Salary;
};
```

Here the structure is been defined with three variables.

```
struct Employee *str_ptr;
str_ptr = (struct Employee *) malloc(sizeof (struct Employee));
```

When this statement is executed, a contiguous block of memory of size 56 bytes (2 bytes for integer employee code, 50 bytes for character type Employee Name and 4 bytes for floating point type Employee Salary) will be allocated.

2.1.2. ALLOCATING MULTIPLE BLOCKS OF MEMORY

The calloc() function works exactly similar to malloc() function except for the fact that it needs two arguments as against one argument required by malloc() function. While malloc() function allocates a single block of memory space, calloc() function allocates multiple blocks of memory, each of the same size, and then sets all bytes to zero. The general form of calloc() function is

ptr = (int_type*) calloc(n sizeof (block_size));

ptr = (int_type*) malloc(n* (sizeof (block_size));

The above statement allocates contiguous space for '*n*' blocks, each of size of block_size bytes. All bytes are initialized to zero and a pointer to the first byte of the allocated memory block is returned. If there is no sufficient memory space, a NULL pointer is returned. For example

ptr = (int *) calloc(25, 4);

ptr = (int *) calloc(25,sizeof (float));

Here, in the first statement the size of data type in byte for which allocation is to be made (4 bytes for a floating point numbers) is specified and 25 specifies the number of elements for which allocation is to be made.

Note : The memory allocated using malloc() function contains garbage values, the memory allocated by calloc() function contains the value zero.

2.1.3. RELEASING THE USED SPACE

Dynamic memory allocation allocates block(s) of memory when it is required and deallocates or releases when it is not in use. It is important and is our responsibility to release the memory block for future use when it is not in use, using free() function.

The free() function is used to deallocate the previously allocated memory using malloc() or calloc() function. The syntax of this function is

free(ptr);

'ptr' is a pointer to a memory block which has already been allocated by malloc() or calloc() functions. Trying to release an invalid pointer may create problems and cause system crash.

2.1.4. RESIZE THE SIZE OF A MEMORY BLOCK

In some situations, the previously allocated memory is insufficient to run the correct application, *i.e.*, we want to increase the memory space. It is also possible that the memory allocated is much larger than necessary, *i.e.*, we want to reduce the memory space. In both the cases we want to change the size of the allocated memory block and this can be done by realloc() function. This process is called reallocation of the memory. The syntax of this function is

ptr = realloc(ptr, New_Size)

Where 'ptr' is a pointer holding the starting address of the allocated memor
And New_Size is the size in bytes that the system is going to reallocate. Followin
will elaborate the concept of reallocation of memory.

ptr = (int *) malloc(sizeof (int));

```
ptr = (int *) realloc(ptr, sizeof (int));   }  Both the statements are same
ptr = (int *) realloc(ptr, 2);               }

ptr = (int *) realloc(ptr, sizeof (float)); }  Both the statements are same
ptr = (int *) realloc(ptr, 4);               }
```

2.2. DYNAMIC MEMORY ALLOCATION IN C++

Although C++ supports all the functions (*i.e.*, malloc, calloc, realloc and free) used in C, it also defines two unary operators *new* and *delete* that performs the task of allocating and freeing the memory in a better and easier way.

An object (or variable) can be created by using *new*, and destroyed by using *delete*, as and when required. A data object created inside a block with *new*, will remain in existence until it is explicitly destroyed by using *delete*. Thus, the lifetime of an object is directly under our control and is unrelated to the block structure of the program.

The new operator can be used to create objects of any type. It takes the following general form:

Pointer_Variable = new data_type;

Here, *Pointer_Variable* is a pointer of type *data_type*. The *new* operator allocates sufficient memory to hold a data object of type *data_type* and returns the address of the object. The *data_type* may be any valid data type. The *Pointer_Variable* holds the address of the memory space allocated. For example:

```
int *Var1 = new int;
float *Var2 = new float;
```

Where Var1 is a pointer of type int and Var2 is a pointer of type float.

When a data object is no longer needed, it is destroyed to release the memory space for reuse. The general form of its use is:

delete *Pointer_Variable;*

The *Pointer_Variable* is the pointer that points to a data object created with new.

```
delete Var1;
delete Var2
```

2.3. FREE STORAGE LIST

Now we have discussed several functions to allocate and freeing storage (or deallocate). To store any data, memory space is allocated dynamically using the function we have discussed in the earlier sections. That is storage allocation is done when the programmer requests it by declaring a structure at the run time.

But freeing storage is not as easy as allocation. When a program or block of program (or function or module) ends, the storage allocated at the beginning of the program will be freed. Dynamically a memory cell can be freed using the operator *delete* in C++.

In memory a special list of unused (including the deallocated) memory cells is maintained to provide (or allocate) memory space. This list, which has its own pointer, is called *list of available space* or the *free storage list* or the *free pool.*

Two problems arise in the context of storage release. One is the accumulation of garbage (called *garbage collection*) and another is that of *dangling reference*, which is discussed in following sections.

2.4. GARBAGE COLLECTION

Suppose some memory space becomes reusable when a node (or a variable) is deleted from a list or an entire list is deleted from a program. Obviously, we would like the space to be made available for future use. One way to bring this about is to immediately reinsert the space into the free-storage list-using delete or free. However, this method may be too time-consuming for the operating system and most of the programming languages, reserve themselves the task of storage release, even if they provide operator like *delete*. So the problem arises when the system considers a memory cell as free storage.

The operating system of a computer may periodically collect all the deleted space onto the free-storage list. Any technique that does this is called garbage collection. Garbage collection usually takes place in two steps. First the computer runs through all lists, tagging those cells which are currently in use, and then the computer runs through the memory, collecting all untagged space onto the free-storage list. The garbage collection may take place when there is only some minimum amount of space or no space at all left in the free-storage list, or when the CPU is idle and has time to do the collection. Generally speaking, the garbage collection is invisible to the programmer. Any future discussion about this topic of garbage collection lies beyond the scope of this text.

2.5. DANGLING REFERENCE

A dangling reference is a pointer existing in a program, which still accesses a block of memory that has been freed. For example consider the following code in C++.

```
int ptr,temp;
--------------------
--------------------
ptr = new int;
--------------------
--------------------
--------------------
--------------------
temp = ptr
--------------------
--------------------
delete ptr;
--------------------
--------------------
```

Here *temp* is the dangling reference. *temp* is a pointer which is pointing to a memory block *ptr,* which is just deleted. This can be overcome by using a reference counters.

2.6. REFERENCE COUNTERS

In the reference-counter method, a counter is kept that records how many pointers have direct access to each memory block. When a memory block is first allocated, its reference counter is set to 1. Each time another link is made pointing to this block, the reference counter is incremented. Each time a link to its block is broken, the reference counter is decremented. When the count reaches 0, the memory block is not accessed by any other pointer and it can be returned to the free list. This technique completely eliminates the dangling reference problem.

2.7. STORAGE COMPACTION

Storage compaction is another technique for reclaiming free storage. Compaction works by actually moving blocks of data from one location in the memory to another so as to collect all the free blocks into one single large block. Once this single block gets too small again, the compaction mechanism is called gain to reclaim the unused storage. Here no storage releasing mechanism is used. Instead, a marking algorithm is used to mark blocks that are still in use. Then instead of freeing each unmarked block by calling a release mechanism to put it on the free list, the compactor simply collects all unmarked blocks into one large block at one end of the memory segment.

2.8. BOUNDARY TAG METHOD

Boundary tag representation is a method of memory management described by Knuth. Boundary tags are data structures on the boundary between blocks in the heap from which memory is allocated. The use of such tags allow blocks of arbitrary size to be used as shown in the Fig. 2.1.

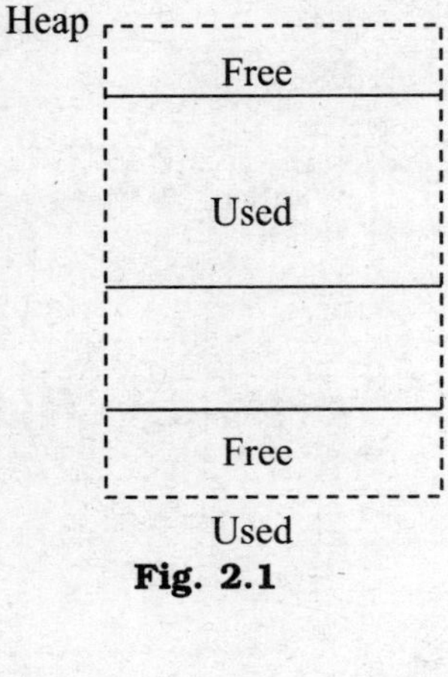

Fig. 2.1

Suppose '*n*' bytes of memory are to be allocated from a large area, in contiguous blocks of varying size, and that no form of compaction or rearrangement of the allocated segments will be used.

To reserve a block of '*n*' bytes of memory, a free space of size '*n*' or larger must be located. If we could locate a large size memory, then the allocation process will divide it into an allocated space, and a new smaller free space. Suppose free space is subdivided in this manner several times, and some of the allocated regions are "released" (after use *i.e.*, deallocated).

If we try to reserve more memory; even though there is a large contiguous chunk of free space, the memory manager perceives it as two smaller segments and so may falsely conclude that it has insufficient free space to satisfy a large request.

For optimal use of the memory, adjacent free segments must be combined. For maximum availability, they must be combined as soon as possible. The task of identifying and merging adjacent free segments should be done when a segment is released, called the boundary tag method. The method consistently applied to ensure that there would never be two adjacent free segments. This guarantees the largest available free space short of compacting the string space.

SELF REVIEW QUESTIONS

1. Explain the representation of array in memory. *[MG - MAY 2004 (BTech)]*
2. Write a note on garbage collection and compaction. *[MG - NOV 2003 (BTech), MG - MAY 2000 (BTech)]*
3. Discuss the garbage collection techniques and drawbacks of each. *[MG - MAY 2002 (BTech)]*
4. Write note on storage allocation and storage release. *[MG - MAY 2002 (BTech)]*
5. Explain the different storage representations for string. *[KERALA - MAY 2001 (BTech), CUSAT - MAY 2000 (BTech)]*
6. What is the need for Garbage collection? Explain a suitable data structure to implement Garbage collection. *[CUSAT - NOV 2002 (BTech)]*
7. Write a note on Storage Management. *[ANNA - DEC 2004 (BE)]*
8. Explain about free storage lists. *[KERALA - DEC 2004 (BTech)]*
9. Explain Storage Compaction. *[KERALA - JUN 2004 (BTech)]*
10. Explain Garbage Collection. *[KERALA - DEC 2003 (BTech)]*
11. What are reference counters ? *[KERALA - MAY 2001 (BTech)]*
12. Explain about boundary tag method. *[KERALA - MAY 2001 (BTech)]*
13. Write in detail the garbage collection and the compaction process. *[KERALA - NOV 2001 (BTech)]*

3 The Stack

A **stack** is one of the most important and useful non-primitive linear data structure in computer science. It is an ordered collection of items into which new data items may be added/inserted and from which items may be deleted at only one end, called the *top* of the stack. As all the addition and deletion in a stack is done from the top of the stack, the last added element will be first removed from the stack. That is why the stack is also called ***Last-in-First-out (LIFO)***. Note that the most frequently accessible element in the stack is the top most elements, whereas the least accessible element is the bottom of the stack The operation of the stack can be illustrated as in Fig. 3.1.

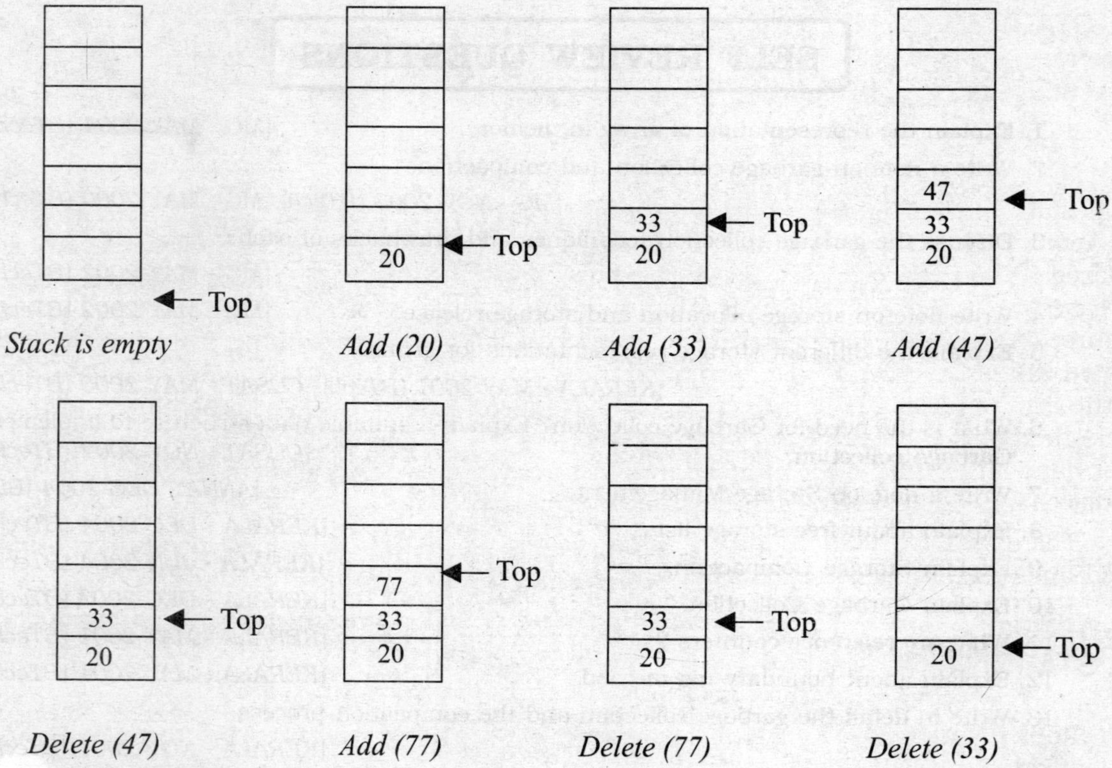

Fig. 3.1. Stack operation.

The insertion (or addition) operation is referred to as *push*, and the deletion (or remove) operation as *pop*. A stack is said to be *empty* or *underflow*, if the stack contains no elements. At this point the top of the stack is present at the bottom of the stack. And it is *overflow* when the stack becomes full, *i.e.*, no other elements can be pushed onto the stack. At this point the top pointer is at the highest location of the stack.

3.1. OPERATIONS PERFORMED ON STACK

The primitive operations performed on the stack are as follows:

PUSH: The process of adding (or inserting) a new element to the top of the stack is called PUSH operation. Pushing an element to a stack will add the new element at the top. After every push operation the top is incremented by one. If the array is full and no new element can be accommodated, then the stack overflow condition occurs.

POP: The process of deleting (or removing) an element from the top of stack is called POP operation. After every pop operation the stack is decremented by one. If there is no element in the stack and the pop operation is performed then the stack underflow condition occurs.

3.2. STACK IMPLEMENTATION

Stack can be implemented in two ways:

1. Static implementation (using arrays)
2. Dynamic implementation (using pointers)

Static implementation uses arrays to create stack. Static implementation using arrays is a very simple technique but is not a flexible way, as the size of the stack has to be declared during the program design, because after that, the size cannot be varied (*i.e.*, increased or decreased). Moreover static implementation is not an efficient method when resource optimization is concerned (*i.e.*, memory utilization). For example a stack is implemented with array size 50. That is before the stack operation begins, memory is allocated for the array of size 50. Now if there are only few elements (say 30) to be stored in the stack, then rest of the statically allocated memory (in this case 20) will be wasted, on the other hand if there are more number of elements to be stored in the stack (say 60) then we cannot change the size array to increase its capacity.

The above said limitations can be overcome by dynamically implementing (is also called linked list representation) the stack using pointers.

3.3. STACK USING ARRAYS

Implementation of stack using arrays is a very simple technique. Algorithm for pushing (or add or insert) a new element at the top of the stack and popping (or delete) an element from the stack is given below.

Algorithm for push

Suppose STACK[SIZE] is a one dimensional array for implementing the stack, which will hold the data items. TOP is the pointer that points to the top most element of the stack. Let DATA is the data item to be pushed.

1. If TOP = SIZE – 1, then:
    (*a*) Display "The stack is in overflow condition"
    (*b*) Exit
2. TOP = TOP + 1
3. STACK [TOP] = ITEM
4. Exit

Algorithm for pop

Suppose STACK[SIZE] is a one dimensional array for implementing the stack, which will hold the data items. TOP is the pointer that points to the top most element of the stack. DATA is the popped (or deleted) data item from the top of the stack.

1. If TOP < 0, then
    (*a*) Display "The Stack is empty"
    (*b*) Exit
2. Else remove the Top most element
3. DATA = STACK[TOP]
4. TOP = TOP – 1
5. Exit

PROGRAM 3.1

```
//THIS PROGRAM IS TO DEMONSTRATE THE OPERATIONS PERFORMED
//ON THE STACK  AND IT IS IMPLEMENTATION USING ARRAYS
//CODED AND COMPILED IN TURBO C

#include<stdio.h>
#include<conio.h>

//Defining the maximum size of the stack
#define MAXSIZE 100

//Declaring the stack array and top variables in a structure
struct stack
{
	int stack[MAXSIZE];
	int Top;
};

//type definition allows the user to define an identifier that would
//represent an existing data type. The user-defined data type identifier
//can later be used to declare variables.
typedef struct stack NODE;
```

```
//This function will add/insert an element to Top of the stack
void push(NODE *pu)
{
int item;
//if the top pointer already reached the maximum allowed size then
//we can say that the stack is full or overflow
if (pu->Top == MAXSIZE–1)
{
    printf("\nThe Stack Is Full");
    getch();
}
//Otherwise an element can be added or inserted by
//incrementing the stack pointer Top as follows
else
{
        printf("\nEnter The Element To Be Inserted = ");
        scanf("%d",&item);
        pu->stack[++pu->Top]=item;
    }
}

//This function will delete an element from the Top of the stack
void pop(NODE *po)
{
        int item;
        //If the Top pointer points to NULL, then the stack is empty
        //That is NO element is there to delete or pop
        if (po->Top == -1)
            printf("\nThe Stack Is Empty");
        //Otherwise the top most element in the stack is popped or
        //deleted by decrementing the Top pointer
        else
        {
            item=po->stack[po->Top--];
            printf("\nThe Deleted Element Is = %d",item);
        }
}
//This function to print all the existing elements in the stack
void traverse(NODE *pt)
{
        int i;
        //If the Top pointer points to NULL, then the stack is empty
```

```
        //That is NO element is there to delete or pop
        if (pt->Top == -1)
            printf("\nThe Stack is Empty");
        //Otherwise all the elements in the stack is printed
        else
        {
            printf("\n\nThe Element(s) In The Stack(s) is/are...");
            for(i=pt->Top; i>=0; i--)
                printf ("\n %d",pt->stack[i]);
        }
}

void main( )
{
        int choice;
        char ch;
        //Declaring an pointer variable to the structure
        NODE *ps;
        //Initializing the Top pointer to NULL
        ps->Top=–1;
        do
        {
            clrscr();
            //A menu for the stack operations
            printf("\n1. PUSH");
            printf("\n2. POP");
            printf("\n3. TRAVERSE");
            printf("\nEnter Your Choice = ");
            scanf ("%d", &choice);
            switch(choice)
            {
                case 1://Calling push() function by passing
                //the structure pointer to the function
                push(ps);
                break;

                case 2://calling pop() function
                pop(ps);
                break;
                case 3://calling traverse() function
                traverse(ps);
                break;
```

```
                default:
                printf("\nYou Entered Wrong Choice") ;
            }
            printf("\n\nPress (Y/y) To Continue = ");
            //Removing all characters in the input buffer
            //for fresh input(s), especially <<Enter>> key
            fflush(stdin);
            scanf("%c",&ch);
        }while(ch == 'Y' || ch == 'y');
}
```

PROGRAM 3.2

```
//THIS PROGRAM IS TO DEMONSTRATE THE OPERATIONS
//PERFORMED ON STACK & IS IMPLEMENTATION USING ARRAYS
//CODED AND COMPILED IN TURBO C++

#include<iostream.h>
#include<conio.h>

//Defining the maximum size of the stack
#define MAXSIZE 100

//A class initialized with public and private variables and functions
class STACK_ARRAY
{
        int stack[MAXSIZE];
        int Top;

        public:
        //constructor is called and Top pointer is initialized to -1
        //when an object is created for the class
            STACK_ARRAY()
            {
                Top=-1;
            }
            void push();
            void pop();
            void traverse();
};
```

```
//This function will add/insert an element to Top of the stack
void STACK_ARRAY::push()
{
        int item;
        //if the top pointer already reached the maximum allowed size then
        //we can say that the stack is full or overflow
        if (Top == MAXSIZE-1)
        {
                cout<<"\nThe Stack Is Full";
                getch();
        }
        //Otherwise an element can be added or inserted by
        //incrementing the stack pointer Top as follows
        else
        {
                cout<<"\nEnter The Element To Be Inserted = ";
                cin>>item;
                stack[++Top]=item;
        }
}

//This function will delete an element from the Top of the stack
void STACK_ARRAY::pop()
{
        int item;
        //If the Top pointer points to NULL, then the stack is empty
        //That is NO element is there to delete or pop
        if (Top == -1)
                cout<<"\nThe Stack Is Empty";
        //Otherwise the top most element in the stack is poped or
        //deleted by decrementing the Top pointer
        else
        {
                item=stack[Top--];
                cout<<"\nThe Deleted Element Is = "<<item;
        }
}

//This function to print all the existing elements in the stack
void STACK_ARRAY::traverse()
{
```

```
        int i;
        //If the Top pointer points to NULL, then the stack is empty
        //That is NO element is there to delete or pop
        if (Top == -1)
                cout<<"\nThe Stack is Empty";
        //Otherwise all the elements in the stack is printed
        else
        {
                cout<<"\n\nThe Element(s) In The Stack(s) is/are...";
                for(i=Top; i>=0; i--)
                        cout<<"\n "<<stack[i];
        }
}

void main()
{
        int choice;
        char ch;
        //Declaring an object to the class
        STACK_ARRAY ps;
        do
        {
                clrscr();
                //A menu for the stack operations
                cout<<"\n1. PUSH";
                cout<<"\n2. POP";
                cout<<"\n3. TRAVERSE";
                cout<<"\nEnter Your Choice = ";
                cin>>choice;

                switch(choice)
                {
                        case 1://Calling push() function by class object
                        ps.push();
                        break;

                        case 2://calling pop() function
                        ps.pop();
                        break;
```

```
                case 3://calling traverse() function
                ps.traverse();
                break;

                default:
                cout<<"\nYou Entered Wrong Choice" ;
            }
            cout<<"\n\nPress (Y/y) To Continue = ";
            cin>>ch;
        }while(ch == 'Y' || ch == 'y');
}
```

3.4. APPLICATIONS OF STACKS

There are a number of applications of stacks; three of them are discussed briefly in the preceding sections. Stack is internally used by compiler when we implement (or execute) any recursive function. If we want to implement a recursive function non-recursively, stack is programmed explicitly. Stack is also used to evaluate a mathematical expression and to check the parentheses in an expression.

3.4.1. RECURSION

Recursion occurs when a function is called by itself repeatedly; the function is called recursive function. The general algorithm model for any recursive function contains the following steps:

1. *Prologue:* Save the parameters, local variables, and return address.
2. *Body:* If the base criterion has been reached, then perform the final computation and go to step 3; otherwise, perform the partial computation and go to step 1 (initiate a recursive call).
3. *Epilogue:* Restore the most recently saved parameters, local variables, and return address.

A flowchart model for any recursive algorithm is given in Fig. 3.2.

It is difficult to understand a recursive function from its flowchart, and the best way is to have an intuitive understanding of the function. The key box in the flowchart contained in the body of the function is the one, which invokes a call to itself. Each time a function call to itself is executed, the prologue of the function saves necessary information required for its proper functioning.

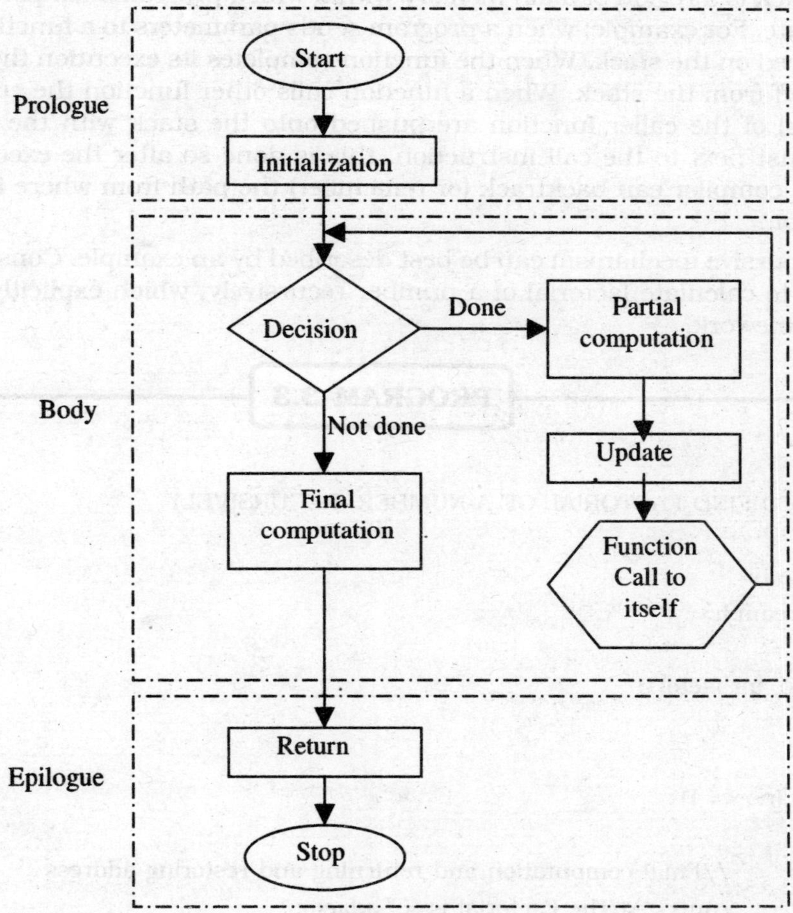

Fig. 3.2. Flowchart model for a recursive algorithm

The Last-in-First-Out characteristics of a recursive function points that the stack is the most obvious data structure to implement the recursive function. Programs compiled in modern high-level languages (even C) make use of a stack for the procedure or function invocation in memory. When any procedure or function is called, a number of words (such as variables, return address and other arguments and its data(s) for future use) are pushed onto the program stack. When the procedure or function returns, this frame of data is popped off the stack.

As a function calls a (may be or may not be another) function, its arguments, return address and local variables are pushed onto the stack. Since each function runs in its own environment or context, it becomes possible for a function to call itself — a technique known as *recursion*. This capability is extremely useful and extensively used — because many problems are elegantly specified or solved in a recursive way.

The stack is a region of main memory within which programs temporarily store data as they execute. For example, when a program sends parameters to a function, the parameters are placed on the stack. When the function completes its execution these parameters are popped off from the stack. When a function calls other function the current contents (ie., variables) of the caller function are pushed onto the stack with the address of the instruction just next to the call instruction, this is done so after the execution of called function, the compiler can backtrack (or remember) the path from where it is sent to the called function.

The recursive mechanism can be best described by an example. Consider the following program to calculate factorial of a number recursively, which explicitly describes the recursive framework.

PROGRAM 3.3

```
//PROGRAM TO FIND FACTORIAL OF A NUMBER, RECURSIVELY

#include<conio.h>
#include<iostream.h>

void fact(int no, int facto)
{
        if (no <= 1)
        {
                //Final computation and returning and restoring address
                cout<<"\nThe Factorial is = "<<facto;
                return;
        }
        else
        {
                //Partiial computation of the program
                facto=facto*no;
                //Function call to itself, that is recursion
                fact(--no,facto);
        }

}
void main()
{
        clrscr();
        int number,factorial;
```

```
    //Initialization of formal parameters, local variables and etc.
    factorial=1;
    cout<<"\nEnter the No = ";
    cin>>number;
    //Starting point of the function, which calls itself
    fact(number,factorial);
    getch();
}
```

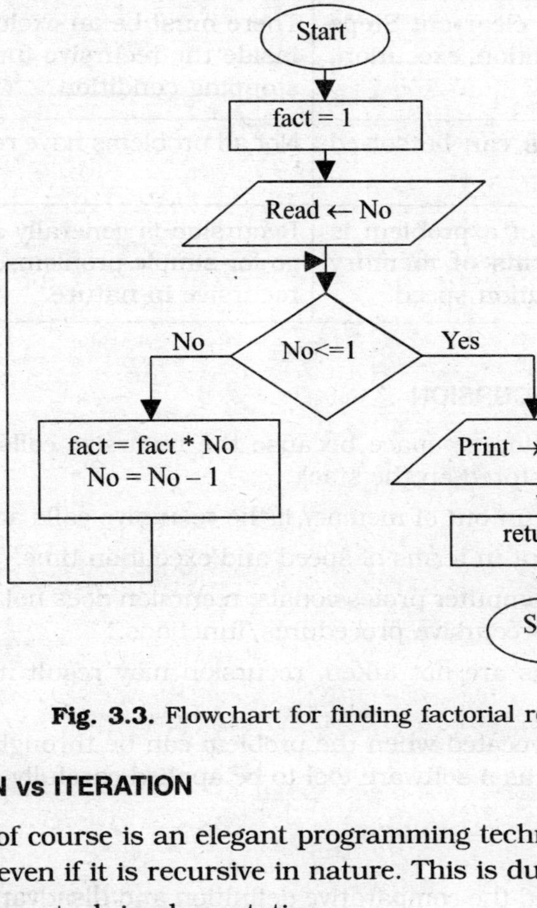

Fig. 3.3. Flowchart for finding factorial recursively

3.4.2. RECURSION vs ITERATION

Recursion of course is an elegant programming technique, but not the best way to solve a problem, even if it is recursive in nature. This is due to the following reasons:

1. It requires stack implementation.
2. It makes inefficient utilization of memory, as every time a new recursive call is made a new set of local variables is allocated to function.
3. Moreover it also slows down execution speed, as function calls require jumps, and saving the current state of program onto stack before jump.

Though inefficient way to solve general problems, it is too handy in several problems as discussed in the starting of this chapter. It provides a programmer with certain pitfalls.

and quite sharp concepts about programming. Moreover recursive functions are often easier to implement d maintain, particularly in case of data structures which are by nature recursive. Such data structures are queues, trees, and linked lists. Given below are some of the important points, which differentiate iteration from recursion.

No.	*Iteration*	*Recursion*
1	It is a process of executing a statement or a set of statements repeatedly, until some specified condition is specified.	Recursion is the technique of defining anything in terms of itself.
2	Iteration involves four clear-cut Steps like initialization, condition, execution, and updating.	There must be an exclusive if statement inside the recursive function, specifying stopping condition.
3	Any recursive problem can be solved iteratively.	Not all problems have recursive solution.
4	Iterative counterpart of a problem is more efficient in terms of memory 1,1tilization and execution speed.	Recursion is generally a worse option to go for simple problems, or problems not recursive in nature.

3.4.3. DISADVANTAGES OF RECURSION

1. It consumes more storage space because the recursive calls along with automatic variables are stored on the stack.
2. The computer may run out of memory if the recursive calls are not checked.
3. It is not more efficient in terms of speed and execution time.
4. According to some computer professionals, recursion does not offer any concrete advantage over non-recursive procedures/functions.
5. If proper precautions are not taken, recursion may result in non-terminating iterations.
6. Recursion is not advocated when the problem can be through iteration. Recursion may be treated as a software tool to be applied carefully and selectively.

3.4.4. TOWER OF HANOI

So far we have discussed the comparative definition and disadvantages of recursion with examples. Now let us look at the Tower of Hanoi problem and see how we can use recursive technique to produce a logical and elegant solution.

The initial setup of the problem is shown below. Here three pegs (or towers) X, Y and Z exists. There will be four different sized disks, say A, B, C and D. Each disk has a hole in the center so that it can be stacked on any of the pegs. At the beginning, the disks are stacked on the X peg, that is the largest sized disk on the bottom and the smallest sized disk on top as shown in Fig. 3.4.

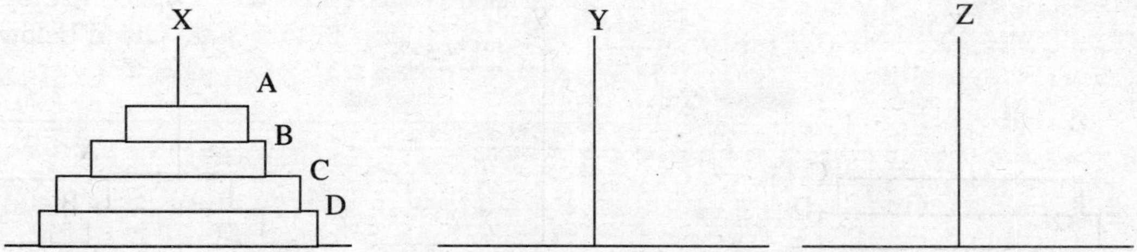

Fig. 3.4. Initial position of the Tower of Hanoi

Here we have to transfer all the disks from source peg X to the destinat[illegible] peg Z by using an intermediate peg Y. Following are the rules to be followed during transfer :

1. Transferring the disks from the source peg to the destination peg such that at any point of transformation no large size disk is placed on the smaller one.
2. Only one disk may be moved at a time.
3. Each disk must be stacked on any one of the pegs.

Now Tower of Hanoi problem can be solved as shown below :

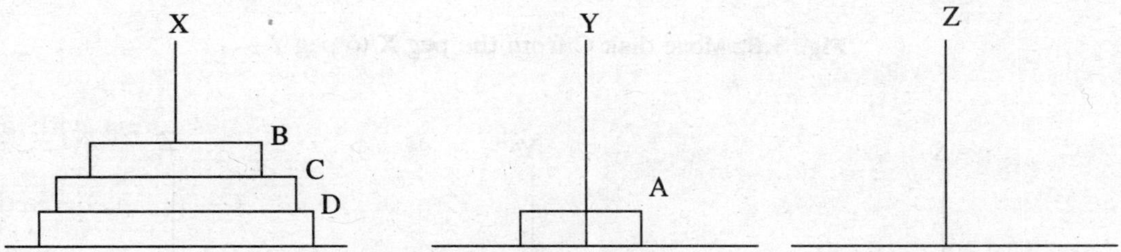

Fig. 3.5. Move disk A from the peg X to peg Y

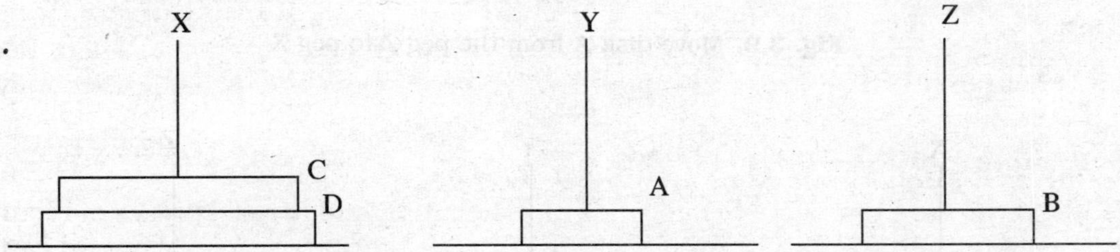

Fig. 3.6. Move disk B from the peg X to peg Z

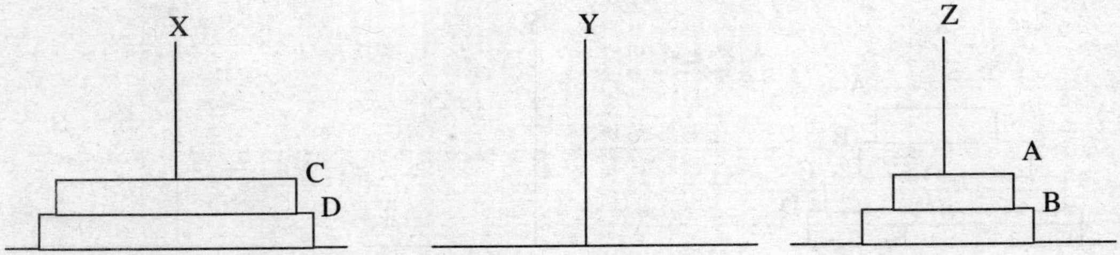

Fig. 3.7. Move disk A from the peg Y to peg Z

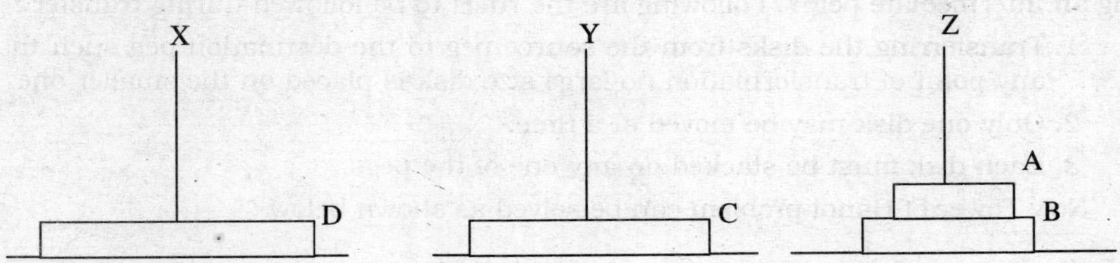

Fig. 3.8. Move disk C from the peg X to peg Y

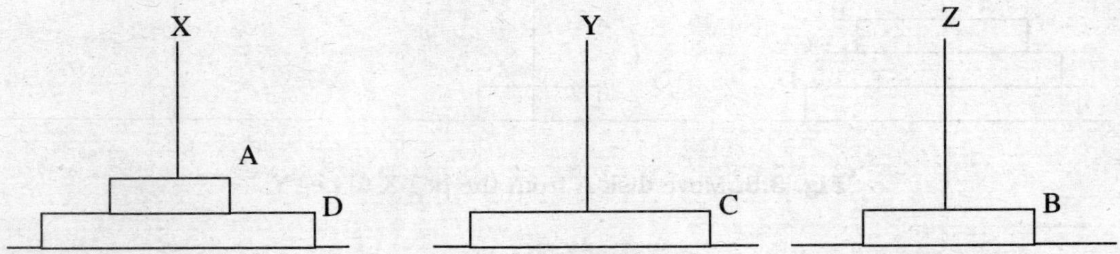

Fig. 3.9. Move disk A from the peg Z to peg X

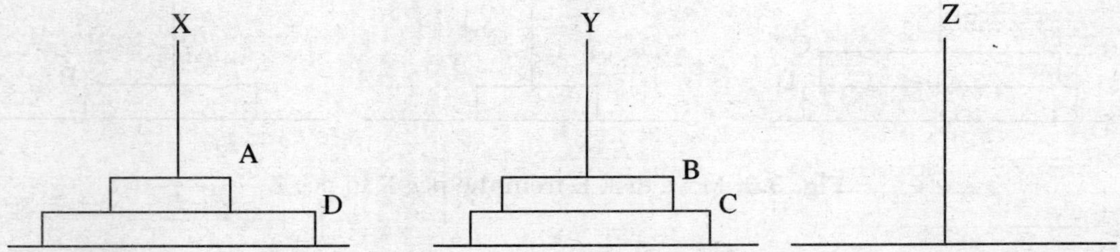

Fig. 3.10. Move disk B from the peg Z to peg Y

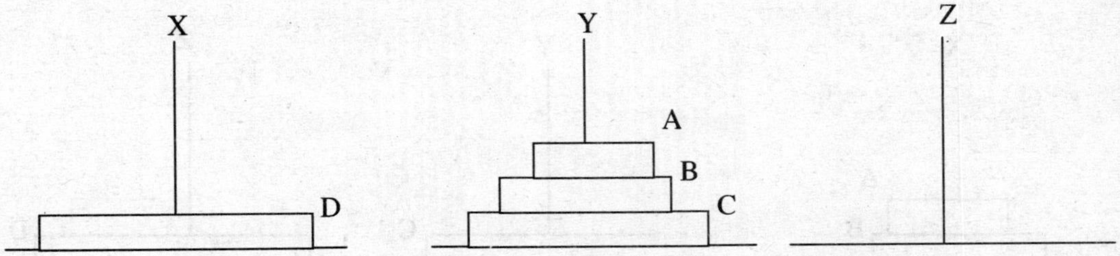

Fig. 3.11. Move disk A from the peg X to peg Y

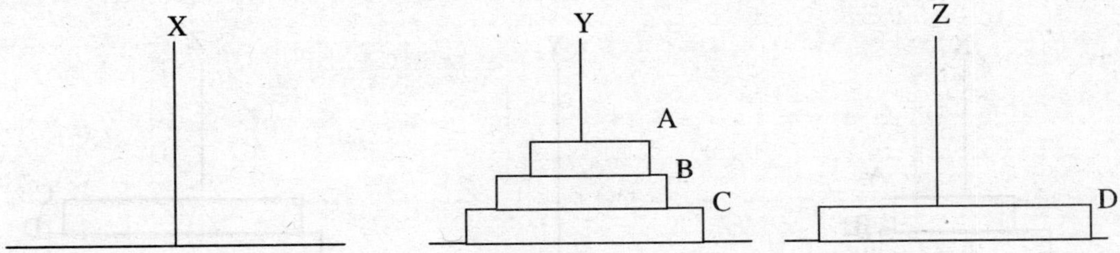

Fig. 3.12. Move disk D from the peg X to peg Z

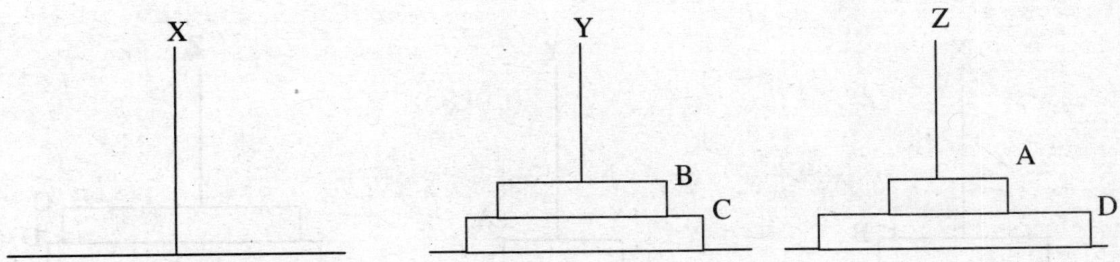

Fig. 3.13. Move disk A from the peg Y to peg Z

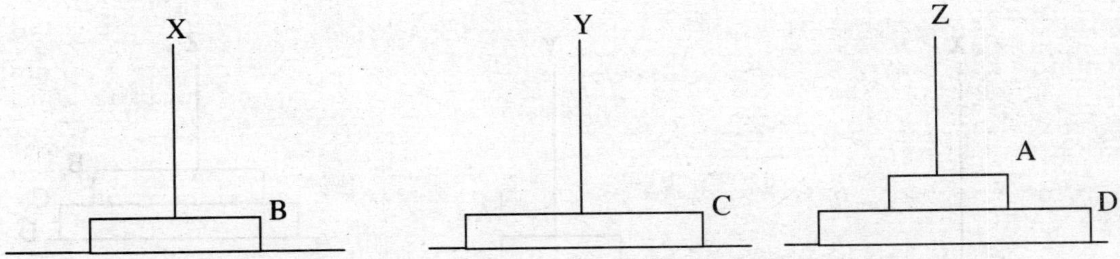

Fig. 3.14. Move disk B from the peg Y to peg X

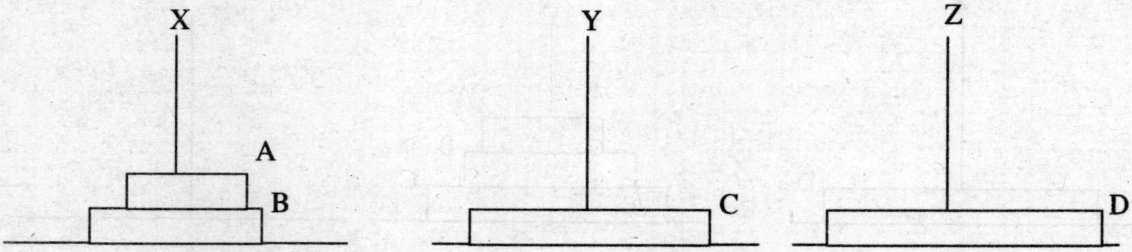

Fig. 3.15. Move disk A from the peg Z to peg X

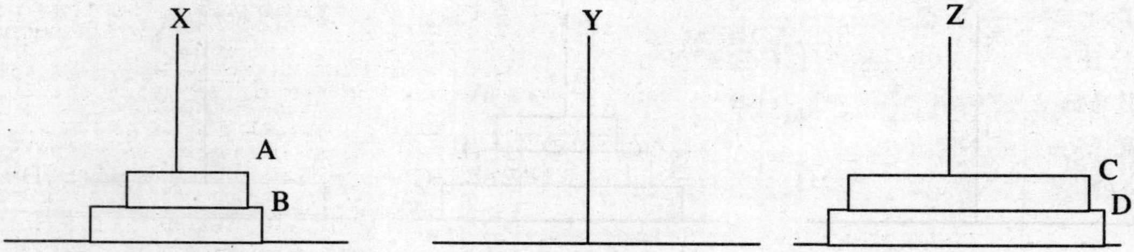

Fig. 3.16. Move disk C from the peg Y to peg Z

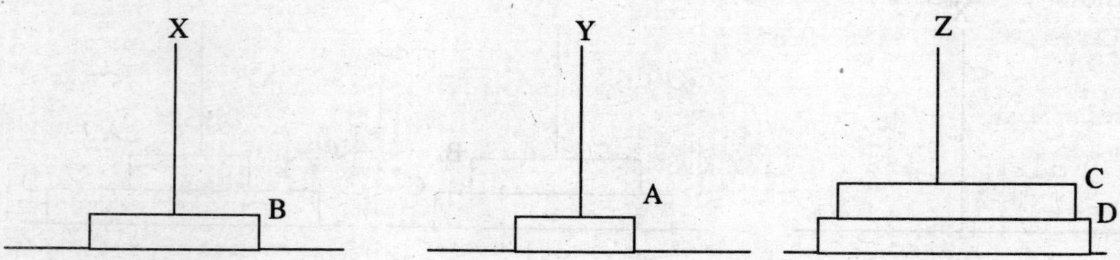

Fig. 3.17. Move disk A from the peg X to peg Y

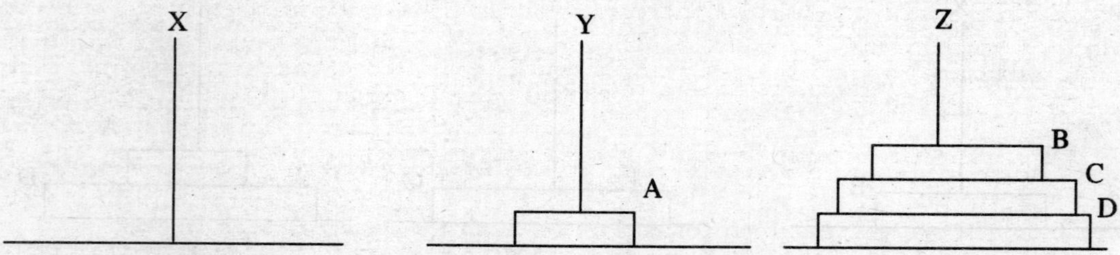

Fig. 3.18. Move disk B from the peg X to peg Z

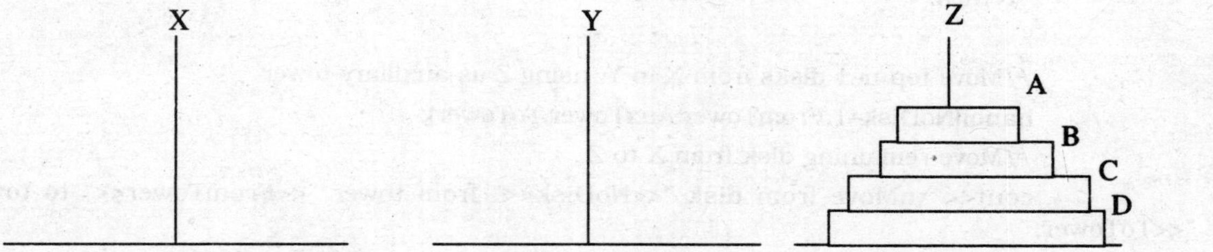

Fig. 3.19. Move disk A from the tower Y to tower Z

We can generalize the solution to the Tower of Hanoi problem recursively as follows :

To move *n* disks from peg X to peg Z, using Y as auxiliary peg:

1. If $n = 1$, move the single disk from X to Z and stop.

2. Move the top($n - 1$) disks from the peg X to the peg Y, using Z as auxiliary.

3. Move *n*th disk to peg Z.

4. Now move $n - 1$ disk from Y to Z, using Z as auxiliary.

PROGRAM 3.4

```
//PROGRAM TO SIMULATE THE TOWER OF HANOI PROBLEM
//CODED AND COMPILED IN TURBO C++

#include<conio.h>
#include<iostream.h>

class tower
{
        //Private variables are declared
        int NoDisk;
        char FromTower,ToTower,AuxTower;

        public:
                void hanoi(int,char,char,char);
};

void tower::hanoi(int NoDisk,char FromTower,char ToTower, char AuxTower)
{
        //if only one disk, make the move and return
        if (NoDisk == 1)
        {
```

```
        cout<<"\nMove from disk 1 from tower "<<FromTower<<" to tower "<<ToTower;
        return;
    }
    //Move top n–1 disks from X to Y, using Z as auxiliary tower
    hanoi(NoDisk–1,FromTower,AuxTower,ToTower);
    //Move remaining disk from X to Z
    cout<<"\nMove from disk "<<NoDisk<<" from tower "<<FromTower<<" to tower
"<<ToTower;
    //Move n–1 disk from Y to Z using X as auxiliary tower
    hanoi(NoDisk–1,AuxTower,ToTower,FromTower);
    return;
}

void main()
{
    int No;
    tower Ob;
    clrscr();
    cout<<"\n\t\t\t--- Tower of Hanoi ---\n";
    //Imput the number of disk in the tower
    cout<<"\n\nEnter the number of disks = ";
    cin>>No;
    //We assume that the towers are X, Y and Z
    Ob.hanoi(No,'X','Z','Y');
    cout<<"\n\nPress any key to continue...";
    getch();
}
```

3.4.5. EXPRESSION

Another application of stack is calculation of postfix expression. There are basically three types of notation for an expression (mathematical expression; An expression is defined as the number of operands or data items combined with several operators.)

1. Infix notation
2. Prefix notation
3. Postfix notation

The *infix notation* is what we come across in our general mathematics, where the operator is written in-between the operands. For example : The expression to add two numbers A and B is written in infix notation as:

$$A + B$$

Note that the operator '+' is written in between the operands A and B.

The *prefix notation* is a notation in which the operator(s) is written before the operands, it is also called polish notation in the honor of the polish mathematician Jan

Lukasiewicz who developed this notation. The same expression when written in prefix notation looks like:

+ A B

As the operator '+' is written before the operands A and B, this notation is called prefix (pre means before).

In the *postfix notation* the operator(s) are written after the operands, so it is called the postfix notation (post means after), it is also known as *suffix notation* or *reverse polish notation.* The above expression if written in postfix expression looks like:

A B +

The prefix and postfix notations are not really as awkward to use as they might look. For example, a C function to return the sum of two variables A and B (passed as argument) is called or invoked by the instruction:

add(A, B)

Note that the operator *add* (name of the function) precedes the operands A and B. Because the postfix notation is most suitable for a computer to calculate any expression (due to its reverse characteristic), and is the universally accepted notation for designing Arithmetic and Logical Unit (ALU) of the CPU (processor). Therefore it is necessary to study the postfix notation. Moreover the postfix notation is the way computer looks towards arithmetic expression, any expression entered into the computer is first converted into postfix notation, stored in stack and then calculated. In the preceding sections we will study the conversion of the expression from one notation to other.

Advantages of using postfix notation

Human beings are quite used to work with mathematical expressions in *infix* notation, which is rather complex. One has to remember a set of nontrivial rules while using this notation and it must be applied to expressions in order to determine the final value. These rules include precedence, BODMAS, and associativity.

Using infix notation, one cannot tell the order in which operators should be applied. Whenever an infix expression consists of more than one operator, the precedence rules (BODMAS) should be applied to decide which operator (and operand associated with that operator) is evaluated first. But in a postfix expression operands appear before the operator, so there is no need for operator precedence and other rules. As soon as an operator appears in the postfix expression during scanning of postfix expression the topmost operands are popped off and are calculated by applying the encountered operator. Place the result back onto the stack; likewise at the end of the whole operation the final result will be there in the stack.

Notation Conversions

Let A + B * C be the given expression, which is an infix notation. To calculate this expression for values 4, 3, 7 for A, B, C respectively we must follow certain rule (called BODMAS in general mathematics) in order to have the right result. For example:

A + B * C = 4 + 3 * 7 = 7 * 7 = 49

The answer is not correct; multiplication is to be done before the addition, because multiplication has higher precedence over addition. This means that an expression is calculated according to the operator's precedence not the order as they look like. The error in the above calculation occurred, since there were no braces to define the precedence of the operators. Thus expression A + B * C can be interpreted as A + (B * C). Using this alternative method we can convey to the computer that multiplication has higher precedence over addition.

Operator precedence

Exponential operator	^	Highest precedence
Multiplication/Division	*, /	Next precedence
Addition/Subtraction	+, -	Least precedence

3.5. CONVERTING INFIX TO POSTFIX EXPRESSION

The method of converting infix expression A + B * C to postfix form is:

A + B * C Infix Form
A + (B * C) Parenthesized expression
A + (B C *) Convert the multiplication
A (B C *) + Convert the addition
A B C * + Postfix form

The rules to be remembered during infix to postfix conversion are:

1. Parenthesize the expression starting from left to light.
2. During parenthesizing the expression, the operands associated with operator having higher precedence are first parenthesized. For example in the above expression B * C is parenthesized first before A + B.
3. The sub-expression (part of expression), which has been converted into postfix, is to be treated as single operand.
4. Once the expression is converted to postfix form, remove the parenthesis.

Problem 3.4.2.1. Give postfix form for A + [(B + C) + (D + E) * F] / G

Solution. Evaluation order is

A + { [(BC +) + (DE +) * F] / G}
A + { [(BC +) + (DE + F *] / G}
A + { [(BC + (DE + F * +] / G} .
A + [BC + DE + F *+ G /]
ABC + DE + F * + G / + Postfix Form

Problem 3.4.2.2. Give postfix form for (A + B) * C / D + E ^ A / B

Solution. Evaluation order is

[(AB +) * C / D] + [(EA ^) / B]
[(AB +) * C / D] + [(EA ^) B /]
[(AB +) C * D /] + [(EA ^) B /]

(AB +) C * D / (EA ^) B / +

AB + C * D / EA ^ B / + Postfix Form

Algorithm

Suppose P is an arithmetic expression written in infix notation. This algorithm finds the equivalent postfix expression Q. Besides operands and operators, P (infix notation) may also contain left and right parentheses. We assume that the operators in P consists of only exponential (^), multiplication (*), division (/), addition (+) and subtraction (-). The algorithm uses a stack to temporarily hold the operators and left parentheses. The postfix expression Q will be constructed from left to right using the operands from P and operators, which are removed from stack. We begin by pushing a left parenthesis onto stack and adding a right parenthesis at the end of P. the algorithm is completed when the stack is empty.

1. Push "(" onto stack, and add")" to the end of P.
2. Scan P from left to right and repeat Steps 3 to 6 for each element of P until the stack is empty.
3. If an operand is encountered, add it to Q.
4. If a left parenthesis is encountered, push it onto stack.
5. If an operator ⊗ is encountered, then:
   (*a*) Repeatedly pop from stack and add P each operator (on the top of stack), which has the same precedence as, or higher precedence than ⊗.
   (*b*) Add ⊗ to stack.
6. If a right parenthesis is encountered, then:
   (*a*) Repeatedly pop from stack and add to P (on the top of stack until a left parenthesis is encountered.
   (*b*) Remove the left parenthesis. [Do not add the left parenthesis to P.]
7. Exit.

Note. Special character ⊗ is used to symbolize any operator in P.

Consider the following arithmetic infix expression P

P = A + (B / C - (D * E ^ F) + G) * H

Fig. 3.20 shows the character (operator, operand or parenthesis) scanned, status of the stack and postfix expression Q of the infix expression P.

Character scanned	*Stack*	*Postfix Expression (Q)*
A	(	A
+	(+	A
(	(+ (	A
B	(+ (	A B
/	(+ (/	A B
C	(+ (/	A B C

–	(+ (-	A B C /
(	(+ (- (	A B C /
D	(+ (- (	A B C / D
*	(+ (- (*	A B C / D
E	(+ (- (*	A B C / D E
^	(+ (- (* ^	A B C / D E
F	(+ (- (* ^	A B C / D E F
)	(+ (-	A B C / D E F ^ *
+	(+ (+	A B C / D E F ^ * -
G	(+ (+	A B C / D E F ^ * - G
)	(+	A B C / D E F ^ * - G +
*	(+ *	A B C / D E F ^ * - G +
H	(+ *	A B C / D E F ^ * - G + H
)		A B C / D E F ^ * - G + H * +

Fig. 3.20

PROGRAM 3.5

```
//THIS PROGRAM IS TO COVERT THE INFIX TO POSTFIX EXPRESSION
//STACK IS USED AND IT IS IMPLEMENTATION USING ARRAYS
//CODED AND COMPILED IN TURBO C

#include<stdio.h>
#include<conio.h>
#include<string.h>

//Defining the maximum size of the stack
#define MAXSIZE 100
//Declaring the stack array and top variables in a structure
struct stack
{
        char stack[MAXSIZE];
        int Top;
};

//type definition allows the user to define an identifier that would
//represent an existing data type. The user-defined data type identifier
//can later be used to declare variables.
typedef struct stack NODE:
```

```
//This function will add/insert an element to Top of the stack
void push(NODE *pu,char item)
{
        //if the top pointer already reached the maximum allowed size then
        //we can say that the stack is full or overflow
        if (pu->Top == MAXSIZE-1)
        {
                printf("\nThe Stack Is Full");
                getch();
        }
        //Otherwise an element can be added or inserted by
        //incrementing the stack pointer Top as follows
        else
                pu->stack[++pu->Top]=item;
}

//This function will delete an element from the Top of the stack
char pop(NODE *po)
{
        char item='#';
        //If the Top pointer points to NULL, then the stack is empty
        //That is NO element is there to delete or pop
        if(po->Top == -1)
                printf("\nThe Stack Is Empty. Invalid Infix expression");
        //Otherwise the top most element in the stack is poped or
        //deleted by decrementing the Top pointer
        else
                item=po->stack[po->Top--];
        return(item);
}


//This function returns the precedence of the operator
int prec(char symbol)

        switch(symbol)
```

```
        case '-':
                return(3);
        case '*':
        case '/':
        case '%':
                return(4);
        case '^':
                return(5);
        default:
                return(0);
    }
}

//This function will return the postfix expression of an infix
void Infix_Postfix(char infix[])
{

    int len,priority;
    char postfix[MAXSIZE],ch;
    //Declaring an pointer variable to the structure
    NODE *ps;
    //Initializing the Top pointer to NULL
    ps->Top=-1;
    //Finding length of the string
    len=strlen(infix);
    //At the end of the string inputting a parenthesis ')'
    infix[len++]=')';
    push(ps,'(');//Parenthesis is pushed to the stack
    for(int i=0,j=0;i<len;i++)
    {
        switch(prec(infix[i]))

            //Scanned char is '(' push to the stack
            case 1:
                push(ps,infix[i]);
                break;
            //Scanned char is ')' pop the operator(s) and add to //the postfix
            expression
            case 2:
                ch=pop(ps);
                while(ch != '(')
                {
```

```
                postfix[j++]=ch;
                ch=pop(ps);
            }
            break;
        //Scanned operator is +,- then pop the higher or same
        //precedence operator to add postfix before pushing
        //the scanned operator to the stack
        case 3:
            ch=pop(ps);
            while(prec(ch) >= 3)
            {
                postfix[j++]=ch;
                ch=pop(ps);
            }
            push(ps,ch);
            push(ps,infix[i]);
            break;
        //Scanned operator is *,/,% then pop the higher or
        //same precedence operator to add postfix before
        //pushing the scanned operator to the stack
        case 4:
            ch=pop(ps);
            while(prec(ch) >= 4)
            {
                postfix[j++]=ch;
                ch=pop(ps);
            }
            push(ps,ch);
            push(ps,infix[i]);
            break;
        //Scanned operator is ^ then pop the same
        //precedence operator to add to postfix before pushing
        //the scanned operator to the stack
        case 5:
            ch=pop(ps);
            while(prec(ch) == 5)
            {
                postfix[j++]=ch;
                ch=pop(ps);
            }
            push(ps,ch);
            push(ps,infix[i]);
            break;
```

```
                //Scanned char is a operand simply add to the postfix
                //expression
                default:
                        postfix[j++]=infix[i];
                        break;
                }
        }
        //Printing the postfix notation to the screen
        printf ("\nThe Postfix expression is = ");
        for(i=0;i<j;i++)
        printf ("%c",postfix[i]);
}

void main()
{
        char choice,infix[MAXSIZE];
        do
        {
                clrscr();
                printf("\n\nEnter the infix expression = ");
                fflush(stdin);
                gets(infix);//Inputting the infix notation
                Infix_Postfix(infix);//Calling the infix to postfix function
                printf("\n\nDo you want to continue (Y/y) =");
                fflush(stdin);
                scanf("%c",&choice);
        }while(choice == 'Y' || choice == 'y');
}
```

PROGRAM 3.6

```
//THIS PROGRAM IS TO COVERT THE INFIX TO POSTFIX EXPRESSION
//AND IT IS IMPLEMENTATION USING ARRAYS
//CODED AND COMPILED IN TURBO C++

#include<iostream.h>
#include<conio.h>
#include<string.h>
```

```
//Defining the maximum size of the stack
#define MAXSIZE 100

//A class initialised with public and private variables and functions
class STACK_ARRAY
{
        int stack[MAXSIZE];
        int Top;

        public:
        //constructor is called and Top pointer is initialised to -1
        //when an object is created for the class
                STACK_ARRAY()
                {
                        Top=-1;
                }
                void push(char);
                char pop();
                int prec(char);
                void Infix_Postfix();

};

//This function will add/insert an element to Top of the stack
void STACK_ARRAY::push(char item)
{
        //if the top pointer already reached the maximum allows size then
        //we can say that the stack is full or overflow
        if (Top == MAXSIZE-1)
        {
                cout<<"\nThe Stack Is Full";
                getch();
        }
        //Otherwise an element can be added or inserted by
        //incrementing the stack pointer Top as follows
        else
                stack[++Top]=item;
}

//This function will delete an element from the Top of the stack
char STACK_ARRAY::pop()
{
```

```
        char item='#';
        //If the Top pointer points to NULL, then the stack is empty
        //That is NO element is there to delete or pop
        if (Top == -1)
                cout<<"\nThe Stack Is Empty. Invalid Infix expression";
        //Otherwise the top most element in the stack is poped or
        //deleted by decrementing the Top pointer
        else
                item=stack[Top--];
        return(item);
}
//This function returns the precedence of the operator
int STACK_ARRAY::prec(char symbol)
{
        switch(symbol)
        {
                case '(':
                        return(1);
                case ')':
                        return(2);
                case '+':
                case '-':
                        return(3);
                case '*':
                case '/':
                case '%':
                        return(4);
                case '^':
                        return(5);
                default:
                        return(0);
        }
}

//This function will return the postfix expression of an infix
void STACK_ARRAY::Infix_Postfix()
{

        int len,priority;
        char infix[MAXSIZE],postfix[MAXSIZE],ch;
        cout<<"\n\nEnter the infix expression = ";
        cin>>infix;//Inputting the infix notation
```

```
//Finding length of the string
len=strlen(infix);
//At the end of the string inputting a parenthesis ')'
infix[len++]=')';
push('(');//Parenthesis is pushed to the stack
for(int i=0,j=0;i<len;i++)
{
    switch(prec(infix[i]))
    {
         //Scanned char is '(' push to the stack
        case 1:
            push(infix[i]);
            break;
    //Scanned char is ')' pop the operator(s) and add to
    //the postfix expression
        case 2:
            ch=pop();
            while(ch != '(')
            {
                postfix[j++]=ch;
                ch=pop();
            }
            break;
    //Scanned operator is +,- then pop the higher or
    //same precedence operator to add postfix before
    //pushing the scanned operator to the stack
        case 3:
            ch=pop();
            while(prec(ch) >= 3)
            {
                postfix[j++]=ch;
                ch=pop();
            }
            push(ch);
            push(infix[i]);
            break;
    //Scanned operator is *,/,% then pop the higher or
    //same precedence operator to add postfix before
    //pushing the scanned operator to the stack
        case 4:
            ch=pop();
            while(prec(ch) >= 4)
            {
```

```
                        postfix[j++]=ch;
                        ch=pop();
                    }
                    push(ch);
                    push(infix[i]);
                    break;
                //Scanned operator is ^ then pop the same
                //precedence operator to add to postfix before
                //pushing the scanned operator to the stack
                case 5:
                    ch=pop();
                    while(prec(ch) == 5)
                    {
                        postfix[j++]=ch;
                        ch=pop();
                    }
                    push(ch);
                    push(infix[i]);
                    break;
                //Scanned char is a operand simply add to the
                //postfix expression
                default:
                    postfix[j++]=infix[i];
                    break;
            }
        }
        //Printing the postfix notation to the screen
        cout<<"\nThe Postfix expression is = ";
        for(i=0;i<j;i++)
        cout<<postfix[i];
}
void main()
{
        char choice;
        INFI_POST ip;
        do
        {
            clrscr();
            ip.Infix_Postfix();//Calling the infix to postfix function
            cout<<"\n\nDo you want to continue (Y/y) =";
            cin>>choice;
        }while(choice == 'Y' || choice == 'y');
```

3.6. EVALUATING POSTFIX EXPRESSION

Following algorithm finds the RESULT of an arithmetic expression P written in postfix notation. The following algorithm, which uses a STACK to hold operands, evaluates P.

Algorithm

1. Add a right parenthesis ")" at the end of P. [This acts as a sentinel.]
2. Scan P from left to right and repeat Steps 3 and 4 for each element of P until the sentinel ")" is encountered.
3. If an operand is encountered, put it on STACK.
4. If an operator ⊗ is encountered, then:
   (*a*) Remove the two top elements of STACK, where A is the top element and B is the next-to-top element.
   (*b*) Evaluate B ⊗ A.
   (*c*) Place the result on to the STACK.
5. Result equal to the top element on STACK.
6. Exit.

PROGRAM 3.7

```
//THIS PROGRAM IS TO EVALUATE POSTFIX EXPRESSION. THE STACK
//IS USED AND IT IS IMPLEMENTATION USING ARRAYS
//CODED AND COMPILED IN TURBO C

#include<stdio.h>
#include<math.h>
#include<conio.h>
#include<string.h>

//Defining the maximum size of the stack
#define MAXSIZE 100

//Declaring the stack array and top variables in a structure
struct stack
{
        int stack[MAXSIZE];
        int Top;
};

//type definition allows the user to define an identifier that would
//represent an existing data type. The user-defined data_type identifier
```

```
//can later be used to declare variables.
typedef struct stack NODE;

//This function will add/insert an element to Top of the stack
void push(NODE *pu,int item)
{
        //if the top pointer already reached the maximum allowed size then
        //we can say that the stack is full or overflow
        if (pu->Top == MAXSIZE-1)
        {
                printf("\nThe Stack Is Full");
                getch();
        }
        //Otherwise an element can be added or inserted by
        //incrementing the stack pointer Top as follows
        else
                pu->stack[++pu->Top]=item;
}

//This function will delete an element from the Top of the stack
int pop(NODE *po)
{
        int item;
        //If the Top pointer points to NULL, then the stack is empty
        //That is NO element is there to delete or pop
        if (po->Top == –1)
                printf("\nThe Stack Is Empty. Invalid Infix expression");
        //Otherwise the top most element in the stack is poped or
        //deleted by decrementing the Top pointer
        else
                item=po->stack[po->Top--];
        return(item);

//This function will return the postfix expres
nt Postfix_Eval(char postfix[])

        int a,b,temp,len;
        //Declaring an r
        NODE *ps;
        //Initializing the
        ps->Top=–1;
```

```
        //Finding length of the string
        len=strlen(postfix);

        for(int i=0;i<len;i++)
        {
                if(postfix[i]<='9' && postfix[i]>='0')
                        //Operand is pushed on the stack
    push(ps,(postfix[i]-48));
                else
                {
                        //Pop the top most two operand for operation
                        a=pop(ps);
                        b=pop(ps);

                        switch(postfix[i])
                        {
                        case '+':
                                temp=b+a; break;
                        case '-':
                                temp=b–a;break;
                        case '*':
                                temp=b*a;break;
                        case '/':
                                temp=b/a;break;
                        case '%':
                                temp=b%a;break;
                        case '^':
                                temp=pow(b,a);
                        }/*End of switch */
                        push(ps,temp);
                }
        ,
        return(pop(ps));
}

void main()
{
        char choice,postfix[MAXSIZE];
        do
        {
                clrscr();
                printf("\n\nEnter the Postfix expression =
```

```
		fflush(stdin);
		gets(postfix);//Inputting the postfix notation
	printf("\n\nThe postfix evaluation is = %d",Postfix_Eval(postfix));
		printf("\n\nDo you want to continue (Y/y) =");
		fflush(stdin);
		scanf("%c",&choice);
	}while(choice == 'Y' || choice == 'y');
}
```

PROGRAM 3.8

```
//THIS PROGRAM IS TO COVERT THE INFIX TO POSTFIX EXPRESSION
//AND IT IS IMPLEMENTATION USING ARRAYS
//CODED AND COMPILED IN TURBO C++

#include<iostream.h>
#include<math.h>
#include<conio.h>
#include<string.h>

//Defining the maximum size of the stack
#define MAXSIZE 100

//A class initialised with public and private variables and functions
class POST_EVAL
{
	int stack[MAXSIZE];
	int Top;

	public:
	//constructor is called and Top pointer is initialised to -1
	//when an object is created for the class
		POST_EVAL()
		{
			Top=-1;
		}
		void push(int);
		int pop();
		int Postfix_Eval();
```

```
};

//This function will add/insert an element to Top of the stack
void POST_EVAL::push(int item)
{
        //if the top pointer already reached the maximum allows size
        //then we can say that the stack is full or overflow
        if (Top == MAXSIZE-1)
        {
                cout<<"\nThe Stack Is Full";
                getch();
        }
        //Otherwise an element can be added or inserted by
        //incrementing the stack pointer Top as follows
        else
                stack[++Top]=item;
}

//This function will delete an element from the Top of the stack
int POST_EVAL::pop()
{
        int item;
        //If the Top pointer points to NULL, then the stack is empty
        //That is NO element is there to delete or pop
        if (Top == -1)
                cout<<"\nThe Stack Is Empty. Invalid Infix expression";
        //Otherwise the top most element in the stack is poped or
        //deleted by decrementing the Top pointer
        else
                item=stack[Top--];
        return(item);
}

//This function will return the postfix expression of an infix
int POST_EVAL::Postfix_Eval()
{
        int a,b,temp,len;
        char postfix[MAXSIZE];
        cout<<"\n\nEnter the Postfix expression = ";
        cin>>postfix;//Inputting the postfix notation

        //Finding length of the string
```

```
        len=strlen(postfix);

        for(int i=0;i<len;i++)
        {
            if (postfix[i]<='9' && postfix[i]>='0')
                push(postfix[i]-48);
            else
            {
                a=pop();
                b=pop();

                switch(postfix[i])
                {
                case '+':
                    temp=b+a; break;
                case '-':
                    temp=b–a;break;
                case '*':
                    temp=b*a;break;
                case '/':
                    temp=b/a;break;
                case '%':
                    temp=b%a;break;
                case '^':
                    temp=pow(b,a);
                }/*End of switch */
                push(temp);
            }/*End of else*/
        }/*End of for */
        return(pop());
}

void main()
{
        char choice;
        int RESULT;
        POST_EVAL ps;
        do
        {
            clrscr();
            RESULT=ps.Postfix_Eval();
            cout<<"\n\nThe postfix evaluation is = "<<RESULT;
```

```
        cout<<"\n\nDo you want to continue (Y/y) =";
        cin>>choice;
    }while(choice == 'Y' || choice == 'y');
}
```

SELF REVIEW QUESTIONS

1. What is meant by recursive algorithm ? *[MG - MAY 2004 (BTech)]*
2. Define and explain the data structure stacks. *[MG - MAY 2004 (BTech)]*
3. What are the operations on stack and an important use for this structure? *[Calicut - APR 1995 (BTech), MG - NOV 2003 (BTech), MG - NOV 2002 (BTech)]*
4. Explain how infix expressions are converted to polish notation. Illustrate the answer with suitable example ? *[CUSAT - DEC 2003 (MCA), MG - MAY 2002 (BTech) ANNA - DEC 2004 (BE), CUSAT - JUL 2002 (MCA) KERALA - MAY 2002 (BTech)]*
5. Discuss the use of a stack in implementing recursive procedures. *[MG - MAY 2002 (BTech)]*
6. Explain recursion with one example. *[ANNA - DEC 2004 (BE), MG - MAY 2000 (BTech)]*
7. Write an algorithm for deleting an element from a stack. *[Calicut - APR 1995 (BTech)]*
9. Show how to evaluate the expression in the postfix using stack. *[Calicut - APR 1995 (BTech)]*
10. Discuss the application of stacks. *[Calicut - APR 1997 (BTech)]*
11. Write an algorithm to transform from prefix to postfix. *[CUSAT - APR 1998 (BTech)]*
12. Explain the principle of recursive algorithm. *[CUSAT - MAY 2000 (BTech)]*
13. Outline an algorithm to convert a given postfix expression to infix form. *[CUSAT - MAY 2000 (BTech)]*
14. Explain the implementation of stack using arrays and linked list. Write appropriate functions to perform valid operations on stack. *[CUSAT - MAY 2000 (BTech)]*
15. What is a Stack? Explain any two operations performed on a Stack with required algorithms. *[KERALA - NOV 2001 (BTech), ANNA - DEC 2004 (BE)]*
16. Convert the following infix expression into postfix form (A + B)* (C + B)* (ElF). *[ANNA - MAY 2004 (MCA)]*
17. What is recursion? Give the application of recursion with programs. *[ANNA - MAY 2003 (BE)]*
18. What are the various stack operations? Explain. *[KERALA - MAY 2003 (BTech), ANNA - MAY 2003 (BE)]*
19. Explain the application of stack for conversion of infix to postfix. *[ANNA - MAY 2003 (BE)]*

20. Write procedures for Push and Prop operations on stacks.

[*KERALA - DEC 2004 (BTech)*]

21. Write procedure to convert infix to portfix expressions.

[*KERALA - JUN 2004 (BTech), KERALA - DEC 2004 (BTech)*
KERALA - NOV 2001 (BTech)]

22. Explain the linked list implementation of a LIFO structure.

[*KERALA - DEC 2002 (BTech)*]

23. Write the prefix and postfix form for: A + B * (C - D) / (E - F).

[*KERALA - MAY 2002 (BTech)*]

24. Which data structure would you use for recursive procedures?

[*KERALA - MAY 2002 (BTech)*]

25. Explain how a postfix expression is evaluated using stack with suitable example ?

[*KERALA - NOV 2001 (BTech)*]

4 The Queues

A queue is logically a *first in first out (FIFO or first come first serve)* linear data structure. The concept of queue can be understood by our real life problems. For example a customer come and join in a queue to take the train ticket at the end (rear) and the ticket is issued from the front end of queue. That is, the customer who arrived first will receive the ticket first. It means the customers are serviced in the order in which they arrive at the service centre.

It is a homogeneous collection of elements in which new elements are added at one end called *rear*, and the existing elements are deleted from other end called *front*.

The basic operations that can be performed on queue are

1. Insert (or add) an element to the queue (push)
2. Delete (or remove) an element from a queue (pop)

Push operation will insert (or add) an element to queue, at the rear end, by incrementing the array index. Pop operation will delete (or remove) from the front end by decrementing the array index and will assign the deleted value to a variable. Total number of elements present in the queue is front-rear+1, when implemented using arrays. Following figure will illustrate the basic operations on queue.

Fig. 4.1. Queue is empty.

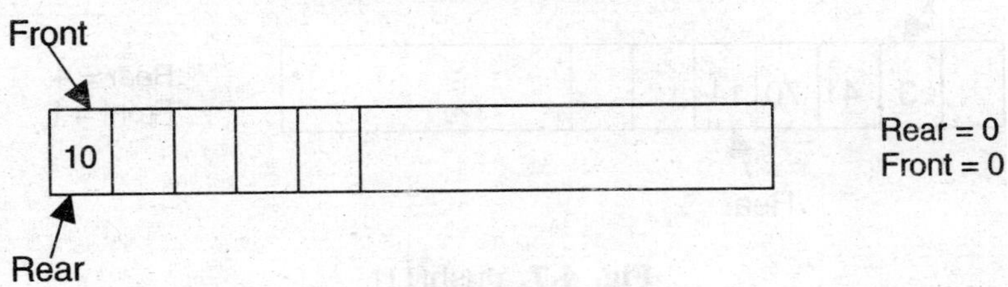

Fig. 4.2. push(10)

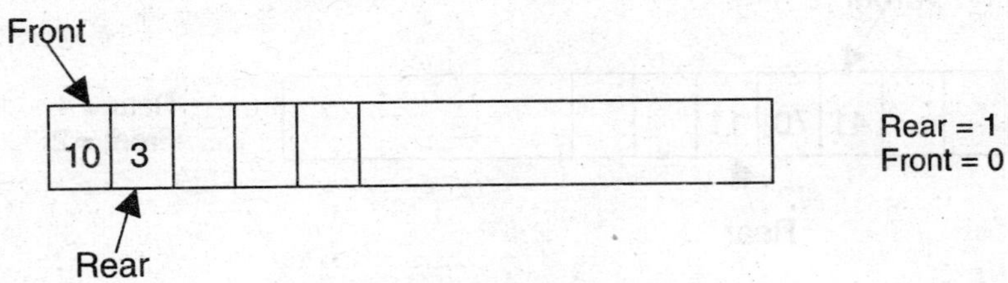

Fig. 4.3. push(3)

Fig. 4.4. push(41)

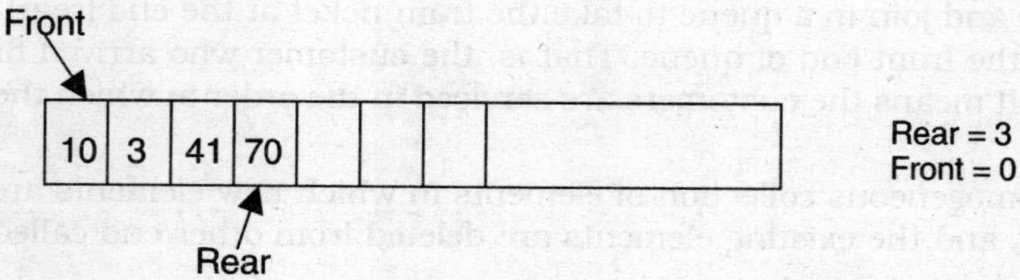

Fig. 4.5. push(70)

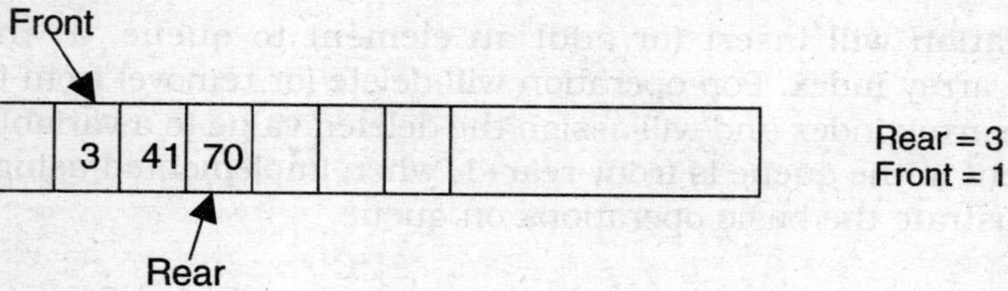

Fig. 4.6. x = pop() (*i.e.*; x = 10)

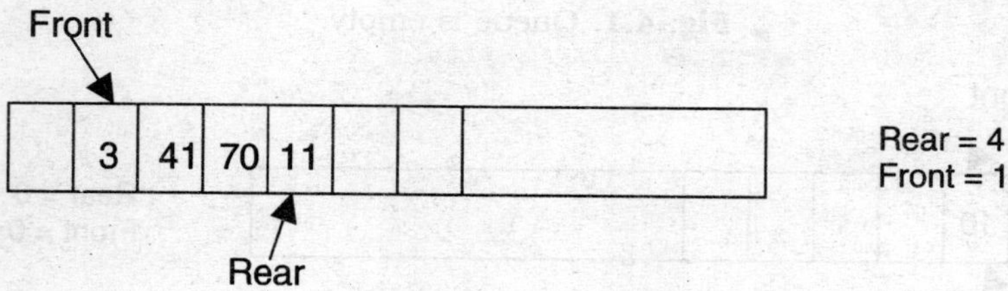

Fig. 4.7. push(11)

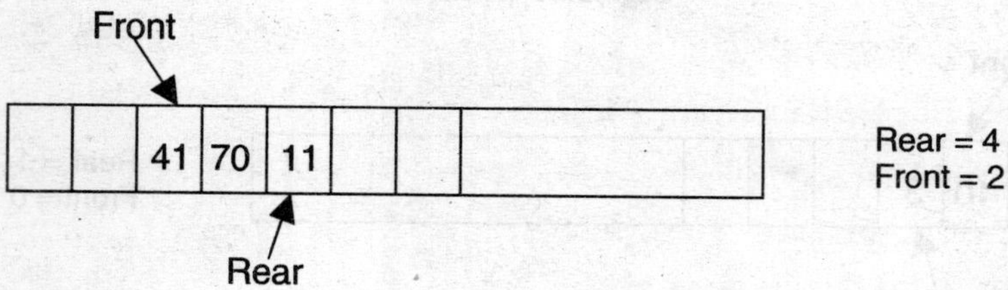

Fig. 4.8. x = pop() (*i.e.*; x = 3)

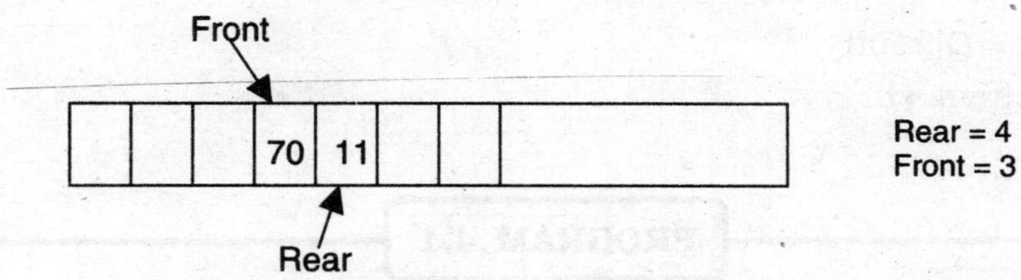

Fig. 4.9. x = pop() (*i.e.*, x = 41)

Queue can be implemented in two ways:

1. Using arrays (static)
2. Using pointers (dynamic)

Implementation of queue using pointers will be discussed in chapter 5. Let us discuss underflow and overflow conditions when a queue is implemented using arrays.

If we try to pop (or delete or remove) an element from queue when it is empty, underflow occurs. It is not possible to delete (or take out) any element when there is no element in the queue.

Suppose maximum size of the queue (when it is implemented using arrays) is 50. If we try to push (or insert or add) an element to queue, overflow occurs. When queue is full it is naturally not possible to insert any more elements

4.1. ALGORITHM FOR QUEUE OPERATIONS

Let Q be the array of some specified size say SIZE

4.1.1. INSERTING AN ELEMENT INTO THE QUEUE

1. Initialize front=0 rear = –1
2. Input the value to be inserted and assign to variable "data"
3. If (rear >= SIZE)
   (*a*) Display "Queue overflow"
   (*b*) Exit
4. Else
   (*a*) Rear = rear +1
5. Q[rear] = data
6. Exit

4.1.2. DELETING AN ELEMENT FROM QUEUE

1. If (rear< front)
   (*a*) Front = 0, rear = –1
   (*b*) Display "The queue is empty"
   (*c*) Exit

2. Else
   (*a*) Data = Q[front]
3. Front = front +1
4. Exit

PROGRAM 4.1

```
//PROGRAM TO IMPLEMENT QUEUE USING ARRAYS
//CODED AND COMPILED USING TURBO C

#include<conio.h>
#include<stdio.h>
#include<process.h>

#define MAX 50

int queue_arr[MAX];
int rear = -1;
int front = -1;

//This function will insert an element to the queue
void insert ()
{
        int added_item;
        if (rear==MAX-1)
        {
                printf("\nQueue Overflow\n");
                getch();
                return;
        }
        else
        {
                if (front==-1)  /*If queue is initially empty */
                        front=0;
                printf("\nInput the element for adding in queue: ");
                scanf("%d", &added_item);
                rear=rear+1;
                //Inserting the element
                queue_arr[rear] = added_item ;

End of insert()*/
```

```
//This function will delete (or pop) an element from the queue
void del()
{
        if (front == -1 || front > rear)
        {
                printf ("\nQueue Underflow\n");
                return;
        }
        else
        {
                //deleteing the element
      printf ("\nElement deleted from queue is : %d\n",
      queue_arr[front]);
                front=front+1;
        }
}/*End of del()*/

//Displaying all the elements of the queue
void display()
{
        int i;
        //Checking whether the queue is empty or not
        if (front == -1 || front > rear)
        {
                printf ("\nQueue is empty\n");
                return;
        }
        else
        {
                printf("\nQueue is :\n");
                for(i=front;i<= rear;i++)
                        printf("%d  ",queue_arr[i]);
                printf("\n");
        }
}/*End of display() */

void main()
{
        int choice;
        while (1)
        {
                clrscr();
```

```
            //Menu options
            printf("\n1.Insert\n");
            printf("2.Delete\n");
            printf("3.Display\n");
            printf("4.Quit\n");
            printf("\nEnter your choice:");
            scanf("%d", & choice);
            switch(choice)
            {
            case 1 :
                    insert();
                    break;
            case 2:
                    del();
                    getch();
                    break;
            case 3:
                    display();
                    getch();
                    break;
            case 4:
                    exit(1);
            default:
                    printf ("\n Wrong choice\n");
                    getch();
            }/*End of switch*/
        }/*End of while*/
}/*End of main()*/
```

Suppose a queue Q has maximum size 5, say 5 elements pushed and 2 elements popped.

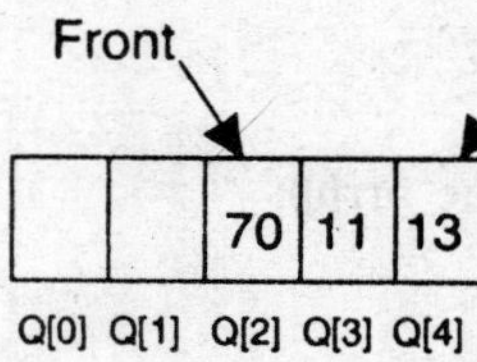

Fig. 4.10

Now if we attempt to add more elements, even though 2 queue cells are free, the elements cannot be pushed. Because in a queue, elements are always inserted at the *rear* end and hence *rear* points to last location of the queue array Q[4]. That is queue is full (overflow condition) though it is empty. This limitation can be overcome if we use circular queue.

4.2. OTHER QUEUES

There are three major variations in a simple queue. They are

1. Circular queue
2. Double ended queue (de-queue)
3. Priority queue

Priority queue is generally implemented using linked list, which is discussed in the section 5.13. The other two queue variations are discussed in the following sections.

4.3. CIRCULAR QUEUE

In circular queues the elements Q[0],Q[1],Q[2] .... Q[n – 1] is represented in a circular fashion with Q[1] following Q[n]. A circular queue is one in which the insertion of a new element is done at the very first location of the queue if the last location at the queue is full.

Suppose Q is a queue array of 6 elements. Push and pop operation can be performed on circular. The following figures will illustrate the same.

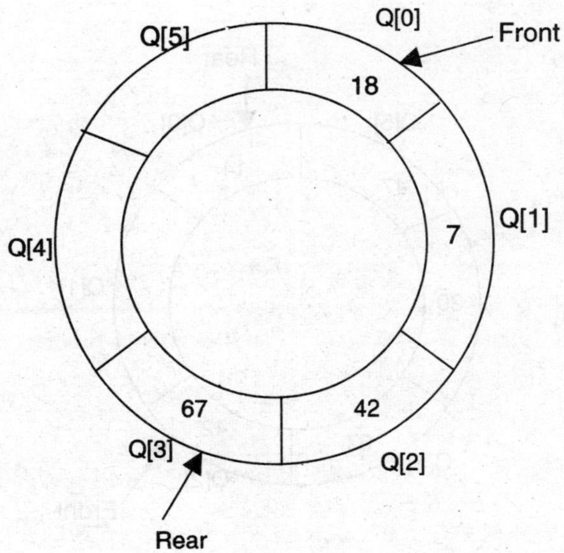

Fig. 4.11. A circular queue after inserting 18, 7, 42, 67.

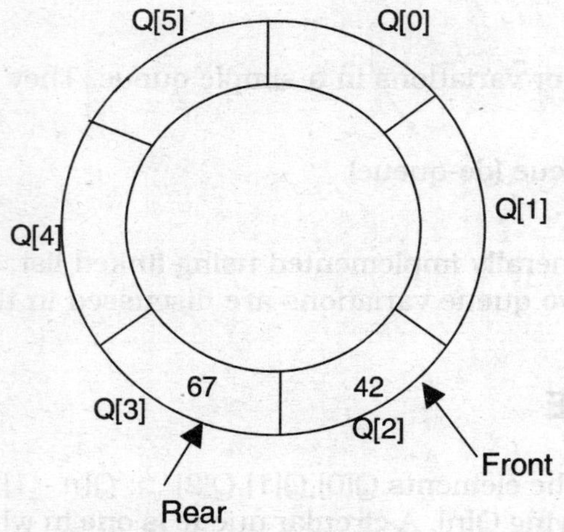

Fig. 4.12. A circular queue after popping 18, 7

After inserting an element at last location Q[5], the next element will be inserted at the very first location (*i.e.*, Q[0]) that is circular queue is one in which the first element comes just after the last element.

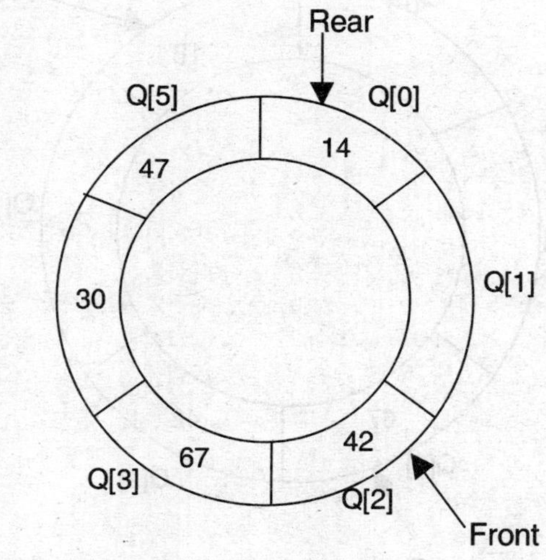

Fig. 4.13. A circular queue after pushing 30, 47, 14

At any time the position of the element to be inserted will be calculated by the relation Rear = (Rear + 1) % SIZE

After deleting an element from circular queue the position of the front end is calculated by the relation Front= (Front + 1) % SIZE

After locating the position of the new element to be inserted, *rear*, compare it with *front*. If (rear = front), the queue is full and cannot be inserted anymore.

4.3.1. ALGORITHMS

Let Q be the array of some specified size say SIZE. FRONT and REAR are two pointers where the elements are deleted and inserted at two ends of the circular queue. DATA is the element to be inserted.

Inserting an element to circular Queue

1. Initialize FRONT = – 1; REAR = 1
2. REAR = (REAR + 1) % SIZE
3. If (FRONT is equal to REAR)
   (*a*) Display "Queue is full"
   (*b*) Exit
4. Else
   (*a*) Input the value to be inserted and assign to variable "DATA"
5. If (FRONT is equal to – 1)
   (*a*) FRONT = 0
   (*b*) REAR = 0
6. Q[REAR] = DATA
7. Repeat steps 2 to 5 if we want to insert more elements
8. Exit

Deleting an element from a circular queue

1. If (FRONT is equal to – 1)
   (*a*) Display "Queue is empty"
   (*b*) Exit
2. Else
   (*a*) DATA = Q[FRONT]
3. If (REAR is equal to FRONT)
   (*a*) FRONT = –1
   (*b*) REAR = –1
4. Else
   (*a*) FRONT = (FRONT +1) % SIZE
5. Repeat the steps 1, 2 and 3 if we want to delete more elements
6. Exit

PROGRAM 4.2

```
/// PROGRAM TO IMPLEMENT CIRCULAR QUEUE USING ARRAY
//CODED AND COMPILED USING TURBO C++
```

```
#include<conio.h>
#include<process.h>
#include<iostream.h>

#define MAX 50

//A class is created for the circular queue
class circular_queue
{
        int cqueue_arr[MAX];
        int front,rear;

        public:
                //a constructor is created to initialize the variables
                circular_queue()
                {
                        front = -1;
                        rear = -1;
                }
                //public function declarations
                void insert();
                void del();
                void display();
};

//Function to insert an element to the circular queue
void circular_queue::insert()
{
        int added_item;
        //Checking for overflow condition
        if ((front == 0 && rear == MAX-1) || (front == rear +1))
        {
                cout<<"\nQueue Overflow \n";
                getch();
                return;
        }
        if (front == -1)  /*If queue is empty */
        {
                front = 0;
                rear = 0;
        }
```

```
        else
                if (rear == MAX-1)/*rear is at last position of queue */
                        rear = 0;
                else
                        rear = rear + 1;
        cout<<"\nInput the element for insertion in queue:";
        cin>>added_item;
        cqueue_arr[rear] = added_item;
}/*End of insert()*/

//This function will delete an element from the queue
void circular_queue::del()
{
        //Checking for queue underflow
        if (front == -1)
        {
                cout<<"\nQueue Underflow\n";
                return;
        }
        cout<<"\nElement deleted from queue is:"<<cqueue_arr[front]<<"\n";
        if (front == rear) /* queue has only one element */
        {
                front = -1;
                rear = -1;
        }
        else
                if(front == MAX-1)
                        front = 0;
                else
                        front = front + 1;
}/*End of del()*/

//Function to display the elements in the queue
void circular_queue::display()
{
        int front_pos = front,rear_pos = rear;
        //Checking whether the circular queue is empty or not
        if (front == -1)
        {
                cout<<"\nQueue is empty\n";
                return;
        }
```

```
        //Displaying the queue elements
        cout<<"\nQueue elements:\n";
        if(front_pos <= rear_pos )
                while(front_pos <= rear_pos)
                {
                        cout<<cqueue_arr[front_pos]<<", ";
                        front_pos++;
                }
        else
        {
                while(front_pos <= MAX-1)
                {
                        cout<<cqueue_arr[front_pos]<<", ";
                        front_pos++;
                }
                front_pos = 0;
                while(front_pos <= rear_pos)
                {
                        cout<<cqueue_arr[front_pos]<<", ";
                        front_pos++;
                }
        }/*End of else*/
        cout<<"\n";
}/*End of display() */

void main()
{
        int choice;
        //Creating the objects for the class
        circular_queue co;
        while(1)
        {
                clrscr();
                //Menu options
                cout <<"\n1.Insert\n";
                cout <<"2.Delete\n";
                cout <<"3.Display\n";
                cout <<"4.Quit\n";
                cout <<"\nEnter your choice: ";
                cin>>choice;

                switch(choice)
```

```
            {
            case 1:
                    co.insert();
                    break;
            case 2 :
                    co.del();
                    getch();
                    break;
            case 3:
                    co.display();
                    getch();
                    break;
            case 4:
                    exit(1);
            default:
                    cout<<"\nWrong choice\n";
                    getch();
            }/*End of switch*/
        }/*End of while*/
}/*End of main()*/
```

4.4. DEQUES

A deque is a homogeneous list in which elements can be added or inserted (called push operation) and deleted or removed from both the ends (which is called pop operation). ie; we can add a new element at the rear or front end and also we can remove an element from both front and rear end. Hence it is called Double Ended Queue.

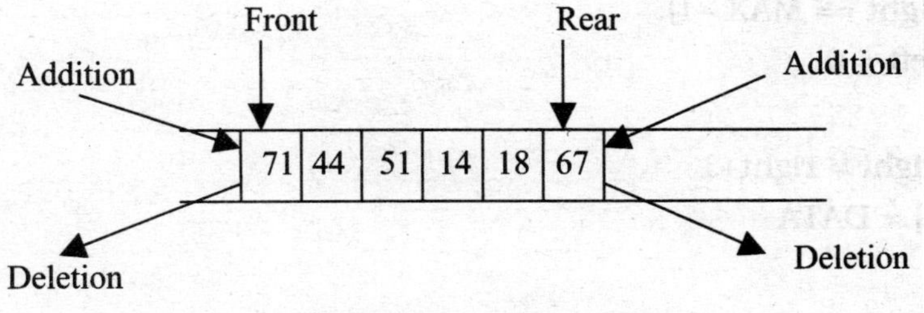

Fig. 4.14. A deque

There are two types of deque depending upon the restriction to perform insertion or deletion operations at the two ends. They are

1. Input restricted deque
2. Output restricted deque

An input restricted deque is a deque, which allows insertion at only 1 end, rear end, but allows deletion at both ends, rear and front end of the lists.

An output-restricted deque is a deque, which allows deletion at only one end, front end, but allows insertion at both ends, rear and front ends, of the lists.

The possible operation performed on deque is

1. Add an element at the rear end
2. Add an element at the front end
3. Delete an element from the front end
4. Delete an element from the rear end

Only 1st, 3rd and 4th operations are performed by input-restricted deque and 1st, 2nd and 3rd operations are performed by output-restricted deque.

4.4.1. ALGORITHMS FOR INSERTING AN ELEMENT

Let Q be the array of MAX elements. *front* (or left) and *rear* (or *right*) are two array index (pointers), where the addition and deletion of elements occurred. Let DATA be the element to be inserted. Before inserting any element to the queue *left* and *right* pointer will point to the – 1.

INSERT AN ELEMENT AT THE RIGHT SIDE OF THE DE-QUEUE

1. Input the DATA to be inserted
2. If ((left == 0 && right == MAX–1) | | (left == right + 1))
   (*a*) Display "Queue Overflow"
   (*b*) Exit
3. If (left == –1)
   (*a*) left = 0
   (*b*) right = 0
4. Else
   (*a*) if (right == MAX –1)
      (*i*) left = 0
   (*b*) else
      (*i*) right = right+1
5. Q[right] = DATA
6. Exit

INSERT AN ELEMENT AT THE LEFT SIDE OF THE DE-QUEUE

1. Input the DATA to be inserted
2. If ((left == 0 && right == MAX–1) | | (left == right+1))
   (*a*) Display "Queue Overflow"
   (*b*) Exit

3. If (left == – 1)
   (*a*) Left = 0
   (*b*) Right = 0
4. Else
   (*a*) if (left == 0)
      (*i*) left = MAX – 1
   (*b*) else
      (*i*) left = left – 1
5. Q[left] = DATA
6. Exit

4.4.2. ALGORITHMS FOR DELETING AN ELEMENT

Let Q be the array of MAX elements. *front* (or *left*) and *rear* (or *right*) are two array index (pointers), where the addition and deletion of elements occurred. DATA will contain the element just deleted.

DELETE AN ELEMENT FROM THE RIGHT SIDE OF THE DE-QUEUE

1. If (left == – 1)
   (*a*) Display "Queue Underflow"
   (*b*) Exit
2. DATA = Q [right]
3. If (left == right)
   (*a*) left = – 1
   (*b*) right = – 1
4. Else
   (*a*) if(right == 0)
      (*i*) right = MAX-1
   (*b*) else
      (*i*) right = right-1
5. Exit

DELETE AN ELEMENT FROM THE LEFT SIDE OF THE DE-QUEUE

1. If (left == – 1)
   (*a*) Display "Queue Underflow"
   (*b*) Exit
2. DATA = Q [left]
3. If(left == right)
   (*a*) left = – 1
   (*b*) right = – 1

4. Else
   (*a*) if (left == MAX-1)
      (*i*) left = 0
   (*b*) Else
      (*i*) left = left +1
5. Exit

PROGRAM 4.3

```
//PROGRAM TO IMPLEMENT INPUT AND OUTPUT
//RESTRICTED DE-QUEUE USING ARRAYS
//CODED AND COMPILED USING TURBO C

#include<conio.h>
#include<stdio.h>
#include<process.h>

#define MAX 50

int deque_arr[MAX];
int left = –1;
int right = –1;

//This function will insert an element at the
//right side of the de-queue
void insert_right()
{
        int added_item;
        if ((left == 0 && right == MAX-1) || (left == right+1))
        {
                printf ("\nQueue Overflow\n");
                getch();
                return;
        }
        if (left == –1)  /* if queue is initially empty */
        {
                left = 0;
                right = 0;
        }
        else
```

```
        if(right == MAX-1)  /*right is at last position of queue */
                right = 0;
        else
                right = right+1;
        printf("\n Input the element for adding in queue: ");
        scanf ("%d", &added_item);
        //Inputting the element at the right
        deque_arr[right] = added_item ;
}/*End of insert_right()*/

//Function to insert an element at the left position
//of the de-queue
void insert_left()
{
        int added_item;
        //Checking for queue overflow
        if ((left == 0 && right == MAX-1) || (left == right+1))
        {
                printf ("\nQueue Overflow \n");
                getch();
                return;
        }
        if (left == -1)/*If queue is initially empty*/
        {
                left = 0;
                right = 0;
        }
        else
        if (left== 0)
                left = MAX -1;
        else
                left = left-1;
        printf("\nInput the element for adding in queue:");
        scanf ("%d", &added_item);
        //inputting at the left side of the queue
        deque_arr[left] = added_item ;
}/*End of insert_left()*/

//This function will delete an element from the queue
//from the left side
void delete_left()
{
```

```
        //Checking for queue underflow
        if (left == -1)
        {
                printf("\nQueue Underflow\n");
                return;
        }
        //deleting the element from the left side
        printf ("\nElement deleted from queue is: %d\n",deque_arr[left]);
        if(left == right) /*Queue has only one element */
        {
                left = -1;
                right=-1;
        }
        else
                if (left == MAX-1)
                        left = 0;
                else
                        left = left+1;
}/*End of delete_left()*/

//Function to delete an element from the right hand
//side of the de-queue
void delete_right()
{
        //Checking for underflow conditions
        if (left == -1)
        {
                printf("\nQueue Underflow\n");
                return;
        }
        printf("\nElement deleted from queue is : %d\n",deque_arr[right]);
        if(left == right) /*queue has only one element*/
        {
                left = -1;
                right=-1;
        }
        else
                if (right == 0)
                        right=MAX-1;
                else
                        right=right-1;
}/*End of delete_right() */
```

```
//Displaying all the contents of the queue
void display_queue()
{
        int front_pos = left, rear_pos = right;
        //Checking whether the queue is empty or not
        if (left == -1)
        {
            printf ("\nQueue is empty\n");
            return;
        }
        //displaying the queue elements
        printf ("\nQueue elements :\n");
        if ( front_pos <= rear_pos )
        {
            while(front_pos <= rear_pos)
            {
                printf ("%d ",deque_arr[front_pos]);
                front_pos++;
            }
        }
        else
        {
            while(front_pos <= MAX-1)
            {
                printf("%d ",deque_arr[front_pos]);
                front_pos++;
            }
            front_pos = 0;
            while(front_pos <= rear_pos)
            {
                printf ("%d ",deque_arr[front_pos]);
                front_pos++;
            }
        }/*End of else */
        printf ("\n");
}/*End of display_queue() */

//Function to implement all the operation of the
//input restricted queue
void input_que()
{
        int choice;
        while(1)
```

```
        {
                clrscr();
                //menu options to input restricted queue
                printf ("\n1.Insert at right\n");
                printf ("2.Delete from left\n");
                printf ("3.Delete from right\n");
                printf ("4.Display\n");
                printf ("5.Quit\n");
                printf ("\nEnter your choice : ");
                scanf ("%d",&choice);

                switch(choice)
                {
                 case 1:
                        insert_right();
                        break;
                 case 2:
                        delete_left();
                        getch();
                        break;
                 case 3:
                        delete_right();
                        getch();
                        break;
                 case 4:
                        display_queue();
                        getch();
                        break;
                 case 5:
                        exit(0);
                 default:
                        printf("\nWrong choice\n");
                        getch();
                }/*End of switch*/
        }/*End of while*/
}/*End of input_que() */

//This function will implement all the operation of the
//output restricted queue
void output_que()
{
        int choice;
```

```
        while(1)
        {
                clrscr();
                //menu options for output restricted queue
                printf ("\n1.Insert at right\n");
                printf ("2.Insert at left\n");
                printf ("3.Delete from left\n");
                printf ("4.Display\n");
                printf ("5.Quit\n");
                printf ("\nEnter your choice:");
                scanf ("%d",&choice);

                switch(choice)
                {
                 case 1:
                        insert_right();
                        break;
                 case 2:
                        insert_left();
                        break;
                 case 3:
                        delete_left();
                        getch();
                        break;
                 case 4:
                        display_queue();
                        getch();
                        break;
                 case 5:
                        exit(0);
                 default:
                        printf("\nWrong choice\n");
                        getch();
                }/*End of switch*/
        }/*End of while*/
}/*End of output_que() */

void main()
{
        int choice;
        clrscr();
        //Main menu options
        printf ("\n1.Input restricted dequeue\n");
```

```
        printf ("2.Output restricted dequeue\n");
        printf ("Enter your choice:");
        scanf ("%d",&choice);

        switch(choice)
        {
         case 1:
               input_que();
               break;
         case 2:
               output_que();
               break;
         default:
               printf("\nWrong choice\n");
        }/*End of switch*/
}/*End of main()*/
```

If we analyze the algorithms in this chapter the time needed to add or delete a data is constant, *i.e.* time complexity is of order O(1).

4.5. APPLICATIONS OF QUEUE

1. Round robin techniques for processor scheduling is implemented using queue.
2. Printer server routines (in drivers) are designed using queues.
3. All types of customer service software (like Railway/Air ticket reservation) are designed using queue to give proper service to the customers.

SELF REVIEW QUESTIONS

1. Write an algorithm to add a new element of information to a circular queue?
   [*Calicut - APR 1995 (BTech), Calicut APR 1997 (BTech), MG - NOV 2002 (BTech)*]
2. Write algorithms for inserting and deleting items from a DEQUE?
   [*MG - MAY 2004 (BTech), MG - MAY 2003 (BTech), MG - NOV 2002 (BTech), CUSAT - JUL 2002 (MCA)*]
3. Distinguish between Queues and Deques? [*MG - NOV 2004 (BTech)*]
4. Describe a circular DEQUEUE? Write algorithms for insertion into front end and deletion from the back end of this structure?
   [*MG - NOV 2003 (BTech), MG - MAY 2000 (BTech)*]
5. Explain the implementation of circular queue using array. How an "empty queue" is distinguished from a "full queue"? Write necessary functions to perform all valid operations on circular queue. [*CUSAT - NOV 2002 (BTech)*]

6. Discuss the advantages of Circular queue with example. *[ANNA - DEC 2003 (BE)]*
7. What are the various queue operations? Explain. *[ANNA - MAY 2003 (BE)]*
8. What are dequeues ? Explain various representations of dequeues.
[KERALA - MAY 2001 (BTech), KERALA - DEC 2003 (BTech)]
9. What are the difference between a stack and a queue?
[KERALA - NOV 2001 (BTech), KERALA - DEC 2002 (BTech)]
10. Write the insertion and deletion procedures in a queue.
[KERALA - NOV 2001 (BTech), KERALA - MAY 2001 (BTech)]
11. Mention and explain various types of queues. Compare them.
[KERALA - MAY 2001 (BTech)]
12. What is meant by circular queue and deque ? *[KERALA - MAY 2002 (BTech)]*

5

Linked List

If the memory is allocated for the variable during the compilation (*i.e.; before execution)* of a program, then it is fixed and cannot be changed. For example, an array A[100] is declared with 100 elements, then the allocated memory is fixed and cannot decrease or increase the SIZE of the array if required. So we have to adopt an alternative strategy to allocate memory only when it is required. There is a special data structure called linked list that provides a more flexible storage system and it does not require the use of arrays.

5.1. LINKED LISTS

A linked list is a linear collection of specially designed data elements, called nodes, linked to one another by means of pointers. Each node is divided into two parts: the first part contains the information of the element, and the second part contains the address of the next node in the linked list. Address part of the node is also called linked or next field. Following Fig 5:1 shows a typical example of node.

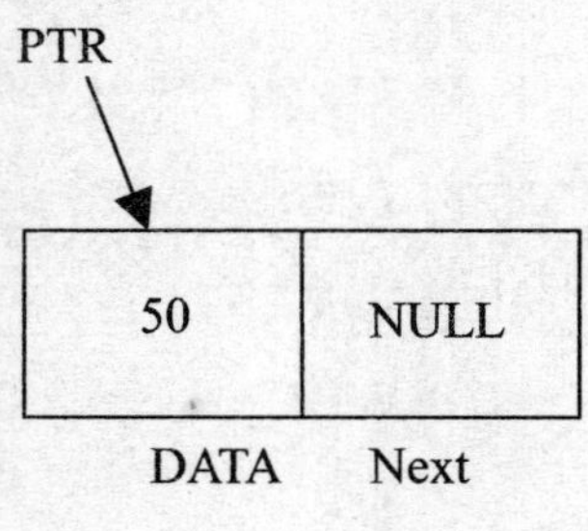

PTR → DATA = 50
PTR → Next = NULL

Fig. 5.1. Nodes.

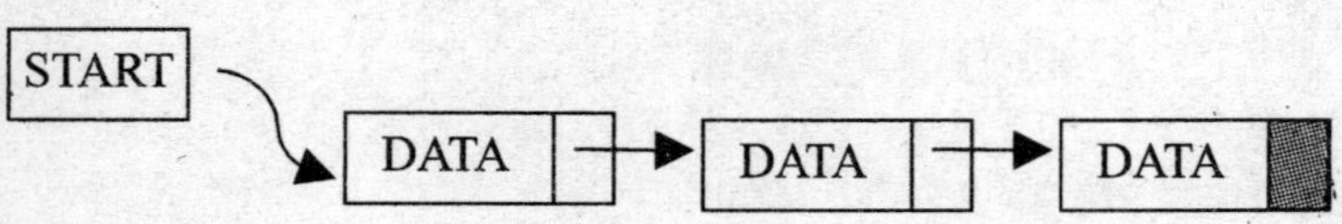

Fig. 5.2. Linked List.

Fig. 5.3. Linked List representation in memory.

Fig. 5.2 shows a schematic diagram of a linked list with 3 nodes. Each node is pictured with two parts. The left part of each node contains the data items and the right part represents the address of the next node; there is an arrow drawn from it to the next node. The next pointer of the last node contains a special value, called the NULL pointer, which does not point to any address of the node. That is NULL pointer indicates the end of the linked list. START pointer will hold the address of the 1st node in the list START = NULL if there is no list (*i.e.*; NULL list or empty list).

5.2. REPRESENTATION OF LINKED LIST

Suppose we want to store a list of integer numbers using linked list. Then it can be schematically represented as

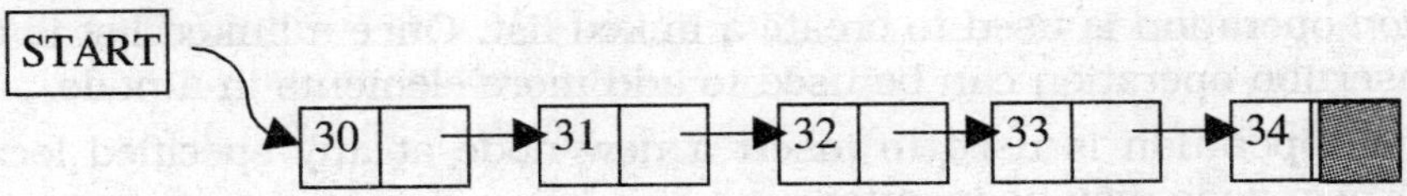

Fig. 5.4. Linked list representation of integers

The linear linked list can be represented in memory with the following declaration.

```
struct Node
{
        int DATA; //Instead of 'DATA' we also use 'Info'
        struct Node *Next; //Instead of 'Next' we also use 'Link'
};
typedef struet Node *NODE;
```

5.3. ADVANTAGES AND DISADVANTAGES

Linked list have many advantages and some of them are:

1. Linked list are dynamic data structure. That is, they can grow or shrink during the execution of a program.
2. Efficient memory utilization: In linked list (or dynamic) representation, memory is not pre-allocated. Memory is allocated whenever it is required. And it is deallocated (or removed) when it is not needed.

3. Insertion and deletion are easier and efficient. Linked list provides flexibility in inserting a data item at a specified position and deletion of a data item from the given position.
4. Many complex applications can be easily carried out with linked list.

Linked list has following disadvantages

1. More memory: to store an integer number, a node with integer data and address field is allocated. That is more memory space is needed.
2. Access to an arbitrary data item is little bit cumbersome and also time consuming.

5.4. OPERATION ON LINKED LIST

The primitive operations performed on the linked list are as follows

1. Creation
2. Insertion
3. Deletion
4. Traversing
5. Searching
6. Concatenation

Creation operation is used to create a linked list. Once a linked list is created with one node, insertion operation can be used to add more elements in a node.

Insertion operation is used to insert a new node at any specified location in the linked list. A new node may be inserted.

(*a*) At the beginning of the linked list

(*b*) At the end of the linked list

(*c*) At any specified position in between in a linked list

Deletion operation is used to delete an item (or node) from the linked list. A node may be deleted from the

(*a*) Beginning of a linked list

(*b*) End of a linked list

(*c*) Specified location of the linked list

Traversing is the process of going through all the nodes from one end to another end of a linked list. In a singly linked list we can visit from left to right, forward traversing, nodes only. But in doubly linked list forward and backward traversing is possible.

Concatenation is the process of appending the second list to the end of the first list. Consider a list A having n nodes and B with m nodes. Then the operation concatenation will place the 1st node of B in the (n+1)th node in A. After concatenation A will contain (n+m) nodes

5.5. TYPES OF LINKED LIST

Basically we can divide the linked list into the following three types in the order in which they (or node) are arranged.

1. Singly linked list
2. Doubly linked list
3. Circular linked list

5.6. SINGLY LINKED LIST

All the nodes in a singly linked list are arranged sequentially by linking with a pointer. A singly linked list can grow or shrink, because it is a dynamic data structure. Following figure explains the different operations on a singly linked list.

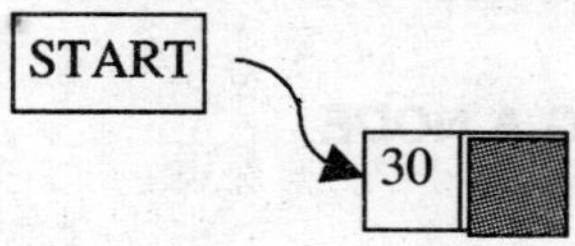

Fig. 5.5. Create a node with DATA(30)

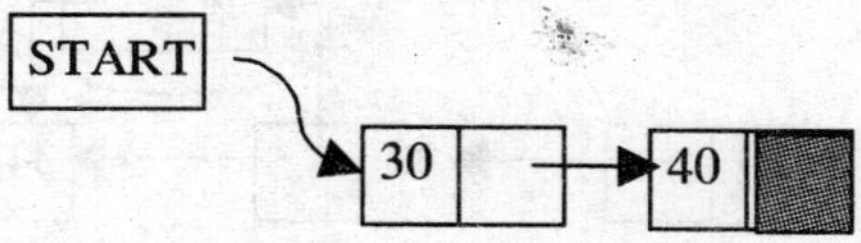

Fig. 5.6. Insert a node with DATA(40) at the end

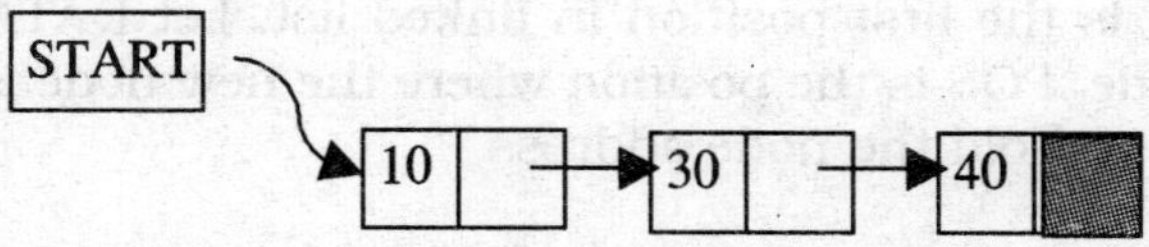

Fig. 5.7. Insert a node with DATA(10) at the beginning

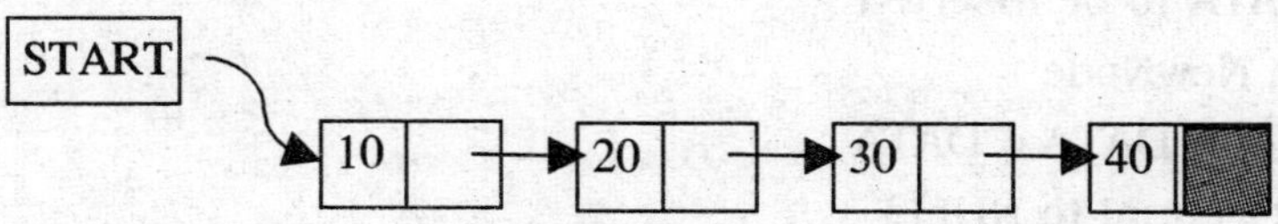

Fig. 5.8. Insert a node with DATA(20) at the 2nd position

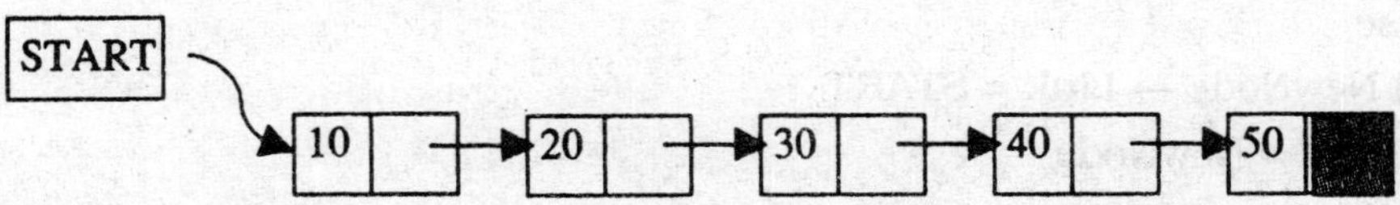

Fig. 5.9. Insert a node with DATA(50) at the end

Output → 10, 20, 30, 40, 50

Fig. 5.10. Traversing the nodes from left to right

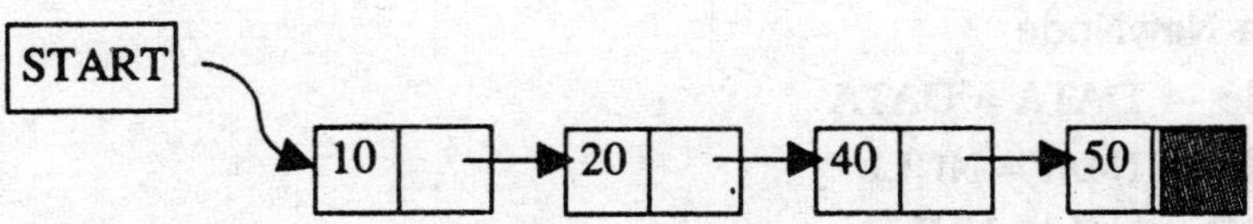

Fig. 5.11. Delete the 3rd node from the list

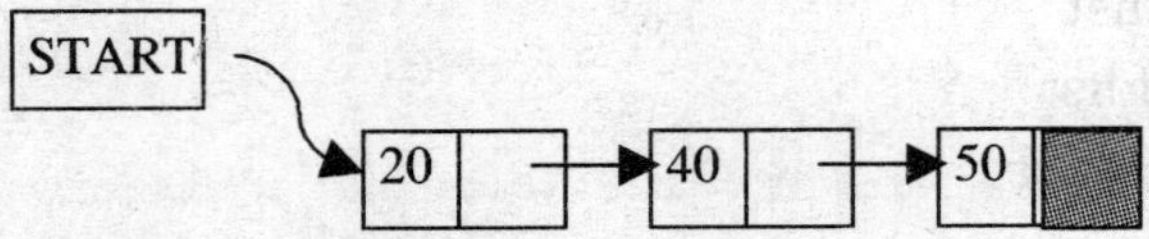

Fig. 5.12. Delete the 1st node

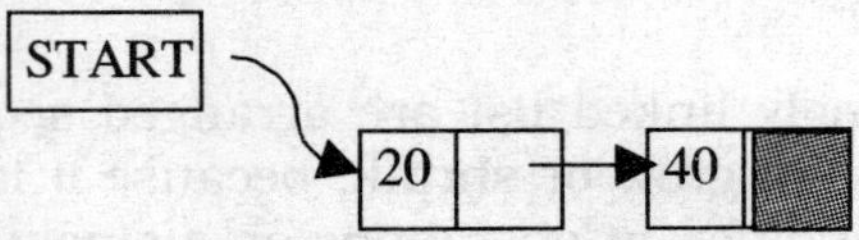

Fig. 5.13. Delete the last node

5.6.1. ALGORITHM FOR INSERTING A NODE

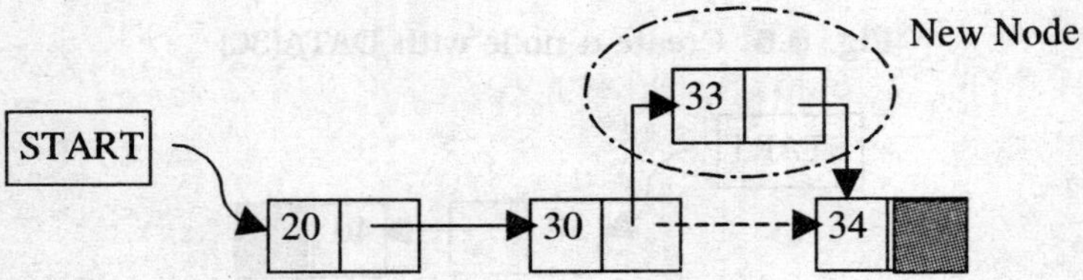

Fig. 5.14. Insertion of New Node

Suppose START is the first position in linked list. Let DATA be the element to be inserted in the new node. POS is the position where the new node is to be inserted. TEMP is a temporary pointer to hold the node address.

Insert a Node at the beginning

1. Input DATA to be inserted
2. Create a NewNode
3. NewNode → DATA = DATA
4. If (SATRT equal to NULL)
   (*a*) NewNode → Link = NULL
5. Else
   (*a*) NewNode → Link = START
6. START = NewNode
7. Exit

Insert a Node at the end

1. Input DATA to be inserted
2. Create a NewNode
3. NewNode → DATA = DATA
4. NewNode → Next = NULL
8. If (SATRT equal to NULL)
   (*a*) START = NewNode

9. Else
   (*a*) TEMP = START
   (*b*) While (TEMP → Next not equal to NULL)
      (*i*) TEMP = TEMP → Next
10. TEMP → Next = NewNode
11. Exit

Insert a Node at any specified position

1. Input DATA and POS to be inserted
2. intialise TEMP = START; and j = 0
3. Repeat the step 3 while(k is less than POS)
   (*a*) TEMP = TEMP è Next
   (*b*) If (TEMP is equal to NULL)
      (*i*) Display "Node in the list less than the position"
      (*ii*) Exit
   (*c*) *k* = *k* + 1
4. Create a New Node
5. NewNode → DATA = DATA
6. NewNode → Next = TEMP → Next
7. TEMP → Next = NewNode
8. Exit

5.6.2. ALGORITHM FOR DELETING A NODE

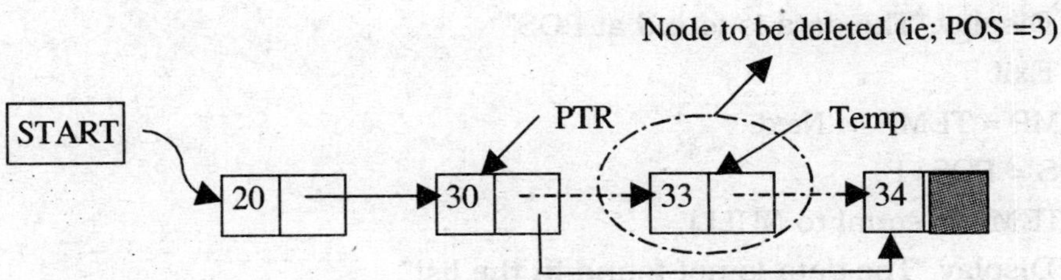

Fig. 5.15. Deletion of a Node.

Suppose START is the first position in linked list. Let DATA be the element to be deleted. TEMP, HOLD is a temporary pointer to hold the node address.

1. Input the DATA to be deleted
2. if ((START → DATA) is equal to DATA)
   (*a*) TEMP = START
   (*b*) START = START → Next
   (*c*) Set free the node TEMP, which is deleted
   (*d*) Exit

3. HOLD = START
4. while ((HOLD → Next → Next) not equal to NULL))
   (*a*) if ((HOLD → NEXT → DATA) equal to DATA)
      (*i*) TEMP = HOLD → Next
      (*ii*) HOLD → Next = TEMP → Next
      (*iii*) Set free the node TEMP, which is deleted
      (*iv*) Exit
   (*b*) HOLD = HOLD → Next
5. if ((HOLD → next → DATA) == DATA)
   (*a*) TEMP = HOLD → Next
   (*b*) Set free the node TEMP, which is deleted
   (*c*) HOLD → Next = NULL
   (*d*) Exit
6. Disply "DATA not found"
7. Exit

5.6.3. ALGORITHM FOR SEARCHING A NODE

Suppose START is the address of the first node in the linked list and DATA is the information to be searched. After searching, if the DATA is found, POS will contain the corresponding position in the list.

1. Input the DATA to be searched
2. Initialize TEMP = START; POS =1;
3. Repeat the step 4, 5 and 6 until (TEMP is equal to NULL)
4. If (TEMP → DATA is equal to DATA)
   (*a*) Display "The data is found at POS"
   (*b*) Exit
5. TEMP = TEMP → Next
6. POS = POS+1
7. If (TEMP is equal to NULL)
   (*a*) Display "The data is not found in the list"
8. Exit

5.6.4. ALGORITHM FOR DISPLAY ALL NODES

Suppose START is the address of the first node in the linked list. Following algo rithm will visit all nodes from the START node to the end.

1. If (START is equal to NULL)
   (*a*) Display "The list is Empty"
   (*b*) Exit
2. Initialize TEMP = START

3. Repeat the step 4 and 5 until (TEMP == NULL)
4. Display "TEMP → DATA"
5. TEMP = TEMP → Next
6. Exit

PROGRAM 5.1

```
//THIS PROGRAM WILL IMPLEMENT ALL THE OPERATIONS
//OF THE SINGLY LINKED LIST
//CODED AND COMPILED IN TURBO C

#include<stdio.h>
#include<conio.h>
#include<malloc.h>
#include<process.h>

//Structure declaration for the node
struct node
{
        int info;
        struct node *link;
    }*start;

    //This function will create a new linked list
    void Create_List(int data)
    {
        struct node *q,*tmp;
        //Dynamic memory is been allocated for a node
        tmp= (struct node*)malloc(sizeof(struct node));
        tmp->info=data;
        tmp->link=NULL;

        if(start==NULL) /*If list is empty*/
            start=tmp;
        else
        {   /*Element inserted at the end*/
            q=start;
            while(q->link!=NULL)
                q=q->link;
            q->link=tmp;
        }
```

```
}/*End of create_list()*/

//This function will add new element at the beginning of the linked list
void AddAtBeg(int data)
{
        struct node *tmp;
        tmp=(struct node*)malloc(sizeof(struct node));
        tmp->info=data;
        tmp->link=start;
        start=tmp;
}/*End of addatbeg()*/

//Following function will add new element at any position
void AddAfter(int data,int pos)
{
        struct node *tmp,*q;
        int i;
        q=start;
        //Finding the position to add new element to the linked list
        for(i=0;i<pos-1;i++)
        {
                q=q->link;
                if(q==NULL)
                {
                        printf ("\n\n There are less than %d elements",pos);
                        getch();
                        return;
                }
        }/*End of for*/

        tmp=(struct node*)malloc(sizeof (struct node));
        tmp->link=q->link;
        tmp->info=data;
        q->link=tmp;
}/*End of addafter()*/

//Delete any element from the linked list
void Del(int data)
{
        struct node *tmp,*q;
        if (start->info == data)
        {
```

```
        tmp=start;
        start=start->link; /*First element deleted*/
        free(tmp);
        return;
    }
    q=start;
    while(q->link->link ! = NULL)
    {
        if(q->link->info == data) /*Element deleted in between*/
        {
            tmp=q->link;
            q->link=tmp->link;
            free(tmp);
            return;
        }
        q=q->link;
    }/*End of while */
    if(q->link->info==data) /*Last element deleted*/
    {
        tmp=q->link;
        free(tmp);
        q->link=NULL;
        return;
    }
    printf ("\n\nElement %d not found",data);
    getch();
}/*End of del()*/

//This function will display all the element(s) in the linked list
void Display()
{
    struct node *q;
    if(start == NULL)
    {
        printf ("\n\nList is empty");
        return;
    }
    q=start;
    printf("\n\nList is : ");
    while(q!=NULL)
    {
        printf ("%d ", q->info);
        q=q->link;
```

```
        }
        printf ("\n");
        getch();
}/*End of display() */

//Function to count the number of nodes in the linked list
void Count()
{
        struct node *q=start;
        int cnt=0;
        while(q!=NULL)
        {
                q=q->link;
                cnt++;
        }
        printf ("Number of elements are %d\n",cnt);
        getch();
}/*End of count()*/

//This function will reverse the linked list
void Rev()
{
        struct node *p1,*p2,*p3;
        if(start->link==NULL)     /*only one element*/
                return;
        p1=start;
        p2=p1->link;
        p3=p2->link;
        p1->link=NULL;
        p2->link=p1;
        while(p3!=NULL)
        {
                p1=p2;
                p2=p3;
                p3=p3->link;
                p2->link=p1;
        }
        start=p2;
}/*End of rev()*/

//Function to search an element from the linked list
void Search(int data)
{
```

```
            struct node *ptr = start;
            int pos = 1;
            //searching for an element in the linked list
            while(ptr!=NULL)
            {
                    if (ptr->info==data)
                    {
                            printf ("\n\nItem %d found at position %d", data, pos);
                            getch();
                            return;
                    }
                    ptr = ptr->link;
                    pos++;
            }
            if (ptr == NULL)
                    printf ("\n\nItem %d not found in list",data);
            getch();
}


void main()
{
            int choice,n,m,position,i;
            start=NULL;
            while(1)
            {
                    clrscr();
                    printf ("1.Create List\n");
                    printf ("2.Add at beginning\n");
                    printf ("3.Add after \n");
                    printf ("4.Delete\n");
                    printf ("5.Display\n");
                    printf ("6.Count\n");
                    printf ("7.Reverse\n");
                    printf ("8.Search\n");
                    printf ("9.Quit\n");
                    printf ("\nEnter your choice:");
                    scanf ("%d",&choice);
                    switch (choice)
                    {
                     case 1:
                            printf ("\n\nHow many nodes you want:");
                            scanf ("%d",&n);
```

```
            for(i = 0;i<n;i++)
            {
                  printf ("\nEnter the element:");
                  scanf ("%d",&m);
                  Create_List(m);
            }
            break;
      case 2:
            printf ("\n\nEnter the element : ");
            scanf ("%d",&m);
            AddAtBeg(m);
            break;
      case 3:
            printf ("\n\nEnter the element:");
            scanf ("%d",&m);
            printf ("\nEnter the position after which this element is inserted:");
            scanf ("%d",&position);
            Add After(m,position);
            break;
      case 4:
            if (start == NULL)
            {
                  printf("\n\nList is empty");
                  continue;
            }
            printf ("\n\nEnter the element for deletion:");
            scanf ("%d",&m);
            Del(m);
            break;
      case 5:
            Display();
            break;
      case 6:
            Count();
            break;
      case 7:
            Rev();
            break;
      case 8:
            printf("\n\nEnter the element to be searched:");
            scanf ("%d",&m);
```

```
                Search(m);
                break;
            case 9:
                exit(0);
            default:
                printf ("\n\nWrong choice");
        }/*End of switch*/
    }/*End of while*/
}/*End of main()*/
```

PROGRAM 5.2

```
//THIS PROGRAM WILL IMPLEMENT ALL THE OPERATIONS
//OF THE SINGLY LINKED LIST
//CODED AND COMPILED IN TURBO C++


#include<iostream.h>
#include<conio.h>
#include<process.h>


class Linked_List
{
    //Structure declaration for the node
    struct node
    {
                int info;
                struct node *link;
    };

            //private structure variable declared
            struct node *start;
        public:
            Linked_List()//Constructor defined
            {
                start = NULL;
            }
            //public fucntion declared
            void Create_List(int);
```

```
                void AddAtBeg(int);
                void AddAfter(int,int);
                void Delete();
                void Count();
                void Search(int);
                void Display();
                void Reverse();
};

//This function will create a new linked list of elements
void Linked_List::Create_List(int data)
{
        struct node *q,*tmp;
        //New node is created with new operator
        tmp= (struct node *)new(struct node);
        tmp->info=data;
        tmp->link=NULL;

        if (start==NULL) /*If list is empty */
                start=tmp;
        else
        {       /*Element inserted at the end */
                q=start;
                while(q->link!=NULL)
                        q=q->link;
                q-> link=tmp;
        }
}/*End of create_list()*/

//following function will add new element at the beginning
void Linked_List::AddAtBeg(int data)
{
        struct node *tmp;
        tmp=(struct node*)new(struct node);
        tmp->info=data;
        tmp->link=start;
        start=tmp;
}/*End of addatbeg()*/

//This function will add new element at any specified position
void Linked_List::AddAfter(int data,int pos)
{
```

```
        struct node *tmp,*q;
        int i;
        q=start;
        //Finding the position in the linked list to insert
        for(i=0;i<pos-1;i++)
        {
                q=q->link;
                if(q==NULL)
                {
                        cout<<"\n\nThere are less than "<<pos<<" elements";
                        getch();
                        return;
                }
        }/*End of for*/

        tmp=(struct node*)new(struct node);
        tmp->link=q->link;
        tmp->info=data;
        q->link=tmp;
}/*End of addafter()*/

//Funtion to delete an element from the list
void Linked_List::Delete()
{
        struct node *tmp,*q;
        int data;
        if(start==NULL)
        {
                cout<<"\n\nList is empty";
                getch();
                return;
        }
        cout<<"\n\nEnter the element for deletion : ";
        cin>>data;

        if(start->info == data)
        {
                tmp=start;
                start=start->link; //First element deleted
                delete(tmp);
                return;
        }
```

```
        q=start;
        while(q->link->link != NULL)
        {
                if(q->link->info==data) //Element deleted in between
                {
                        tmp=q->link;
                        q->link=tmp->link;
                        delete(tmp);
                        return;
                }
                q=q->link;
        }/*End of while */
        if(q->link->info==data) //Last element deleted
        {
                tmp=q->link;
                delete(tmp);
                q->link=NULL;
                return;
        }
        cout<<"\n\nElement "<<data<<" not found";
        getch();
}/*End of del()*/

void Linked_List::Display()
{
        struct node *q;
        if(start == NULL)
        {
                cout<<"\n\nList is empty";
                return;
        }
        q=start;
        cout<<"\n\nList is : ";
        while(q!=NULL)
        {
                cout<<q->info;
                q=q->link;
        }
        cout<<"\n";
        getch();
}/*End of display() */
```

```
void Linked_List::Count()
{
        struct node *q=start;
        int cnt=0;
        while(q!=NULL)
        {
                q=q->link;
                cnt++;
        }
        cout<<"Number of elements are \n"<<cnt;
        getch();
}/*End of count() */

void Linked_List::Reverse()
{
        struct node *p1,*p2,*p3;
        if(start->link==NULL)    /*only one element*/
                return;
        p1=start;
        p2=p1->link;
        p3=p2->link;
        p1->link=NULL;
        p2->link=p1;
        while(p3!=NULL)
        {
                p1=p2;
                p2=p3;
                p3=p3->link;
                p2->link=p1;
        }
        start=p2;
}/*End of rev()*/

void Linked_List::Search(int data)
{
        struct node *ptr = start;
        int pos = 1;
        while(ptr!=NULL)
        {
                if(ptr->info==data)
                {
                        cout<<"\n\nItem "<<data<<" found at position "<<pos;
```

```
                getch();
                return();
            }
            ptr = ptr->link;
            pos++;
        }
        if(ptr == NULL)
            cout<<"\n\nItem "<<data<<" not found in list";
        getch();
}

void main()
{
        int choice,n,m,position,i;
        Linked_List po;
        while(1)
        {
            clrscr();
            cout<<"1.Create List\n";
            cout<<"2.Add at begining\n";
            cout<<"3.Add after \n";
            cout<<"4.Delete\n";
            cout<<"5.Display\n";
            cout<<"6.Count\n";
            cout<<"7.Reverse\n";
            cout<<"8.Search\n";
            cout<<"9.Quit\n";
            cout<<"\nEnter your choice:";
            cin>>choice;
            switch(choice)
            {
             case 1:
                cout<<"\n\nHow many nodes you want:";
                cin>>n;
                for(i=0;i<n;i++)
                {
                    cout<<"\nEnter the element:";
                    cin>>m;
                    po.Create_List(m);
                }
                break;
```

```
		case 2:
			cout<<"\n\nEnter the element:";
			cin>>m;
			po.AddAtBeg(m);
			break;
		case 3:
			cout<<"\n\nEnter the element:";
			cin>>m;
			cout<<"\nEnter the position after which this element is inserted:";
			cin>>position;
			po.AddAfter(m,position);
			break;
		case 4:
			po.Delete();
			break;
		case 5:
			po.Display();
			break;
		case 6:
			po.Count();
			break;
		case 7:
			po.Reverse();
			break;
		case 8:
			cout<<"\n\nEnter the element to be searched:";
			cin>>m;
			po.Search(m);
			break;
		case 9:
			exit(0);
		default:
			cout<<"\n\nWrong choice";
		}/*End of switch */
	}/*End of while */
}/*End of main()*/
```

5.7. STACK USING LINKED LIST

In chapter 3, we have discussed what a stack means and its different operations. And we have also discussed the implementation of stack using array, *i.e.*, static memory allocation. Implementation issues of the stack (Last In First Out - LIFO) using linked list is illustrated in following figures.

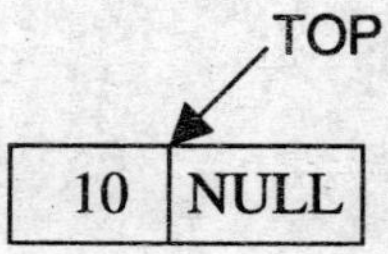

Fig. 5.11. push (10)

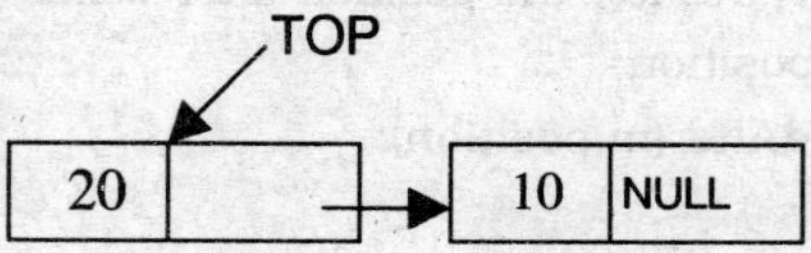

Fig. 5.12. push (20)

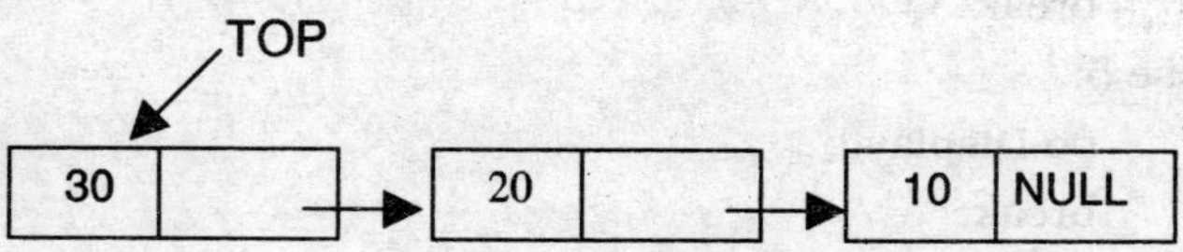

Fig. 5.13. push (30)

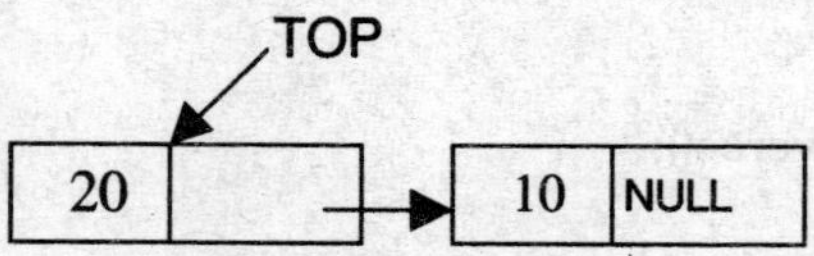

Fig. 5.14. X = pop() (ie; X = 30)

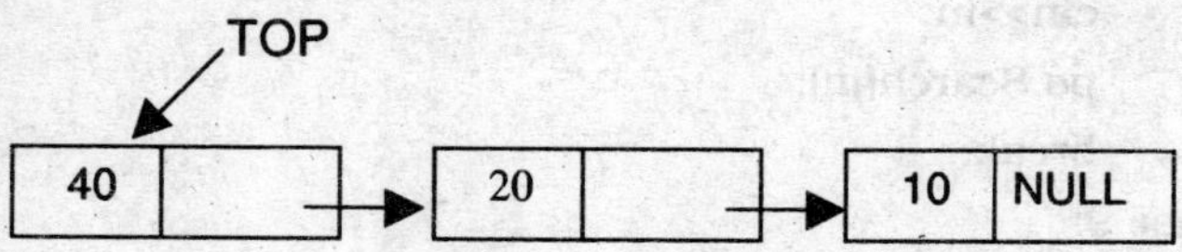

Fig. 5.15. push (40)

5.7.1. ALGORITHM FOR PUSH OPERATION

Suppose TOP is a pointer, which is pointing towards the topmost element of the stack. TOP is NULL when the stack is empty. DATA is the data item to be pushed.

1. Input the DATA to be pushed
2. Creat a New Node
3. NewNode → DATA = DATA
4. NewNode → Next = TOP
5. TOP = NewNode
6. Exit

5.7.2. ALGORITHM FOR POP OPERATION

Suppose TOP is a pointer, which is pointing towards the topmost element of the stack. TOP is NULL when the stack is empty. TEMP is pointer variable to hold any nodes address. DATA is the information on the node which is just deleted.

1. if (TOP is equal to NULL)
   (*a*) Display "The stack is empty"
2. Else
   (*a*) TEMP = TOP
   (*b*) Display "The popped element TOP → DATA"
   (*c*) TOP = TOP → Next
   (*d*) TEMP → Next = NULL
   (*e*) Free the TEMP node
3. Exit

PROGRAM 5.3

```
//THIS PROGRAM IS TO DEMONSTRATE THE OPERATIONS
//PERFORMED ON THE STACK INPLEMENTED USING LINKED LIST
//CODED AND COMPILED IN TURBO C
#include<conio.h>
#include<stdio.h>
#include<malloc.h>
#include<process.h>

//Structure is created a node
struct node
{
        int info;
        struct node *link;//A link to the next node
};

//A variable named NODE is been defined for the structure
typedef struct node *NODE;

//This function is to perform the push operation
NODE push(NODE top)
{
        NODE NewNode;
        int pushed_item;
        //A new node is created dynamically
```

```
		NewNode = (NODE)malloc(sizeof(struct node));
		printf("\nInput the new value to be pushed on the stack:");
		scanf("%d",&pushed_item);
		NewNode->info=pushed_item;//Data is pushed to the stack
		NewNode->link=top;//Link pointer is set to the next node
		top=NewNode;//Top pointer is set
		return(top);
}/*End of push()*/

//Following function will implement the pop operation
NODE pop(NODE top)
{
		NODE tmp;
		if(top == NULL)//checking whether the stack is empty or not
			printf ("\nStack is empty\n");
		else
		{
	tmp=top;//popping the element
			printf("\nPopped item is %d\n",tmp->info);
			top=top->link;//resetting the top pointer
			tmp->link=NULL
			free(tmp);//freeing the popped node
		}
		return(top);

}/*End of pop()*/

//This is to display the entire element in the stack
void display(NODE top)
{
		if(top==NULL)
			printf("\nStack is empty\n");
		else
		{
			printf("\nStack elements:\n");
			while(top != NULL)
			{
				printf("%d\n",top->info);
				top = top->link;
			}/*End of while */
		}/*End of else*/
/*End of display()*/
```

```
void main()
{
        char opt;
        int choice;
        NODE Top=NULL;
        do
        {
                clrscr();
                printf("\n1.PUSH\n");
                printf("2.POP\n");
                printf("3.DISPLAY\n");
                printf("4.EXIT\n");
                printf("\nEnter your choice:");
                scanf("%d", &choice);
                switch(choice)
                {
                case 1:
                        Top=push(Top);
                        break;
                case 2:
                        Top=pop(Top);
                        break;
                case 3:
                        display(Top);
                        break;
                case 4:
                        exit(1);
                default:
                        printf("\nWrong choice\n");
                }/*End of switch*/

                printf ("\n\nDo you want to continue (Y/y) = ");
                fflush(stdin);
                scanf("%c",&opt);
        }while((opt == 'Y') || (opt == 'y'));
}/*End of main() */
```

PROGRAM 5.4

```
//THIS PROGRAM IS TO DEMONSTRATE THE OPERATIONS
//PERFORMED ON THE STACK IMPLEMENTATION
```

```
//USING LINKED LIST
//CODED AND COMPILED IN TURBO C++

#include<conio.h>
#include<iostream.h>
#include<process.h>

//Class is created for the linked list
class Stack_Linked
{
        //Structure is created for the node
        struct node
        {
                int info;
                struct node *link;//A link to the next node
        };

        //A variable top is been declared for the structure
        struct node *top;
        //NODE is defined as the data type of the structure node
        typedef struct node *NODE;

        public:
                //Constructer is defined for the class
                Stack_Linked()
                {
                        //top pointer is initialized
                        top=NULL;
                }
                //function declarations
                void push();
                void pop();
                void display();
};

//This function is to perform the push operation
void Stack_Linked::push()
{
        NODE NewNode;
        int pushed_item;
        //A new node is created dynamically
        NewNode=(NODE)new(struct node);
        cout<<"\nInput the new value to be pushed on the stack:";
```

```
        cin>>pushed_item;
        NewNode->info=pushed_item;//Data is pushed to the stack
        NewNode->link=top;//Link pointer is set to the next node
        top=NewNode;//Top pointer is set
}/*End of push()*/

//Following function will implement the pop operation
void Stack_Linked::pop()
{
        NODE tmp;
        if(top == NULL)//checking whether the stack is empty or not
                cout<<"\nStack is empty\n";
        else
        {       tmp=top;//popping the element
                cout<<"\nPopped item is:"<<tmp->info;
                top=top->link;//resetting the top pointer
                tmp->link=NULL;
                delete(tmp);//freeing the popped node
        }
}/*End of pop()*/

//This is to display all the element in the stack
void Stack_Linked::display()
{
        if(top==NULL)//Checking whether the stack is empty or not
                cout<<"\nStack is empty\n";
        else
        {
                NODE ptr=top;
                cout<<"\nStack elements:\n";
                while(ptr != NULL)
                {
                        cout<<"\n"<<ptr->info;
                        ptr = ptr->link;
                }/*End of while */
        }/*End of else*/
}/*End of display()*/

void main()
{
        char opt;
        int choice;
```

```
        Stack_Linked So;
        do
        {
                clrscr();
                //The menu options are listed below
                cout<<"\n1.PUSH\n";
                cout<<"2.POP\n";
                cout<<"3.DISPLAY\n";
                cout<<"4.EXIT\n";
                cout<<"\nEnter your choice : ";
                cin>>choice;

                switch(choice)
                {
                case 1:
                        So.push();//push function is called
                        break;
                case 2:
                        So.pop();//pop function is called
                        break;
                case 3:
                        So.display();//display function is called
                        break;
                case 4:
                        exit(1);
                default:
                        cout<<"\nWrong choice\n";
                }/*End of switch */

                cout<<"\n\nDo you want to continue (Y/y) = ";
                cin>>opt;
        }while((opt == 'Y') || (opt == 'y'));
}/*End of main() */
```

5.8. QUEUE USING LINKED LIST

Queue is a First In First Out [FIFO] data structure. In chapter 4, we have discussed about stacks and its different operations. And we have also discussed the implementation of stack using array, ie; static memory allocation. Implementation issues of the stack (Last In First Out - LIFO) using linked list is illustrated in the following figures.

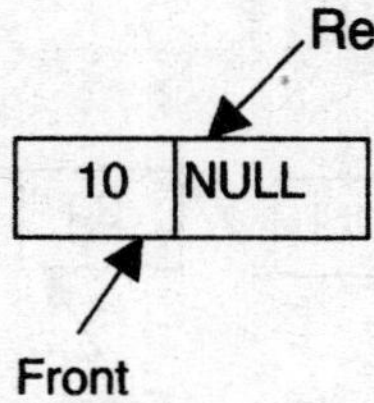

Fig. 5.16. push (10)

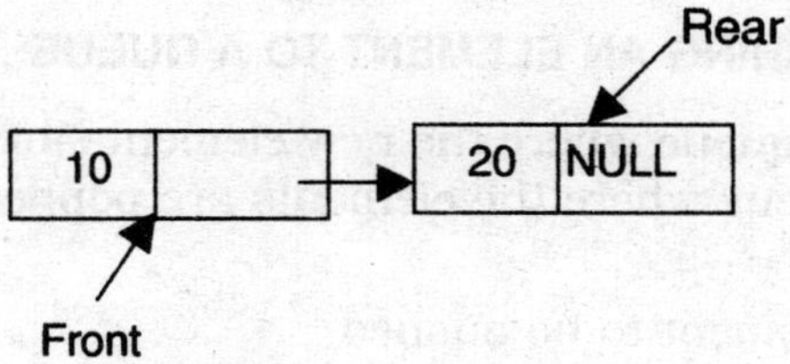

Fig. 5.17. push (20)

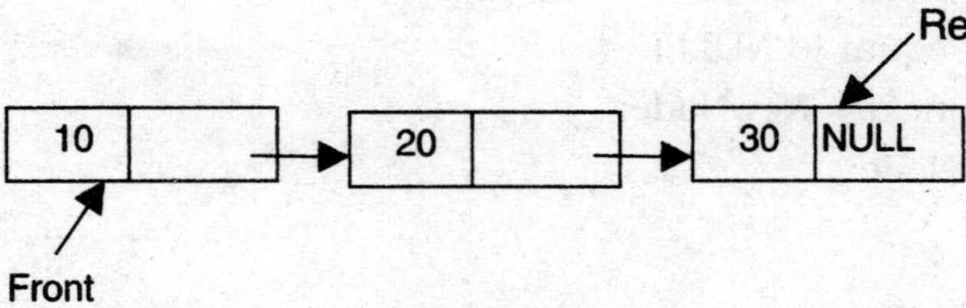

Fig. 5.18. push (30)

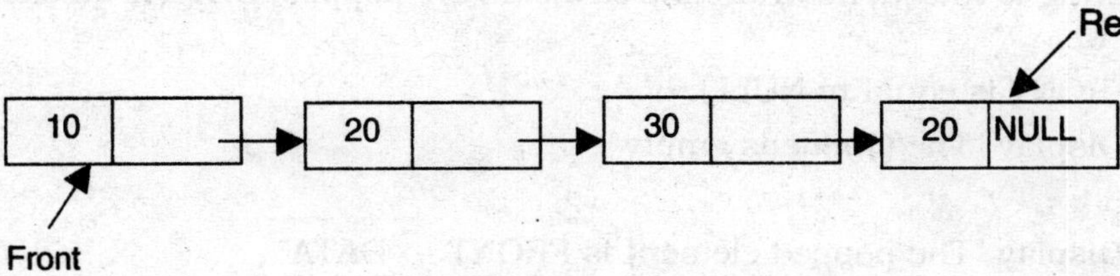

Fig. 5.19. push (40)

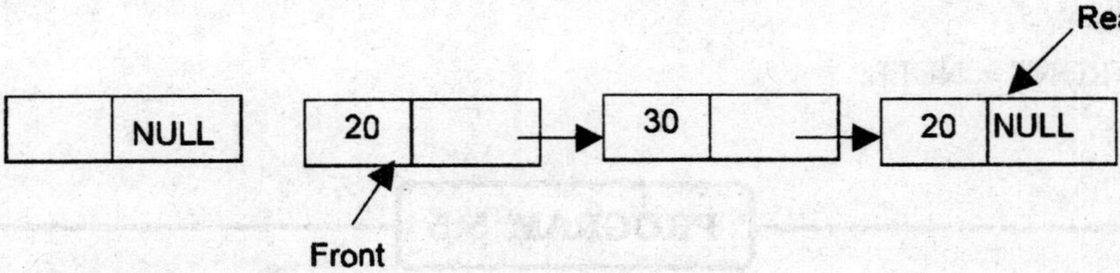

Fig. 5.20. X = pop() (*i.e.*; X = 10)

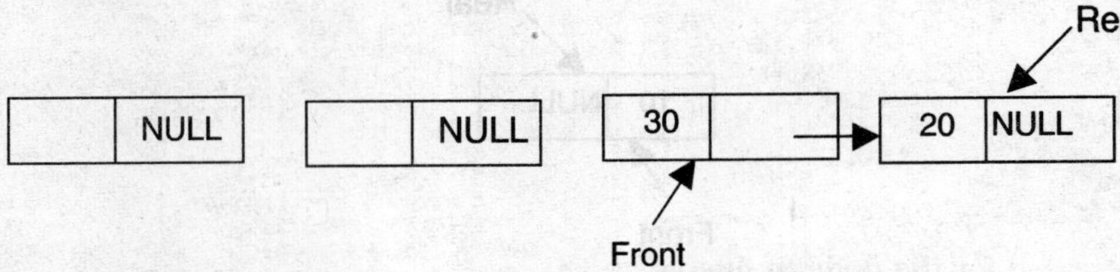

Fig. 5.21. X = pop() (*i.e.*; X = 20)

5.8.1. ALGORITHM FOR PUSHING AN ELEMENT TO A QUEUE

REAR is a pointer in queue where the new elements are added. FRONT is a pointer, which is pointing to the queue where the elements are popped. DATA is an element to be pushed.

1. Input the DATA element to be pushed
2. Create a New Node
3. NewNode → DATA = DATA
4. NewNode → Next = NULL
5. If(REAR not equal to NULL)
   (*a*) REAR → next = NewNode;
6. REAR =NewNode;
7. Exit

5.8.2. ALGORITHM FOR POPPING AN ELEMENT FROM A QUEUE

REAR is a pointer in queue where the new elements are added. FRONT is a pointer, which is pointing to the queue where the elements are popped. DATA is an element popped from the queue.

1. If (FRONT is equal to NULL)
   (*a*) Display "The Queue is empty"
2. Else
   (*a*) Display "The popped element is FRONT → DATA"
   (*b*) If(FRONT is not equal to REAR)
      (*i*) FRONT = FRONT → Next
   (*c*) Else
   (*d*) FRONT = NULL;
3. Exit

PROGRAM 5.5

```
//THIS PROGRAM WILL IMPLEMENT ALL THE OPERATIONS
//OF THE QUEUE, IMPLEMENTED USING LINKED LIST
```

```
//CODED AND COMPILED IN TURBO C

#include<stdio.h>
#include<conio.h>
#include<malloc.h>

//A structure is created for the node in queue
struct queu
{
	int info;
	struct queu *next;//Next node address
};

typedef struct queu *NODE;

//This function will push an element into the queue
NODE push(NODE rear)
{
	NODE NewNode;
	//New node is created to push the data
	NewNode=(NODE)malloc(sizeof(struct queu)),
	printf ("\nEnter the no to be pushed = ");
	scanf ("%d",&NewNode->info);
	NewNode->next=NULL;
	//setting the rear pointer
	if (rear != NULL)
		rear->next=NewNode;
	rear=NewNode;
	return(rear);
}

//This function will pop the element from the queue
NODE pop(NODE f,NODE r)
{
	//The Queue is empty when the front pointer is NULL
	if(f==NULL)
		printf ("\nThe Queue is. empty");
	else
	{
		printf ("\nThe poped element is = %d",f->info);
		if(f ! = r)
			f=f->next;
```

```
		else
			f=NULL;
	}
	return(f);
}

//Function to display the element of the queue
void traverse(NODE fr,NODE re)
{
	//The queue is empty when the front pointer is NULL
	if (fr==NULL)
		printf ("\nThe Queue is empty");
	else
	{
		printf ("\nThe element(s) is/are = ");
		while(fr != re)
		{
			printf("%d ",fr->info);
			fr=fr->next;
		};
		printf ("%d",fr->info);
	}
}

void main()
{
	int choice;
	char option;
	//declaring the front and rear pointer
	NODE front, rear;
	//Initializing the front and rear pointer to NULL
	front = rear = NULL;
	dos
	{
		clrscr();
		printf ("1. Push\n");
		printf ("2. Pop\n");
		printf ("3. Traverse\n");
		printf ("\n\nEnter your choice = ");
		scanf ("%d",&choice);
		switch(choice)
		{
```

```
                case 1:
                        //calling the push function
                        rear = push(rear);
                        if (front==NULL)
                        {
                                front=rear;
                        }
                        break;
                case 2:
                        //calling the pop function by passing
                        //front and rear pointers
                        front = pop(front,rear);
                        if (front == NULL)
                                rear = NULL;
                        break;
                case 3:
                        traverse(front,rear);
                        break;
                }
                printf ("\n\nPress (Y/y) to continue = ");
                fflush(stdin);
                scanf ("%c",&option);
        }while(option == 'Y' || option == 'y');
}
```

PROGRAM 5.6

```
//THIS PROGRAM WILL IMPLEMENT ALL THE OPERATIONS
//OF THE QUEUE, IMPLEMENTED USING LINKED LIST
//CODED AND COMPILED IN TURBO C++

#include<iostream.h>
#include<conio.h>
#include<malloc.h>

//class is created for the queue
class Queue_Linked
{
        //A structure is created for the node in queue
        struct queu
```

```
		{
			int info;
			struct queu *next;//Next node address
		};

		struct queu *front;
		struct queu *rear;
		typedef struct queu *NODE;

		public:
			//Constructor is created
			Queue_Linked()
			{
				front = NULL;
				rear = NULL;
			}
			void push();
			void pop();
			void traverse();
};
//This function will push an element into the queue
void Queue_Linked::push()
{
		NODE NewNode;
		//New node is created to push the data
		NewNode=(NODE)malloc(sizeof(struct queu));
		cout<<"\nEnter the no to be pushed = ";
		cin>>NewNode->info;
		NewNode->next=NULL;
		//setting the rear pointer
		if (rear != NULL)
			rear->next = NewNode;
		rear=NewNode;
		if (front == NULL)
			front = rear;
}

//This function will pop the element from the queue
void Queue_Linked::pop()
{
		//The Queue is empty when the front pointer is NULL
		if (front == NULL)
```

```
        {
                cout<<"\nThe Queue is empty";
                rear = NULL;
        }
        else
        {
                //Front element in the queue is popped
                cout<<"\nThe popped element is = "<<front->info;
                if (front != rear)
                        front=front->next;
                else
                        front = NULL;
        }
}

//Function to display the element of the queue
void Queue_Linked::traverse()
{
        //The queue is empty when the front pointer is NULL
        if (front==NULL)
                cout<<"\nThe Queue is empty";
        else
        {
                NODE Temp_Front=front;
                cout<<"\nThe element(s) is/are = ";
                while(Temp_Front ! = rear)
                {
                        cout<<Temp_Front->info;
                        Temp_Front=Temp_Front->next;
                };
                cout<<Temp_Front->info;
        }
}

void main()
{
        int choice;
        char option;
        Queue_Linked Qo;
        do
        {
                clrscr();
```

```
            cout<<"\n1. PUSH\n";
            cout<<"2. POP\n";
            cout<<"3. DISPLAY\n";
            cout<<"\n\nEnter your choice = ";
            cin>>choice;
            switch(choice)
            {
                case 1:
                    //calling the push function
                    Qo.push();
                    break;
                case 2:
                    //calling the pop function by passing
                    //front and rear pointers
                    Qo.pop();
                    break;
                case 3:
                    Qo.traverse();
                    break;
            }
            cout<<"\n\nPress (Y/y) to continue = ";
            cin>>option;
        }while(option == 'Y' || option == 'y');
}
```

5.9. QUEUE USING TWO STACKS

A queue can be implemented using two stacks. Suppose STACK1 and STACK2 are the two stacks. When an element is pushed on to the queue, push the same on STACK1. When an element is popped from the queue, pop all elements of STACK1 and push the same on STACK2. Then pop the topmost element of STACK2; which is the first (front) element to be popped from the queue. Then pop all elements of STACK2 and push the same on STACK1 for next operation (*i.e., push or pop*). PROGRAM 5:5 gives the program to implement the queue using two stacks by singly linked list, coded in C language.

PROGRAM 5.7

```
//IMPLEMENTING THE QUEUE USING TWO STACKS
//BY SINGLY LINK LIST
//CODED AND COMPILED USING TURBO C
```

```
#include<stdio.h>
#include<conio.h>
#include<stdlib.h>

//Stack node is created with structure
struct stack
{
        int info;
        struct stack *next;
};

typedef struct stack *NODE;

//A new element is pushed to the stack
NODE push(NODE top)
{
        NODE NewNode;
        //New node is created
        NewNode=(NODE)malloc(sizeof(struct stack));
        NewNode->next=top;

        printf("\nEnter the no: to be pushed = ");
        scanf("%d",&NewNode->info);

        top=NewNode;
        return(top);
}

NODE pop(NODE top1)
{
        //checking for whether the queue is empty or not
        if(top1 == NULL)
        {
                printf("\nThe Queu is empty");
                return(top1);
        }

        //when top1->next == NULL the queue contains only one element
        if(top1->next == NULL)
        {
                //popping the only one element present in the queue
                printf("\nThe popped element is = %d",top1->info);
```

```
        free(top1);
        top1=NULL;
        return(top1);
    }

    NODE NewNode,top2,TEMP;

    //popping the elements from the first stack and pushing the
    //same element to the second stack
    top2=NULL;
    while(top1 != NULL)
    {

        TEMP=top1;
        //Creating the new node for the second stack
        NewNode=(NODE)malloc(sizeof(struct stack));
        NewNode->next=top2;
        NewNode->info=top1->info;
        top2=NewNode;
        top1=top1->next;
        free(TEMP);
    };

    //popping the top most element from the stack so as to
    //pop an element from the queue
    printf("\nThe popped element is = %d",top2->info);
    top2=top2->next;

    //popping rest of the element from the second stack and
    //pushing the same elements to the first stack
    top1=NULL;
    while(top2 != NULL)
    {
        TEMP=top2;
        //creating new nodes for the first stack
        NewNode=(NODE)malloc(sizeof(struct stack));
        NewNode->next=top1;
        NewNode->info=top2->info;
        top1=NewNode;
        top2=top2->next;
        free(TEMP);//freeing the nodes
};
return(top1);
```

```
}

//this function is to display all the elements in the queue
void traverse(NODE top)
{
        if(top == NULL)
        {
                printf("\nThe Queue is empty");
                return;
        }

        printf ("\nThe element(s) in the Queue is/are =");
        do
        {
                printf (" %d",top->info);
                top=top->next;
        }while(top != NULL);

        return;
    }

    void main()
    {
        int choice;
        char ch;
        NODE top;
        top=NULL;
        do
        {
                clrscr();
                //A menu for the stack operations
                printf("\n1. PUSH");
                printf("\n2. POP");
                printf("\n3. TRAVERSE");
                printf("\nEnter Your Choice = ");
                scanf ("%d", &choice);

                switch(choice)
                {
                        case 1://Calling push() function by passing
                                //the structure pointer to the function
                                top=push(top);
```

```
                    break;

                case 2://calling pop() function
                    top=pop(top);
                    break;

                case 3://calling traverse() function
                    traverse(top);
                    break;

                default:
                    printf("\nYou Entered Wrong Choice");
                    break;
            }

            printf("\n\nPress (Y/y) To Continue = ");
            //Removing all characters in the input buffer
            //for fresh input(s), especially <<Enter>> key
            fflush(stdin);
            scanf("%c",&ch);
        }while(ch == 'Y' || ch == 'y');
}
```

5.10. POLYNOMIALS USING LINKED LIST

Different operations, such as addition, subtraction, division and multiplication of polynomials can be performed using linked list. In this section, we discuss about polynomial addition using linked list. Consider two polynomials $f(x)$ and $g(x)$; it can be represented using linked list as follows in Fig. 5.22.

$$f(x) = ax^3 + bx + c$$

$$g(x) = mx^4 + nx^3 + ox^2 + px + q$$

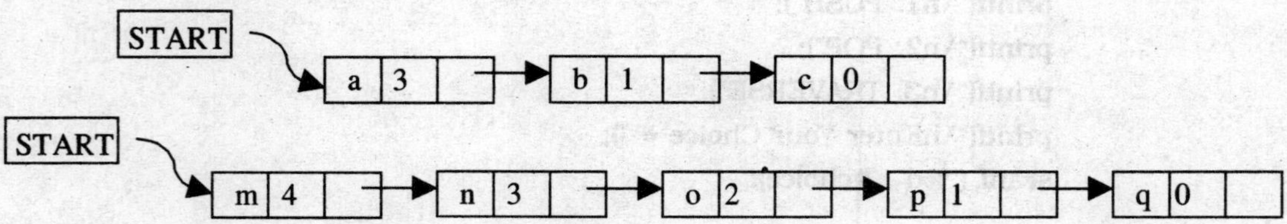

Fig. 5.22. Polynomial Representation

These two polynomials can be added by

$$h(x) = f(x) + g(x) = mx^4 + (a + n)\ x^3 + ox^2 + (b + p)x + (c + q)$$

i.e.; adding the constants of the corresponding polynomials of the same exponentials. $h(x)$ can be represented as in Fig. 5.23.

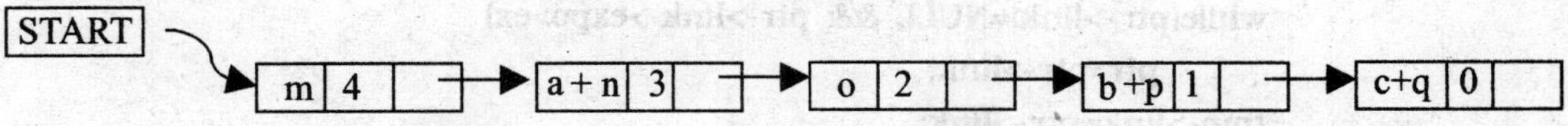

Fig. 5.23

PROGRAM 5.8

```
//Program of polynomial addition using linked list
//CODED AND COMPILED IN TURBO C

#include<stdio.h>
#include<malloc.h>

//structure is created for the node
struct node
{
        float coef;
        int expo;
        struct node *link;
};

typedef struct node *NODE;
//Function to add any node to the linked list
NODE insert(NODE start,float co,int ex)
{
        NODE ptr,tmp;
        //a new node is created
        tmp= (NODE)malloc(sizeof(struct node));
        tmp->coef=co;
        tmp->expo=ex;

        /*list empty or exp greater than first one */
        if(start==NULL || ex>start->expo)
        {
                tmp->link=start;//setting the start
                start=tmp;
        }
        else
```

```
        {
                ptr=start;
                while(ptr->link!=NULL && ptr->link->expo>ex)
                        ptr=ptr->link;
                tmp->link=ptr->link;
                ptr->link=tmp;
                if(ptr->link==NULL)  /*item to be added in the end */
                        tmp->link=NULL;
        }
        return start;
}/*End of insert()*/

//This function is to add two polynomials
NODE poly_add(NODE p1,NODE p2)
{
        NODE p3_start,p3,tmp;
        p3_start=NULL;
        if(p1==NULL && p2==NULL)
                return p3_start;

        while(p1!=NULL && p2!=NULL )
        {
                //New node is created
                tmp=(NODE)malloc(sizeof(struct node));
                if(p3_start==NULL)
                {
                        p3_start=tmp;
                        p3=p3_start;
                }
                else
                {
                        p3->link=tmp;
                        p3=p3->link;
                }
                if(p1->expo > p2->expo)
                {
                        tmp->coef=p1->coef;
                        tmp->expo=p1->expo
                        p1=p1->link;
                }
                else
                        if(p2->expo > p1->expo)
```

```
            {
                    tmp->coef=p2->coef;
                    tmp->expo=p2->expo;
                    p2=p2->link;
            }
            else
                    if(p1->expo == p2->expo)
                    {
                            tmp->coef=p1->coef + p2->coef;
                            tmp->expo=p1->expo;
                            p1=p1->link;
                            p2=p2->link;
                    }
}/*End of while*/
while(p1!=NULL)
{
            tmp=(NODE)malloc(sizeof(struct node));
            tmp->coef=p1->coef;
            tmp->expo=p1->expo;
            if (p3_start==NULL) /*poly 2 is empty*/
            {
                    p3_start=tmp;
                    p3=p3_start;
            }
            else
            {
                    p3->link=tmp;
                    p3=p3->link;
            }
            p1=p1->link;
        }/*End of while */
        while(p2!=NULL)
        {
            tmp=(NODE)malloc(sizeof(struct node));
            tmp->coef=p2->coef;
            tmp->expo=p2->expo;
            if (p3_start==NULL) /*poly 1 is empty*/
            {
                    p3_start=tmp;
                    p3=p3_start;
            }
            else
```

```
                {
                        p3->link=tmp;
                        p3=p3->link;
                }
                p2=p2->link;
        }/*End of while*/
        p3->link=NULL;
        return p3_start;
}/*End of poly_add() */

//Inputting the two polynomials
NODE enter(NODE start)
{
        int i,n,ex;
        float co;
        printf("\nHow many terms u want to enter:");
        scanf("%d",&n);
        for(i=1;i<=n;i++)
        {
                printf("\nEnter coeficient for term %d:",i);
                scanf("%f",&co);
                printf("Enter exponent for term %d:",i);
                scanf("%d",&ex);
                start=insert(start,co,ex);
        }
        return start;
}/*End of enter()*/

//This function will display the two polynomials and its
//added polynomials
void display(NODE ptr)
{
        if (ptr==NULL)
        {
                printf ("\nEmpty\n");
                return;
        }
        while(ptr!=NULL)
        {
                printf ("(%.1fx^%d) + ", ptr->coef,ptr->expo);
                ptr=ptr->link;
        }
```

```
        printf ("\b\b \n"); /* \b\b to erase the last + sign*/
}/*End of display()*/

void main()
{
        NODE p1_start,p2_start,p3_start;

        p1_start=NULL;
        p2_start=NULL;
        p3_start=NULL;

        printf("\nPolynomial 1 :\n");
        p1_start=enter(p1_start);

        printf("\nPolynomial 2 :\n");
        p2_start=enter(p2_start);
        //polynomial addition function is called
        p3_start=poly_add(p1_start,p2_start);

        clrscr();
        printf("\nPolynomial 1 is: ");
        display(p1_start);
        printf ("\nPolynomial 2 is: ");
        display(p2_start);
        printf ("\nAdded polynomial is: ");
        display(p3_start);
        getch();
}/*End of main()*/
```

5.11. DOUBLY LINKED LIST

A doubly linked list is one in which all nodes are linked together by multiple links which help in accessing both the successor (next) and predecessor (previous) node for any arbitrary node within the list. Every nodes in the doubly linked list has three fields: LeftPointer, RightPointer and DATA. Fig. 5.22 shows a typical doubly linked list.

LPoint	DATA	RPoint

Fig. 5.24. A typical doubly linked list node

LPoint will point to the node in the left side (or previous node) that is LPoint will hold the address of the previous node. RPoint will point to the node in the right side (or next node) that is RPoint will hold the address of the next node. DATA will store the information of the node.

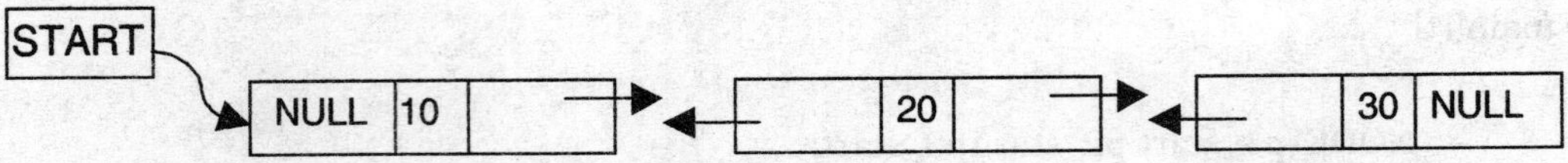

Fig. 5.25. Doubly Linked List

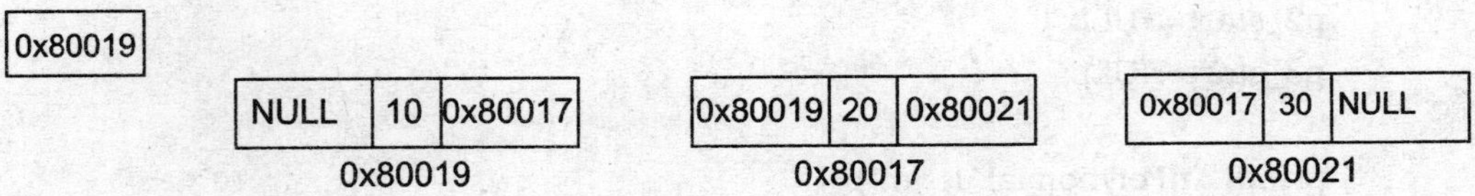

Fig. 5.26. Memory Representation of Doubly Linked List

5.11.1. REPRESENTATION OF DOUBLY LINKED LIST

A node in the doubly linked list can be represented in memory with the following declarations.

```
struct Node
{
    int DATA;
    struct Node *RChild;
    struct Node *LChild;
};
    typedef struct Node *NODE;
```

All the operations performed on singly linked list can also be performed on doubly linked list. Following figure will illustrate the insertion and deletion of nodes.

Fig. 5.27. Add(20)

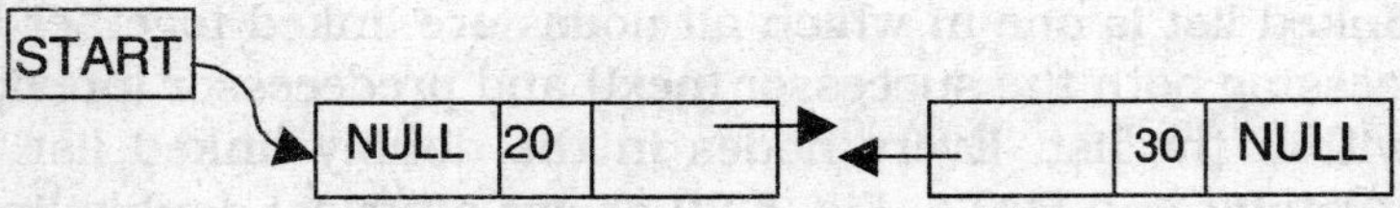

Fig 5.28. Insert (30) at the end

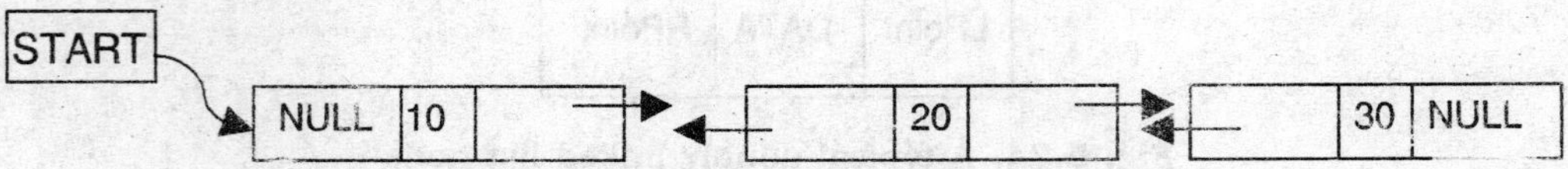

Fig 5.29. Insert (10) at the beginning

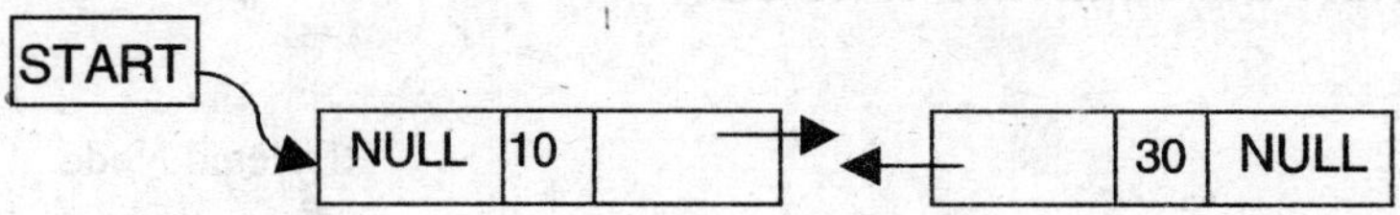

Fig 5.30. Delete a node at the 2nd position

5.11.2. ALGORITHM FOR INSERTING A NODE

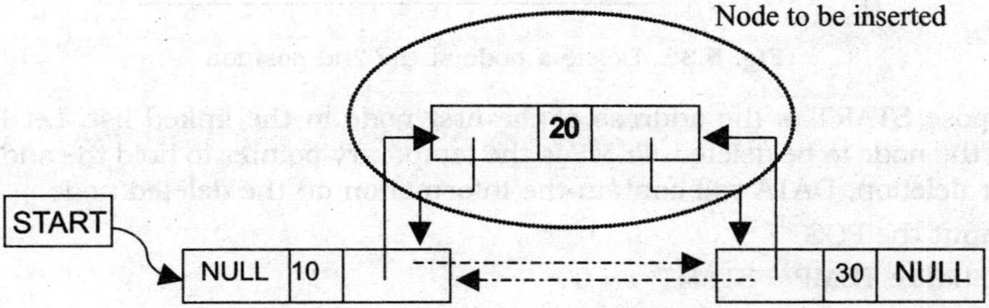

Fig. 5.31. Insert a node at the 2nd position

Suppose START is the first position in linked list. Let DATA be the element to be inserted in the new node. POS is the position where the NewNode is to be inserted. TEMP is a temporary pointer to hold the node address.

1. Input the DATA and POS
2. Initialize TEMP = START; i = 0
3. Repeat the step 4 if (i less than POS) and (TEMP is not equal to NULL)
4. TEMP = TEMP → RPoint; i = i +1
5. If (TEMP not equal to NULL) and (i equal to POS)
   (*a*) Create a New Node
   (*b*) NewNode → DATA = DATA
   (*c*) NewNode → RPoint = TEMP → RPoint
   (*d*) NewNode → LPoint = TEMP
   (*e*) (TEMP → RPoint) → LPoint = NewNode
   (*f*) TEMP → RPoint = New Node
6. Else
   (*a*) Display "Position NOT found"
7. Exit

5.11.3. ALGORITHM FOR DELETING A NODE

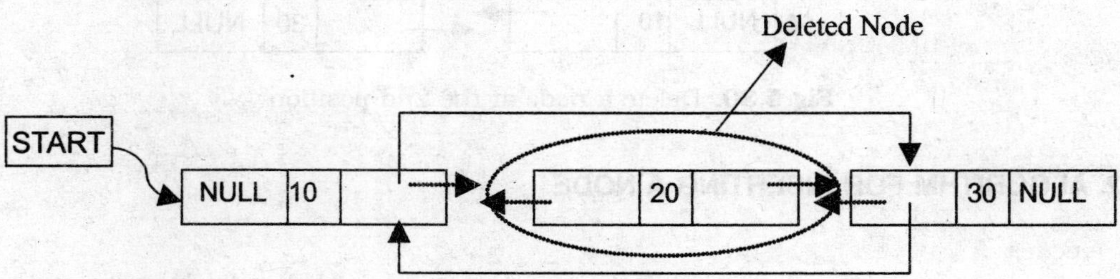

Fig. 5.32. Delete a node at the 2nd position

Suppose START is the address of the first node in the linked list. Let POS is the position of the node to be deleted. TEMP is the temporary pointer to hold the address of the node. After deletion, DATA will contain the information on the deleted node.

1. Input the POS
2. Initialize TEMP = START; i = 0
3. Repeat the step 4 if (i less than POS) and (TEMP is not equal to NULL)
4. TEMP = TEMP → RPoint; i = i +1
5. If (TEMP not equal to NULL) and (i equal to POS)
   (*a*) Create a New Node
   (*b*) NewNode → DATA = DATA
   (*c*) NewNode → RPoint = TEMP → RPoint
   (*d*) NewNode → LPoint = TEMP
   (*e*) (TEMP → RPoint) → LPoint = NewNode
   (*f*) TEMP → RPoint = New Node
6. Else
   (*a*) Display "Position NOT found"
7. Exit

PROGRAM 5.9

```
// PROGRAM TO IMPLEMENT ALL THE OPERATIONS IN THE
//DOUBLY LINKED LIST
//CODED AND COMPILED IN TURBO C

#include<conio.h>
#include<stdio.h>
#include<malloc.h>
#include<process.h>
```

```
//Structure is created for the node
struct node
{
        struct node *prev;
        int info;
        struct node *next;
    }*start;

    typedef struct node *NODE;

    //fucntion to create a doubly linked list
    void create_list(int num)
    {
        NODE q,tmp;
        //a new node is created
        tmp=(NODE)malloc(sizeof(struct node));
        tmp->info=num;//assigning the data to the new node
        tmp->next=NULL;
        if(start==NULL)
        {
            tmp->prev=NULL;
            start->prev=tmp;
            start=tmp;
        }
        else
        {
            q=start;
            while(q->next!=NULL)
                q=q->next;
            q->next=tmp;
            tmp->prev=q;
        }
}/*End of create_list()*/

//Function to add new node at the beginning
void addatbeg(int num)
{
        NODE tmp;
        //a new node is created for inserting the data
        tmp=(NODE)malloc(sizeof(struct node));
        tmp->prev=NULL;
        tmp->info=num;
```

```
        tmp->next=start;
        start->prev=tmp;
        start=tmp;
}/*End of addatbeg()*/

//This fucntion will insert a node in any specific position
void addafter(int num,int pos)
{
        NODE tmp,q;
        int i;
        q=start;
        //Finding the position to be inserted
        for(i=0;i<pos-1;i++)
        {
                q=q->next;
                if(q==NULL)
                {
                        printf ("\nThere are less than %d elements\n",pos);
                        return;
                }
        }
        //a new node is created
        tmp=(NODE)malloc(sizeof(struct node) );
        tmp->info=num;
        q->next->prev=tmp;
        tmp->next=q->next;
        tmp->prev=q;
        q->next=tmp;
}/*End of addafter() */

//Function to delete a node
void del(int num)
{
        NODE tmp,q;
        if(start->info==num)
        {
                tmp=start;
                start=start->next;  /*first element deleted*/
                start->prev = NULL;
                free(tmp);//Freeing the deleted node
                return;
        }
```

```
        q=start;
        while(q->next->next!=NULL)
        {
                if(q->next->info==num)      /*Element deleted in between*/
                {
                        tmp=q->next;
                        q->next=tmp->next;
                        tmp->next->prev=q;
                        free(tmp);
                        return;
                }
                q=q->next;
        }
        if (q->next->info==num)     /*last element deleted*/
        {       tmp=q->next;
                free(tmp);
                q->next=NULL;
                return;
        }
        printf("\nElement %d not found\n",num);
}/*End of del()*/

//Displaying all data(s) in the node
void display()
{
        NODE q;
        if(start==NULL)
        {
                printf("\nList is empty\n");
                return;
        }
        q=start;
        printf("\nList is :\n");
        while(q!=NULL)
        {
                printf("%d ", q->info);
                q=q->next;
        }
        printf("\n");
}/*End of display() */

//Function to count the number of nodes in the linked list
```

```
void count()
{
        NODE q=start;
        int cnt=0;
        while(q!=NULL)
        {
                q=q->next;
                cnt++;
        }
        printf("\nNumber of elements are %d\n",cnt);
}/*End of count()*/

//Reversing the linked list
void rev()
{
        NODE p1,p2;
        p1=start;
        p2=p1->next;
        p1->next=NULL;
        p1->prev=p2;
        while(p2!=NULL)
        {
                p2->prev=p2->next;
                p2->next=p1;
                p1=p2;
                p2=p2->prev; /*next of p2 changed to prev */
        }
        start=p1;
}/*End of rev()*/

void main()
{
        int choice,n,m,po,i;
        start=NULL;
        while(1)
        {
                //Menu options for the doubly linked list operation
                clrscr();
                printf("\n1.Create List\n");
                printf("2.Add at begining\n");
                printf("3.Add after\n");
                printf("4.Delete\n");
```

```
            printf("5.Display\n");
            printf("6.Count\n");
            printf("7.Reverse\n");
            printf("8.exit\n");
            printf("\nEnter your choice:");
            scanf("%d",&choice);
            //switch instruction is called to execute
            //correspoding function
            switch(choice)
            {
             case 1:
                printf("\nHow many nodes you want:");
                scanf("%d",&n);
                for(i=0;i<n;i++)
                {
                    printf("\nEnter the element:");
                    scanf("%d",&m);
                    //create linked list function is called
                    create_list(m);
                }
                break;
             case 2:
                printf("\nEnter the element:");
                scanf("%d",&m);
                addatbeg(m);
                break;
             case 3:
                printf("\nEnter the element:");
                scanf("%d",&m);
    printf("\nEnter the position after which this element is inserted:");
                scanf("%d",&po);
                addafter(m,po);
                break;
             case 4:
                printf("\nEnter the element for deletion:");
                scanf("%d",&m);
                //Delete a node fucntion is called
                del(m);
                break;
             case 5:
                display();
                getch();
```

```
                break;
            case 6:
                count();
                getch();
                break;
            case 7:
                rev();
                break;
            case 8:
                exit(0);
            default:
                printf("\nWrong choice\n");
                getch();
        }/*End of switch*/
    }/*End of while*/
}/*End of main()*/
```

5.12. CIRCULAR LINKED LIST

A circular linked list is one, which has no beginning and no end. A singly linked list can be made a circular linked list by simply storing the address of the very first node in the linked field of the last node. A circular linked list is shown in Fig. 5.33. Implementation of circular linked list is in PROGRAM 5:8.

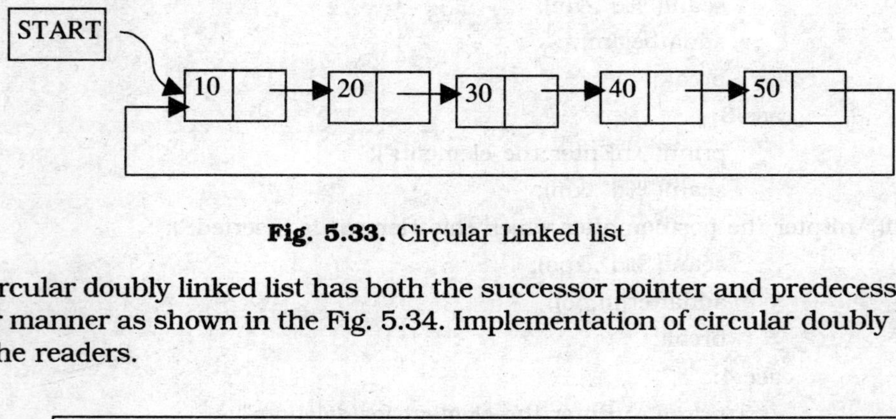

Fig. 5.33. Circular Linked list

A circular doubly linked list has both the successor pointer and predecessor pointer in circular manner as shown in the Fig. 5.34. Implementation of circular doubly linked list is left to the readers.

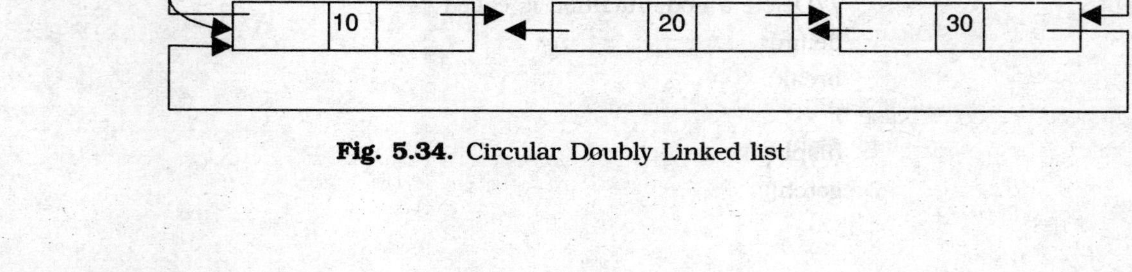

Fig. 5.34. Circular Doubly Linked list

PROGRAM 5.10

```
// PROGRAM TO IMPLEMENT CIRCULAR SINGLY LINKED LIST
//CODED AND COMPILED INTO TURBO C++
#include<iostream.h>
#include<process.h>

//class is created for the circular linked list
class Circular_Linked
{
        //structure node is created
        struct node
        {
                int info;
                struct node *link;
        };
        struct node *last;
        typedef struct node *NODE;

        public:
                //Constructor is defined
                Circular_Linked()
                {
                        last=NULL;
                }

                void create_list(int);
                void addatbeg(int);
                void addafter(int,int);
                void del();
                void display();
};

//A circular list created in this function
void Circular_Linked::create_list(int num)
{
        NODE q,tmp;
        //New node is created
        tmp = (NODE)new(struct node);
        tmp->info = num;
```

```
        if (last == NULL)
        {
                last = tmp;
                tmp->link = last;
        }
        else
        {
                tmp->link = last->link; /*added at the end of list*/
                last->link = tmp;
                last = tmp;
        }
}/*End of create_list()*/

//This function will add new node at the beginning
void Circular_Linked::addatbeg(int num)
{
        NODE tmp;
        tmp = (NODE)new(struct node);
        tmp->info = num;
        tmp->link = last->link;
        last->link = tmp;
}/*End of addatbeg()*/

//Function to add new node at any position of the circular list
void Circular_Linked::addafter(int num,int pos)
{
        NODE tmp,q;
        int i;
        q = last->link;
        //finding the position to insert a new node
        for(i=0; i < pos-1; i++)
        {
                q = q->link;
                if (q == last->link)
                {
                        cout<<"There are less than "<<pos<<" elements\n";
                        return;
                }
        }/*End of for*/
        //creating the new node
        tmp = (NODE)new(struct node);
        tmp->link = q->link;
```

```
        tmp->info = num;
        q->link = tmp;
        if(q==last)    /*Element inserted at the end*/
                last=tmp;
}/*End of addafter()*/

//Function to delete a node from the circular linked list
void Circular_Linked::del()
{
        int num;
        if(last == NULL)
        {
                cout<<"\nList underflow\n";
                return;
        }
        cout<<"\nEnter the number for deletion:";
        cin>>num;

        NODE tmp,q;
        if( last->link == last && last->info == num)  /*Only one element*/
        {
                tmp = last;
                last = NULL;
                //deleting the node
                delete(tmp);
                return;

        q = last->link;
        if(q->info == num)
        {
                tmp = q;
                last->link = q->link;
                //deleting the node
                delete(tmp);
                return;
        }
        while(q->link != last)
        {
                if(q->link->info == num)    /*Element deleted in between*/
                {
                        tmp = q->link;
                        q->link = tmp->link;
```

```
                delete(tmp);
                cout<<"\n"<<num<<" deleted\n";
                return;
            }
            q = q->link;
        }/*End of while*/
        if(q->link->info == num)    /*Last element deleted q->link=last*/
        {
            tmp = q->link;
            q->link = last->link;
            delete(tmp);
            last = q;
            return;
        }
        cout<<"\nElement "<<num<<" not found\n";
}/*End of del()*/

//Function to display all the nodes in the circular linked list
void Circular_Linked::display()
{
        NODE q;
        if(last == NULL)
        {
            cout<<"\nList is empty\n";
            return;
        }
        q = last->link;
        cout<<"\nList is:\n";
        while(q != last)
        {
            cout<< q->info;
            q = q->link;
        }
        cout<<"\n"<<last->info;
}/*End of display()*/

void main()
{
        int choice,n,m,po,i;
        Circular_Linked co;//Object is created for the class
        while(1)
        {
            //Menu options
```

```
cout<<"\n1.Create List\n";
cout<<"2.Add at begining\n";
cout<<"3.Add after \n";
cout<<"4.Delete\n";
cout<<"5.Display\n";
cout<<"6.Quit\n";
cout<<"\nEnter your choice:";
cin>>choice;

switch(choice)
{
case 1:
        cout<<"\nHow many nodes you want:";
        cin>>n;
        for(i=0; i < n;i++)
        {
                cout<<"\nEnter the element:";
                cin>>m;
                co.create_list(m);
        }
        break;
case 2:
        cout<<"\nEnter the element:";
        cin>>m;
        co.addatbeg(m);
        break;
case 3:
        cout<<"\nEnter the element:";
        cin>>m;
        cout<<"\nEnter the position after which this element is inserted:";
        cin>>po;
        co.addafter(m,po);
        break;
case 4:
        co.del();
        break;
case 5:
        co.display();
        break;
```

```
                cout<<"\nWrong choice\n";
            }/*End of switch*/
        }/*End of while*/
}/*End of main()*/
```

5.13. PRIORITY QUEUES

Priority Queue is a queue where each element is assigned a priority. In priority queue, the elements are deleted and processed by following rules.

1. An element of higher priority is processed before any element of lower priority.
2. Two elements with the same priority are processed according to the order in which they were inserted to the queue.

For example, Consider a manager who is in a process of checking and approving files in a first come first serve basis. In between, if any urgent file (with a high priority) comes, he will process the urgent file next and continue with the other low urgent files.

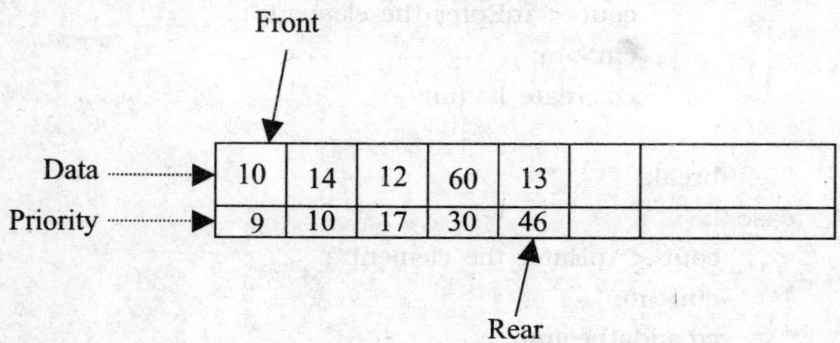

Fig. 5.35. Priority queue representation using arrays

Above Fig. 5.35 gives a pictorial representation of priority queue using arrays after adding 5 elements (10,14,12,60,13) with its corresponding priorities (9,10,17,30,46). Here the priorities of the data(s) are in ascending order. Always we may not be pushing the data in an ascending order. From the mixed priority list it is difficult to find the highest priority element if the priority queue is implemented using arrays. Moreover, the implementation of priority queue using array will yield n comparisons (in liner search), so the time complexity is O(n), which is much higher than the other queue (ie; other queues takes only O(1)) for inserting an element. So it is always better to implement the priority queue using linked list - where a node can be inserted at anywhere in the list - which is discussed in this section.

A node in the priority queue will contain DATA, PRIORITY and NEXT field. DATA field will store the actual information; PRIORITY field will store its corresponding priority of the DATA and NEXT will store the address of the next node. Fig. 5.36 shows the linked list representation of the node when a DATA (*i.e.*, 12) and PRIORITY (*i.e.*, 17) is inserted in a priority queue.

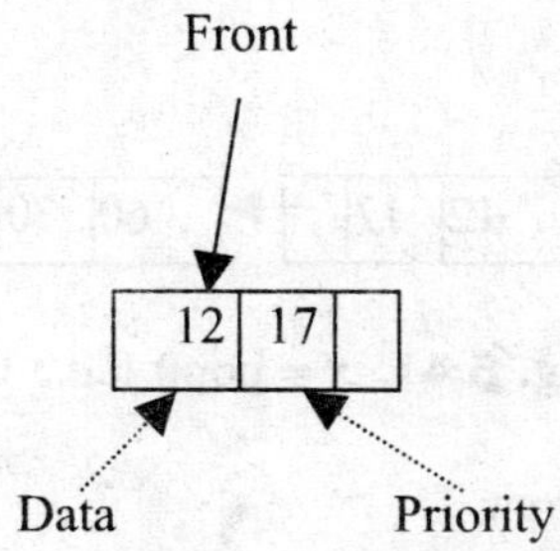

Fig. 5.36. Linked list representation of priority queue

When an element is inserted into the priority queue, it will check the priority of the element with the element(s) present in the linked list to find the suitable position to insert. The node will be inserted in such a way that the data in the priority field(s) is in ascending order. We do not use rear pointer when it is implemented using linked list, because the new nodes are not always inserted at the rear end. Following figures will illustrate the push and pop operation of priority queue using linked list.

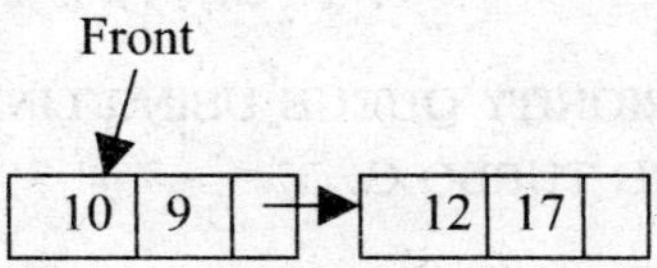

Fig. 5.37. push(DATA =10, PRIORITY = 9)

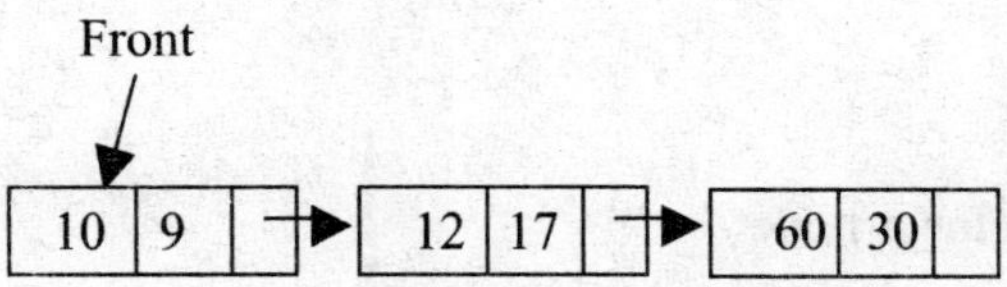

Fig. 5.38. push(DATA = 60, PRIORITY = 30)

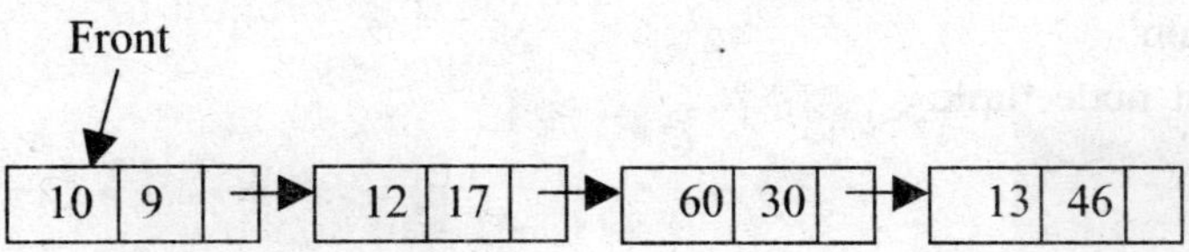

Fig. 5.39. push(DATA = 13, PRIORITY = 46)

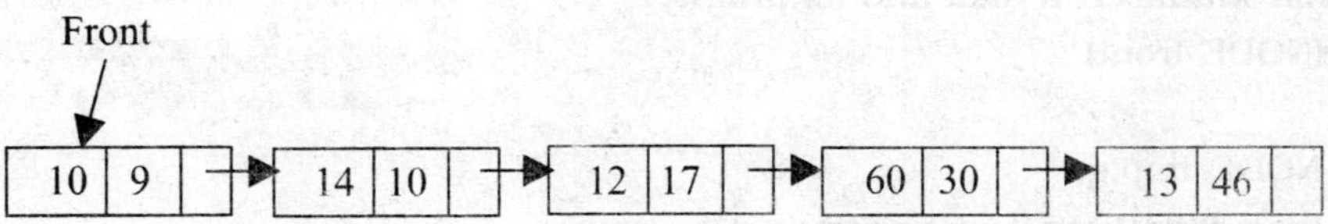

Fig. 5.40. push(DATA = 14, PRIORITY = 10)

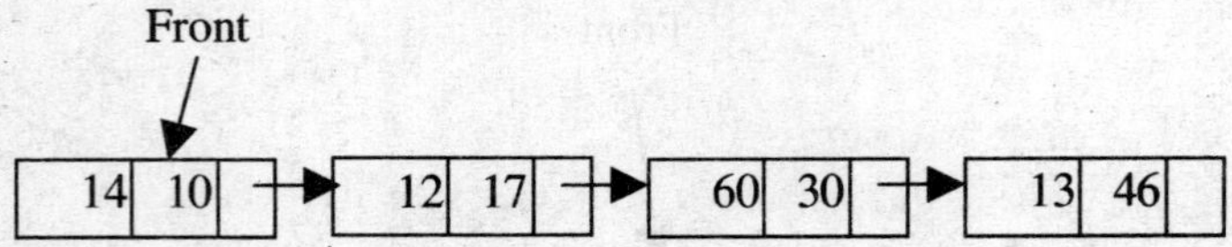

Fig. 5.41. x = pop() (*i.e.*, 10)

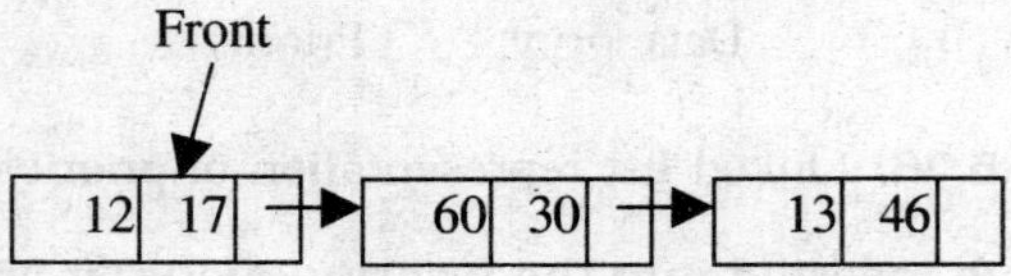

Fig. 5.42. x = pop() (*i.e.*, 14)

PROGRAM 5.11

```
//PROGRAM TO IMPLEMENT PRIORITY QUEUE USING LINKED LIST
//CODED AND COMPILED USING TURBO C

#include<conio.h>
#include<stdio.h>
#include<malloc.h>
#include<process.h>

//A structure is created for a node
struct node
{
        int priority;
        int info;
        struct node *link;
};

typedef struct node *NODE;

//This function will insert a data and its priority
NODE insert(NODE front)
{
        NODE tmp,q;
        int added_item,item_priority;
        //New node is created
```

```
        tmp = (NODE)malloc(sizeof(struct node));
        printf("\nInput the item value to be added in the queue:");
        scanf("%d",&added_item);
        printf("\nEnter its priority:");
        scanf("%d",&item_priority);
        tmp->info = added_item;
        tmp->priority = item_priority;
        /*Queue is empty or item to be added has priority more than first item*/
        if(front == NULL || item_priority < front->priority)
        {
                tmp->link = front;
                front = tmp;
        }
        else
        {
                q = front;
                while(q->link != NULL && q->link->priority <= item_priority)
                        q=q->link;
                tmp->link = q->link;
                q->link = tmp;
        }/*End of else*/
        return(front);
}/*End of insert()*/

//Following function is to delete a node from the priority queue
NODE del(NODE front)
{
        NODE tmp;
        if(front == NULL)
                printf("\nQueue Underflow\n");
        else
        {
                tmp = front;
                printf("\nDeleted item is %d\n",tmp->info);
                front = front->link;
                free(tmp);
        }
        return(front);
}/*End of del()*/

void display(NODE front)
{
```

```
        NODE ptr;
        ptr = front;
        if(front == NULL)
                printf("\nQueue is empty\n");
        else
        {       printf("\nQueue is:\n");
                printf("\nPriority Item\n");
                while(ptr != NULL)
                {
                        printf("%5d %5d\n",ptr->priority,ptr->info);
                        ptr = ptr->link;
                }
        }/*End of else */
}/*End of display() */


void main()
{
        int choice;
        NODE front=NULL;
        while(1)
        {
                clrscr();
                //Menu options
                printf("\n1.Insert\n");
                printf("2.Delete\n");
                printf("3.Display\n");
                printf("4.Quit\n");
                printf("\nEnter your choic");
                scanf("%d", &choice);

                switch(choice)
                {
                case 1:
                        front=insert(front);
                        break;
                case 2:
                        front=del(front);
                        getch();
                        break;
                case 3:
                        display(front);
```

```
                getch();
                break;
            case 4:
                exit(1);
            default :
                printf("\nWrong choice\n");
        }/*End of switch*/
    }/*End of while*/
}/*End of main()*/
```

SELF REVIEW QUESTIONS

1. Write an algorithm to count the number of nodes in a singly linked list?

   [*Calicut - APR 1997 (BTech), MG - MAY 2000 (BTech)*]

2. Write an algorithm to insert a node in a linked list? [*MG - MAY 2004 (BTech)*]

3. Describe how a polynomial is represented using singly linked lists. Write an algorithm to add two polynomials represented using linked list?

   [*MG - MAY 2004 (BTech), MG - MAY 2003 (BTech), MG - NOV 2003 (BTech), MG - NOV 2002 (BTech), MG - MAY 2002 (BTech), MG - MAY 2000 (BTech) CUSAT - DEC 2003 (MCA)*]

4. What is doubly linked list? Write an algorithm to add and delete a node from it?

   [*MG - NOV 2004 (BTech), MG - MAY 2000 (BTech) ANNA - DEC 2003 (BE), CUSAT - DEC 2003 (MCA) ANNA - MAY 2004 (MCA), ANNA - DEC 2004 (BE) KERALA - MAY 2003 (BTech)*]

5. Explain the array representation of a priority queue? Write an algorithm for deleting and inserting in a priority queue? Mention its Applications?

   [*MG - NOV 2004 (BTech), MG - MAY 2003 (BTech), MG - NOV 2003 (BTech), CUSAT - NOV 2002 (BTech), MG - NOV 2002 (BTech)*]

6. Discuss the advantages and disadvantages of singly linked list?

   [*MG - MAY 2003 (BTech)*]

7. Explain the structure of a doubly linked list. Write a general algorithm for inserting and deleting nodes in the middle? [*MG - MAY 2003 (BTech), MG - NOV 2002 (BTech)*]

8. Compare and distinguish between singly linked lists and doubly linked lists?

   [*CUSAT - APR 1998 (BTech), MG - NOV 2003 (BTech), KERALA - MAY 2001 (BTech), CUSAT - JUL 2002 (MCA)*]

9. Discuss the advantages and disadvantages of linked list over arrays?

   [*MG - NOV 2002 (BTech)*]

10. Write down the steps to invert a singly-linked circular linked list?
[CUSAT - MAY 2000 (BTech), MG - MAY 2002 (BTech)
11. How do you use circular queue in programming? *[MG - MAY 2000 (BTech)]*
12. How doubly linked list can be used for dynamic storage? *[MG - MAY 2000 (BTech)]*
13. What is a Priority queue? How is it represented in the memory?
[ANNA - DEC 2004 (BE), CUSAT - APR 1998 (BTech)]
14. What is a linked list? What are its advantages over array? How is linked list implemented in the memory? *[CUSAT - APR 1998 (BTech)]*
15. Develop an algorithm to insert a node to the right of kth node of a singly linked linear list.
[CUSAT - APR 1998 (BTech)]
16. Evaluate the complexity of the algorithm to add two polynomials in the form of linked lists *[CUSAT - MAY 2000 (BTech)]*
17. Compare linear data structures with linked storage data types.
[CUSAT - MAY 2000 (BTech)]
18. Explain the representation of polynomials using linked lists.
[CUSAT - NOV 2002 (BTech)]
19. Write algorithms for adding and deleting elements from a circular queue implemented as linked list. *[CUSAT - DEC 2003 (MCA)]*
20. Explain any three operations on a linked list. Write algorithms for these operations.
[ANNA - DEC 2003 (BE)]
21. Discuss the advantage of circular queue with examples. *[ANNA - MAY 2004 (MCA)]*
22. Explain how pointers are used to implement linked list structures.
[ANNA - MAY 2004 (BE)]
23. Differentiate singly linked list and circularly linked list.
[KERALA - DEC 2003 (BTech), ANNA - MAY 2003 (BE)]
24. Write an algorithm to traverse elements in a singly linked list
[KERALA - DEC 2004 (BTech)]
25. Explain about frequency count and give an example. Write procedures for circular queue operations. *[KERALA - JUN 2004 (BTech)]*
26. Write procedure for searching an element in a singly linked list.
[KERALA - JUN 2004 (BTech)]
27. What is the advantage of a doubly linked list compared to a singly linked list?
[KERALA - MAY 2002 (BTech)]

6 Sorting Techniques

The operation of sorting is the most common task performed by computers today. Sorting is used to arrange names and numbers in meaningful ways. For example; it is easy to look in the dictionary for a word if it is arranged (or sorted) in alphabetic order .

Let A be a list of *n* elements A1, A2, ... An in memory. Sorting of list A refers to the operation of rearranging the contents of A so that they are in increasing (or decreasing) order (numerically or lexicographically); A1 < A2 < A3 < ...... < An.

Since A has *n* elements, the contents in A can appear in *n*! ways. These ways correspond precisely to the *n*! permutations of 1,2,3, ... *n*. Each sorting algorithm must take care of these *n*! possibilities.

For example

Suppose an array A contains 7 elements, 42, 33, 23, 74, 44, 67, 49. After sorting, the array A contains the elements as follows 23, 33, 42, 44, 49, 67, 74. Since A consists of 7 elements, there are 7! =.5040 ways that the elements can appear in A.

The elements of an array can be sorted in any specified order *i.e.*, either in ascending order or descending order. For example, consider an array A of size 7 elements 42, 33, 23, 74, 44, 67, 49. If they are arranged in ascending order, then sorted array is 23, 33, 42, 44, 49, 67, 74 and if the array is arranged in descending order then the sorted array is 74, 67, 49, 44, 42, 33, 23. In this chapter all the sorting techniques are discussed to arrange in ascending order.

Sorting can be performed in many ways. Over a time several methods (or algorithms) are being developed to sort data(s). Bubble sort, Selection sort, Quick sort, Merge sort, Heap sort, Binary sort, Shell sort and Radix sort are the few sorting techniques discussed in this chapter.

It is very difficult to select a sorting algorithm over another. And there is no sorting algorithm better than all others in all circumstances. Some sorting algorithm will perform well in some situations, so it is important to have a selection of sorting algorithms. Some factors that play an important role in selection processes are the time complexity of the algorithm (use of computer time), the size of the data structures (for Eg: an array) to be sorted (use of storage space), and the time it takes for a programmer to implement the algorithms (programming effort).

For example, a small business that manages a list of employee names and salary could easily use an algorithm such as bubble sort since the algorithm is simple to implement and the data to be sorted is relatively small. However a large public limited with ten thousands of employees experience horrible delay, if we try to sort it with bubble sort algorithm. More efficient algorithm, like Heap sort is advisable.

6.1. COMPLEXITY OF SORTING ALGORITHMS

The complexity of sorting algorithm measures the running time of n items to be sorted. The operations in the sorting algorithm, where A1, A2 ..... An contains the items to be sorted and B is an auxiliary location, can be generalized as:

(*a*) Comparisons- which tests whether Ai < Aj or test whether Ai < B

(*b*) Interchange- which switches the contents of Ai and Aj or of Ai and B

(*c*) Assignments- which set B = A and then set Aj = B or Aj = Ai

Normally, the complexity functions measure only the number of comparisons, since the number of other operations is at most a constant factor of the number of comparisons.

6.2. BUBBLE SORT

In bubble sort, each element is compared with its adjacent element. If the first element is larger than the second one, then the positions of the elements are interchanged, otherwise it is not changed. Then next element is compared with its adjacent element and the same process is repeated for all the elements in the array until we get a sorted array.

Let A be a linear array of n numbers. Sorting of A means rearranging the elements of A so that they are in order. Here we are dealing with ascending order. *i.e.*, A[1] < A[2] < A[3] < ...... A[n].

Suppose the list of numbers A[1], A[2], ... A[n] is an element of array A. The bubble sort algorithm works as follows:

Step 1: Compare A[1] and A[2] and arrange them in the (or desired) ascending order, so that A[1] < A[2].that is if A[1] is greater than A[2] then interchange the position of data by swap = A[1]; A[1] = A[2]; A[2] = swap. Then compare A[2] and A[3] and arrange them so that A[2] < A[3]. Continue the process until we compare A[N – 1] with A[N].

Note: Step1 contains $n - 1$ comparisons *i.e.*, the largest element is "bubbled up" to the nth position or "sinks" to the nth position. When step 1 is completed A[N] will contain the largest element.

Step 2: Repeat step 1 with one less comparisons that is, now stop comparison at A [$n - 1$] and possibly rearrange A[N – 2] and A[N – 1] and so on.

Note: in the first pass, step 2 involves n–2 comparisons and the second largest element will occupy A[n-1]. And in the second pass, step 2 involves $n - 3$ comparisons and the 3rd largest element will occupy A[$n - 2$] and so on.

Step $n - 1$: compare A[1]with A[2] and arrange them so that A[1] < A[2]

After $n - 1$ steps, the array will be a sorted array in increasing (or ascending) order.

The following figures will depict the various steps (or PASS) involved in the sorting of an array of 5 elements. The elements of an array A to be sorted are: 42, 33, 23, 74, 44

FIRST PASS

33 swapped	33	33	33
42	23 swapped	23	23
23	42	42 no swapping	42
74	74	74	44 swapped
44	44	44	74

23 swapped	23	23
33	33 no swapping	33
42	42	42 no swapping
44	44	44
74	74	74

23 no swapping	23
33	33 no swapping
42	42
44	44
74	74

23 no swapping
33
42
44
74

Thus the sorted array is 23, 33, 42, 44, 74.

ALGORITHM

Let A be a linear array of *n* numbers. Swap is a temporary variable for swapping (or interchange) the position of the numbers.

1. Input *n* numbers of an array A
2. Initialise $i = 0$ and repeat through step 4 if $(i < n)$
3. Initialize $j = 0$ and repeat through step 4 if $(j < n - i - 1)$
4. If (A[*j*] > A[*j* + 1])
   (*a*) Swap = A[*j*]
   (*b*) A[*j*] = A[*j* + 1]
   (*c*) A[*j* + 1] = Swap
5. Display the sorted numbers of array A
6. Exit.

PROGRAM 6.1

```
//PROGRAM TO IMPLEMENT BUBBLE SORT USING ARRAYS
//STATIC MEMORY ALLOCATION
//CODED AND COMPILED IN TURBO C

#include<conio.h>
#include<stdio.h>
```

```
#define MAX 20
void main()
{
        int arr[MAX],i,j,k,temp,n,xchanges;
        clrscr();
        printf ("\nEnter the number of elements : ");
        scanf ("%d",&n);
        for (i = 0; i < n; i++)
        {
                printf ("E\nnter element %d : ",i+1);
                scanf ("%d",&arr[i]);
        }
        printf ("\nUnsorted list is :\n");
        for (i = 0; i < n; i++)
                printf ("%d ", arr[i]);
        printf ("\n");

        /* Bubble sort*/
        for (i = 0; i < n-1 ; i++)
        {
                xchanges=0;
                for (j = 0; j <n-1-i; j++)
                {
                        if (arr[j] > arr[j+1])
                        {
                                temp = arr[j];
                                arr[j] = arr[j+1];
                                arr[j+1] = temp;
                                xchanges++;
                        }/*End of if*/
                }/*End of inner for loop*/
                if (xchanges==0) /*If list is sorted*/
                        break;
                printf("\nAfter Pass %d elements are : ",i+1);
                for (k = 0; k < n; k++)
                        printf("%d ", arr[k]);
                printf("\n");
        }/*End of outer for loop*/
        printf("\nSorted list is :\n");
        for (i = 0; i < n; i++)
                printf("%d ", arr[i]);
        getch();
}/*End of main()*/
```

PROGRAM 6.2

```
//PROGRAM TO IMPLEMENT BUBBLE SORT
//USING DYNAMIC MEMORY ALLOCATION
//CODED AND COMPILED IN TURBO C

#include<stdio.h>
#include<conio.h>
#include<malloc.h>

//this function will bubble sort the input
void bubblesort(int *a,int n)
{
	int i,j,k,temp;
	for(i=1;i < n;i++)
	for(j=0;j < n-1;j++)
		if (a[j] > a[j+1])
		{
			temp=a[j];
			a[j]=a[j+1];
			a[j+1]=temp;
		}
}

void main()
{
	int *a,n,*l,*temp;
	clrscr();
	printf ("\nEnter the number of elements :");
	scanf ("%d",&n);
	//allocating the array of memory dynamically
	a=((int*)malloc(n*sizeof (int)));
	temp=a;//storing the memnory address
	l=a+n;
	printf ("\nEnter the elements\n");
	while(a < l)
	{
		scanf ("%d",a);
		a++;
	}
```

```
        bubblesort(temp,n);
        printf ("\nSorted array is : ");
        a=temp;
        while(a < l)
        {
                printf ("  %d",*a);
                a++;
        }
        getch();
    }
```

TIME COMPLEXITY

The time complexity for bubble sort is calculated in terms of the number of comparisons $f(n)$ (or of number of loops); here two loops (outer loop and inner loop) iterates (or repeated) the comparisons. The number of times the outer loop iterates is determined by the number of elements in the list which is asked to sort (say it is n). The inner loop is iterated one less than the number of elements in the list (*i.e.*, n-1 times) and is reiterated upon every iteration of the outer loop

$$f(n) = (n - 1) + (n - 2) + \ldots\ldots + 2 + 1$$
$$= n(n - 1) = O(n2).$$

BEST CASE

In this case you are asked to sort a sorted array by bubble sort algorithm. The inner loop will iterate with the 'if' condition evaluating time, that is the swap procedure is never called. In best case outer loop will terminate after one iteration, *i.e.*, it involves performing one pass, which requires n–1 comparisons

$$f(n) = O(n)$$

WORST CASE

In this case the array will be an inverted list (*i.e.*, 5, 4, 3, 2, 1, 0). Here to move first element to the end of the array, n–1 times the swapping procedure is to be called. Every other element in the list will also move one location towards the start or end of the loop on every iteration. Thus n times the outer loop will iterate and n (n-1) times the inner loop will iterate to sort an inverted array

$$f(n) = (n(n - 1))/2 = O(n2)$$

AVERAGE CASE

Average case is very difficult to analyse than the other cases. In this case the input data(s) are randomly placed in the list. The exact time complexity can be calculated only if we know the number of iterations, comparisons and swapping. In general, the complexity of average case is:

$$f(n) = (n(n-1))/2 = O(n2).$$

6.3. SELECTION SORT

Selection sort algorithm finds the smallest element of the array and interchanges it with the element in the first position of the array. Then it finds the second smallest element from the remaining elements in the array and places it in the second position of the array and so on.

Let A be a linear array of '*n*' numbers, A [1], A [2], A [3],......A [*n*].

Step 1: Find the smallest element in the array of *n* numbers A[1], A[2], ... A[*n*]. Let LOC is the location of the smallest number in the array. Then interchange A[LOC] and A[1] by swap = A[LOC]; A[LOC] = A[1]; A[1] = Swap.

Step 2: Find the second smallest number in the sub list of *n* – 1 elements A [2] A [3] ...... A [*n* – 1] (first element is already sorted). Now we concentrate on the rest of the elements in the array. Again A [LOC] is the smallest element in the remaining array and LOC the corresponding location then interchange A [LOC] and A [2].Now A [1] and A [2] is sorted, since A [1] less than or equal to A [2].

Step 3: Repeat the process by reducing one element each from the array

Step n – 1: Find the *n* – 1 smallest number in the sub array of 2 elements (*i.e.*, A(*n*–1), A (*n*)). Consider A [LOC] is the smallest element and LOC is its corresponding position. Then interchange A [LOC] and A(*n*– 1). Now the array A [1], A [2], A [3], A [4],..........A [*n*] will be a sorted array.

Following figure is generated during the iterations of the algorithm to sort 5 numbers 42, 33, 23, 74, 44 :

				First Pass			Second Pass	
A[1]	42		A[1]	23		23	
A[2]	33		A[2]	33	LOC = 2	33	LOC = 2
A[3]	23	LOC = 3	A[3]	42		42	
A[4]	74		A[4]	74		74	
A[5]	44		A[5]	44		44	

Third Pass		Fourth Pass	
23		23	
33		33	
42	LOC = 3	42	
74		44	
44		74	LOC = 5

ALGORITHM

Let A be a linear array of *n* numbers A [1], A [2], A [3], ...A [k], A [k+1], ... A [n]. *Swap* be a temporary variable for swapping (or interchanging) the position of the numbers. *Min* is the variable to store smallest number and *Loc* is the location of the smallest element.

1. Input *n* numbers of an array A
2. Initialize *i* = 0 and repeat through step5 if (*i* < *n* – 1)
   (*a*) min = *a*[*i*]
   (*b*) loc = *i*

3. Initialize $j = i + 1$ and repeat through step 4 if $(j < n - 1)$
4. if (a[*j*] < min)
   (*a*) min = a[*j*]
   (*b*) loc = *j*
5. if (loc ! = i)
   (*a*) swap = *a*[*i*]
   (*b*) *a*[*i*] = *a*[loc]
   (*c*) *a*[loc] = swap
6. display "the sorted numbers of array A"
7. Exit

PROGRAM 6.3

```
//PROGRAM TO IMPLEMENT SELECTION SORT
//USING STATIC MEMORY ALLOCATION, THAT IS USING ARRAYS
//CODED AND COMPILED IN TURBO C

#include<conio.h>
#include<stdio.h>

#define MAX 20

void main()
{
    int arr[MAX], i,j,k,n,temp,smallest;
    clrscr();
    printf ("\nEnter the number of elements : ");
    scanf ("%d", & n);
    for (i = 0; i < n; i++)
    {
        printf ("\nEnter element %d : ",i+1);
        scanf ("%d", &arr[i]);
    }
    printf ("\nUnsorted list is : \n");
    for (i = 0; i < n; i++)
        printf ("%d ", arr[i]);
    printf ("\n");
    /*Selection sort*/
    for (i = 0; i < n - 1 ; i++)
    {
```

```
            /*Find the smallest element*/
            smallest = i;
            for(k = i + 1; k < n ; k++)
            {
                  if (arr[smallest] > arr[k])
                        smallest = k ;
            }
            if ( i != smallest )
            {
                  temp = arr [i];
                  arr[i] = arr[smallest];
                  arr[smallest] = temp ;
            }
            printf ("\nAfter Pass %d elements are :  ",i+1);
            for (j = 0; j < n; j++)
                  printf ("%d ", arr[ j]);
            printf ("\n");
      }/*End of for*/
      printf ("\nSorted list is : \n");
      for (i = 0; i < n; i++)
            printf ("%d ", arr[i]);
      getch();
}/*End of main()*/
```

PROGRAM 6.4

```
//PROGRAM TO IMPLEMENT SELECTION SORT
//USING DYNAMIC MEMORY ALLOCATION
//CODED AND COMPILED USING TURBO C

#include<stdio.h>
#include<conio.h>
#include<malloc.h>

//this function will sort the input elements using selection sort
void selectionsort(int *a,int n)
{
      int i,j,temp;
      for(i=0;i< n-1;i++)
      for(j=i+1;j < n;j++)
```

```
        if (a[i]>a[j])
        {
                temp=a[i];
                a[i]=a[j];
                a[j]=temp;
        }
}

void main()
{
        int *a,n,*l,*temp;
        clrscr();
        printf ("\nEnter the number of elements\n");
        scanf ("%d",&n);

        //dynamically allocate the memory array block
        a=((int*)malloc(n*sizeof (int)));
        temp=a;
        l=a+n;
        printf ("\nEnter the elements\n");
        while(a < l)
        {
                scanf ("%d",a);
                a++;
        }

        //calling the selection sort fucntion
        selectionsort(temp,n);
        printf ("\nSorted array :  ");
        a=temp;
        while(a < l)
        {
                printf (" %d",*a);
                a++;
        }
        getch();
}
```

TIME COMPLEXITY

Time complexity of a selection sort is calculated in terms of the number of comparisons $f(n)$. In the first pass it makes $n - 1$ comparisons; the second pass makes $n - 2$

comparisons and so on. The outer *for loop* iterates for $(n - 1)$ times. But the inner loop iterates for $n*(n - 1)$ times to complete the sorting.

$$f(n) = (n-1) + (n-2) + \ldots\ldots + 2 + 1$$
$$= (n(n-1))/2$$
$$= O(n_2)$$

Readers can go through the algorithm and analyse it for different types of input to find their (efficiency) Time complexity for best, worst and average case. That is in best case how the algorithm is performed for sorted arrays as input.

In worst case we can analyse how the algorithm is performed for reverse sorted array as input. Average case is where we input general (mixed sorted) input to the algorithm. Following table will summarise the efficiency of algorithm in different case :

Best case	*Worst case*	*Average case*
$n - 1 = O(n)$	$\frac{n(n-1)}{2} = O(n^2)$	$\frac{n(n-1)}{2} = O(n)$

6.4. INSERTION SORT

Insertion sort algorithm sorts a set of values by inserting values into an existing sorted file. Compare the second element with first, if the first element is greater than second, place it before the first one. Otherwise place is just after the first one. Compare the third value with second. If the third value is greater than the second value then place it just after the second. Otherwise place the second value to the third place. And compare third value with the first value. If the third value is greater than the first value place the third value to second place, otherwise place the first value to second place. And place the third value to first place and so on.

Let A be a linear array of n numbers A [1], A [2], A [3], ... A[*n*]. The algorithm scan the array A from A [1] to A [n], by inserting each element A[k], into the proper position of the previously sorted sub list. A [1], A [2], A [3], ... A [*k* – 1]

Step 1: As the single element A [1] by itself is sorted array.

Step 2: A [2] is inserted either before or after A [1] by comparing it so that A[1], A[2] is sorted array.

Step 3: A [3] is inserted into the proper place in A [1], A [2], that is A [3] will be compared with A [1] and A [2] and placed before A [1], between A [1] and A [2], or after A [2] so that A [1], A [2], A [3] is a sorted array.

Step 4: A [4] is inserted in to a proper place in A [1], A [2], A [3] by comparing it; so that A [1], A [2], A [3], A [4] is a sorted array.

Step 5: Repeat the process by inserting the element in the proper place in array

Step n : A [*n*] is inserted into its proper place in an array A [1], A [2], A [3], ... A [*n* – 1] so that A [1], A [2], A [3], ... ,A [*n*] is a sorted array.

To illustrate the insertion sort methods, consider a following array with five elements 42, 33, 23, 74, 44 :

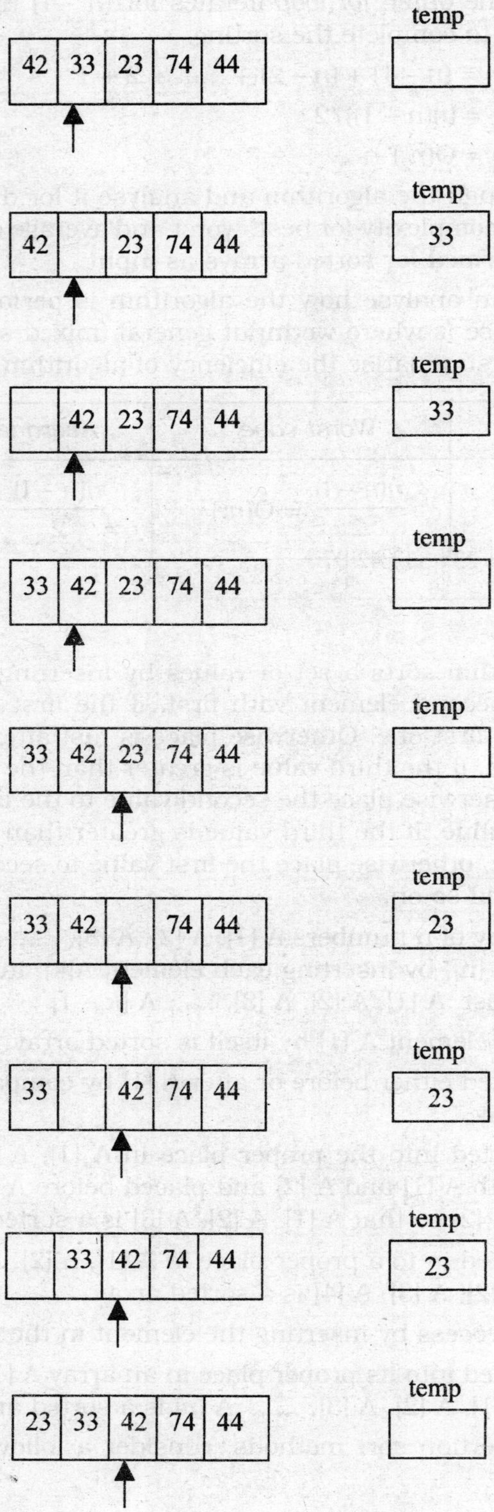
temp
42 33 23 74 44
temp
42 23 74 44
33
temp
42 23 74 44
33
temp
33 42 23 74 44
temp
33 42 23 74 44
temp
33 42 74 44
23
temp
33 42 74 44
23
temp
33 42 74 44
23
temp
23 33 42 74 44

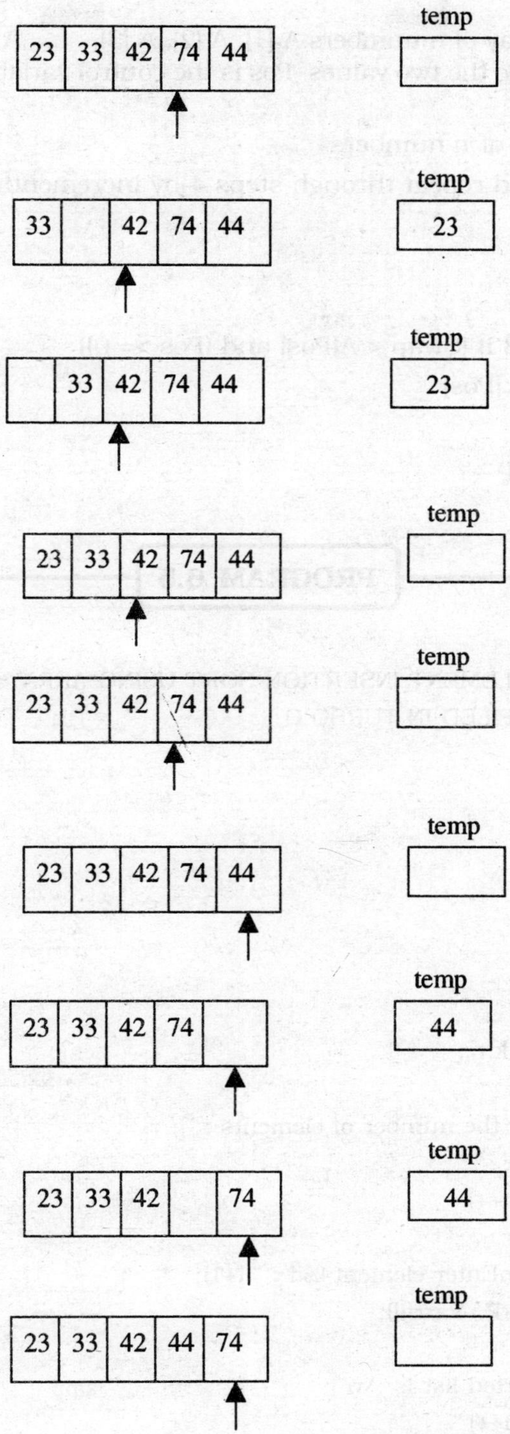
temp
23 33 42 74 44
temp
33 42 74 44
23
temp
33 42 74 44
23
temp
23 33 42 74 44
temp
23 33 42 74 44
temp
23 33 42 74 44
temp
23 33 42 74
44
temp
23 33 42 74
44
temp
23 33 42 44 74

ALGORITHM

Let A be a linear array of n numbers A [1], A [2], A [3], ... ,A [n]......Swap be a temporary variable to interchange the two values. Pos is the control variable to hold the position of each pass.

1. Input an array A of n numbers
2. Initialize $i = 1$ and repeat through steps 4 by incrementing i by one.
   (a) If $(i <= n - 1)$
   (b) Swap = A [I],
   (c) Pos = $i - 1$
3. Repeat the step 3 if (Swap < A[Pos] and (Pos >= 0))
   (a) A [Pos+1] = A [Pos]
   (b) Pos = Pos-1
4. A [Pos +1] = Swap
5. Exit

PROGRAM 6.5

```
//PROGRAM TO IMPLEMENT INSERTION SORT USING ARRAYS
//CODED AND COMPILED IN TURBO C

#include<conio.h>
#include<stdio.h>

#define MAX 20

void main()
{
	int arr[MAX],i,j,k,n;
	clrscr();
	printf ("\nEnter the number of elements : ");
	scanf ("%d",&n);
	for (i = 0; i < n; i++)
	{
		printf ("\nEnter element %d : ",i+1);
		scanf ("%d", &arr[i]);
	}
	printf ("\nUnsorted list is :\n");
	for (i = 0; i < n; i++)
		printf ("%d ", arr[i]);
	printf ("\n");
```

```
/*Insertion sort*/
for(j=1;j < n;j++)
{
        k=arr[j]; /*k is to be inserted at proper place*/
        for(i=j-1;i>=0 && k<arr[i];i--)
                arr[i+1]=arr[i];
        arr[i+1]=k;
        printf ("\nPass %d, Element inserted in proper place: %d\n",j,k);
        for (i = 0; i < n; i++)
                printf ("%d ", arr[i]);
        printf ("\n");
}
printf ("\nSorted list is :\n");
for (i = 0; i < n; i++)
        printf ("%d ", arr[i]);
getch();
}/*End of main()*/
```

TIME COMPLEXITY

In the insertion sort algorithm $(n-1)$ times the loop will execute for comparisons and interchanging the numbers. The inner while loop iterates maximum of $((n-1) \times (n-1))/2$ times to computing the sorting.

WORST CASE

The worst case occurs when the array A is in reverse order and the inner while loop must use the maximum number $(n-1)$ of comparisons. Hence

$$f(n) = (n-1) + \ldots\ldots.\ 2 + 1$$
$$= (n(n-1))/2$$
$$= O(n^2).$$

AVERAGE CASE

On the average case there will be approximately $(n-1)/2$ comparisons in the inner while loop. Hence the average case

$$f(n) = (n-1)/2 + \ldots\ldots + 2/2 + 1/2$$
$$= n(n-1)/4$$
$$= O(n^2).$$

BEST CASE

The best case occurs when the array A is in sorted order and the outer for loop will iterate for $(n-1)$ times. And the inner while loop will not execute because the given array is a sorted array

i.e., $f(n) = O(n)$.

6.5. SHELL SORT

Shell Sort is introduced to improve the efficiency of simple insertion sort. Shell Sort is also called *diminishing increment sort.* In this method, sub-array, contain *k*th element of the original array, are sorted.

Let A be a linear array of *n* numbers A [1], A [2], A [3], ... A [n].

Step 1: The array is divided into *k* sub-arrays consisting of every *k*th element. Say *k* = 5, then five sub-array, each containing one fifth of the elements of the original array.

Sub array 1 → A[0] A[5] A[10]
Sub array 2 → A[1] A[6] A[11]
Sub array 3 → A[2] A[7] A[12]
Sub array 4 → A[3] A[8] A[13]
Sub array 5 → A[4] A[9] A[14]

Note : The ith element of the *j*th sub array is located as A [(*i*–1) × *k*+*j*–1]

Step 2: After the first *k* sub array are sorted (usually by insertion sort) , a new smaller value of *k* is chosen and the array is again partitioned into a new set of sub arrays.

Step 3: And the process is repeated with an even smaller value of *k*, so that A [1], A [2], A [3], ... A [*n*] is sorted.

To illustrate the shell sort, consider the following array with 7 elements 42, 33, 23, 74, 44, 67, 49 and the sequence K = 4, 2, 1 is chosen.

Pass = 1

Span = *k* = 4

42, 33, 23, 74, 44, 67, 49

Pass = 2

span = *k* = 2

42, 33, 23, 74, 44, 67, 49

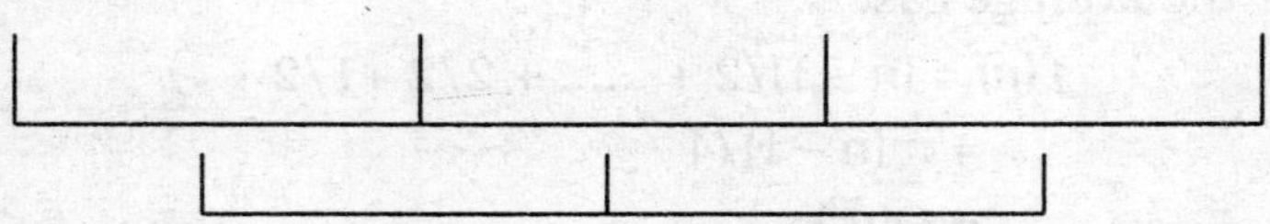

Pass = 3

Span = *k* = 1

23, 33, 42, 67, 44, 74, 49

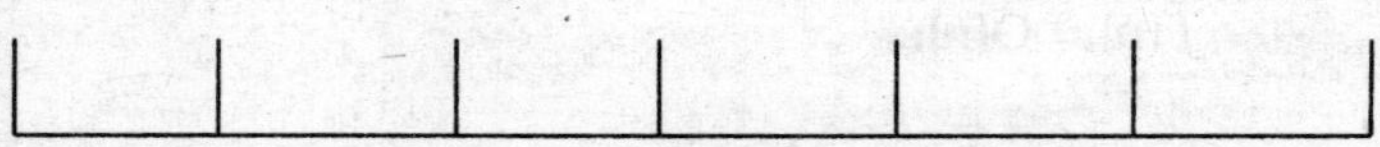

23, 33, 42, 44, 49, 67, 74

ALGORITHM

Let A be a linear array of *n* elements, A [1], A [2], A [3], ... A[*n*] and *Incr* be an array of sequence of span to be incremented in each pass. X is the number of elements in the array *Incr. Span* is to store the span of the array from the array Incr.

1. Input *n* numbers of an array A
2. Initialise *i* = 0 and repeat through step 6 if (*i* < *x*)
3. Span = Incr[*i*]
4. Initialise *j* = span and repeat through step 6 if (*j* < *n*)
   (*a*) Temp = A [*j*]
5. Initialise *k* = *j*-span and repeat through step 5 if (*k* > = 0) and (temp < A [*k*])
   (*a*) A [*k* + span] = A [*k*]
6. A [*k* + span] = temp
7. Exit

PROGRAM 6.6

```
//PROGRAM TO IMPLEMENT SHELL SORT USING ARRAYS
//CODED AND COMPILED IN TURBO C

#include<conio.h>
#include<stdio.h>

#define MAX 20

void main()
{
        int arr[MAX], i,j,k,n,incr;
        clrscr();
        printf ("\nEnter the number of elements : ");
        scanf ("%d",&n);
        for (i=0;i < n;i++)
        {
                printf ("\nEnter element %d : ",i+1);
                scanf ("%d",&arr[i]);
        }
        printf ("\nUnsorted list is :\n");
        for (i = 0; i < n; i++)
                printf ("%d ", arr[i]);
        printf ("\nEnter maximum increment (odd value) : ");
```

```
        scanf ("%d",&incr);
        /*Shell sort algorithm is applied*/
        while(incr>=1)
        {
                for (j=incr;j<n;j++)
                {
                        k=arr[ j];
                        for(i = j–incr; i > = 0 && k < arr[i]; i = i–incr)
                                arr[i+incr]=arr[i];
                        arr[i+incr]=k;
                }
                printf ("\nIncrement=%d \n",incr);
                for (i = 0; i < n; i++)
                        printf("%d ", arr[i]);
                printf ("\n");
                incr=incr–2; /*Decrease the increment*/
        }/*End of while*/
        printf ("\nSorted list is :\n");
        for (i = 0; i < n; i++)
                printf ("%d ", arr[i]);
        getch();
}/*End of main()*/
```

TIME COMPLEXITY

The detailed efficiency analysis of the shell sort is mathematically involved and beyond the scope of this book. The time complexity depends on the number of elements in the array increment (*i.e.*, number of spans) and on their actual values. One requirement is that the elements of increments should be relatively prime (*i.e.*, no common divisor other than 1). This guarantees that after successive iteration of the sub arrays, the entire array is almost sorted when the span = 1 (*i.e.*, in the last iteration). If an appropriate sequence of increments is classified, then the order of the shell sort is

$$f(n) = O(n (\log n)^2)$$

6.6. QUICK SORT

It is one of the widely used sorting techniques and it is also called the partition-exchange sort. Quick sort is an efficient algorithm and it passes a very good time complexity in average case. This is developed by C.A.R. Hoare. It is an algorithm of the divide-and-conquer type.

The quick sort algorithm works by partitioning the array to be sorted. And each partitions are internally sorted recursively. In partition the first element of an array is chosen as a key value. This key value can be the first element of an array. That is, if A is an array then key = A (0), and rest of the elements are grouped into two portions such that, (*a*) One partition contains elements smaller than key value

(*b*) Another partition contains elements larger than the key value

Two pointers, up and low, are initialized to the upper and lower bounds of the sub array. During execution, at any point each element in a position above up is greater than or equal to key value and each element in a position below low pointer is less than or equal to the key. Up pointer will move in a decrement and low in an increment fashion.

Let A be an array A [1], A [2], A [3], ... ,A [n] of n number to be sorted. Then,

Step 1: Choose the first elements of the array (or sub-array) as the key *i.e.*, key = A(1).

Step 2: Place the low pointer in second position of the array and up pointer in the last position of the array *i.e.*, low = 2 and up = *n*.

Step 3: Repeatedly increase the pointer low by one position until (A [low] > key).

Step 4: Repeatedly decrease the pointer up by one position until (A [up] < = key).

Step 5: If up > low, interchange A [low] with A [up], Swap = A [low]; A [low] = A [up]; A [up] = Swap.

Step 6: Repeat the step 3, 4, and 5 until the condition in step 5 fails (*i.e.*, up < = low), then interchange A [up] with key.

NOTE: Now the given array is partitioned into two sub-arrays. The sub-array A [1], A [2], A [3], ... ,A [*k* –1] is less than A [*k*] (*i.e.*, key) and the second sub array A [*k* + 1], A [*k* + 2], A [k + 3], ... ,A [*n*) which is greater than the key value A (*k*). We can repeatedly apply this procedure on each of these sub-arrays until the entire array is sorted.

To illustrate the quick sort algorithm, consider the following array with 7 elements 42, 33, 23, 74, 44, 67, 49. Select the first value of the array as key, here the key = 42. and locate the low and up pointers.

```
          low→                             up
42,       33 ,    23,    74,    44,   67,   49
```

Move the low pointers by repeatedly incrementing the pointer by one position until (A[low] > key).

```
                 low→                      up
42,       33 ,    23,    74,    44,   67,   49
```

```
                        low→               up
42,       33 ,    23,    74,    44,   67,   49
```

Here (A [low] > key) *i.e.*, 74 > 42. Now decrease the pointer up by one position until (A [up] < = key).

```
                        low               ←up
42,       33 ,    23,    74,    44,   67,   49
```

			low		←up	
42,	33 ,	23,	74,	44,	67,	49

			low ←up			
42,	33 ,	23,	74,	44,	67,	49

		← up	low			
42,	33 ,	23,	74,	44,	67,	49

	← up		low			
42,	33 ,	23,	74,	44,	67,	49

		up	low			
42,	33 ,	23,	74,	44,	67,	49

23, 33 , (Value < 42)   42,   74, 44, 67, 49 (Value > 42)

ALGORITHM

Let A be a linear array of *n* elements A (1), A (2), A (3)......A (*n*), low represents the lower bound pointer and up represents the upper bound pointer. Key represents the first element of the array, which is going to become the middle element of the sub-arrays.

1. Input *n* number of elements in an array A
2. Initialize low = 2, up = *n* , key = A[(low + up)/2]
3. Repeat through step 8 while (low < = up)
4. Repeat step 5 while(A [low] > key)
5. low = low + 1
6. Repeat step 7 while(A [up] < key)
7. up = up–1
8. If (low < = up)
   (*a*) Swap = A [low]
   (*b*) A [low] = A [up]
   (*c*) A [up] = swap
   (*d*) low=low+1

(*e*) up=up–1

9. If (1 < up) Quick sort (A, 1, up)
10. If (low < *n*) Quick sort (A, low, *n*)
11. Exit

PROGRAM 6.7

```
//PROGRAM TO IMPLEMENT QUICK SORT
//USING ARRAYS RECURSIVELY
//CODED AND COMPILED IN TURBO C

#include<conio.h>
#include<stdio.h>

#define MAX 30

enum bool {FALSE,TRUE};

//Function display the array
void display(int arr[],int low,int up)
{
	int i;
	for(i=low;i<=up;i++)
		printf ("%d ",arr[i]);
}

//This function will sort the array using Quick sort algorithm
void quick(int arr[],int low,int up)
{
	int piv,temp,left,right;
	enum bool pivot_placed=FALSE;
	//setting the pointers
	left=low;
	right=up;
	piv=low; /*Take the first element of sublist as piv */

	if (low>=up)
		return;
	printf ("\nSublist : ");
	display(arr,low,up);
```

```
        /*Loop till pivot is placed at proper place in the sublist*/
        while(pivot_placed==FALSE)
        {
            /*Compare from right to left  */
            while( arr[piv]<=arr[right] && piv!=right )
                right=right-1;
            if ( piv==right )
                pivot_placed=TRUE;
            if ( arr[piv] > arr[right] )
            {
                temp=arr[piv];
                arr[piv]=arr[right];
                arr[right]=temp;
                piv=right;
            }
            /*Compare from left to right */
            while( arr[piv]>=arr[left] && left!=piv )
                left=left+1;
            if (piv==left)
                pivot_placed=TRUE;
            if ( arr[piv] < arr[left] )
            {
                temp=arr[piv];
                arr[piv]=arr[left];
                arr[left]=temp;
                piv=left;
            }
        }/*End of while */

        printf ("-> Pivot Placed is %d -> ",arr[piv]);
        display(arr,low,up);
        printf ("\n");
        quick(arr,low,piv-1);
        quick(arr,piv+1,up);
}/*End of quick()*/

void main()
{
        int array[MAX],n,i;
        clrscr();
        printf ("\nEnter the number of elements : ");
        scanf ("%d",&n);
```

```
        for (i=0;i<n;i++)
        {
                printf ("\nEnter element %d : ",i+1);
                scanf ("%d",&array[i]);
        }

        printf ("\nUnsorted list is :\n");
        display(array,0,n-1);
        printf ("\n");

        quick (array,0,n-1);
        printf ("\nSorted list is :\n");
        display(array,0,n-1);
        getch();
}/*End of main() */
```

TIME COMPLEXITY

The time complexity of quick sort can be calculated for any of the following case. It is usually measured by the number $f(n)$ of comparisons required to sort n elements.

WORST CASE

The worst case occurs when the list is already sorted. In this case the given array is partitioned into two sub arrays. One of them is an empty array and another one is an array. After partition, when the first element is checked with other element, it will take n comparison to recognize that it remain in the position so as $(n - 1)$ comparisons for the second position.

$$f(n) = n + (n-1) + \ldots\ldots + 2 + 1$$
$$= (n(n+1))/2$$
$$= O(n^2)$$

AVERAGE CASE

In this case each reduction step of the algorithm produces two sub arrays. Accordingly :

(*a*) Reducing the array by placing one element and produces two sub arrays.

(*b*) Reducing the two sub-arrays by placing two elements and produces four sub-arrays.

(*c*) Reducing the four sub-arrays by placing four elements and produces eight sub-arrays.

And so on. Reduction step in the *k*th level finds the location at 2^{k-1} elements; however there will be approximately $\log_2 n$ levels at reduction steps. Furthermore each level uses at most n comparisons,

so $$f(n) = O(n \log n)$$

BEST CASE

The base case analysis occurs when the array is always partitioned in half, That key = A [(low+up)/2]

$$
\begin{aligned}
f(n) &= Cn + f(n/2) + f(n/2) \\
&= Cn + 2f(n/2) \\
&= O(n) \qquad \text{where C is a constant.}
\end{aligned}
$$

6.7. MERGE SORT

Merging is the process of combining two or more sorted array into a third sorted array. It was one of the first sorting algorithms used on a computer and was developed by John Von Neumann. Divide the array into approximately $n/2$ sub-arrays of size two and set the element in each sub array. Merging each sub-array with the adjacent sub-array will get another sorted sub-array of size four. Repeat this process until there is only one array remaining of size n.

Since at any time the two arrays being merged are both sub-arrays of A, lower and upper bounds are required to indicate the sub-arrays of a being merged. l1 and $u1$ represents the lower and upper bands of the first sub-array and l2 and $u2$ represents the lower and upper bands of the second sub-array respectively.

Let A be an array of n number of elements to be sorted A[1], A[2] ...... A[n].

Step 1: Divide the array A into approximately $n/2$ sorted sub-array of size 2. *i.e.*, the elements in the (A [1], A [2]), (A [3], A [4]), (A [k], A [k + 1]), (A [n – 1], A [n]) sub-arrays are in sorted order.

Step 2: Merge each pair of pairs to obtain the following list of sorted sub-array of size 4; the elements in the sub-array are also in the sorted order.

(A [1], A [2], A [3], A [4]),...... (A [k – 1], A [k], A [k + 1], A [k + 2]),
...... (A [n – 3], A [n – 2], A [n – 1], A [n]).

Step 3: Repeat the step 2 recursively until there is only one sorted array of size n.

To illustrate the merge sort algorithm consider the following array with 7 elements [42], [33], [23], [74], [44], [67], [49]

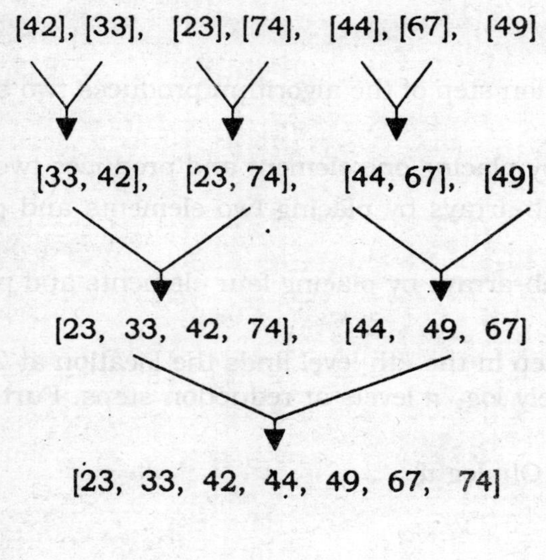

ALGORITHM

Let A be a linear array of size *n*, A [1], A [2], A [3] ...... A [*n*], l1 and *u*1 represent lower and upper bounds of the first sub-array and l2 and *u*2 represent the lower and upper bound of the second sub-array. *Aux* is an auxiliary array of size *n*. *Size* is the *sizes* of merge files.

1. Input an array of *n* elements to be sorted
2. Size = 1
3. Repeat through the step 13 while (Size < *n*)
   (*a*) set l1 = 0; *k* = 0
4. Repeat through step 10 while ((l1+Size) < *n*)
   (*a*) l2 = l1+Size
   (*b*) u1 = l2–1
5. If ((l2+Size–1) < n)
   (*i*) *u*2 = l2+Size–1
   (*b*) Else
   (*i*) *u*2 = n-1
6. Initialize *i* = l1; *j* = l2 and repeat through step 7 if (*i* <= u1) and (j < = *u*2)
7. If (A [i] < = A[j])
   (*i*) Aux [*k*] = A [i++]
   (*b*) Else
   (*i*) Aux [*k*] = A [j++]
8. Repeat the step 8 by incrementing the value of *k* until (*i* < = *u*1)
   (*a*) Aux [*k*] = A [I++]
9. Repeat the step 9 by incrementing the value of *k* until (*j* < = *u*2)
   (*a*) Aux [*k*] = A [*j*++]
10. L1=*u*2+1
11. Initialize I = l1 and repeat the step 11 if (k < n) by incrementing I by one
    (*a*) Aux [k++] = A[I]
12. Initialize I=0 and repeat the step 12 if (I < n) by incrementing I by one
    (*a*) A [i] = A [I]
13. Size = Size*2
14. Exit

PROGRAM 6.8

```
//PROGRAM TO IMPLEMENT MERGING OF TWO SORTED ARRAYS
//INTO A THIRD SORTED ARRAY
//CODED AND COMPILED IN TURBO C
```

```
#include<conio.h>
#include<stdio.h>
void main()
{
	int arr1[20],arr2[20],arr3[40];
	int i,j,k;
	int max1,max2;
	clrscr();

	printf ("\nEnter the number of elements in list1 : ");
	scanf ("%d",&max1);
	printf ("\nTake the elements in sorted order :\n");
	for (i=0;i<max1;i++)
	{
		printf ("\nEnter element %d : ",i+1);
		scanf ("%d",&arr1[i]);
	}
	printf ("\nEnter the number of elements in list2 : ");
	scanf ("%d",&max2);
	printf ("\nTake the elements in sorted order :\n");
	for (i=0;i<max2;i++)
	{
		printf ("\nEnter element %d : ",i+1);
		scanf ("%d",&arr2[i]);
	}
	/* Merging */
	i=0;	/*Index for first array*/
	j=0;	/*Index for second array*/
	k=0;	/*Index for merged array*/
	while( (i < max1) && (j < max2) )
	{
		if ( arr1[i] < arr2[j] )
			arr3[k++]=arr1[i++];
		else
			arr3[k++]=arr2[j++];
	}/*End of while*/
	/*Put remaining elements of arr1 into arr3*/
	while( i < max1 )
		arr3[k++]=arr1[i++];
	/*Put remaining elements of arr2 into arr3*/
```

```
	while( j < max2 )
		arr3[k++]=arr2[j++];

	/*Merging completed*/
	printf ("\nList 1 :  ");
	for (i=0;i<max1;i++)
		printf ("%d ",arr1[i]);
	printf ("\nList 2 :  ");
	for (i=0;i<max2;i++)
		printf("%d ",arr2[i]);
	printf ("\nMerged list : ");
	for( i=0;i<max1+max2;i++)
		printf ("%d ",arr3[i]);
	getch();
}/*End of main()*/
```

PROGRAM 6.9

```
//PROGRAM TO IMPLEMENT MERGE SORT WITHOUT RECURSION
//CODED AND COMPILED IN TURBO C
#include<stdio.h>
#include<conio.h>

#define MAX 30

void main()
{
	int arr[MAX],temp[MAX],i,j,k,n,size,l1,h1,l2,h2;
	clrscr();
	printf ("\nEnter the number of elements : ");
	scanf ("%d",&n);
	for (i=0;i<n;i++)
	{
		printf ("\nEnter element %d : ",i+1);
		scanf ("%d",&arr[i]);
	}
	printf ("\nUnsorted list is : ");
	for ( i = 0 ; i<n ; i++)
		printf("%d ", arr[i]);

	/*l1 lower bound of first pair and so on*/
```

```
for (size=1; size < n; size=size*2 )
{
        l1 = 0;
        k = 0;  /*Index for temp array*/
        while( l1+size < n)
        {
                h1=l1+size-1;
                l2=h1+1;
                h2=l2+size-1;
                if ( h2>=n ) /* h2 exceeds the limlt of arr */
                        h2=n-1;
                /*Merge the two pairs with lower limits l1 and l2*/
                i=l1;
                j=l2;
                while(i<=h1 && j<=h2 )
                {
                        if ( arr[i] <= arr[ j] )
                                temp[k++]=arr[i++];
                        else
                                temp[k++]=arr[ j++];
                }
                while(i<=h1)
                        temp[k++]=arr[i++];
                while( j<=h2)
                        temp[k++]=arr[ j++];
                /**Merging completed**/
                l1 = h2+1; /*Take the next two pairs for merging */
        }/*End of while*/

        for (i=l1; k<n; i++) /*any pair left */
                temp[k++]=arr[i];

        for(i=0;i<n;i++)
            arr[i]=temp[i];

        printf ("\nSize=%d \nElements are : ",size);
        for ( i = 0 ; i<n ; i++)
                printf ("%d ", arr[i]);
}/*End of for loop */
printf ("\nSorted list is :\n");
for ( i = 0 ; i<n ; i++)
        printf ("%d ", arr[i]);
```

```
        getch();
}/*End of main()*/
```

PROGRAM 6.10

```
//PROGRAM TO IMPLEMENT MERGE SORT THROUGH RECURSION
//CODED AND COMPILED IN TURBO C

#include<stdio.h>
#include<conio.h>

#define MAX 20

int array[MAX];
//Function to merge the sub  files or arrays
void merge(int low, int mid, int high )
{
        int temp[MAX];
        int i = low;
        int j = mid +1 ;
        int k = low ;

        while( (i < = mid) && (j < =high) )
        {
                if (array[i] < = array[ j])
                        temp[k++] = array[i++] ;
                else
                        temp[k++] = array[ j++] ;
        }/*End of while*/
        while( i <= mid )
                temp[k++]=array[i++];
        while( j <= high )
                temp[k++]=array[j++];

        for (i= low; i < = high ; i++)
                array[i]=temp[i];
}/*End of merge()*/

//Function which call itself to sort an array
void merge_sort(int low, int high )
```

```
{
        int mid;
        if ( low ! = high )
        {
                mid = (low+high)/2;
                merge_sort( low , mid );
                merge_sort( mid+1, high );
                merge(low, mid, high );
        }
}/*End of merge_sort*/

void main()
{
        int i,n;
        clrscr();
        printf ("\nEnter the number of elements : ");
        scanf ("%d",&n);
        for (i=0;i<n;i++)
        {
                printf ("\nEnter element %d : ",i+1);
                scanf ("%d",&array[i]);
        }

        printf ("\nUnsorted list is :\n");
        for ( i = 0 ; i<n ; i++)
                printf ("%d ", array[i]);

        merge_sort( 0, n-1);

        printf ("\nSorted list is :\n");
        for ( i = 0 ; i<n ; i++)
                printf ("%d ", array[i]);
        getch();
}/*End of main()*/
```

TIME COMPLEXITY

Let $f(n)$ denote the number of comparisons needed to sort an n element array A using the merge sort algorithm. The algorithm requires almost log n passes, each involving n or fewer comparisons.

In average and worst case the merge sort requires $O(n \log n)$ comparisons.

The main drawback of merge sort is that it requires $O(n)$ additional space for the auxiliary array.

6.8. RADIX SORT

Radix sort or bucket sort is a method that can be used to sort a list of numbers by its base. If we want to sort list of English words, where radix or base is 26, then 26 buckets is used to sort the words.

To sort an array of decimal numbers, where the radix or base is 10, we need 10 buckets and can be numbered as 0, 1, 2, 3, 4, 5, 6, 7, 8, 9. Number of passes required to have a sorted array depends upon the number of digits in the largest element. To illustrate the radix sort, consider the following array with 7 elements :

42, 133, 7, 23, 74, 670, 49

In this array the biggest element is 670 and the number of digit is 3. So 3 passes are required to sort the array. Read the element(s) and compare the first position (2 is in first position of 42) digit with the digit of the bucket and place it.

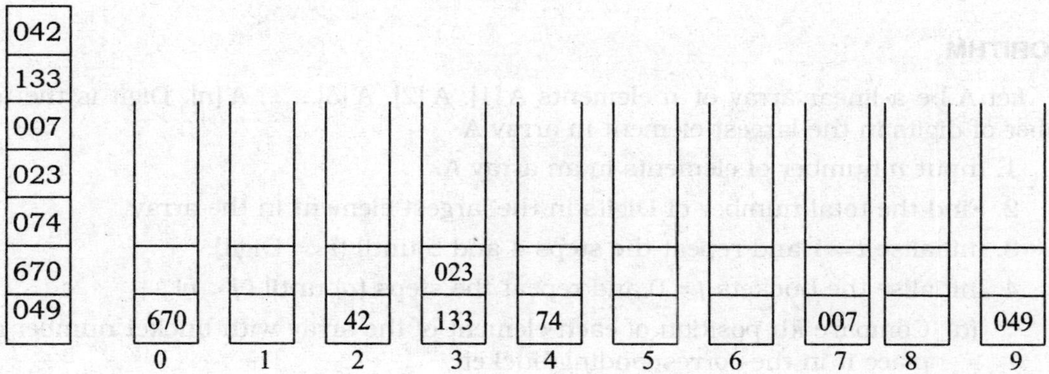

Now read the elements from left to right and bottom to top of the buckets and place it in array for the next pass. Read the array element and compare the second position (4 is in second position of the element 042) digit with the number of the bucket and place it.

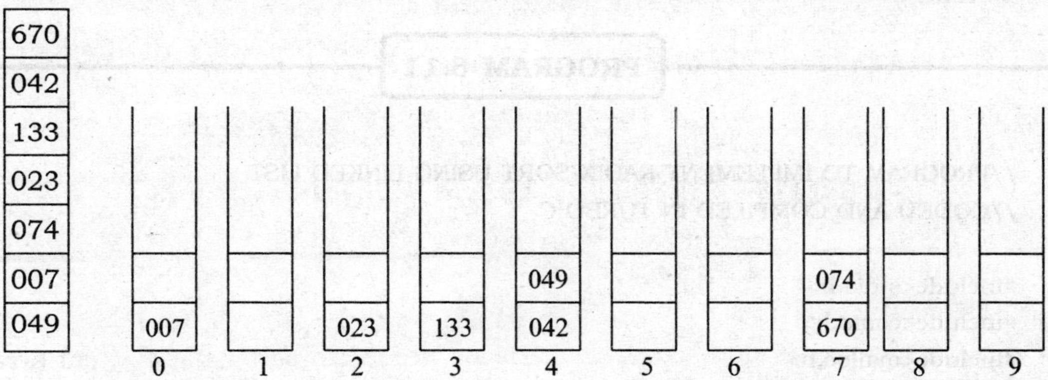

Again read the element from left to right and from bottom to top to get an array for the third pass. (0 is in the third position of 042) Compare the third position digit in each element with the bucket digit and place it wherever it matches.

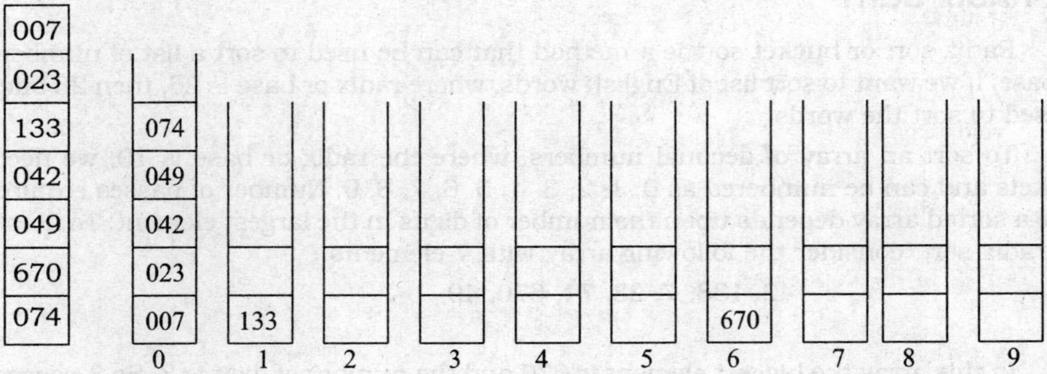

Read the element from the bucket from left to right and from bottom to top for the sorted array. *i.e.*, 7 23, 42, 49, 74, 133, 670.

ALGORITHM

Let A be a linear array of *n* elements A [1], A [2], A [3],...... A [*n*]. Digit is the total number of digits in the largest element in array A.

1. Input *n* number of elements in an array A.
2. Find the total number of Digits in the largest element in the array.
3. Initialise *i* = 1 and repeat the steps 4 and 5 until (*i* <= Digit).
4. Initialise the buckets *j* = 0 and repeat the steps (*a*) until (*j* < *n*)
   (*a*) Compare *i*th position of each element of the array with bucket number and place it in the corresponding bucket.
5. Read the element(s) of the bucket from 0th bucket to 9th bucket and from first position to higher one to generate new array A.
6. Display the sorted array A.
7. Exit.

PROGRAM 6.11

```
//PROGRAM TO IMPLEMENT RADIX SORT USING LINKED LIST
//CODED AND COMPILED IN TURBO C

#include<stdio.h>
#include<conio.h>
#include<malloc.h>

struct node
{
	int info ;
```

```
        struct node *link;
}*start=NULL;

//Display the array elements
void display()
{
        struct node *p=start;
        while( p !=NULL)
        {
                printf ("%d ", p->info);
                p= p->link;
        }
        printf ("\n");
}/*End of display()*/

/* This function finds number of digits in the largest element of the list */
int large_dig(struct node *p)
{
        int large = 0,ndig = 0 ;

        while (p != NULL)
        {
                if (p ->info > large)
                        large = p->info;
                p = p->link ;
        }
        printf ("\nLargest Element is %d , ",large);
        while (large != 0)
        {
                ndig++;
                large = large/10 ;
        }

        printf ("\nNumber of digits in it are %d\n",ndig);
        return(ndig);
} /*End of large_dig()*/

/*This function returns kth digit of a number*/
int digit(int number, int k)
{
        int digit, i ;
        for (i = 1 ; i <=k ; i++)
```

```
    {
        digit = number % 10 ;
        number = number /10 ;
    }
    return(digit);
}/*End of digit()*/

//Function to implement the radix sort algorithm
void radix_sort()
{
    int i,k,dig,maxdig,mindig,least_sig,most_sig;
    struct node *p, *rear[10], *front[10];

    least_sig=1;
    most_sig=large_dig(start);

    for (k = least_sig; k <= most_sig ; k++)
    {
        printf ("\nPASS %d : Examining %dth digit from right   ",k,k);
        for(i = 0 ; i <= 9 ; i++)
        {
            rear[i] = NULL;
            front[i] = NULL ;
        }
        maxdig=0;
        mindig=9;
        p = start ;
        while( p != NULL)
        {
            /*Find kth digit in the number*/
            dig = digit(p->info, k);
            if (dig>maxdig)
                maxdig=dig;
            if (dig<mindig)
                mindig=dig;

            /*Add the number to queue of dig*/
            if (front[dig] == NULL)
                front[dig] = p ;
            else
                rear[dig]->link = p ;
            rear[dig] = p ;
```

```
                p=p->link;/*Go to next number in the list*/
            }/*End while */
            /* maxdig and mindig are the maximum amd minimum
               digits of the kth digits of all the numbers*/
            printf ("\nmindig=%d   maxdig=%d\n",mindig,maxdig);
            /*Join all the queues to form the new linked list*/
            start=front[mindig];
            for i=mindig;i<maxdig;i++)
            {
                if (rear[i+1]!=NULL)
                    rear[i]->link=front[i+1];
                else
                    rear[i+1]=rear[i];
            }
            rear[maxdig]->link=NULL;
            printf ("\nNew list : ");
            display();
        }/* End for */

    }/*End of radix_sort*/

    void main()
    {
        struct node *tmp,*q;
        int i,n,item;
        clrscr();
        printf ("\nEnter the number of elements in the list : ");
        scanf ("%d", &n);

        for (i=0;i<n;i++)
        {
            printf ("\nEnter element %d : ",i+1);
            scanf ("%d",&item);

            /* Inserting elements in the linked list */
            tmp=(struct node*)malloc(sizeof(struct node));
            tmp->info=item;
            tmp->link=NULL;

            if (start==NULL) /* Inserting first element */
                start=tmp;
            else
```

```
            {
                q=start;
                while(q->link!=NULL)
                        q=q->link;
                q->link=tmp;
            }
        }/*End of for*/

        printf ("\nUnsorted list is :\n");
        display();
        radix_sort();
        printf ("\nSorted list is :\n");
        display ();
        getch();
    }/*End of main()*/
```

TIME COMPLEXITY

Time requirement for the radix sorting method depends on the number of digits and the elements in the array. Suppose A is an array of n elements A1, A2..........An and let r denote the radix (for example $r = 10$ for decimal digits, $r = 26$ for English letters and $r = 2$ for bits). If Ai is the largest number then Ai can be represented as

$$Ai = a_{is}\ a_{is-1} \ldots\ldots a_{ik} \ldots\ldots a_{i2}\ a_{i1}$$

Then radix sort algorithm requires s passes. In pass k, a_{ik} of the each element is compared with the bucket element. So radix sort requires the total comparison $f(n)$ of:

$$f(n) <= r \times s \times n$$

WORST CASE

In the worst case $s = n$ so

$$f(n) = O(n^2)$$

BEST CASE

In the best case $s = \log_d n$

So $f(n) = O(n \log n)$

AVERAGE CASE

In the average case, it is very hard to define the time complexity. Because it will depend on the choice of the radix r and also the number of digits on the largest element (*i.e.*, number of passes) But on an average ($\log_d n$) comparison is required. So

$$f(n) = O(n \log n)$$

In other words, radix sort performs well only when the number s of digits in the representation of the A_i is small. The main disadvantage of radix sort is that, it need $d \times n$

memory location to store bucket information. However this drawback may be minimized to 2 × *n* memory locations by using linked list rather than arrays.

6.9. HEAP

A heap is defined as an almost complete binary tree of n nodes such that the value of each node is less than or equal to the value of the father. It can be sequentially represented as

$$A[j] <= A[(j-1)/2]$$

for $\quad 0 <= [(j-1)/2] < j <= n-1$

The root of the binary tree (*i.e.*, the first array element) holds the largest key in the heap. This type of heap is usually called descending heap or mere heap, as the path from the root node to a terminal node forms an ordered list of elements arranged in descending order. Fig. 6.1 shows a heap.

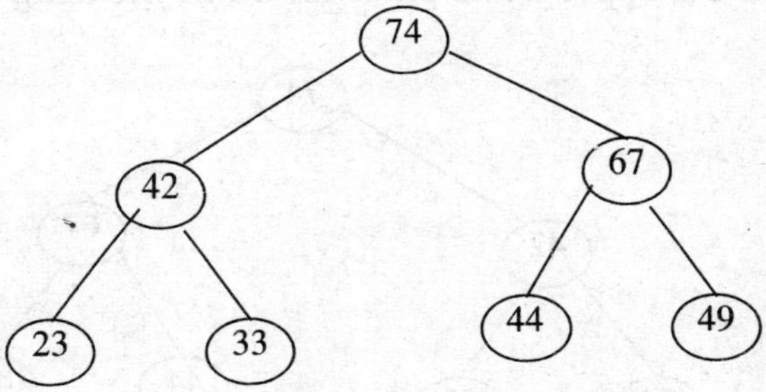

Fig. 6.1. Heap representation

74	42	67	23	33	44	49

Fig. 6.2. Sequential representation

We can also define an ascending heap as an almost complete binary tree in which the value of each node is greater than or equal to the value of its father. This root node has the smallest element of the heap. This type of heap is also called min heap.

6.9.1. HEAP AS A PRIORITY QUEUE

A heap is very useful in implementing priority queue. The priority queue is a data structure in which the intrinsic ordering of the data items determines the result of its basic operations. Primarily queues can be classified into two types:

1. Ascending priority queue
2. Descending priority queue

An ascending priority queue can be defined as a group of elements to which new elements are inserted arbitrarily but only the smallest element is deleted from it. On the other hand a descending priority queue can be defined as a group of elements to which new elements are inserted arbitrarily but only the largest element is deleted from it.

The implementation of the Heap as a priority queue is left to the readers.

6.9.2. HEAP SORT

A heap can be used to sort a set of elements. Let H be a heap with *n* elements and it can be sequentially represented by an array A. Inset an element *data* into the heap H as follows:

1. First place *data* at the end of H so that H is still a complete tree, but not necessarily a heap.

2. Then the data be raised to its appropriate place in H so that H is finally a heap.

To understand the concept of insertion of data into a heap is illustrated with following two examples:

INSERTING AN ELEMENT TO A HEAP

Consider the heap H in Fig. 6.1. Say we want to add a data = 55 to H.

Step 1: First we adjoin 55 as the next element in the complete tree as shown in Fig. 6.2. Now we have to find the appropriate place for 55 in the heap by rearranging it.

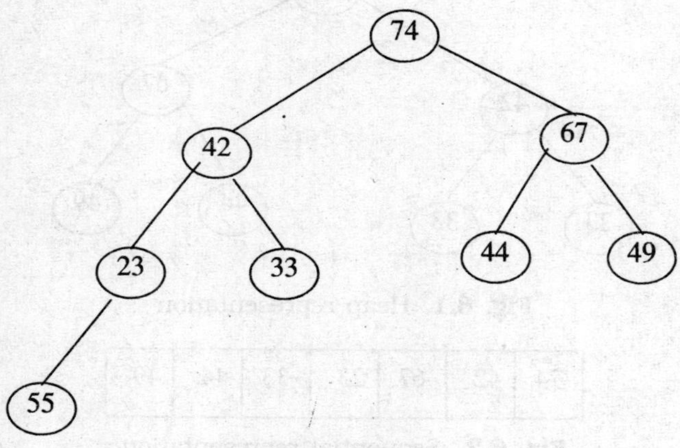

Fig. 6.2.

Step 2: Compare 55 with its parent 23. Since 55 is greater than 23, interchange 23 and 55. Now the heap will look like as in Fig. 6.3.

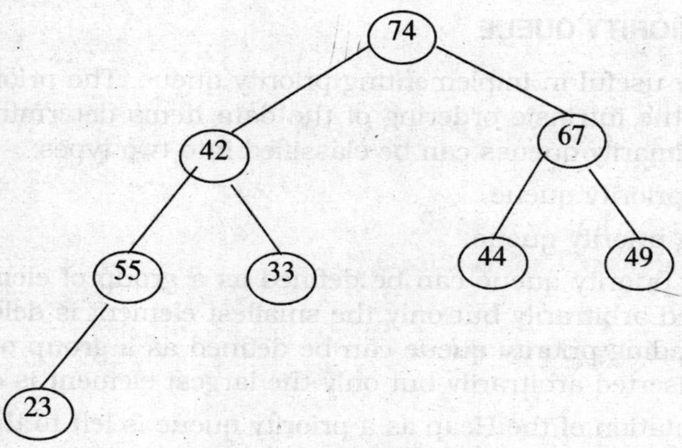

Fig. 6.3

Step 3: Compare 55 with its parent 42. Since 55 is greater than 42, interchange 55 and 42. Now the heap will look like as in Fig. 6.4.

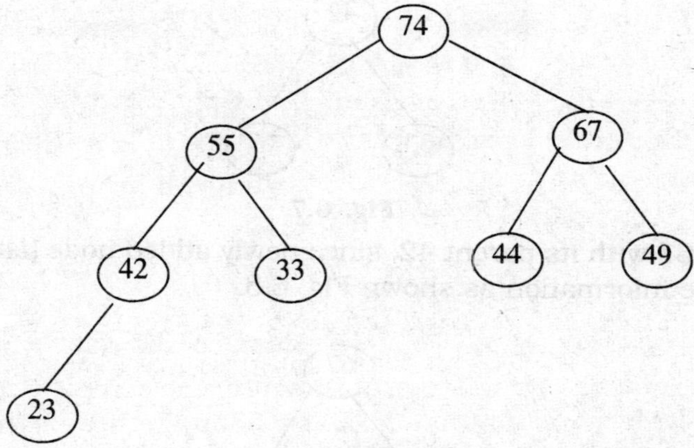

Fig. 6.4

Step 4: Compare 55 with its new parent 74. Since 55 is less than 74, it is the appropriate place of node 55 in the heap H. Fig. 6.4 shows the final heap tree.

CREATING A HEAP

A heap H can be created from the following list of numbers 33, 42, 67, 23, 44, 49, 74 as illustrated below :

Step 1: Create a node to insert the first number (*i.e.*, 33) as shown Fig 6:5

Fig. 6.5

Step 2: Read the second element and add as the left child of 33 as shown Fig. 6.6. Then restructure the heap if necessary.

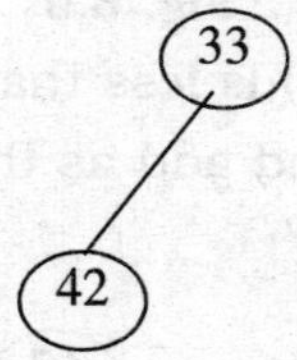

Fig. 6.6

Compare the 42 with its parent 33, since newly added node (*i.e.*, 42) is greater than 33 interchange node information as shown Fig. 6.7.

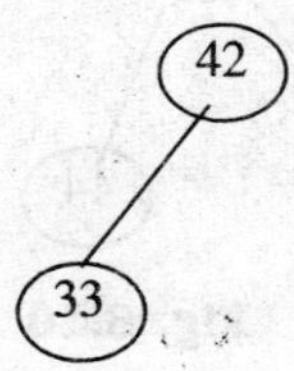

Step 3: Read the 3rd element and add as the right child of 42 as shown Fig. 6.8. Then restructure the heap if necessary.

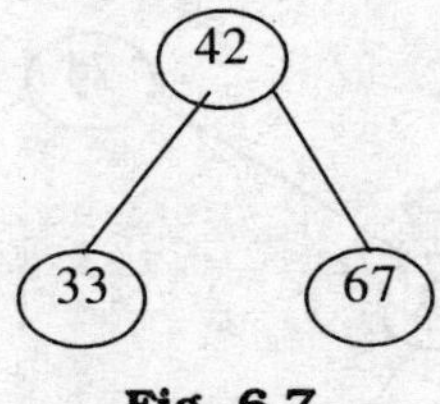

Fig. 6.7

Compare the 67 with its parent 42, since newly added node (*i.e.*, 67) is greater than 42 interchange node information as shown Fig. 6.8.

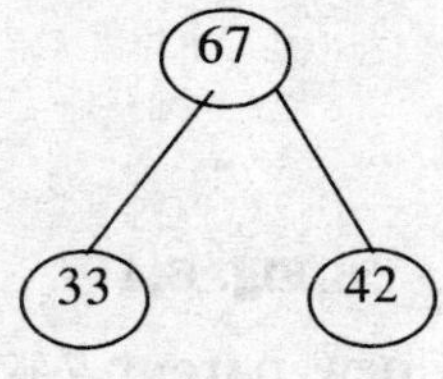

Fig. 6.8

Step 4: Read the 4th element and add as the left child of 33 as shown Fig. 6.9. Then restructure the heap if necessary.

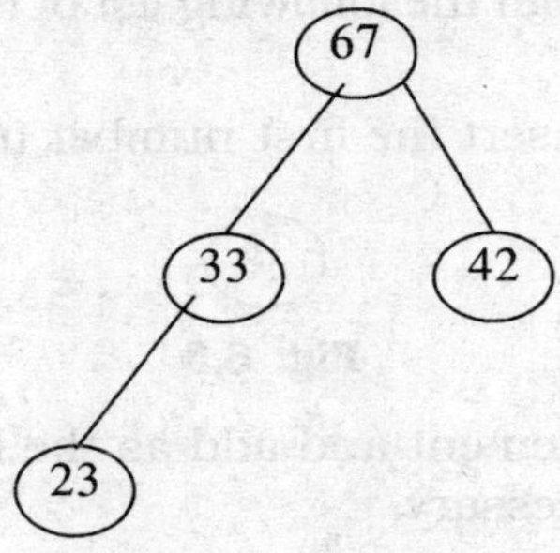

Fig. 6.9

Since newly added node (*i.e.*, 23) is less than its parent 33, no interchange.

Step 5: Read the 5th element and add as the right child of 33 as shown Fig. 6.10. Then restructure the heap if necessary.

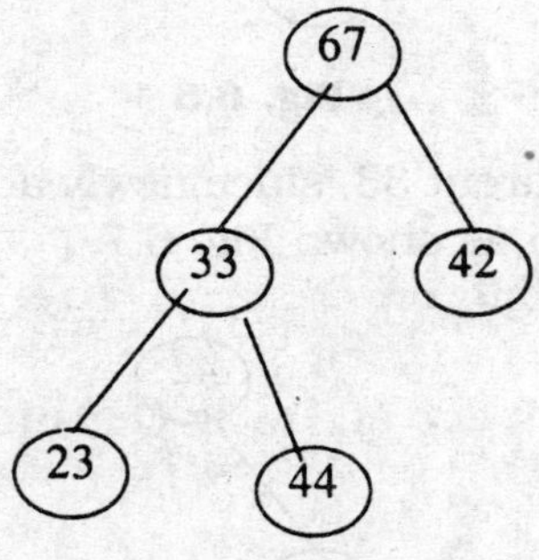

Fig. 6.10

Compare the 44 with its parent 33, since newly added node (*i.e.*, 44) is greater than 33 interchange node information as shown Fig. 6.11.

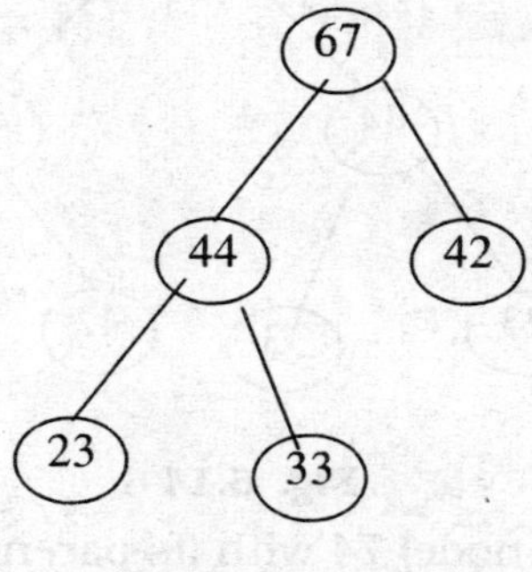

Fig. 6.11

Step 6: Read the 6th element and add as the left child of 42 as shown Fig. 6.12. Then restructure the heap if necessary.

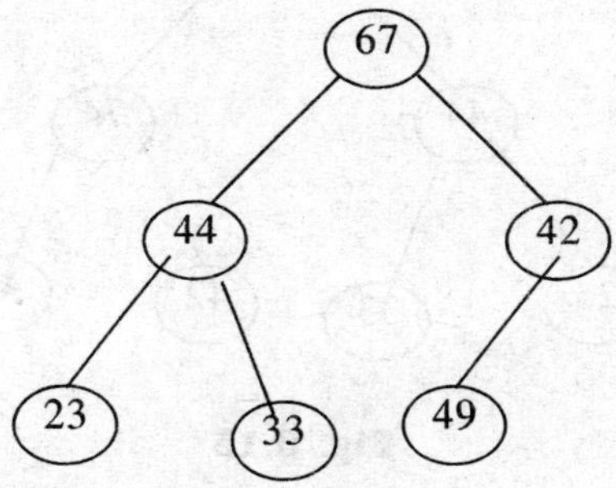

Fig. 6.12

Compare the (newly added node) 49 with its parent 42, since newly added node (*i.e.*, 49) is greater than 42 interchange node information as shown Fig. 6.13.

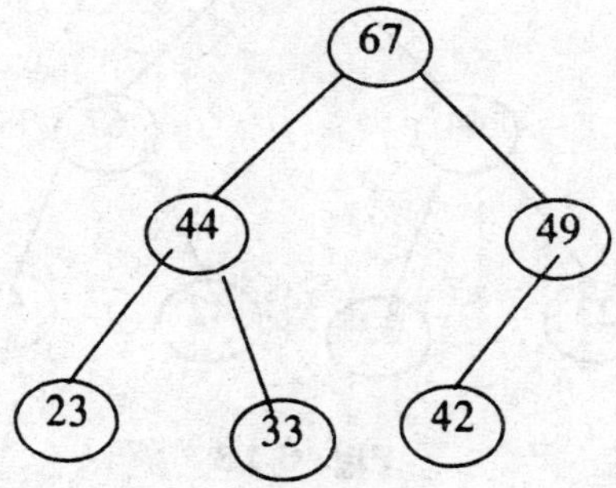

Fig. 6.13

Step 7: Read the 7th element and add as the left child of 49 as shown Fig. 6.14. Then restructure the heap if necessary.

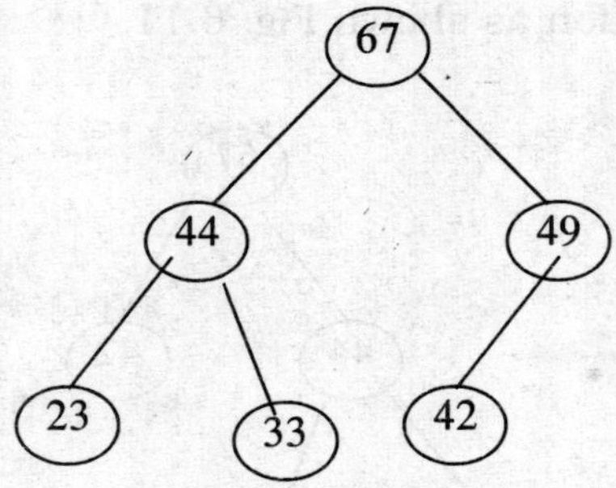

Fig. 6.14

Compare the (newly added node) 74 with its parent 49, since newly added node (*i.e.*, 74) is greater than 49 interchange node information as shown Fig. 6.15.

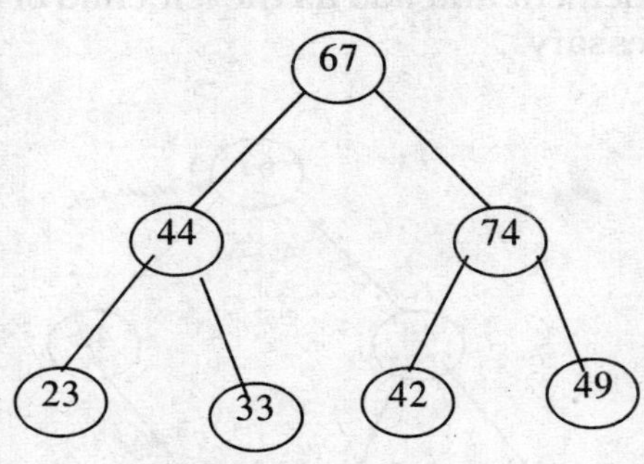

Fig. 6.15

Compare the recently changed node 74 with its parent 67, since it is greater than 67 interchange node information as shown Fig. 6.16.

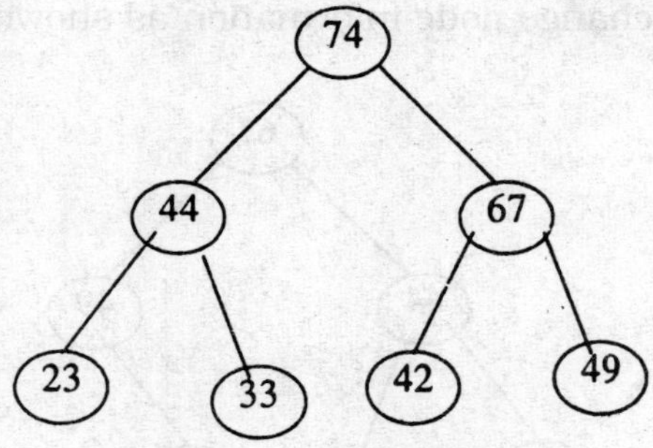

Fig. 6.16

ALGORITHM

Let H be a heap with *n* elements stored in the array HA. This procedure will insert a new element *data* in H. LOC is the present location of the newly added node. And PAR denotes the location of the parent of the newly-added node.

1. Input n elements in the heap H.
2. Add new node by incrementing the size of the heap H: $n = n + 1$ and LOC = n
3. Repeat step 4 to 7 while (LOC < 1)
4. PAR = LOC/2
5. If (data <= HA[PAR])

(*a*) HA[LOC] = data

(*b*) Exit

6. HA[LOC] = HA[PAR]
7. LOC = PAR
8. HA[1] = data
9. Exit

DELETING THE ROOT OF A HEAP

Let H be a heap with n elements. The root R of H can be deleted as follows:

(*a*) Assign the root R to some variable data.

(*b*) Replace the deleted node R by the last node (or recently added node) L of H so that H is still a complete tree, but not necessarily a heap.

(*c*) Now rearrange H in such a way by placing L (new root) at the appropriate place, so that H is finally a heap.

Consider the heap H in Fig. 6.4 where R = 74 is the root and L = 23 is the last node (or recently added node) of the tree. Suppose we want to delete the root node R = 74. Apply the above rules to delete the root. Delete the root node R and assign it to *data* (*i.e.*, data = 74) as shown in Fig. 6.17.

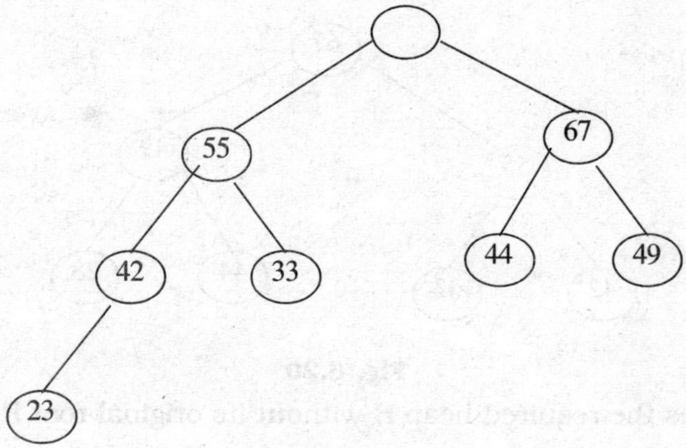

Fig. 6.17

Replace the deleted root node R by the last node L as shown in the Fig. 6.18.

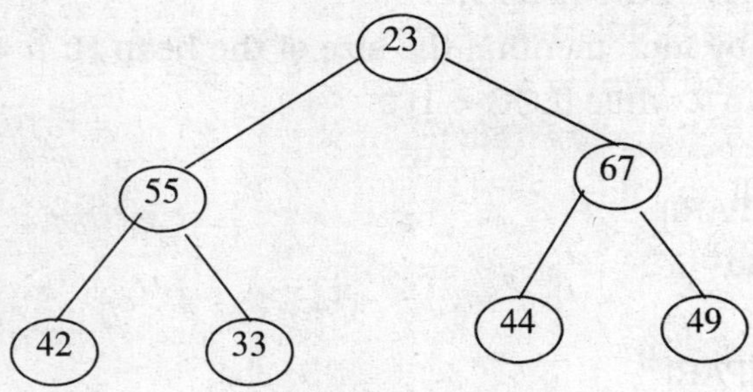

Fig. 6.18

Compare 23 with its new two children 55 and 67. Since 23 is less than the largest child 67, interchange 23 and 67. The new tree looks like as in Fig. 6.19.

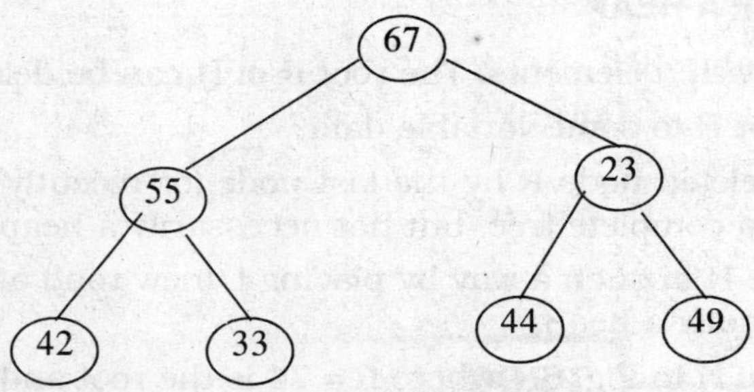

Fig. 6.19

Again compare 23 with its new two children, 44 and 49. Since 23 is less than the largest child 49, interchange 23 and 49as shown in Fig. 6.20.

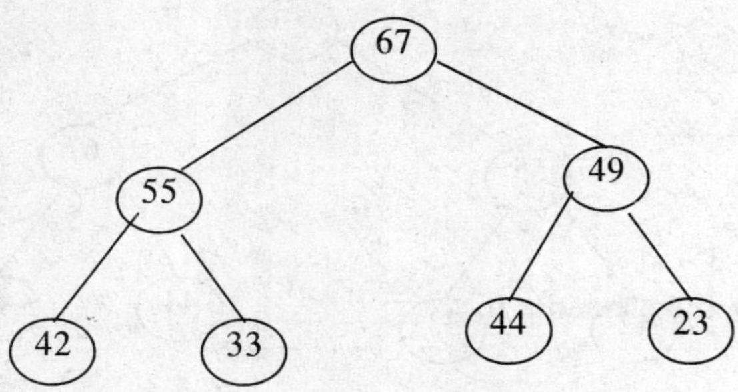

Fig. 6.20

The Fig. 6.20 is the required heap H without its original root R.

ALGORITHM

Let H be a heap with *n* elements stored in the array HA. *data* is the item of the node to be removed. *Last* gives the information about last node of H. The LOC, left, right gives the location of Last and its left and right children as the Last rearranges in the appropriate place in the tree.

1. Input *n* elements in the heap H
2. Data = HA[1]; last = HA[*n*] and *n* = *n* – 1
3. LOC = 1, left = 2 and right = 3
4. Repeat the steps 5, 6 and 7 while (right <= *n*)
5. If (last >= HA[left]) and (last >= HA[right])
   (*a*) HA[LOC] = last
   (*b*) Exit
6. If (HA[right] <= HA[left])
   (*i*) HA[LOC] = HA[left]
   (*ii*) LOC = left
   (*b*) Else
   (*i*) HA[LOC] = HA[right]
   (*ii*) LOC = right
7. left = 2 × LOC; right = left +1
8. If (left = *n*) and (last < HA[left])
   (*a*) LOC = left
9. HA[LOC] = last
10. Exit

PROGRAM 6.12

```
//PROGRAM TO IMPLEMENT HEAP SORT USING ARRAYS
//CODED AND IMPLEMENTED IN TURBO C

#include<conio.h>
#include<stdio.h>

int arr[20],n;

//Function to display the elements in the array
void display()
{     int i;
      for(i=0;i<n;i++)
            printf ("%d  ",arr[i]);
      printf ("\n");
}/*End of display()*/

//Function to insert an element to the heap
void insert(int num,int loc)
```

```
        int par;
        while(loc>0)
        {
                par=(loc-1)/2;
                if (num<=arr[par])
                {
                        arr[loc]=num;
                        return;
                }
                arr[loc]=arr[par];
                loc=par;
        }/*End of while*/
        arr[0]=num;
}/*End of insert()*/

//This function to create a heap
void create_heap()
{
        int i;
        for(i=0;i<n;i++)
                insert(arr[i],i);
}/*End of create_heap()*/

//Function to delete the root node of the tree
void del_root(int last)
{
        int left,right,i,temp;
        i=0; /*Since every time we have to replace root with last*/
        /*Exchange last element with the root */
        temp=arr[i];
        arr[i]=arr[last];
        arr[last]=temp;

        left=2*i+1; /*left child of root*/
        right=2*i+2;/*right child of root*/

        while( right < last)
        {
                if ( arr[i]>=arr[left] && arr[i]>=arr[right] )
                        return;
                if ( arr[right]<=arr[left] )
                {
```

```
                    temp=arr[i];
                    arr[i]=arr[left];
                    arr[left]=temp;
                    i=left;
                }
                else
                {
                    temp=arr[i];
                    arr[i]=arr[right];
                    arr[right]=temp;
                    i=right;
                }
                left=2*i+1;
                right=2*i+2;
        }/*End of while*/
        if ( left==last-1 && arr[i]<arr[left] )/*right==last*/
        {
                temp=arr[i];
                arr[i]=arr[left];
                arr[left]=temp;
        }
    }/*End of del_root*/

    //Function to sort an element in the heap
    void heap_sort()
    {
        int last;
        for(last=n-1; last>0; last--)
            del_root(last);
    }/*End of del_root*/

    void main()
    {
        int i;
        clrscr();
        printf ("\nEnter number of elements : ");
        scanf ("%d",&n);
        for(i=0;i<n;i++)
        {
                printf ("\nEnter element %d : ",i+1);
                scanf ("%d",&arr[i]);
        }
```

```
        printf ("\nEntered list is :\n");
        display();

        create_heap();

        printf ("\nHeap is :\n");
        display();

        heap_sort();
        printf ("\nSorted list is :\n");
        display();
        getch();
}/*End of main()*/
```

TIME COMPLEXITY

When we calculate the time complexity of the heap sort algorithm, we need to analyse the two phases separately.

Phase 1: Let H be a heap and suppose you want to insert a new element data in H. Then few comparisons are required to locate the appropriate place, and it cannot exceed the depth of H. Since H is a complete tree, its depth is bounded by log m where m is the number of elements in H. Then

$$f(n) = O(n \log n)$$

Note that the number of comparison in the worst case is $O(n \log n)$

In the second phase we analyse the complexity of the algorithm to delete a root element from the heap H with n elements.

Phase 2: Suppose H is a complete tree with $n - 1 = m$ elements, and suppose the left and right sub tree of H are heaps and L is the root of H. Rearranging the node L will take four comparisons to move one step down in the tree H. Since the depth of H does not exceed $\log_2 m$, rearranging will take at most $4 \log_2 m$ comparisons to find the appropriate place of L in the tree H.

$$f(n) = 4n \log_2 n$$

6.10. EXTERNAL SORT

In the previous section, we discussed different internal sorting algorithms and its importance. Now we will discuss about external sorting. These are methods employed to sort elements (or items), which are too large to fit in the main memory of the computer. That is any sort algorithm that uses external memory, such as tape or disk, during the sort is called external sort. Since most common sort algorithms assume high-speed random access to all intermediate memory, they are unsuitable if the values to be sorted do not fit in main memory. Internal sorting refers to the sorting of an array of data which is in RAM. The main concern with external sorting is to minimize external disk access since reading a disk block takes about a million times longer than accessing an item in RAM.

To study external sorting, we need to study the various external memory devices in addition to external sorting algorithms. The involvement of external storage device makes sorting algorithms more complex because of the following reasons:

1. The cost of accessing an item is much higher than any computational cost.
2. Different procedures and methods have to be implemented and executed for different external storage devices.

In this section, we will discuss some data storage devices and sorting algorithms for external storage devices. A cards reader (or punch) can be considered as a primitive external storage. However, this section deals with devices that allow more rapid data transfer and more convenient storage medium than punch cards. External storage devices can be categorized into two types based on the access method. They are:

- Sequential Access Devices (*e.g.*, Magnetic tapes)
- Random Access Devices (*e.g.*, Disks)

6.10.1. MAGNETIC TAPES

The principle behind magnetic tapes is similar to audio tape recorders. Magnetic tape is wound on a spool. Tracks run across the length of the tape. Usually there are 7 to 9 tracks across the tape width and the data is recorded on the tape in a sequence of bits. The number that can be written per inch of track is called the tape density — measured in bits per inch.

Information on tapes is usually grouped into blocks, which may be of fixed or variable size. Blocks are separated by an inter-block gap. Because request to read or write blocks do not arrive at a tape drive at constant rate, there must be a gap between each pair of blocks forming a space to be passed over as the tape accelerates to read/write speed. The medium is not strong enough to withstand the stress that it would sustain with instantaneous starts and stops. Because the tape is not moving at a constant speed, a gap cannot contain user data. Data is usually read/written from tapes in terms of blocks. This is shown in following Fig. 6.21 :

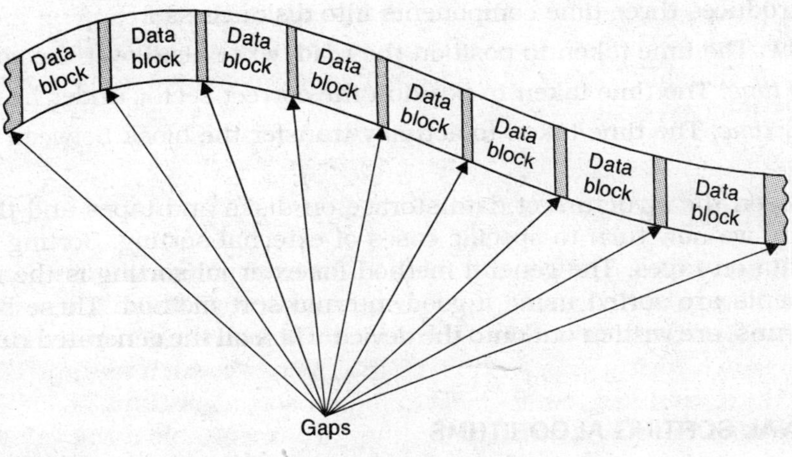

Fig. 6.21. Interblock gaps

In order to read or write data to a tape the block length and the address in memory to/from which the data is to be transferred must be specified. These areas in memory from/to which data is transferred will be called *buffers*. The block size (or length) will respond to its buffer size. And it is a crucial factor in tape access. A large block size is preferred because of the following reasons:

1. Consider a tape with a tape density of 600 bdp and an inter block gap of ¾ inch; generally this gap is enough to write 450 characters. With a small block size, the number of blocks per tape length will increase. This means a larger number of inter block gaps, *i.e.*, bits of data, which cannot be utilized for data storage, and thus tape utilization decreased. Thus the larger the block size, fewer the number of blocks, fewer the number of inter block gaps and better the tape utilization.
2. Larger block size reduces the input/output time. The delay time in tape access is the time needed to cross the inter block gap. This delay time is larger when a tape starts from rest than when the tape is already moving. With a small block size the number of halts in a read are considerable causing the delay time to be incurred each time.

6.10.2. DISKS

Disks are an example of direct access storage devices. In contrast to the way information is recorded on a gramophone record, data are recorded on disk platter in concentric tracks. A disk has two surfaces on which data can be recorded. Disk packs have several such disks or platters rigidly mounted on a common spinder. Data is read/written to the disk by a read/write head. A disk pack would have one such head per surface.

Each disk surface has a number of concentric circles called tracks. In a disk pack, the set of parallel tracks on each surface is called a cylinder. Tracks are further divided into sectors. A sector is the smallest addressable segment of a track.

Data is stored along the tracks in blocks. Therefore to access a disk, the track or cylinder number and the sector number of the starting block must be specified. For disk packs, the surface must also be specified. The read/write head moves horizontally to position itself over the correct track for accessing disk data.

This introduces three time components into disk access :

Seek time: The time taken to position the read/write head over the correct cylinder.

Latency time: The time taken to position the correct sector under head.

Transfer time: The time taken to actually transfer the block between main memory and the disk.

Having seen the structure of data storage on disks and tapes and the methods of accessing them, we now turn to specific cases of external sorting. Sorting data on disks and sorting data on tapes. The general method for external sorting is the merge sort. In this, file segments are sorted using a good internal sort method. These sorted file segments, called runs, are written out onto the device. Then all the generated runs are merged into one run.

6.10.3. EXTERNAL SORTING ALGORITHMS

Perhaps the simplest form of external sorting is to use a fast internal sort with good locality of reference (which means that it tends to reference nearby items, not widely scattered items). Quicksort is one sort algorithm that is generally very fast and has good locality of reference. If the file is too huge, even virtual memory might be unable to fit it. Also, the performance may not be too great due to the large amount of time it takes to access data on disk.

Merge sort is an ideal candidate for external sorting because it satisfies the two criteria for developing an external sorting algorithm. Merge sort can be implemented either top-down or bottom-up. The top-down strategy is typically used for internal sorting, whereas the bottom-up strategy is typically used for external sorting.

The top-down strategy works by:

1. Dividing the data in half
2. Sorting each half
3. Merging the two halves

Merge sort typically break a large data file into a number of shorter, sorted runs. These can be produced by repeatedly reading a section of the data file into RAM, sorting it with ordinary quicksort, and writing the sorted data to disk. After the sorted runs have been generated, a merge algorithm is used to combine sorted files into longer sorted files. The simplest scheme is to use a 2-way merge: merge 2 sorted files into one sorted file, and then merge 2 more, and so on until there is just one large sorted file.

One example of external sorting is the external mergesort algorithm. For the sake of clarity, let us assume that 900 megabyte of data needs to be sorted using only 100 megabytes of RAM.

1. Read 100 MB of the data in main memory and sort by some conventional method (usually quicksort).
2. Write the sorted data to disk.
3. Repeat steps 1 and 2 until all of the data is sorted in chunks of 100 MB. Now you need to merge them into one single sorted output file.
4. Read the first 10 MB of each sorted chunk (call them input buffers) in main memory (90 MB total) and allocate the remaining 10 MB for output buffer.
5. Perform a 9-way merging and store the result in the output buffer. If the output buffer is full, write it to the final sorted file. If any of the 9 input buffers gets empty, fill it with the next 10 MB of its associated 100 MB sorted chunk or otherwise mark it as exhausted if there is no more data in the sorted chunk, do not use it for merging.

Let us analyse how the merge sort algorithm responds when it is practically applied to run using slow tape drives as input and output devices. It requires very little memory, and the memory required does not change with the number of data elements. If you have four tape drives, it works as follows:

1. Divide the data to be sorted in half and put half on each of two tapes.
2. Merge individual pairs of records from the two tapes; write two-record chunks alternately to each of the two output tapes.
3. Merge the two-record chunks from the two output tapes into four-record chunks; write these alternately to the original two input tapes.
4. Merge the four-record chunks into eight-record chunks; write these alternately to the original two output tapes.

5. Repeat until you have one chunk containing all the data, sorted --- that is, for log *n* passes, where *n* is the number of records.

On tape drives that can run both backwards and forwards, you can run merge passes in both directions, avoiding rewind time. For the same reason it is also very useful for sorting data on disk that is too large to fit entirely into primary memory.

The above described algorithm can be generalized by assuming that the amount of data to be sorted exceeds the available memory by a factor of K. Then, K chunks of data need to be sorted and a K-way merge has to be completed. If X is the amount of main memory available, there will be K input buffers and 1 output buffer of size X/(K+1) each. Depending on various factors (how fast the hard drive is, what is the value of K) better performance can be achieved if the output buffer is made larger (for example twice as large as one input buffer).

Note that you do not want to jump back and forth between 2 or more files in trying to merge them (while writing to a third file). This would likely produce a lot of time-consuming disk seeks. Instead, on a single-user PC, it is better to read a block of each of the 2 (or more) files into RAM and carry out the merge algorithm there, with the output also kept in a buffer in RAM until the buffer is filled (or we are out of data) and only then writing it out to disk. When the merge algorithm exhausts one of the blocks of data, refill it by reading from disk another block of the associated file. This is called buffering. On a larger machine where the disk drive is being shared among many users, it may not make sense to worry about this as the read/write head is going to be seeking all over the place anyway.

```
mergesort(int a[], int left, int right)
    {
        int i, j, k, mid;

        if (right > left) {
            mid = (right + left) / 2;
            mergesort(a, left, mid);
            mergesort(a, mid+1, right);
            /* copy the first run into array b */
            for (i = left, j = 0; i <= mid; i++, j++)
                b[ j] = a[i];
            b[j] = MAX_INT;
            /* copy the second run into array c */
            for (i = mid+1, j = 0; i <=right; i++, j++)
                c[ j] = a[i];
            c[ j] = MAX_INT;
            /* merge the two runs */
            i = 0;
            j = 0;
            for (k = left; k <= right; k++)
```

```
                a[k] = (b[i] < c[ j]) ? b[i++] : c[ j++];
            }
        }
```

The bottom-up strategy for merge sort works by:

1. Scanning through data performing 1-by-1 merges to get sorted lists of size 2.
2. Scanning through the size 2 sub-lists and perform 2-by-2 merges to get sorted lists of size 4.
3. Continuing the process of scanning through size *n* sub-lists and performing n-by-*n* merges to get sorted lists of size 2*n* until the file is sorted (*i.e.*, 2*n* >= N, where N is the size of the file).

6.10.4. Mergesort Performance

Mergesort has an average and worst-case performance of O(n log n). In the worst case, merge sort does about 30% fewer comparisons than quicksort does in the average case; thus merge sort very often needs to make fewer comparisons than quicksort. In terms of moves, merge sort's worst case complexity is O(*n* log *n*); the same complexity as quicksort's best case, and merge sort's best case takes about half as much time as the worst case.

However, merge sort performs 2*n* – 1 method calls in the worst case, compared to quicksort's *n*, thus has roughly twice as much recursive overhead as quicksort. Mergesort's most common implementation does not sort in place, that is memory size of the input must be allocated for the sorted output to be stored in. Sorting in-place is possible but requires an extremely complicated implementation.

Although merge sort can sort linked list, it is also much more efficient than quicksort if the data to be sorted can only be efficiently accessed sequentially. Unlike some optimized implementations of quicksort, merge sort is a stable sort, as long as the merge operation is implemented properly.

More precisely, merge sort does between $[n \log n - n + 1]$ and $[n \log n - 0.914 \cdot n]$ comparisons in the worst case.

SELF REVIEW QUESTIONS

1. Explain the method of external sorting with disks. *[MG - MAY 2004 (BTech)]*
2. Write and explain insertion sort algorithm. What is the complexity of the algorithm? *[MG - MAY 2004 (BTech), MG - NOV 2004 (BTech)]*
3. Explain quick sort algorithm. What is the complexity of your algorithm? *[CUSAT - JUL 2002 (MCA), MG - MAY 2004 (BTech) KERALA - MAY 2001 (BTech)]*
4. Explain the method of external sorting with tapes? *[KERALA - DEC 2003 (BTech), MG - NOV 2004 (BTech) KERALA - MAY 2001 (BTech)]*
5. Explain merging of sequential files. *[MG - MAY 2003 (BTech)]*

6. What is external sorting methods?

[*KERALA - DEC 2003 (BTech), KERALA - JUN 2004 (BTech)*

MG - NOV 2003 (BTech), MG - MAY 2000 (BTech)

ANNA - DEC 2004 (BE), ANNA - MAY 2004 (MCA)]

7. Write the Quick sort algorithm. [*MG - NOV 2003 (BTech)*]
8. With suitable example, explain radix sort.

[*CUSAT - APR 1998 (BTech), MG - NOV 2002 (BTech)*]

9. Explain bubble sort with example. Construct Heap sort for the initial key set 42 23 74 11 65 58 94 36 99 87. [*Calicut - APR 1995 (BTech)*]
10. Explain Heap sort with an example. [*Calicut - APR 1997 (BTech)*]
11. Explain quicksort algorithm? Write an iterative program fragment for quicksort?

[*KERALA - JUN 2004 (BTech), CUSAT - NOV 2002 (BTech)*]

12. Write an algorithm for merging two sorted list of numbers represented as linked lists. No new memory space may be used. The merged list should be also sorted.

[*CUSAT - DEC 2003 (MCA)*]

13. For the following input list explain how Merge sort works. What is the time complexity involved in the algorithm? [*CUSAT - JUL 2002 (MCA)*]
14. Differentiate between heap sort and Radix sort. [*ANNA - MAY 2004 (MCA)*]
15. Distinguish between internal sorting and external sorting.

[*KERALA - DEC 2004 (BTech), ANNA - MAY 2004 (MCA)*

KERALA - DEC 2002 (BTech), KERALA - MAY 2003 (BTech)]

16. How many key comparisons and interchanges are required to sort a file of size n using bubble sort? [*ANNA - DEC 2004 (BE)*]
17. What is an external storage device? Explain in detail about any two devices.

[*ANNA - DEC 2004 (BE)*]

18. Explain Internal sorting Methods.

[*KERALA - DEC 2003 (BTech), KERALA - JUN 2004 (BTech)*]

19. Write an algorithm for merge sort method. [*KERALA - JUN 2004 (BTech)*]
20. Write a procedure for bubble sort method with example.

[*KERALA - DEC 2002 (BTech), KERALA - DEC 2003 (BTech)*]

21. Write an algorithm to sort elements by partition exchange method.

[*KERALA - MAY 2003 (BTech)*]

22. Compare merge sort and insertion sort methods. [*KERALA - MAY 2001 (BTech)*]
23. When is the bubble sort better than quick sort? [*KERALA - MAY 2002 (BTech)*]
24. Write a function to implement the queue operation using two stacks.

[*KERALA - NOV 2001 (BTech)*]

25. Write an algorithm for selection sort method. [*KERALA - NOV 2001 (BTech)*]

7

Searching and Hashing

Searching is a process of checking and finding an element from a list of elements. Let A be a collection of data elements, *i.e.*, A is a linear array of say *n* elements. If we want to find the presence of an element "*data*" in A, then we have to search for it. The search is successful if *data* does appear in A and unsuccessful if otherwise. There are several types of searching techniques; one has some advantage(s) over other. Following are the three important searching techniques :

1. Linear or Sequential Searching
2. Binary Searching
3. Fibanocci Search

7.1. LINEAR OR SEQUENTIAL SEARCHING

In linear search, each element of an array is read one by one sequentially and it is compared with the desired element. A search will be unsuccessful if all the elements are read and the desired element is not found.

7.1.1. ALGORITHM FOR LINEAR SEARCH

Let A be an array of *n* elements, A[1],A[2],A[3], ... A[*n*]. "*data*" is the element to be searched. Then this algorithm will find the location "*loc*" of data in A. Set *loc* = – 1,if the search is unsuccessful.

1. Input an array A of n elements and "data" to be searched and initialise *loc* = – 1.
2. Initialise *i* = 0; and repeat through step 3 if (*i* < *n*) by incrementing *i* by one .
3. If (data = A[*i*])
   (*a*) loc = *i*
   (*b*) GOTO step 4
4. If (loc > 0)
   (*a*) Display "data is found and searching is successful"
5. Else
   (*a*) Display "data is not found and searching is unsuccessful"
6. Exit

PROGRAM 7.1

```
//PROGRAM TO IMPLEMENT SEQUENTIAL SEARCHING
//CODED AND COMPILED USING TURBO C

#include<conio.h>
#include<stdio.h>

void main()
{
	char opt;
	int arr[20],n,i,item;
	clrscr();
	printf ("\nHow many elements you want to enter in the array : ");
	scanf ("%d",&n);

	for(i=0; i < n;i++)
	{
		printf ("\nEnter element %d : ",i+1);
		scanf ("%d", &arr[i]);
	}
	printf ("\n\nPress any key to continue....");
	getch();
	do
	{
		clrscr();
		printf ("\nEnter the element to be searched : ");
		scanf ("%d",&item); //Input the item to be searched
		for(i=0;i < n;i++)
		{
			if item == arr[i])
			{
				printf ("\n%d found at position %d\n",item,i+1);
				break;
			}
		}/*End of for*/
		if (i == n)
			printf ("\nItem %d not found in array\n",item);
		printf ("\n\nPress (Y/y) to continue : ");
		fflush(stdin);
```

```
        scanf ("%c",&opt);
    }while(opt == 'Y' || opt == 'y');
}
```

7.1.2. TIME COMPLEXITY

Time Complexity of the linear search is found by number of comparisons made in searching a record.

In the best case, the desired element is present in the first position of the array, *i.e.*, only one comparison is made. So $f(n) = O(1)$.

In the Average case, the desired element is found in the half position of the array, then $f(n) = O[(n + 1)/2]$.

But in the worst case the desired element is present in the nth (or last) position of the array, so n comparisons are made. So $f(n) = O(n + 1)$.

7.2. BINARY SEARCH

Binary search is an extremely efficient algorithm when it is compared to linear search. Binary search technique searches "data" in minimum possible comparisons. Suppose the given array is a sorted one, otherwise first we have to sort the array elements. Then apply the following conditions to search a "data".

1. Find the middle element of the array (*i.e.*, $n/2$ is the middle element if the array or the sub-array contains n elements).
2. Compare the middle element with the data to be searched, then there are following three cases.
   (*a*) If it is a desired element, then search is successful.
   (*b*) If it is less than desired data, then search only the first half of the array, *i.e.*, the elements which come to the left side of the middle element.
   (*c*) If it is greater than the desired data, then search only the second half of the array, *i.e.*, the elements which come to the right side of the middle element.

Repeat the same steps until an element is found or exhaust the search area.

7.2.1. ALGORITHM FOR BINARY SEARCH

Let A be an array of n elements A[1],A[2],A[3],...... A[*n*]. "Data" is an element to be searched. "mid" denotes the middle location of a segment (or array or sub-array) of the element of A. LB and UB is the lower and upper bound of the array which is under consideration.

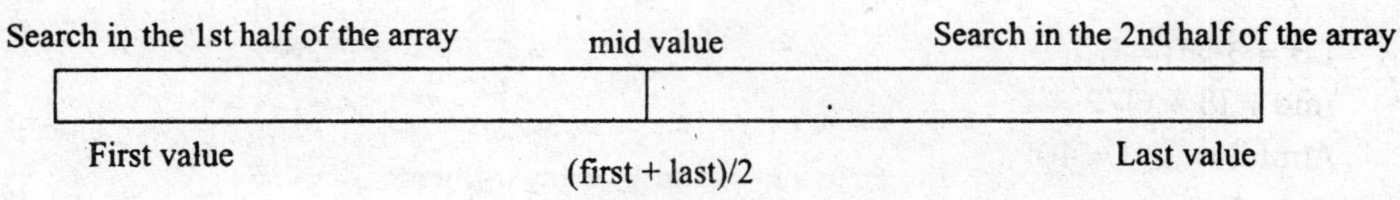

Fig. 7.1

1. Input an array A of n elements and "data" to be sorted

2. LB = 0, UB = *n*; mid = int ((LB+UB)/2)
3. Repeat step 4 and 5 while (LB <= UB) and (A[mid] ! = data)
4. If (data < A[mid])
   (*a*) UB = mid–1
5. Else
   (*a*) LB = mid + 1
6. Mid = int ((LB + UB)/2)
7. If (A[mid]== data)
   (*a*) Display "the data found"
8. Else
   (*a*) Display "the data is not found"
9. Exit

Suppose we have an array of 7 elements

9	10	25	30	40	45	70
0	1	2	3	4	5	6

Following steps are generated if we binary search a data = 45 from the above array.

Step 1:

LB						UB
9	10	25	30	40	45	70
0	1	2	3	4	5	6

LB = 0; UB = 6

mid = (0 + 6)/2 = 3

A[mid] = A[3] = 30

Step 2:

Since (A[3] < data) - *i.e.,* 30 < 45 - reinitialise the variable LB, UB and mid

			LB			UB
9	10	25	30	40	45	70
0	1	2	3	4	5	6

LB = 3 UB = 6

mid = (3 + 6)/2 = 4

A[mid] = A[4] = 40

Step 3:

Since (A[4] < data) - *i.e.,* 40 < 45 - reinitialise the variable LB, UB and mid

				LB		UB
9	10	25	30	40	45	70
0	1	2	3	4	5	6

LB = 4 UB = 6

mid = (4 + 6)/2 = 5

A[mid] = A[5] = 45

Step 4:

Since (A[5] == data) - *i.e.,* 45 == 45 - searching is successful.

PROGRAM 7.2

```
//PROGRAM TO IMPLEMENT THE BINARY SEARCH
//CODED AND COMPILED USING TURBO C

#include<conio.h>
#include<stdio.h>

void main()
{
	char opt;
	int arr[20],start,end,middle,n,i,item;
	clrscr();
	printf ("\nHow many elements you want to enter in the array : ");
	scanf ("%d",&n);
	for(i=0; i < n; i++)
	{
		printf ("\nEnter element %d : ",i+1);
		scanf ("%d",&arr[i]);
	}
	printf ("\n\nPress any key to continue...");
	getch();
	do
	{
		clrscr();
		printf ("\nEnter the element to be searched : ");
		scanf ("%d",&item);
		start=0;
		end=n – 1;
		middle=(start + end)/2;
```

```
        while(item != arr[middle] && start <= end)
        {
            if (item > arr[middle])
                start=middle+1;
            else
                end=middle-1;
            middle=(start+end)/2;
        }
        if (item==arr[middle])
            printf("\n%d found at position %d\n",item,middle + 1);
        if (start>end)
            printf ("\n%d not found in array\n",item);
        printf ("\n\nPree (Y/y) to continue : ");
        fflush(stdin);
        scanf ("%c",&opt);
    }while(opt == 'Y' || opt == 'y');
}/*End of main()*/
```

7.2.2. TIME COMPLEXITY

Time Complexity is measured by the number $f(n)$ of comparisons to locate "data" in A, which contain n elements. Observe that in each comparison the size of the search area is reduced by half. Hence in the worst case, at most $\log_2 n$ comparisons required. So $f(n) = O([\log_2 n]+1)$.

Time Complexity in the average case is almost approximately equal to the running time of the worst case.

7.3. INTERPOLATION SEARCH

Another technique for searching an ordered array is called interpolation search. This method is even more efficient than binary search, if the elements are uniformly distributed (or sorted) in an array A.

Consider an array A of n elements and the elements are uniformly distributed (or the elements are arranged in a sorted array). Initially, as in binary search, low is set to 0 and high is set to n – 1.

Now we are searching an element key in an array between A[low] and A[high]. The key would be expected to be at mid, which is an approximately position.

$$mid = low + (high - low) \times ((key - A[low])/(A[high] - A[low]))$$

If key is lower than A[mid], reset high to mid–1; else reset low to mid+1. Repeat the process until the key has found or low > high.

Interpolation search can be explained with an example below. Consider 7 numbers :

2, 25, 35, 39, 40, 47, 50

CASE 1: Say we are searching 50 from the array

Here $n = 7$ Key = 50

low = 0

high = $n - 1 = 6$

mid = 0+(6–0) × ((50–2)/(50–2))

= 6 × (48/48)

= 6

if (key == A[mid])

⇒ key == A[6]

⇒ 50 == 50

⇒ key is found.

CASE 2: Say we are searching 25 from the array

Here $n = 7$ Key = 25

low = 0

high = $n - 1 = 6$

mid = 0 + (6–0) × ((25–2)/(50–2))

= 6 × (23/48)

= 2.875 Here we consider only the integer part of the mid

i.e., mid = 2

if (key == A[mid])

⇒ key == A[2]

⇒ 25 == 25

⇒ key is found.

CASE 3: Say we are searching 34 from the array

Here $n = 7$ Key = 34

low = 0

high = $n - 1 = 6$

mid = 0 + (6 – 0) × ((34 – 2)/(34 – 2))

= 6 × (32/48)

= 4

if(key < A[mid])

⇒ key < A[4]

⇒ 34 < 40

so reset high = mid–1

⇒ 3

low = 0

high = 3

Since(low < high)

mid = 0+(3–0) × ((34–2)/(39–2))

= 3 × (32/37)

= 2.59 Here we consider only the integer part of the mid

i.e., mid = 2

if (key < A[mid])
⇒ key < A[2]
⇒ 34 < 35
so reset high = mid–1
⇒ 1
low = 0
high = 1
Since (low < high)
mid = 0+(1–0) × ((34–2)/(25–2))
= 3 × (32/23)
= 1
here (key > A[mid])
⇒ key > A[1]
⇒ 34 > 25
so reset low = mid+1
⇒ 2
low = 2
high = 1
Since (low > high)
DISPLAY " The key is not in the array"
STOP

ALGORITHM

Suppose A be array of sorted elements and key is the elements to be searched and low represents the lower bound of the array and high represents higher bound of the array.

1. Input a sorted array of *n* elements and the key to be searched
2. Initialise low = 0 and high = n – 1
3. Repeat the steps 4 through 7 until if(low < high)
4. Mid = low + (high – low) × ((key – A[low]) / (A[high] – A[low]))
5. If(key < A[mid])
   (*a*) high = mid–1
6. Elseif (key > A[mid])
   (*a*) low = mid + 1
7. Else
   (*a*) DISPLAY " The key is not in the array"
   (*b*) STOP
8. STOP

PROGRAM 7.3

```
//PROGRAM TO IMPLEMENT INTERPOLATION SEARCH
//CODED AND COMPILED USING TURBO C++

#include<conio.h>
#include<iostream.h>

class interpolation
{
	int Key;
	int Low,High,Mid;
	public:
		void InterSearch(int*,int);
};

//This function will search the element using interpolation search
void interpolation::InterSearch(int *Arr,int No)
{
	int Key;
	//Assigning the pointer low and high
	Low=0;High=No-1;
	//Inputting the element to be searched
	cout<<"\n\nEnter the Number to be searched = ";
	cin>>Key;

	while(Low < High)
	{
		//Finding the Mid position of the array to be searched
		Mid=Low+(High-Low)*((Key-Arr[Low])/(Arr[High]-Arr[Low]));
		if (Key < Arr[Mid])
			//Re-initializing the high pointer if the
			//key is greater than the mid value
			High=Mid-1;
		else if (Key > Arr[Mid])
			//Re initializing the low pointer if the
			//key is less than the mid value
			Low=Mid+1;
		else
		{
			//if the key value is equal to the mid value
```

```
                    //of the array, the key is found
                    cout<<"\nThe key "<<Key<<" is found at the location "<<Mid;
                    return;
                }
        };
        cout<<"\n\nThe Key "<<Key<<" is NOT found";
}

void main()
{
        int *a,n,*b;
        interpolation Ob;
        clrscr();
        cout<<"\n\nEnter the number of elements : ";
        cin>>n;

        a=new int[n];
        b=a;
        //Input the elements in the array
        for (int i=0;i<n;i++)
        {
                cout<<"\nEnter the "<<i<<" element : ";
                cin>>*a;
                a++;
        }
        //calling the InterSearch function using objects
        Ob.InterSearch(b,n);
        cout<<"\n\nPress any key to continue...";
        getch();
}
```

7.4. FIBONACCI SEARCH

A possible improvement in binary search is not to use the middle element at each step, but to guess more precisely where the key being sought falls within the current interval of interest. This improved version is called fibonacci search. Instead of splitting the array in the middle, this implementation splits the array corresponding to the fibonacci numbers, which are defined in the following manner:

$$F_0 = 0,\ F_1 = 1$$
$$F_n = F_{n-1} + F_{n-2} \text{ for } n >= 2.$$

Let's assume that our array has the F_{n-1} ($n = F_{n-1}$) elements. Now we divide the array into two subsets according to the both preceding fibonacci numbers and compare 'item' to the element at the position F_{n-2}. If 'item' is greater than the element, we continue in the right subset, otherwise in the left subset. In this algorithm we don't have to make a division to calculate the middle element, but we get along only with additions and subtractions. In our implementation we assumed that the fibonacci numbers are given explicitly (*e.g.*, as constants in the frame program).

PROGRAM 7.4

```
//PROGRAM TO IMPLEMENT THE FIBONACCI SEARCH
//CODED AND COMPILED IN TURBO C

#include<iostream.h>
#include<conio.h>

//This function will find the fibonacci number
int fib(int n)
{
	int f1,f2,temp;
	f1=0;f2=1;
	for (int i=0;i<n;i++)
	{
		temp=f2;
		f2=f1+f2;
		f1=temp;
	}
	return(f2);
}

//Function to search an item using fibonacci numbers
int fibonacci_search(int list[],int n,int item)
{
	int f1,f2,t,mid;

	for (int j=1;fib(j)<n;j++);
	f1=fib(j-2);		//find lower fibonacci numbers
	f2=fib(j-3);		//f1=fib(j-2), f2=fib(j-3)
	mid=n-f1+1;
	while (item != list[mid])	//if not found
		if (mid<0 || item > list[mid])
		{		//look in lower half
			if (f1==1)
				return(-1);
```

```
                mid=mid+f2; //decrease fibonacci numbers
                f1 = f1-f2;
                f2 = f2-f1;
            }
            else
            {           //look in upper half
                if (f2==0)     //if not found return -1
                        return(-1);
                mid=mid-f2; //decrease fibonacci numbers
                t=f1-f2;              //this time, decrease more
                f1=f2;         //for smaller list
                f2=t;
            }
            return(mid);
}

void main()
{
        int loc,n,item,list[50];
        cout<<"\n\nEnter the total number of list : ";
        cin>>n;

        cout<<"\nEnter the elements in the list:";
        for (int i=0;i<n;i++)
        {
                cout<<"\nInput "<<i<<" th number : ";
                cin>>list[i];
        }

        cout<<"\nEnter the number to be searched :";
        cin>>item;
        loc=fibonacci_search(list,n,item);
        if (loc != -1)
                cout<<"\nThe number is in the list";
        else
                cout<<"\nThe number is not in the list";
        getch();
}
```

WORST CASE PERFORMANCE

Beginning with an array containing F_{j-1} elements, the length of the subset is bounded to F_{j-1}-1 elements. To search through a range with a length of F_{n-1} at the beginning we have to make n comparisons in the worst case. F_n = (1/sqrt(5))*((1+sqrt(5))/2)n, that's approximately c*1,618n (with a constant c). For N+1 = c*1,618n elements we need n comparisons, *i.e.*, the maximum number of comparisons is O (ld N).

7.5. HASHING

The searching time of the each searching technique, that were discussed in the previous section, depends on the comparison. *i.e.*, n comparisons required for an array A with n elements. To increase the efficiency, *i.e.*, to reduce the searching time, we need to avoid unnecessary comparisons.

Hashing is a technique where we can compute the location of the desired record in order to retrieve it in a single access (or comparison). Let there is a table of n employee records and each employee record is defined by a unique employee code, which is a key to the record and employee name. If the key (or employee code) is used as the array index, then the record can be accessed by the key directly. If L is the memory location where each record is related with the key. If we can locate the memory address of a record from the key then the desired record can be retrieved in a single access. For notational and coding convenience, we assume that the keys in k and the address in L are (decimal) integers. So the location is selected by applying a function which is called *hash function* or *hashing function* from the key k. Unfortunately such a function H may not yield different values (or index or many address); it is possible that two different keys k_1 and k_2 will yield the same hash address. This situation is called *Hash Collision*, which is discussed in the next topic.

7.5.1. HASH FUNCTION

The basic idea of hash function is the transformation of the key into the corresponding location in the hash table. A Hash function H can be defined as a function that takes key as input and transforms it into a hash table index. Hash functions are of two types:

1. Distribution- Independent function
2. Distribution- Dependent function

We are dealing with Distribution - Independent function. Following are the most popular Distribution - Independent hash functions :

1. Division method
2. Mid Square method
3. Folding method.

7.5.1.1. Division Method

TABLE is an array of database file where the employee details are stored. Choose a number m, which is larger than the number of keys k. *i.e.*, m is greater than the total number of records in the TABLE. The number m is usually chosen to be prime number to minimize the collision. The hash function H is defined by

$$H(k) = k \pmod{m}$$

Where H(*k*) is the hash address (or index of the array) and here *k* (mod *m*) means the remainder when *k* is divided by *m*.

For example:

Let a company has 90 employees and 00, 01, 02, ... 99 be the two digit 100 memory address (or index or hash address) to store the records. We have employee code as the key.

Choose *m* in such a way that it is grater than 90. Suppose *m* = 93. Then for the following employee code (or key *k*) :

H(*k*) = H(2103) = 2103 (mod93) = 57

H(*k*) = H(6147) = 6147 (mod 93) = 9

H(*k*) = H(3750) = 3750 (mod93) = 30

Then a typical employee hash table will look like as in Fig. 7.2.

Hash Address	*Employee Code (keys)*	*Employee Name and other Details*
0		
1		
..		
..		
..		
9	6147	Anish
..		
..		
30	3750	Saju
..		
..		
57	2103	Rarish
..		
..		
99		

Fig. 7.2. Hash table

So if you enter the employee code to the hash function, we can directly retrieve TABLE[H(*k*)] details directly. Note that if the memory address begins with 01-*m* instead of 00-*m*, then we have to choose the hash function

$$H(k) = k \ (\text{mod } m)+1.$$

7.5.1.2. Mid Square Method

The key k is squared. Then the hash function H is defined by

$$H(k) = k^2 = l$$

Where l is obtained by digits from both the end of k^2 starting from left. Same number of digits must be used for all of the keys. For example consider following keys in the table and its hash index :

K	4147	3750	2103
K^2	17197609	14062500	4422609
$H(k)$	97	62	22

17197609

14062500

4422609

Hash Address	*Employee Code (keys)*	*Employee Name and other Details*
0		
1		
..		
..		
..		
22	2103	Giri
..		
..		
62	3750	Sunt
..		
..		
..		
97	4147	Renjith
..		
99		

Fig. 7.3. Hash table with mid square division

7.5.1.3. Folding Method

The key K, k_1, k_2,...... k_r is partitioned into number of parts. The parts have same number of digits as the required hash address, except possibly for the last part. Then the parts are added together, ignoring the last carry. That is

$$H(k) = k_1 + k_2 + \ldots\ldots + k_r$$

Here we are dealing with a hash table with index form 00 to 99, *i.e.*, two-digit hash table. So we divide the K numbers of two digits.

K	2103	7148	12345
$k_1\ k_2\ k_3$	21, 03	71, 46	12, 34, 5
$H(k)$ $= k_1 + k_2 + k_3$	H(2103) = 21+03 = 24	H(7148) = 71+46 = 19	H(12345) = 12+34+5 = 51

Fig. 7.4

Extra milling can also be applied to even numbered parts, k_2, k_4, ... are each reversed before the addition.

K	2103	7148	12345
k_1, k_2, k_3	21, 03	71, 46	12, 34, 5
Reversing k_2, k_4	21, 30	71, 64	12, 43, 5
$H(k)$ $= k_1 + k_2 + k_3$	H(2103) = 21+30 = 51	H(7148) = 71+64 = 55	H(12345) = 12+43+5 = 60

Fig. 7.5

H(7148) = 71 + 64 = 155, here we will eliminate the leading carry (*i.e.*, 1). So H(7148) = 71 + 64 = 55.

7.5.2. HASH COLLISION

It is possible that two non-identical keys K_1, K_2 are hashed into the same hash address. This situation is called Hash Collision.

Location	*(Keys)*	*Records*
0	210	
1	111	
2		
3	883	
4	344	
5		
6		

7		
8	488	
9		

Fig. 7.6

Let us consider a hash table having 10 locations as shown in Fig. 7.6. Division method is used to hash the key.

$$H(k) = k \pmod{m}$$

Here m is chosen as 10. The Hash function produces any integer between 0 and 9 inclusions, depending on the value of the key. If we want to insert a new record with key 500 then

$$H(500) = 500(\text{mod } 10) = 0.$$

The location 0 in the table is already filled (*i.e.*, not empty). Thus collision occurred. Collisions are almost impossible to avoid but it can be minimized considerably by introducing any one of the following three techniques:

1. Open addressing
2. Chaining
3. Bucket addressing

7.5.2.1. Open Addressing

In open addressing method, when a key is colliding with another key, the collision is resolved by finding a nearest empty space by probing the cells.

Suppose a record R with key K has a hash address $H(k) = h$. then we will linearly search $h + i$ (where $i = 0, 1, 2, \ldots\ldots m$) locations for free space (*i.e.*, h, $h + 1$, $h + 2$, $h + 3$ ...... hash address).

To understand the concept, let us consider a hash collision which is in the hash table shown in Fig. 7.6.

If we try to insert a new record with a key 500 then

$$H(500) = 500(\text{mod } 10) = 0.$$

The array index 0 is already occupied by H(210). With open addressing we resolve the hash collision by inserting the record in the next available free or empty location in the table. Here next location, *i.e.*, array hash index 1, is also occupied by the key 111. Next available free location in the table is array index 2 and we place the record in this free location.

Location	*(Keys)*	*Records*
0	210	
1	111	
2	500	
3	883	
4	344	
5		
6		
7		
8	488	
9		

Fig. 7.7

The position in which a key can be stored is found by sequentially searching all positions starting from the position calculated by the hash function until an empty cell is found. This type of probing is called *Linear Probing.*

The main disadvantage of Linear Probing is that substantial amount of time will take to find the free cell by sequential or linear searching the table. Other two techniques, which are discussed in the following sections, will minimize this searching time considerably.

QUADRATIC PROBING

Suppose a record with R with key k has the hash address $H(k) = h$. Then instead of searching the location with address h, $h + 1$, $h + 2$,...... $h + i$ ......, we search for free hash address h, $h + 1$, $h + 4$, $h + 9$, $h + 16$, ... $h + i^2$,...... .

DOUBLE HASHING

Second hash function H_1 is used to resolve the collision. Suppose a record R with key k has the hash address $H(k) = h$ and $H1(k) = h^1$, which is not equal to m. Then we linearly search for the location with addresses

h, $h + h^1$, $h + 2h^1$, $h + 3h^1$, ... $h + i\,(h^1)^2$ (where $i = 0, 1, 2,$ ......).

Note : The main drawback of implementing any open addressing procedure is the implementation of deletion.

7.5.2.2. Chaining

In chaining technique the entries in the hash table are dynamically allocated and entered into a linked list associated with each hash key. The hash table in Fig. 7.8 can represented using linked list as in Fig. 7.9.

Location	*(Keys)*	*Records*
0	210	30
1	111	12
2		
3	883	14
4	344	18
5		
6	546	32
7		
8	488	31
9		

Fig. 7.8

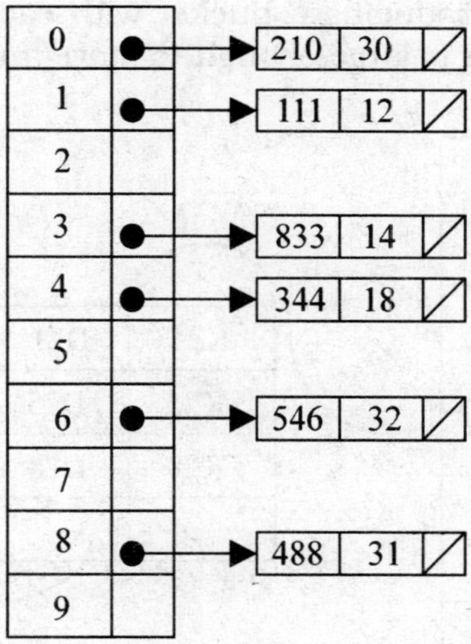

Fig. 7.9

If we try to insert a new record with a key 500 then H(500) = 500(mod 10) = 0.

Then the collision occurs in normal way because there exists a record in the 0th position. But in chaining corresponding linked list can be extended to accommodate the new record with the key as shown in Fig. 7.10.

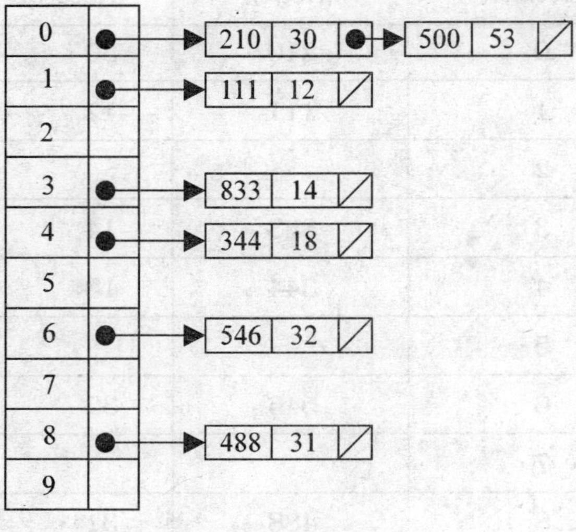

Fig. 7.10

7.5.2.3. Bucket Addressing

Another solution to the hash collision problem is to store colliding elements in the same position in table by introducing a bucket with each hash address. A bucket is a block of memory space, which is large enough to store multiple items.

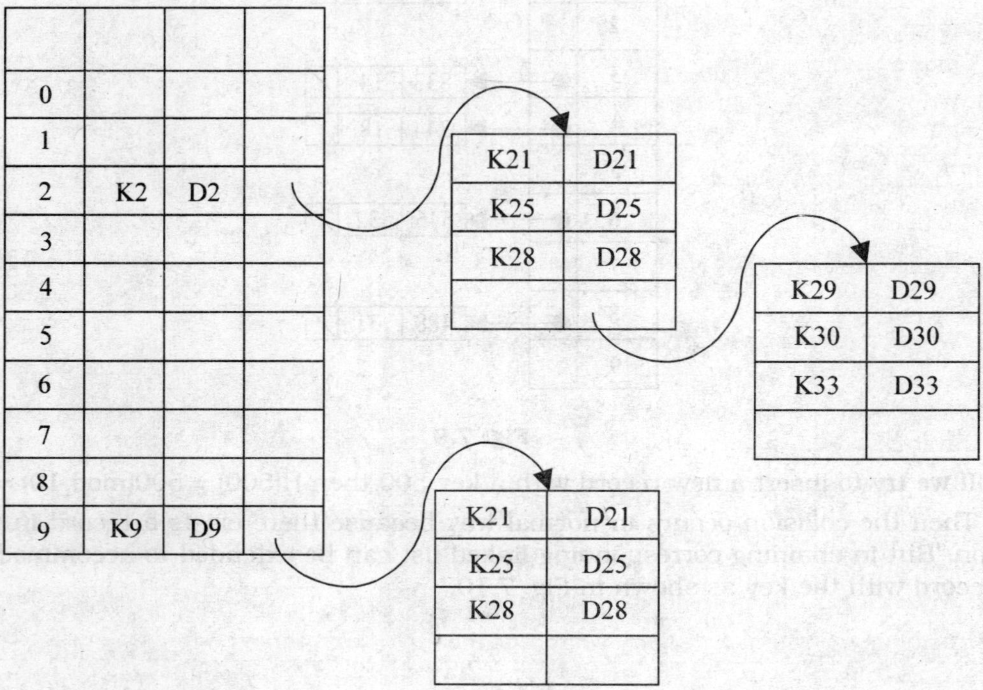

Fig. 7.11. Avoiding collision using buckets

Fig. 7.11 shows how hash collision can be avoided using buckets. If a bucket is full, then the colliding item can be stored in the new bucket by incorporating its link to previous bucket.

7.5.3. HASH DELETION

A data can be deleted from a hash table. In chaining method, deleting an element leads to the deletion of a node from a linked list. But in linear probing, when a data is deleted with its key the position of the array index is made free. The situation is same for other open addressing methods.

SELF REVIEW QUESTIONS

1. Write an algorithm for binary search and discuss its speed compared with linear search. *[MG - MAY 2003 (BTech)]*
2. Write a general algorithm for inserting a name into the structure using hashing techniques. *[MG - MAY 2003 (BTech)]*
3. Compare and contrast between sequential search and binary search. *[ANNA - DEC 2003 (BE), MG - MAY 2002 (BTech) KERALA - DEC 2002 (BTech), ANNA - DEC 2004 (BE)]*
4. Write about the complexities of linear search, binary search and fibonaci search. *[MG - MAY 2000 (BTech)]*
5. What is hashing ? Explain with illustrative examples. Discuss any two hashing techniques you are familiar with. *[ANNA - DEC 2003 (BE), Calicut - APR 1995 (BTech)]*
6. Write a note on Hashing functions. *[CUSAT - MAY 2000 (BTech), Calicut - APR 1997 (BTech) ANNA - MAY 2003 (BE), ANNA - MAY 2004 (MCA) KERALA - MAY 2002 (BTech), KERALA - DEC 2002 (BTech)]*
7. Explain the organization of hash table. How are collisions handled? *[CUSAT - NOV 2002 (BTech)]*
8. What is clustering in a Hash table? Describe two methods for collision resolution. *[ANNA - DEC 2003 (BE)]*
9. Write down the binary search algorithm and obtain the complexities of both worst and average cases. *[ANNA - DEC 2004 (BE)]*
10. Describe various hashing techniques. *[KERALA - DEC 2003 (BTech), ANNA - MAY 2003 (BE)]*
11. Explain (i) hash collision (ii) Linear Searching. *[KERALA - JUN 2004 (BTech)]*
12. Write a recursive procedure for binary search method. *[KERALA - JUN 2004 (BTech)]*
13. Write an algorithm for binary search method by iteration method. *[KERALA - MAY 2003 (BTech)]*
14. What are the hash collision resolution techniques? *[KERALA - NOV 2001 (BTech), KERALA - DEC 2002 (BTech)]*

15. What is searching ? Compare various search methods. [*KERALA - MAY 2001 (BTech)*]
16. Write an algorithm for a hashing method. [*KERALA - MAY 2001 (BTech)*]
17. Describe in detail one hash table method with a suitable method. Explain different probing technique. [*KERALA - MAY 2002 (BTech)*]
18. What is meant by collision processing ? [*KERALA - NOV 2001 (BTech)*]
19. Explain open addressing technique. [*KERALA - NOV 2001 (BTech)*]

8

The Trees

In this chapter we will discuss one of the important non-liner data structure in computer science, Trees. Many real life problems can be represented and solved using trees.

Trees are very flexible, versatile and powerful non-liner data structure that can be used to represent data items possessing hierarchical relationship between the grand father and his children and grand children as so on.

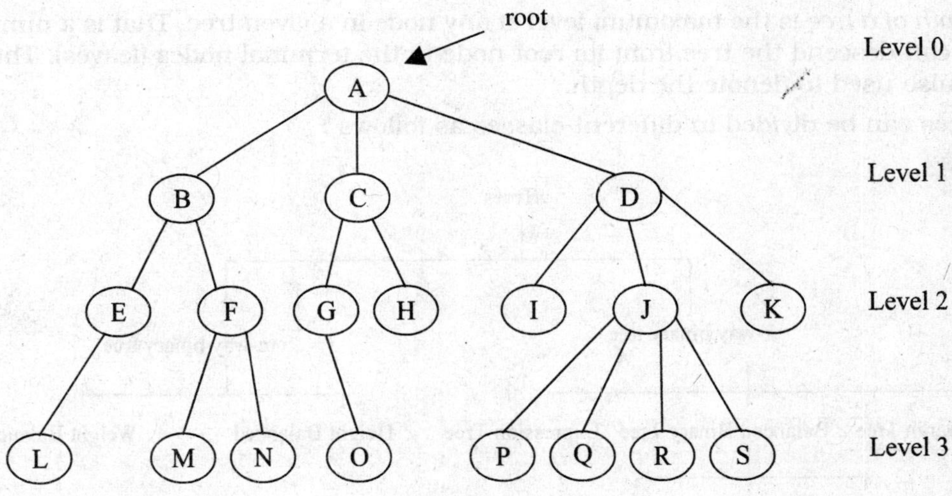

Fig. 8.1. A tree

A tree is an ideal data structure for representing hierarchical data. A tree can be theoretically defined as a finite set of one or more data items (or nodes) such that :

1. There is a special node called the root of the tree.

2. Removing nodes (or data item) are partitioned into number of mutually exclusive (*i.e.*, disjoined) subsets each of which is itself a tree, are called sub tree.

8.1. BASIC TERMINOLOGIES

Root is a specially designed node (or data items) in a tree. It is the first node in the hierarchical arrangement of the data items. 'A' is a root node in the Fig. 8.1. Each data item in a tree is called a *node*. It specifies the data information and links (branches) to other data items.

Degree of a node is the number of subtrees of a node in a give tree. In Fig. 8.1

The degree of node A is 3

The degree of node B is 2

The degree of node C is 2

The degree of node D is 3

The *degree of a tree* is the maximum degree of node in a given tree. In the above tree, degree of a node J is 4. All the other nodes have less or equal degree. So the degree of the above tree is 4. A node with degree zero is called a *terminal node* or a *leaf*. For example in the above tree Fig. 8.1. M, N, I, O etc. are leaf node. Any node whose degree is not zero is called *non-terminal node*. They are intermediate nodes in traversing the given tree from its root node to the terminal nodes.

The tree is structured in different *levels*. The entire tree is leveled in such a way that the root node is always of level 0. Then, its immediate children are at level 1 and their immediate children are at level 2 and so on up to the terminal nodes. That is, if a node is at level *n*, then its children will be at level *n* + 1.

Depth of a tree is the maximum level of any node in a given tree. That is a number of level one can descend the tree from its root node to the terminal nodes (leaves). The term *height* is also used to denote the depth.

Trees can be divided in different classes as follows :

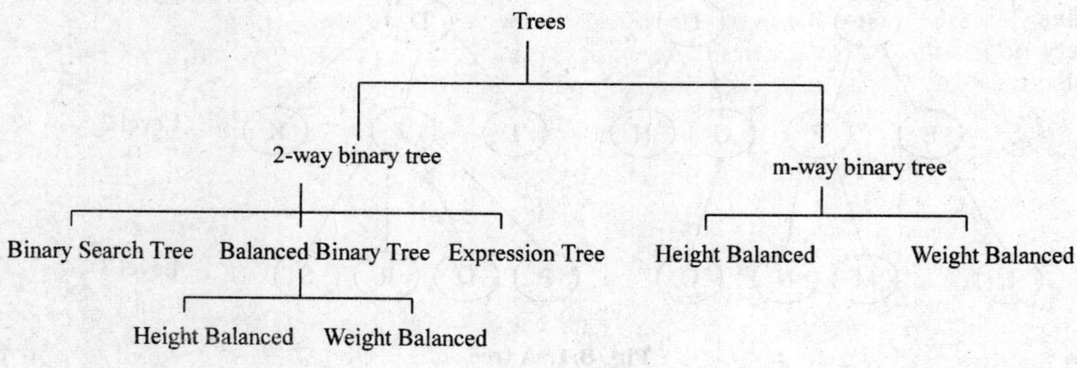

Fig. 8.2

8.2. BINARY TREES

A binary tree is a tree in which no node can have more than two children. Typically these children are described as "left child" and "right child" of the parent node.

A binary tree T is defined as a finite set of elements, called nodes, such that :

1. T is empty (*i.e.*, if T has no nodes called the *null tree* or *empty tree*).

2. T contains a special node R, called root node of T, and the remaining nodes of T form an ordered pair of disjoined binary trees T1 and T2, and they are called left and right sub tree of R. If T1 is non empty then its root is called the left successor of R, similarly if T2 is non empty then its root is called the right successor of R.

Consider a binary tree T in Fig. 8.3. Here 'A' is the root node of the binary tree T. Then 'B' is the left child of 'A' and 'C' is the right child of 'A' *i.e.*, 'A' is a father of 'B' and 'C'. The node 'B' and 'C' are called brothers, since they are left and right child of the same father. If a node has no child then it is called a leaf node. Nodes P,H,I,F,J are leaf node in Fig. 8.3.

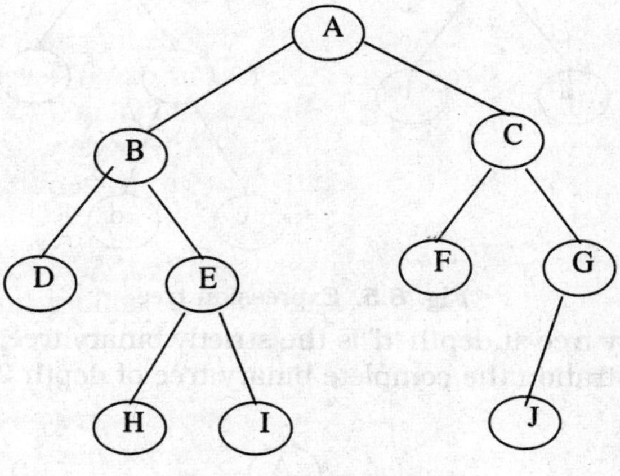

Fig. 8.3. Binary tree

The tree is said to be *strictly binary tree*, if every non-leaf made in a binary tree has non-empty left and right sub trees. A strictly binary tree with *n* leaves always contains 2*n*–1 nodes. The tree in Fig. 8.4 is strictly binary tree, where as the tree in Fig. 8.3 is not. That is every node in the strictly binary tree can have either no children or two children. They are also called 2-*tree* or *extended binary tree.*

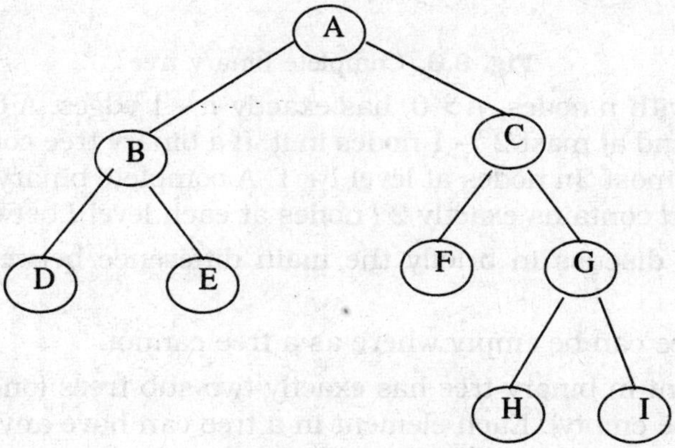

Fig. 8.4. Strictly binary tree

The main application of a 2-tree is to represent and compute any algebraic expression using binary operation.

For example, consider an algebraic expression E.

$$E = (a + b)/((c - d)*e)$$

E can be represented by means of the extended binary tree T as shown in Fig. 8.5. Each variable or constant in E appears as an internal node in T whose left and right sub tree corresponds to the operands of the operation.

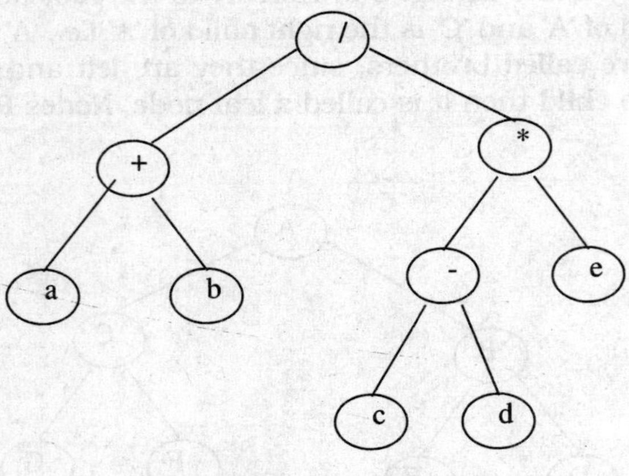

Fig. 8.5. Expression tree

A complete binary tree at depth '*d*' is the strictly binary tree, where all the leaves are at level *d*. Fig. 8.6 illustration the complete binary tree of depth 2.

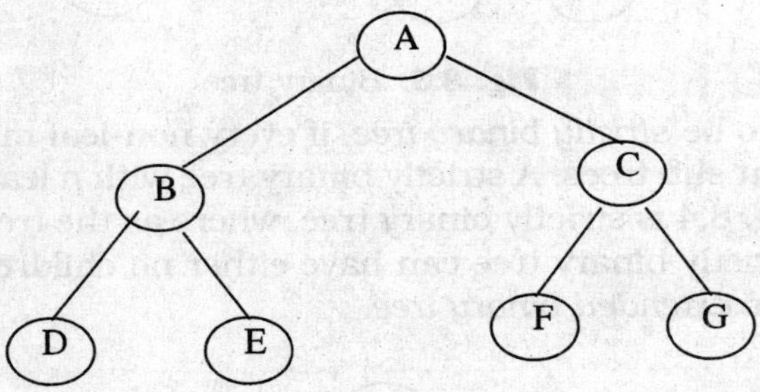

Fig. 8.6. Complete binary tree

A binary tree with *n* nodes, $n > 0$, has exactly $n - 1$ edges. A binary tree of depth *d*, $d > 0$, has at least *d* and at mast $2^d - 1$ nodes in it. If a binary tree contains *n* nodes at level 1, then it contains at most 2*n* nodes at level $l + 1$. A complete binary tree of depth *d* is the binary tree of depth *d* contains exactly 2 *l* nodes at each level *l* between 0 and *d*.

Finally, let us discuss in briefly the main difference between a binary tree and ordinary tree is:

1. A binary tree can be empty where as a tree cannot.
2. Each element in binary tree has exactly two sub trees (one or both of these sub trees may be empty). Each element in a tree can have any number of sub trees.
3. The sub tree of each element in a binary tree are ordered, left and right sub trees. The sub trees in a tree are unordered.

If a binary tree has only left sub trees, then it is called left skewed binary tree. Fig. 8.7(*a*) is a left skewed binary tree.

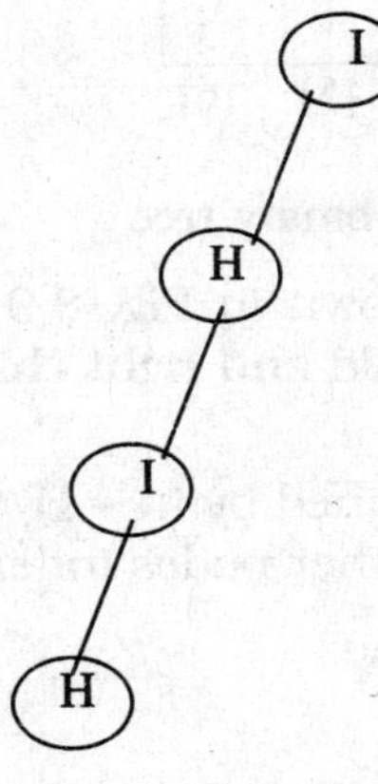

Fig. 8.7(a). Left skewed

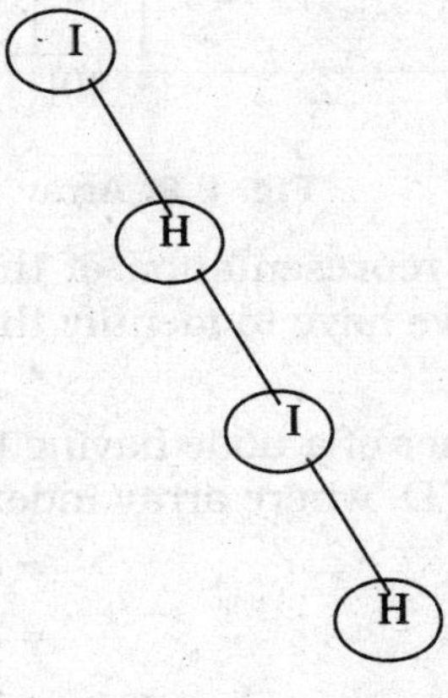

Fig. 8.7(b). Right skewed

If a binary tree has only right sub trees, then it is called right skewed binary tree. Fig. 8.7(*b*) is a right skewed binary tree.

8.3. BINARY TREE REPRESENTATION

This section discusses two ways of representing binary tree T in memory :

1. Sequential representation using arrays
2. Linked list representation

8.3.1. ARRAY REPRESENTATION

An array can be used to store the nodes of a binary tree. The nodes stored in an array of memory can be accessed sequentially.

Suppose a binary tree T of depth *d*. Then at most 2^{d-1} nodes can be there in T.(*i.e.*, SIZE = 2^d–1) So the array of size "SIZE" to represent the binary tree. Consider a binary tree in Fig. 8.8 of depth 3. Then SIZE = $2^3 - 1 = 7$. Then the array A[7] is declared to hold the nodes.

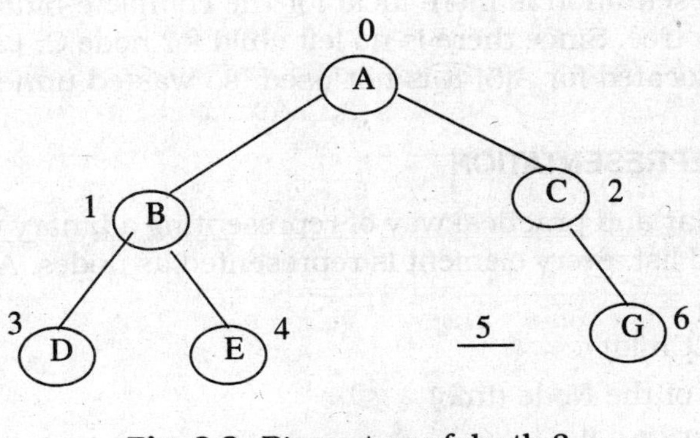

Fig. 8.8. Binary tree of depth 3

A[ ]	A	B	C	D	E		F
	[0]	[1]	[2]	[3]	[4]	[5]	[6]

Fig. 8.9. Array representation of the binary tree

The array representation of the binary tree is shown in Fig. 8.9. To perform any operation often we have to identify the father, the left child and right child of an arbitrary node.

1. The father of a node having index n can be obtained by $(n - 1)/2$. For example to find the father of D, where array index $n = 3$. Then the father nodes index can be obtained

$$= (n - 1)/2$$
$$= 3 - 1/2$$
$$= 2/2$$
$$= 1$$

i.e., A[1] is the father D, which is B.

2. The left child of a node having index n can be obtained by (2n+1). For example to find the left child of C, where array index $n = 2$. Then it can be obtained by

$$= (2n\ +1)$$
$$= 2*2 + 1$$
$$= 4 + 1$$
$$= 5$$

i.e., A[5] is the left child of C, which is NULL. So no left child for C.

3. The right child of a node having array index n can be obtained by the formula $(2n + 2)$. For example to find the right child of B, where the array index $n = 1$. Then

$$= (2n + 2)$$
$$= 2*1 + 2$$
$$= 4$$

i.e., A[4] is the right child of B, which is E.

4. If the left child is at array index n, then its right brother is at $(n + 1)$. Similarly, if the right child is at index n, then its left brother is at $(n - 1)$.

The array representation is more ideal for the complete binary tree. The Fig. 8.8 is not a complete binary tree. Since there is no left child for node C, *i.e.*, A[5] is vacant. Even though memory is allocated for A[5] it is not used, so wasted unnecessarily.

8.3.2. LINKED LIST REPRESENTATION

The most popular and practical way of representing a binary tree is using linked list (or pointers). In linked list, every element is represented as nodes. A node consists of three fields such as :

(*a*) Left Child (LChild)

(*b*) Information of the Node (Info)

(*c*) Right Child (RChild)

The L Child links to the left child node of the parent node, Info holds the information of every node and R Child holds the address of right child node of the parent node. Fig. 8.10 shows the structure of a binary tree node.

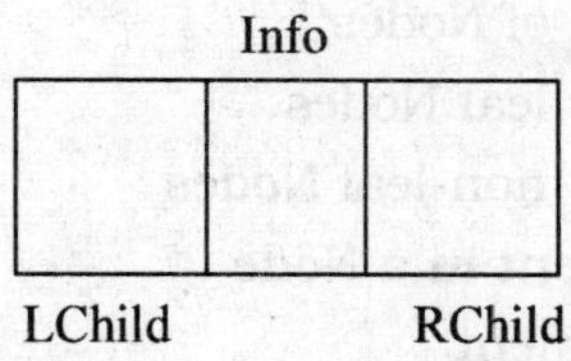

Fig. 8.10

Following figure (Fig. 8.11) shows the linked list representation of the binary tree in Fig. 8.8.

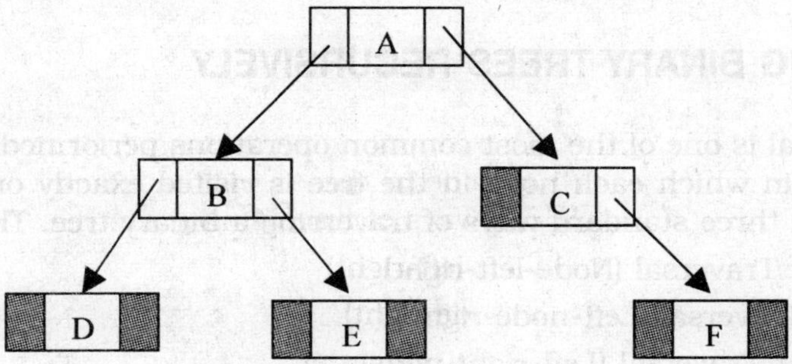

Fig. 8.11

If a node has left or/and right node, corresponding L Child or R Child is assigned to NULL. The node structure can be logically represented in C/C++ as:

```
struct Node
{
        int Info;
        struct Node *Lchild;
        struct Node *Rchild;
};

typedef struct Node *NODE;
```

8.4. OPERATIONS ON BINARY TREE

The basic operations that are commonly performed an binary tree is listed below :

1. Create an empty Binary Tree
2. Traversing a Binary Tree
3. Inserting a New Node

4. Deleting a Node
5. Searching for a Node
6. Copying the mirror image of a tree
7. Determine the total no: of Nodes
8. Determine the total no: leaf Nodes
9. Determine the total no: non-leaf Nodes
10. Find the smallest element in a Node
11. Finding the largest element
12. Find the Height of the tree
13. Finding the Father/Left Child/Right Child/Brother of an arbitrary node

Some primitive operations are discussed in the following sections. Implementation other operations are left to the reader.

8.5. TRAVERSING BINARY TREES RECURSIVELY

Tree traversal is one of the most common operations performed on tree data structures. It is a way in which each node in the tree is visited exactly once in a systematic manner. There are three standard ways of traversing a binary tree. They are:

1. Pre Order Traversal (Node-left-right)
2. In order Traversal (Left-node-right)
3. Post Order Traversal (Left-right-node)

8.5.1. PRE ORDERS TRAVERSAL RECURSIVELY

To traverse a non-empty binary tree in pre order following steps one to be processed

1. Visit the root node
2. Traverse the left sub tree in preorder
3. Traverse the right sub tree in preorder

That is, in preorder traversal, the root node is visited (or processed) first, before traveling through left and right sub trees recursively. It can be implement in C/C++ function as below :

```
void preorder (Node * Root)
{
	If (Root != NULL)
	{
		printf ("%d\n",Root → Info);
	preorder(Root → L child);
		preorder(Root → R child);
	}
}
```

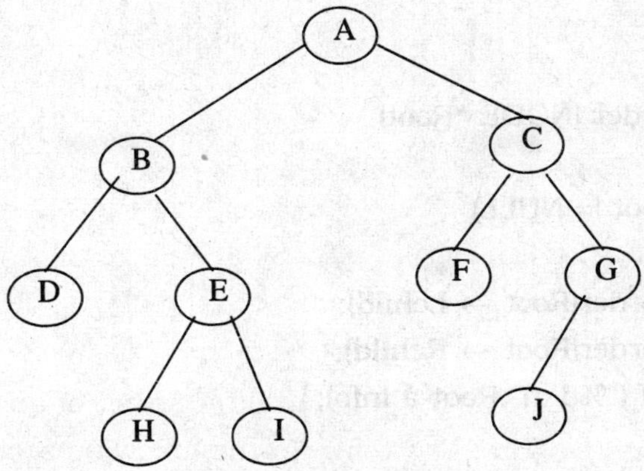

Fig. 8.12

The preorder traversal of a binary tree in Fig. 8.12 is A, B, D, E, H, I, C, F, G, J.

8.5.2. IN ORDER TRAVERSAL RECURSIVELY

The in order traversal of a non-empty binary tree is defined as follows :

1. Traverse the left sub tree in order
2. Visit the root node
3. Traverse the right sub tree in order

In order traversal, the left sub tree is traversed recursively, before visiting the root. After visiting the root the right sub tree is traversed recursively, in order fashion. The procedure for an in order traversal is given below :

```
void inorder (NODE *Root)
{
        If (Root != NULL)
        {
        inorder(Root → L child);
        printf ("%d\n",Root → info);
        inorder(Root → R child);
        }
}
```

The in order traversal of a binary tree in Fig. 8.12 is D, B, H, E, I, A, F, C, J, G.

8.5.3. POST ORDER TRAVERSAL RECURSIVELY

The post order traversal of a non-empty binary tree can be defined as :

1. Traverse the left sub tree in post order
2. Traverse the right sub tree in post order
3. Visit the root node

In Post Order traversal, the left and right sub tree(s) are recursively processed before visiting the root.

```
void postorder (NODE *Root)
{
        If (Root != NULL)
        {
        postorder(Root → Lchild);
        postorder(Root → Rchild);
        printf ("%d\n",Root à info);
}
        }
```

The post order traversal of a binary tree in Fig. 8.12 is D, H, I, E, B, F, J, G, C, A

PROGRAM 8.1

```
//PROGRAM TO IMPLEMENT THE INSERTION AND DELETION IN B TREE
//CODED AND COMPILED USING TURBO C

#include<stdlib.h>
#include<malloc.h>
#include<conio.h>
#include<stdio.h>

#define M 5

//Structure is defined
struct node{
        int n; /* n < M No. of keys in node will always less than order of B tree */
        int keys[M-1]; /*array of keys*/
        struct node *p[M];   /* (n+1 pointers will be in use) */
}*root=NULL;

typedef struct node *NODE;
enum Key Status { Duplicate,Search Failure,Success,InsertIt,Less Keys };

//Function declrations
void insert(int key);
void display(NODE root,int);
```

```
void DelNode(int x);
void search(int x);
enum KeyStatus ins(NODE r, int x, int* y, NODE * u);
int searchPos(int x,int *key_arr, int n);
enum KeyStatus del(NODE r, int x);

void main()
{
        int key;
        int choice;
        while(1)
        {
                clrscr();//Clear the screen
                //Menu options
                printf ("\n1.Insert\n");
                printf ("2.Delete\n");
                printf ("3.Search\n");
                printf ("4.Display\n");
                printf ("5.Quit\n");
                printf ("\nEnter your choice : ");
                scanf ("%d",&choice);

                switch(choice)
                {
                        case 1:
                                printf ("\nEnter the key : ");
                                scanf ("%d",&key);
                                insert(key);
                                break;
                        case 2:
                                printf ("\nEnter the key : ");
                                scanf ("%d",&key);
                                DelNode(key);
                                break;
                        case 3:
                                printf ("\nEnter the key : ");
                                scanf ("%d",&key);
                                search(key);
                                getch();
                                break;
                        case 4:
                                printf ("\nBtree is :\n");
```

```
                    display(root,0);
                    getch();
                    break;
                case 5:
                    exit(1);
                default:
                    printf ("\nWrong choice\n");
                    getch();
                    break;
            }/*End of switch*/
        }/*End of while*/
}/*End of main()*/

void insert(int key)
{
        NODE newnode;
        int upKey;
        enum KeyStatus value;
        value = ins(root, key, &upKey, &newnode);
        //Cheking for duplicate keys
        if (value == Duplicate)
        {
                printf("\nKey already available\n");
                getch();
        }

        if (value == InsertIt)
        {
                NODE uproot = root;
                //Allocating memory
                root=(NODE)malloc(sizeof(struct node));
                root->n = 1;
                root->keys[0] = upKey;
                root->p[0] = uproot;
                root->p[1] = newnode;
        }/*End of if */
}/*End of insert()*/

enum KeyStatus ins(NODE ptr, int key, int *upKey,NODE *newnode)
{
        NODE newPtr,lastPtr;
        int pos, i, n,splitPos;
```

```
int newKey, lastKey;
enum KeyStatus value;
if (ptr == NULL)
{
        *newnode = NULL;
        *upKey = key;
        return InsertIt;
}
n = ptr->n;
pos = searchPos(key, ptr->keys, n);
if (pos < n && key == ptr->keys[pos])
        return Duplicate;
value = ins(ptr->p[pos], key, &newKey, &newPtr);
if (value != InsertIt)
        return value;
/*If keys in node is less than M-1 where M is order of B tree*/
if (n < M - 1)
{
        pos = searchPos(newKey, ptr->keys, n);
        /*Shifting the key and pointer right for inserting the new key*/
        for (i=n; i>pos; i--)
        {
                ptr->keys[i] = ptr->keys[i-1];
                ptr->p[i+1] = ptr->p[i];
        }
        /*Key is inserted at exact location*/
        ptr->keys[pos] = newKey;
        ptr->p[pos+1] = newPtr;
        ++ptr->n; /*incrementing the number of keys in node*/
        return Success;
}/*End of if */
/*If keys in nodes are maximum and position of node to be inserted is last*/
if (pos == M - 1)
{
        lastKey = newKey;
        lastPtr = newPtr;
}
else /*If keys in node are maximum and position of node to be inserted is not last*/
{
        lastKey = ptr->keys[M-2];
        lastPtr = ptr->p[M-1];
        for (i=M-2; i>pos; i--)
```

```
            {
                ptr->keys[i] = ptr->keys[i-1];
                ptr->p[i+1] = ptr->p[i];
            }
            ptr->keys[pos] = newKey;
            ptr->p[pos+1] = newPtr;
        }
        splitPos = (M - 1)/2;
       (*upKey) = ptr->keys[splitPos];

        (*newnode)=(NODE)malloc(sizeof(struct node));/*Right node after split*/
        ptr->n = splitPos; /*No. of keys for left splitted node*/
        (*newnode)->n = M-1-splitPos;/*No. of keys for right splitted node*/
        for (i=0; i < (*newnode)->n; i++)
        {
            (*newnode)->p[i] = ptr->p[i + splitPos + 1];
            if(i < (*newnode)->n - 1)
                (*newnode)->keys[i] = ptr->keys[i + splitPos + 1];
            else
                (*newnode)->keys[i] = lastKey;
        }
        (*newnode)->p[(*newnode)->n] = lastPtr;
        return InsertIt;
}/*End of ins()*/

void display(NODE ptr, int blanks)
{
        if (ptr)
        {
            int i;
            for(i=1;i<=blanks;i++)
                printf (" ");
            for (i=0; i < ptr->n; i++)
                printf ("%d ",ptr->keys[i]);
            printf ("\n");
            for (i=0; i <= ptr->n; i++)
                display(ptr->p[i], blanks+10);
        }/*End of if*/
}/*End of display()*/

void search(int key)
{
```

```
        int pos, i, n;
        NODE ptr = root;
        printf ("\nSearch path:\n");
        while (ptr)
        {
                n = ptr->n;
                for (i=0; i < ptr->n; i++)
                        printf (" %d",ptr->keys[i]);
                printf ("\n");
                pos = searchPos(key, ptr->keys, n);
                if (pos < n && key == ptr->keys[pos])
                {
                        printf ("\nKey %d found in position %d of last dispalyed node\n",key,i);
                        return;
                }
                ptr = ptr->p[pos];
        }
        printf ("\nKey %d is not available\n",key);
}/*End of search()*/

int searchPos(int key, int *key_arr, int n)
{
        int pos=0;
        while (pos < n && key > key_arr[pos])
                pos++;
        return pos;
}/*End of searchPos()*/

void DelNode(int key)
{
        NODE uproot;
        enum KeyStatus value;
        value = del(root,key);
        switch (value)
        {
        case SearchFailure:
                printf("\nKey %d is not available\n",key);
                break;
        case LessKeys:
                uproot = root;
                root = root->p[0];
                free(uproot);
```

```
                break;
        }/*End of switch*/
}/*End of delnode()*/

enum KeyStatus del(NODE ptr, int key)
{
        int pos, i, pivot, n ,min;
        int *key_arr;
        enum KeyStatus value;
        NODE *p,lptr,rptr;

        if (ptr == NULL)
                return SearchFailure;
        /*Assigns values of node*/
        n=ptr->n;
        key_arr = ptr->keys;
        p = ptr->p;
        min = (M - 1)/2;/*Minimum number of keys*/

        pos = searchPos(key, key_arr, n);
        if (p[0] == NULL)
        {
                if (pos == n || key < key_arr[pos])
                        return SearchFailure;
                /*Shift keys and pointers left*/
                for (i=pos+1; i < n; i++)
                {
                        key_arr[i-1] = key_arr[i];
                        p[i] = p[i+1];
                }
                return  --ptr->n >= (ptr==root ? 1 : min) ? Success : LessKeys;
        }/*End of if */

        if (pos < n && key == key_arr[pos])
        {
                struct node *qp = p[pos], *qp1;
                int nkey;
                while(1)
                {
                        nkey = qp->n;
                        qp1 = qp->p[nkey];
                        if (qp1 == NULL)
```

```
                    break;
                qp = qp1;
            }/*End of while*/
            key_arr[pos] = qp->keys[nkey-1];
            qp->keys[nkey - 1] = key;
        }/*End of if */
        value = del(p[pos], key);
        if (value != LessKeys)
            return value;

        if (pos > 0 && p[pos-1]->n > min)
        {
            pivot = pos - 1; /*pivot for left and right node*/
            lptr = p[pivot];
            rptr = p[pos];
            /*Assigns values for right node*/
            rptr->p[rptr->n + 1] = rptr->p[rptr->n];
            for (i=rptr->n; i>0; i--)
            {
                rptr->keys[i] = rptr->keys[i-1];
                rptr->p[i] = rptr->p[i-1];
            }
            rptr->n++;
            rptr->keys[0] = key_arr[pivot];
            rptr->p[0] = lptr->p[lptr->n];
            key_arr[pivot] = lptr->keys[--lptr->n];
            return Success;
        }/*End of if */
        if (pos<n && p[pos+1]->n > min)
        {
            pivot = pos; /*pivot for left and right node*/
            lptr = p[pivot];
            rptr = p[pivot+1];
            /*Assigns values for left node*/
            lptr->keys[lptr->n] = key_arr[pivot];
            lptr->p[lptr->n + 1] = rptr->p[0];
            key_arr[pivot] = rptr->keys[0];
            lptr->n++;
            rptr->n--;
            for (i=0; i < rptr->n; i++)
            {
                rptr->keys[i] = rptr->keys[i+1];
```

```
                rptr->p[i] = rptr->p[i+1];
            }/*End of for*/
            rptr->p[rptr->n] = rptr->p[rptr->n + 1];
            return Success;
        }/*End of if */

        if(pos == n)
            pivot = pos-1;
        else
            pivot = pos;

        lptr = p[pivot];
        rptr = p[pivot+1];
        /*merge right node with left node*/
        lptr->keys[lptr->n] = key_arr[pivot];
        lptr->p[lptr->n + 1] = rptr->p[0];
        for (i=0; i < rptr->n; i++)
        {
            lptr->keys[lptr->n + 1 + i] = rptr->keys[i];
            lptr->p[lptr->n + 2 + i] = rptr->p[i+1];
        }
        lptr->n = lptr->n + rptr->n +1;
        free(rptr); /*Remove right node*/
        for (i=pos+1; i < n; i++)
        {
            key_arr[i-1] = key_arr[i];
            p[i] = p[i+1];
        }
        return --ptr->n >= (ptr == root ? 1 : min) ? Success : LessKeys;
    }/*End of del()*/
```

8.6. TRAVERSING BINARY TREE NON-RECURSIVELY

In this section we will discuss the implementation of three standard traversals algorithms, which were defined recursively in the last section, non-recursively using stack.

8.6.1. PREORDER TRAVERSAL NON-RECURSIVELY

The preorder traversal non-recursively algorithms uses a variable PN (Present Node), which will contain the location of the node currently being scanned. Left(R) denotes the left child of the node R and Right(R) denoted the right child of R. A stack is used to hold the addresses of the nodes to be processed. Info(R) denotes the information of the node R.

Preorder traversal starts with root node of the tree *i.e.*, PN = ROOT. Then repeat the following steps until PN = NULL.

Step 1: Process the node PN. If any right child is there for PN, push the Right (PN) into the top of the stack and proceed down to left by PN = Left (PN), if any left child is there (*i.e.*, Left (PN) not equal to NULL).

Repeat the step 2 until there is no left child (*i.e.*, Left (PN) = NULL).

Step 2: Now we have to go back to the right node(s) by backtracking the tree. This can be achieved by popping the top most element of the stack. Pop the top element from the stack and assigns to PN.

Step 3: If (PN is not equal to NULL) go to the Step 1

Step 4: Exit

The implementation of the preorder non-recursively traversal algorithm can be illustrated with an example. Consider a binary tree in Fig. 8.13. Following steps are generated when the algorithm is applied to the following binary tree :

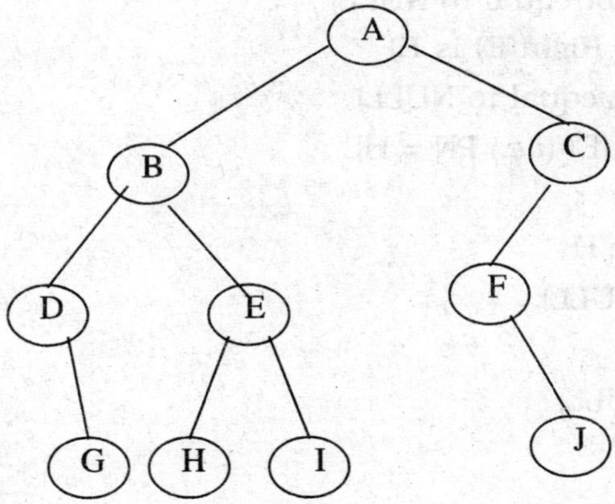

Fig. 8.13

1. Initialize the Root node to PN

   SATCK :

   PN = ROOT (*i.e.*, PN = A)

2. Process the node PN (*i.e.*, A)

   If PN has the right child push it into stack (*i.e.*, C)

   If PN has the left child proceed down to left by PN = Left(A) (*i.e.*, PN = B)

   STACK: C

3. Process the node PN (*i.e.*, B)

   If PN has the right child (*i.e.*, Right (PN) not equal to NULL) then push the right child of PN into the stack (*i.e.*, Right(B) is E)

   If PN has the left child proceed down to left by PN = Left(B) (*i.e.*, Now PN = D)

   STACK: C, E

4. Process or display the node PN (*i.e.*, D)

   If PN has the right child, then push the right child of PN into the stack (*i.e.*, Right(D) is G)

If PN has the left child proceed down to left. Here Left(PN) is equal to NULL, so no left child.

STACK: C, E, G

5. Now the backtracking process will start (*i.e.*, when Left(PN) = NULL)

Pop the top element G from the stack and assign it to PN (*i.e.*, PN = G)

STACK: C, E

6. Process the node G

Check for right child of PN (*i.e.*, G) No right child (*i.e.*, Right(G) = NULL

Check for left child of PN (*i.e.*, G) No left child also (*i.e.*, Left(G) = NULL)

STACK: C, E

7. Again pop the top element E from the stack and assign it to PN (*i.e.*, PN = E)

STACK: C

8. Process the node E (PN)

Since (Right(E) is not equal to NULL)

Push(Right(E)) (*i.e.*, Right(E) is E)

Since (Left(E) is not equal to NULL)

PN = Left(PN) = Left(E) (*i.e.*, PN = H)

STACK: C, I

9. Process the node H

Since (Right(H) = NULL)

Do nothing

Since (Left(H) = NULL)

Do nothing

STACK: C, I

10. Backtracking to right sub tree elements

Pop the top element I from the stack and assign it to PN (*i.e.*, PN = I)

STACK: C

11. Process the node I

No left child for I

No right child for I

STACK: C

12. Again backtracking

Pop the top element C and assign it to PN (*i.e.*, PN=C)

STACK:

13. Display (or process) the node C

Since (Right(C) = NULL)

Do nothing

Since (Left(C) is not equal to NULL)

PN = Left(PN) = Left(C) (*i.e.*, PN = F)

STACK:

14. Display the node F

Since (Right(F) is not equal to NULL)

Push Right(F) to the stack (*i.e.*, J)

Since (Left(F) = NULL)

Do Nothing

STACK: J

15. Backtracking to right node(s)

Pop the top element J and assign it to PN (*i.e.*, PN = J)

STACK:

16. Display the node J

(Right(J) = NULL)

(Right(J) = NULL)

STACK:

17. Backtracking for right nodes. Now the top pointer is pointing to NULL. Assign the top value to PN. (*i.e.*, PN=NULL)

18. When (PN = NULL) STOP

The nodes are processed or displayed in the order A, B, D, G, E, H, I, C, F, J.

ALGORITHM

An array STACK is used to hold the addresses of nodes. TOP pointer points to the top most element of the STACK. ROOT is the root node of tree to be traversed. PN is the address of the present node under scanning. Info(PN) if the information contained in the node PN.

1. Initialize TOP = NULL, PN = ROOT
2. Repeat step 3 to 5 until (PN = NULL)
3. Display Info(PN)
4. If (Right(PN) not equal to NULL)
   (*a*) TOP = TOP+1
   (*b*) STACK(TOP) = Right(PN);
5. If(Left(PN) not equal to NULL)
   (*a*) PN = Left(PN)
6. Else
   (*a*) PN = STACK[TOP]
   (*b*) TOP = TOP–1
7. Exit

PROGRAM 8.2

```
//FUNCTION TO IMPLEMENT NON RECURSIVE PRE ORDER TRAVERSAL
//CODED AND COMPILED IN TURBO C++

void preorder(struct tnode *p)
{
        struct node *stack[100];
        int top;
        top = -1;
        if(p != NULL)
        {
                cout<<" "<<p->info;
                if(p->rchild != NULL)
{
                        top++;
                stack[top] = p->rchild;
                }
                p = p->lchild;
                while(top >= -1)
                {
while ( p!= NULL)/* push the left child onto stack*/
{
printf("%d\t",p->data);
                                if(p->rchild != NULL)
{
                        top++;
                stack[top] = p->rchild;
                        }
                        p = p->lchild;
                        }
                        p = stack[top];
                top--;
                }
        }
}
```

8.6.2. IN ORDER TRAVERSAL NON-RECURSIVELY

The in-order traversal algorithm uses a variable PN, which will contain the location of the node currently being scanned. Info (R) denotes the information of the node R, Left (R) denotes the left child of the node R and Right (R) denotes the right child of the node R.

In-order traversal starts from the ROOT node of the tree (*i.e.*, PN = ROOT). Then repeat the following steps until PN = NULL :

Step 1: Proceed down to left most node of the tree by pushing the root node onto the stack.

Step 2: Repeat the step 1 until there is no left child for a node.

Step 3: Pop the top element of the stack and process the node. PN = STACK[TOP]

Step 4: If the stack is empty then go to step 6.

Step 5: If the popped element has right child then PN = Right(PN). Then repeat the step from 1.

Step 6: Exit.

The in-order traversal algorithm can be illustrated with an example. Consider a binary tree in Fig. 8.13. Following steps may generate if we try to traverse the tree in in-order fashion :

1. Initialize root Node to PN (*i.e.*, PN = ROOT = A)

    STACK:

2. Since(Left(PN) is not equal to NULL

Push (PN) to the stack

PN = Left(PN) (*i.e.*, = B)

    STACK: A

3. Since(Left(PN) is not equal to NULL

Push (PN) to the stack (*i.e.*, = B)

PN = Left(PN) (*i.e.*, = D

    STACK: A, B

4. Since(Left(PN) = NULL

Display the node D

    STACK: A, B

5. Since(Right(PN) is not equal to NULL

PN = Right(PN) = G

    STACK: A, B

6. Since(Left(PN) = NULL

Display the node G

    STACK: A, B

7. Since(Right(PN) = NULL)

Pop the topmost element of the stack

PN = STACK[TOP] (*i.e.*, = B)

Display the node B

    STACK: A

8. Since(Right(PN) is not equal to NULL)

PN = Right(PN) = E

    STACK: A

9. Since(Left(PN) is not equal to NULL
Push(PN) to the stack (*i.e.*, E)
PN = Left(PN) = H
STACK: A, E

10 Since(Left(PN) = NULL)
Display the node H
STACK: A, E

11. Since(Right(PN) = NULL
Pop the topmost element of the stack
PN = STACK[TOP] = E
Display the node E
STACK: A

12. Since(Right(PN) is not equal to NULL)
PN = Right(PN) = I
STACK: A

13. Since(Left(PN) = NULL)
Display the node I
STACK: A

14. Since(Right(PN) = NULL)
Pop the topmost element of the stack
PN = STACK[TOP] = A
Display the node A
STACK:

15. Since(Right(PN) not equal to NULL)
PN = Right(PN) = C
STACK:

16. Since(Left(PN) is not equal to NULL)
Push(PN) to the stack (*i.e.*, = C)
PN = Left(PN) = F
STACK: C

17. Since(Left(PN) = NULL)
Display the node F
STACK: C

18. Since(Right(PN) is not equal to NULL)
PN = Right(PN) = J
STACK: C

19. Since(Left(PN) = NULL
Display the node J
STACK: C

20. Since(Right(PN) = NULL)

Pop the element from the stack

PN = STACK[TOP] = C

Display the node C

STACK:

21. Since(Right(PN) = NULL)

Try to pop an element from the stack. Since the stack is empty PN=NULL and Stop

The nodes are displayed in the order of D, G, B, H, E, I, A, F, J, C.

ALGORITHM

An array STACK is used to temporarily store the addresses of the nodes. TOP pointer always points to the topmost element of the STACK.

1. Initialize TOP = NULL and PN = ROOT
2. Repeat the Step 3, 4 and 5 until (PN = NULL)
3. TOP = TOP +1
4. STACK[TOP] = PN
5. PN = Left(PN)
6. PN = STACK[TOP]
7. TOP = TOP–1
8. Repeat steps 9, 10, 11 and 12 until (PN = NULL)
9. Display Info(PN)
10. If(Right(PN) is not equal to NULL
    (*a*) PN = Right(PN)
    (*b*) Go to Step 6
11. PN = STACK[TOP]
12. TOP = TOP –1
13. Exit

PROGRAM 8.3

```
//FUNCTION TO IMPLEMENT NON RECURSIVE IN ORDER TRAVERSAL
//CODED AND COMPILED IN TURBO C++
void inorder(struct tnode *p)
{
	struct tnode *stack[100];
	int top;
	top = –1;
	if(p != NULL)
	{
```

```
        top++;
        stack[top] = p;
        p = p->lchild;
        while(top >= 0)
        {
while ( p!= NULL)/* push the left child onto stack*/
{
            top++;
                stack[top] =p;
            p = p->lchild;
            }
            p = stack[top];
        top--;
            cout<<" "<<p->data;
        p = p->rchild;
            if ( p != NULL) /* push right child*/
            {
                top++;
            stack[top] = p;
                p = p->lchild;
            }
        }
    }
}
```

8.6.3. POSTORDER TRAVERSAL NON-RECURSIVELY

The post-order traversal algorithm uses a variable PN, which will contain the location of the node currently being scanned. Left (R) denotes the left child of the node R and Right (R) denotes the right child of the node R. Info (R) denotes the information of the node R.

The post-order traversal algorithm is more complicated than the proceeding two algorithms, because here we have to push the information of the node PN to stack in two different situations. These two situations are distinguished between by pushing Left(PN) and - Right(PN) on to stack. That is whenever a negative node sees in the stack; it means that it was a right child of a node. Post-order traversal starts from the ROOT node of the tree (*i.e.*, PN = ROOT).

Step 1: Proceed down to left most node of the tree by pushing the root node and - Right(PN) on the stack.

Step 2: Repeat the Step 1 until there is no left child for the node.

Step 3: Pop and display the positive nodes on the stack.

Step 4: If the stack is empty, go to Step 6

Step 5: If a negative node is popped, then PN = – PN (*i.e.*, to remove the negative sign in the node) and go to Step 1.

Step 6: Exit.

The post-order traversal algorithm can be illustrated with a binary tree in Fig. 8.13.

1. Initialize ROOT Node to PN (*i.e.*, PN = A)

STACK:

2. Push(PN) to the stack

Since(Right(A) is not equal to NULL)

Push(-Right(A)) to the stack

Then If(Left(A) is not equal to NULL)

PN = Left(PN) (*i.e.*, PN=B)

STACK: A, – C

3. Push (B) to the stack

Since (Right(B) is not equal to NULL)

Push(-Right(B)) to the stack

Then If(Left(B) is not equal to NULL)

PN=Left(PN) (*i.e.*, PN =D)

STACK : A, – C, B, –E

4. Push (D) to the stack

Since (Right(D) is not equal to NULL)

Push(-Right(D)) to the stack

Since(Left(D) = NULL)

STACK : A, – C, B, – E, D, –G

Next step is pop and display all the positive elements from the top until a negative element is reached. Here the top element is a negative one, so only the top of the stack is popped (*i.e.*, -G) and assigned to PN. Now PN= – G. Set PN = – PN (*i.e.*, PN = G)

STACK: A, – C, B, – E, D

5. Push(G) to the stack

If(Right(G) = NULL)

Do nothing

If(Left(G) = NULL)

STACK: A, – C, B, – E, D, G

Pop and display all the positive elements from the top of the stack until a negative element is reached. Here the G, D are popped and displayed. – E is popped and assigned it to PN then PN = – PN = E

STACK: A, – C, B,

6. Push(E) to the stack

Since(Right(E) is not equal to NULL)

Push(– Right(E)) to the stack

Since(Left(E) is not equal to NULL)

PN=Left(PN) (*i.e.*, PN=H)

STACK: A, – C, B, E, – I

7. Push(H) to the stack

If(Right(H) = NULL)

Do nothing

If(Left(H) = NULL)

STACK: A, – C, B, E, – I, H

Pop and display H then pop and assign I to PN (*i.e.*, PN = I)

STACK: A, – C, B, E,

8. Push(I) to the stack

If(Right(I) = NULL)

Do nothing

If(Left(I) = NULL)

STACK: A, – C, B, E, I

Pop and display all positive elements of stack from top, until a negative number is reached. Here I, E, B are popped and displayed. And – C is popped and assigned to PN (*i.e.*, PN = C)

STACK: A,

9. Push(C) to the stack

If(Right(C) = NULL)

Do nothing

If(Left(C) = NULL)

PN = Left(C) = F

STACK: A, C

10. Push(F) to the stack

Since(Right(F) is not equal to NULL)

Push(-Right(F))s

Since(Left(F) = NULL)

STACK: A, C, F, – J

Pop the top element and assign it to PN. (*i.e.*, PN = J)

11. Push(J) to the stack

Since(Right(J) = NULL)

Do nothing

Since(Left(J) = NULL)

Pop all positive elements from top, until a negative element is reached. Here all the elements J, F, C, A are popped and displayed. Now the stack is empty and PN = NULL and STOP.

The nodes are displayed in the following order G, D, H, I, E, B, J, F, C, A.

ALGORITHM

An array STACK is used to temporarily store the addresses of the nodes. TOP pointer always points to the top most element of the stack.

1. Initialize TOP = NULL and PN = ROOT
2. Repeat the steps 3 to 6 until (PN = NULL)
3. TOP = TOP+1
4. SATCK(TOP)=PN
5. If (Right(PN) is not equal to NULL)
   (*a*) TOP = TOP+1
   (*b*) STACK(TOP) = – Right(PN)
6. PN = Left(PN)
7. PN = STACK(TOP)
8. TOP = TOP–1
9. Repeat the step 9 until (PN less than or equal to 0)
   (*a*) Display Info(PN)
   (*b*) PN = STACK(TOP)
   (*c*) TOP = TOP=1
10. If(PN < 0)
    (*a*) PN = – PN
    (*b*) Go to step 2
11. Exit

PROGRAM 8.3

```
//FUNCTION TO IMPLEMENT NON RECURSIVE POST ORDER TRAVERSAL
//CODED AND COMPILED IN TURBO C++

void postorder(struct node *p)
{
        struct node *stack[100];
        int top,sig, sign[100];
        top = –1;
        if(p != NULL)
        {
            top++;
            stack[top] = p;
    sign[top]=1;
        if(p->rchild != NULL)
                {
                        top++;
                        stack[top] = p->rchild;
                        sign[top]=–1
```

```
p = p->lchild;
while(top >= 0)
{
        while ( p!= NULL)/* push the left child onto stack*/
        {
                top++;
                stack[top] = p;
                sign[top]=1;
                if(p->rchild != NULL)
                {
                        top++;
                        stack[top] = p->rchild;
                        sign[top]=-1;
                }
                p = p->lchild;
        }

        p = stack[top];
        sig=sign[top];
        top--;

        while((sig > 0) && (top >= -1))
        {
                cout<<" "<<p->info;
                p = stack[top];
                sig=sign[top];
                top--;
        }


        }
    }
}
```

8.7. BINARY SEARCH TREES

A Binary Search Tree is a binary tree, which is either empty or satisfies the following properties :

1. Every node has a value and no two nodes have the same value (*i.e.*, all the values are unique).

2. If there exists a left child or left sub tree then its value is less than the value of the root.

3. The value(s) in the right child or right sub tree is larger than the value of the root node.

All the nodes or sub trees of the left and right children follows above rules. The Fig. 8.14 shows a typical binary search tree. Here the root node information is 50. Note that the right sub tree node's value is greater than 50, and the left sub tree nodes value is less than 50. Again right child node of 25 has large values than 25 and left child node has small values than 25. Similarly right child node of 75 has large values than 75 and left child node has small values that 75 and so on.

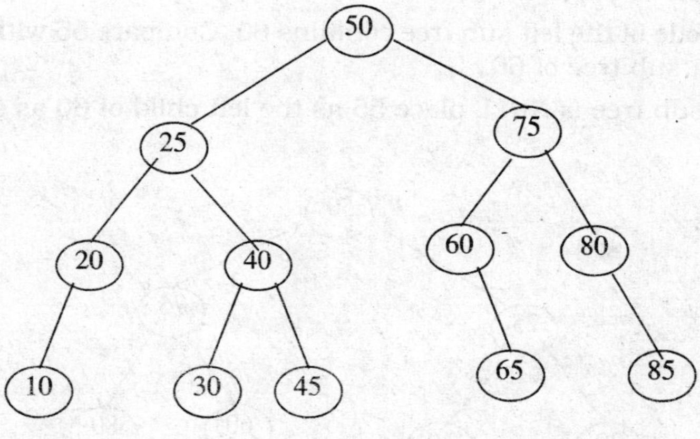

Fig. 8.14

The operations performed on binary tree can also be applied to Binary Search Tree (BST). But in this section we discuss few other primitive operators performed on BST :

1. Inserting a node
2. Searching a node
3. Deleting a node

Another most commonly performed operation on BST is, traversal. The tree traversal algorithm (pre-order, post-order and in-order) are the standard way of traversing a binary search tree.

8.7.1. INSERTING A NODE

A BST is constructed by the repeated insertion of new nodes to the tree structure. Inserting a node in to a tree is achieved by performing two separate operations.

1. The tree must be searched to determine where the node is to be inserted.
2. Then the node is inserted into the tree.

Suppose a "DATA" is the information to be inserted in a BST.

Step 1: Compare DATA with root node information of the tree

(*i*) If (DATA < ROOT → Info)

Proceed to the left child of ROOT

(*ii*) If (DATA > ROOT → Info)

Proceed to the right child of ROOT

Step 2: Repeat the Step 1 until we meet an empty sub tree, where we can insert the DATA in place of the empty sub tree by creating a new node.

Step 3: Exit

For example, consider a binary search tree in Fig. 8.14. Suppose we want to insert a DATA = 55 in to the tree, then following steps one obtained :

1. Compare 55 with root node info (*i.e.*, 50) since 55 > 50 proceed to the right sub tree of 50.

2. The root node of the right sub tree contains 75. Compare 55 with 75. Since 55 < 75 proceed to the left sub tree of 75.

3. The root node of the left sub tree contains 60. Compare 55 with 60. Since 55 < 60 proceed to the right sub tree of 60.

4. Since left sub tree is NULL place 55 as the left child of 60 as shown in Fig. 8.15.

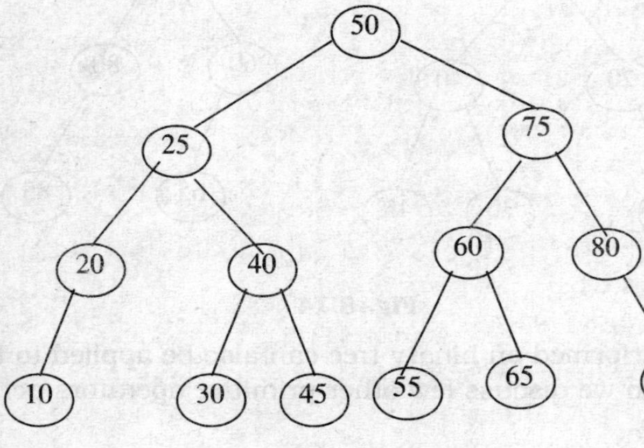

Fig. 8.15

ALGORITHM

NEWNODE is a pointer variable to hold the address of the newly created node. DATA is the information to be pushed.

1. Input the DATA to be pushed and ROOT node of the tree.
2. NEWNODE = Create a New Node.
3. If (ROOT == NULL)
   (*a*) ROOT=NEW NODE
4. Else If (DATA < ROOT → Info)
   (*a*) ROOT = ROOT → Lchild
   (*b*) GoTo Step 4
5. Else If (DATA > ROOT → Info)
   (*a*) ROOT = ROOT → Rchild
   (*b*) GoTo Step 4

6. If (DATA < ROOT → Info)

   (a) ROOT → LChild = NEWNODE

7. Else If (DATA > ROOT → Info)

   (a) ROOT → RChild = NEWNODE

8. Else

   (a) Display ("DUPLICATE NODE")

   (b) EXIT

9. NEW NODE → Info = DATA

10. NEW NODE → LChild = NULL

11. NEW NODE → RChild = NULL

12. EXIT

8.7.2. SEARCHING A NODE

Searching a node was part of the operation performed during insertion. Algorithm to search as element from a binary search tree is given below.

ALGORITHM

1. Input the DATA to be searched and assign the address of the root node to ROOT.

2. If (DATA == ROOT → Info)

   (a) Display "The DATA exist in the tree"

   (b) GoTo Step 6

3. If (ROOT == NULL)

   (a) Display "The DATA does not exist"

   (b) GoTo Step 6

4. If(DATA > ROOT→Info)

   (a) ROOT = ROOT→RChild

   (b) GoTo Step 2

5. If(DATA < ROOT→Info)

   (a) ROOT = ROOT→Lchild

   (b) GoTo Step 2

6. Exit

Suppose a binary search tree contains *n* data items, A1, A2, A3..........A*n*. There are *n*! permutations of the *n* items. The average depth of the n! tree is approximately C log 2 *n*, where C=1.4. The average running time *f*(*n*) to search for an item in a binary tree with *n* elements is proportional to $Log_2\ n$, that is

$$f(n) = O(Log_2\ n)$$

8.7.3. DELETING A NODE

This section gives an algorithm to delete a DATA of information from a binary search tree. First search and locate the node to be deleted. Then any one of the following conditions arises :

1. The node to be deleted has no children
2. The node has exactly one child (or sub tress, left or right sub tree)
3. The node has two children (or two sub tress, left and right sub tree)

Suppose the node to be deleted is N. If N has no children then simply delete the node and place its parent node by the NULL pointer.

If N has one child, check whether it is a right or left child. If it is a right child, then find the smallest element from the corresponding right sub tree. Then replace the smallest node information with the deleted node. If N has a left child, find the largest element from the corresponding left sub tree. Then replace the largest node information with the deleted node.

The same process is repeated if N has two children, *i.e.*, left and right child. Randomly select a child and find the small/large node and replace it with deleted node. NOTE that the tree that we get after deleting a node should also be a binary search tree.

Deleting a node can be illustrated with an example. Consider a binary search tree in Fig. 8.15. If we want to delete 75 from the tree, following steps are obtained :

Step 1: Assign the data to be deleted in DATA and NODE = ROOT.

Step 2: Compare the DATA with ROOT node, *i.e.*, NODE, information of the tree.

Since (50 < 75)

NODE = NODE → RChild

Step 3: Compare DATA with NODE. Since (75 = 75) searching successful. Now we have located the data to be deleted, and delete the DATA. (See Fig. 8.16)

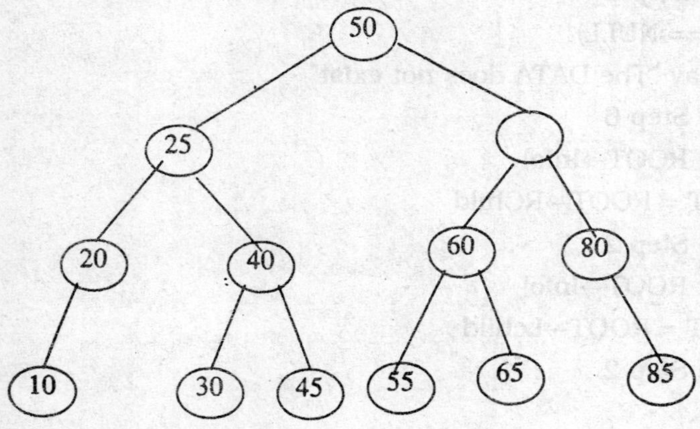

Fig. 8.16

Step 4: Since NODE (*i.e.*, node where value was 75) has both left and right child choose one. (Say Right Sub Tree) - If right sub tree is opted then we have to find the smallest node. But if left sub tree is opted then we have to find the largest node.

Step 5: Find the smallest element from the right sub tree (*i.e.*, 80) and replace the node with deleted node. (See Fig. 8.17)

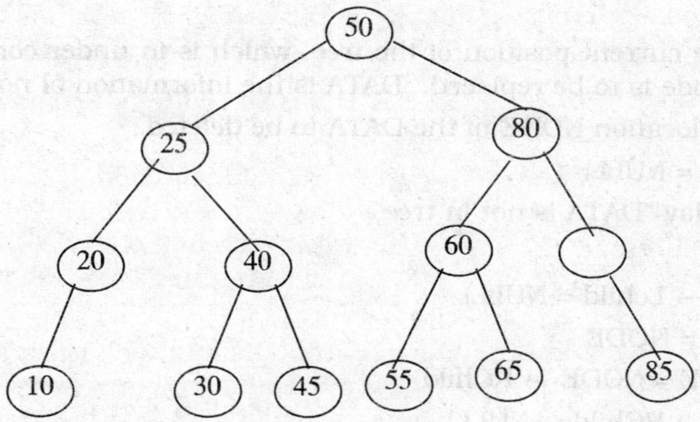

Fig. 8.17

Step 6: Again the (NODE → Rchild is not equal to NULL) find the smallest element from the right sub tree (Which is 85) and replace it with empty node. (See Fig. 8.18)

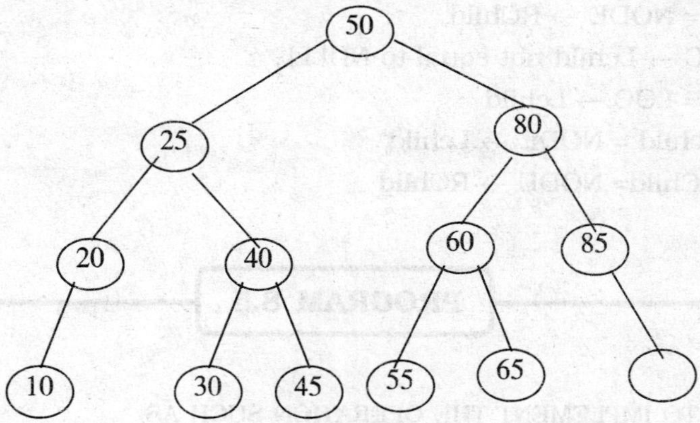

Fig. 8.18

Step 7: Since (NODE→Rchild = NODE→Lchild = NULL) delete the NODE and place NULL in the parent node. (See Fig. 8.19)

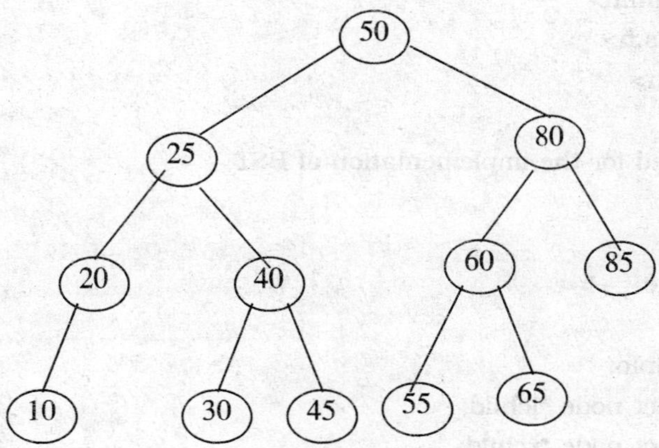

Fig. 8.19

Step 8: Exit.

ALGORITHM

NODE is the current position of the tree, which is in under consideration. LOC is the place where node is to be replaced. DATA is the information of node to be deleted.

1. Find the location NODE of the DATA to be deleted.
2. If (NODE = NULL)
   (*a*) Display "DATA is not in tree"
   (*b*) Exit
3. If(NODE → Lchild = NULL)
   (*a*) LOC = NODE
   (*b*) NODE = NODE → RChild
4. If(NODE → RChild= =NULL)
   (*a*) LOC = NODE
   (*b*) NODE = NODE → LChild
5. If((NODE → Lchild not equal to NULL) && (NODE → Rchild not equal to NULL))
   (*a*) LOC = NODE → RChild
6. While(LOC → Lchild not equal to NULL)
   (*a*) LOC = LOC → Lchild
7. LOC → Lchild = NODE → Lchild
8. LOC → RChild= NODE → RChild
9. Exit

PROGRAM 8.5

```
//PROGRAM TO IMPLEMENT THE OPERATION SUCH AS
//INSERTION, DELETION AND TRAVERSAL IN BINARY SEARCH TREE
//CODED AND COMPILED USING TURBO C++

#include<iostream.h>
#include<process.h>
#include<conio.h>

//Class is created for the implementation of BST
class BST
{
	struct node
	{
		int info;
		struct node *lchild;
		struct node *rchild;
```

```
        };
        typedef struct node *NODE;

        public:
                struct node *root;
                BST()
                {
                        root=NULL;
                }
                //public functions declarations
                void find(int,NODE *,NODE *);
                void case_a(NODE,NODE);
                void case_b(NODE,NODE);
                void case_c(NODE,NODE);
                void insert(int);
                void del(int);
                void preorder(NODE);
                void inorder(NODE);
                void postorder(NODE);
                void display(NODE,int);
};

//Function to find the item form the tree
void BST::find(int item,NODE *par,NODE *loc)
{
        NODE ptr,ptrsave;

        if(root==NULL)  /*tree empty*/
        {
                *loc=NULL;
                *par=NULL;
                return;
        }
        if(item==root->info) /*item is at root*/
        {
                *loc=root;
                *par=NULL;
                return;
        }
        /*Initialize ptr and ptrsave*/
        if(item<root->info)
                ptr=root->lchild;
```

```
    else
            ptr=root->rchild;
    ptrsave=root;

    while(ptr!=NULL)
    {
            if(item==ptr->info)
            {       *loc=ptr;
                    *par=ptrsave;
                    return;
            }
            ptrsave=ptr;
            if(item<ptr->info)
                    ptr=ptr->lchild;
            else
                    ptr=ptr->rchild;
    }/*End of while */
    *loc=NULL;   /*item not found*/
    *par=ptrsave;
}/*End of find()*/

void BST::case_a(NODE par,NODE loc )
{
    if(par==NULL) /*item to be deleted is root node*/
            root=NULL;
    else
            if(loc==par->lchild)
                    par->lchild=NULL;
            else
                    par->rchild=NULL;
}/*End of case_a()*/

void BST::case_b(NODE par,NODE loc)
{
    NODE child;

    /*Initialize child*/
    if(loc->lchild!=NULL) /*item to be deleted has lchild */
            child=loc->lchild;
    else                /*item to be deleted has rchild */
            child=loc->rchild;
```

```
        if(par==NULL )   /*Item to be deleted is root node*/
                root=child;
        else
                if( loc==par->lchild)   /*item is lchild of its parent*/
                        par->lchild=child;
                else                    /*item is rchild of its parent*/
                        par->rchild=child;
}/*End of case_b()*/

void BST::case_c(NODE par,NODE loc)
{
        NODE ptr,ptrsave,suc,parsuc;

        /*Find inorder successor and its parent*/
        ptrsave=loc;
        ptr=loc->rchild;
        while(ptr->lchild!=NULL)
        {
                ptrsave=ptr;
                ptr=ptr->lchild;
        }
        suc=ptr;
        parsuc=ptrsave;

        if(suc->lchild==NULL && suc->rchild==NULL)
                case_a(parsuc,suc);
        else
                case_b(parsuc,suc);

        if(par==NULL) /*if item to be deleted is root node */
                root=suc;
        else
                if(loc==par->lchild)
                        par->lchild=suc;
                else
                        par->rchild=suc;

        suc->lchild=loc->lchild;
        suc->rchild=loc->rchild;
}/*End of case_c()*/

//This function will insert an element to the tree
```

```
void BST::insert(int item)
{       NODE tmp,parent,location;
        find(item,&parent,&location);
        if(location!=NULL)
        {
                cout<<"\nItem already present";
                getch();
                return;
        }
        //creating new node to insert
        tmp=(NODE)new(struct node);
        tmp->info=item;
        tmp->lchild=NULL;
        tmp->rchild=NULL;

        if(parent==NULL)
                root=tmp;
        else
                if(item<parent->info)
                        parent->lchild=tmp;
                else
                        parent->rchild=tmp;
}/*End of insert()*/

//Function to delete a node
void BST::del(int item)
{
        NODE parent,location;
        if(root==NULL)
        {
                cout<<"\nTree is empty";
                getch();
                return;
        }

        find(item,&parent,&location);
        if(location==NULL)
        {
                cout<<"\nItem not present in tree";
                return;
        }
```

```
        if(location->lchild==NULL && location->rchild==NULL)
                case_a(parent,location);
        if(location->lchild!=NULL && location->rchild==NULL)
                case_b(parent,location);
        if(location->lchild==NULL && location->rchild!=NULL)
                case_b(parent,location);
        if(location->lchild!=NULL && location->rchild!=NULL)
                case_c(parent,location);
        delete(location);
}/*End of del()*/

//Function to traverse in a preorder fashion
void BST::preorder(NODE ptr)
{
        if(root==NULL)
        {
                cout<<"\nTree is empty";
                getch();
                return;
        }
        if(ptr!=NULL)
        {
                cout<<"  "<<ptr->info;
                preorder(ptr->lchild);
                preorder(ptr->rchild);
        }
}/*End of preorder()*/

//Function for Inorder traversal
void BST::inorder(NODE ptr)
{
        if(root==NULL)
        {
                cout<<"Tree is empty";
                getch();
                return;
        }
        if(ptr!=NULL)
        {
                inorder(ptr->lchild);
                cout<<"  "<<ptr->info;
                inorder(ptr->rchild);
```

```
        }
}

//This function will travel in a postorder fashion
void BST::postorder(NODE ptr)
{
        if(root==NULL)
        {
                cout<<"\nTree is empty";
                getch();
                return;
        }
        if(ptr!=NULL)
        {
                postorder(ptr->lchild);
                postorder(ptr->rchild);
                cout<<"  "<<ptr->info;
        }
}/*End of postorder()*/

//Function to display all the nodes of the tree
void BST::display(NODE ptr,int level)
{
        int i;
        if ( ptr!=NULL )
        {
                display(ptr->rchild, level+1);
                cout<<"\n";
                for (i = 0; i < level; i++)
                        cout<<"    ";
                cout<<ptr->info;
                display(ptr->lchild, level+1);
        }/*End of if*/
}/*End of display()*/

void main()
{
        int choice,num;
        BST bo;
        while(1)
        {
                clrscr();
```

```
//Menu options
cout<<"\n1.Insert\n";
cout<<"2.Delete\n";
cout<<"3.Inorder Traversal\n";
cout<<"4.Preorder Traversal\n";
cout<<"5.Postorder Traversal\n";
cout<<"6.Display\n";
cout<<"7.Quit\n";
cout<<"\nEnter your choice : ";
cin>>choice;

switch(choice)
{
 case 1:
        cout<<"\nEnter the number to be inserted : ";
        cin>>num;
        bo.insert(num);
        break;
 case 2:
        cout<<"\nEnter the number to be deleted : ";
        cin>>num;
        bo.del(num);
        break;
 case 3:
        bo.inorder(bo.root);
        getch();
        break;
 case 4:
        bo.preorder(bo.root);
        getch();
        break;
 case 5:
        bo.postorder(bo.root);
        getch();
        break;
 case 6:
        bo.display(bo.root,1);
        getch();
        break;
 case 7:
```

```
            cout<<"\nWrong choice\n";
            getch();
        }/*End of switch */
    }/*End of while */
}/*End of main()*/
```

8.8. THREADED BINARY TREE

Traversing a binary tree is a common operation and it would be helpful to find more efficient method for implementing the traversal. Moreover, half of the entries in the Lchild and Rchild field will contain NULL pointer. These fields may be used more efficiently by replacing the NULL entries by special pointers which points to nodes higher in the tree. Such types of special pointers are called threads and binary tree with such pointers are called threaded binary tree.

Fig. 8.20 shows the threaded binary tree with threads replacing NULL pointer of binary tree in Fig. 8.13. The threads are drawn with dotted lines to differentiate then from tree pointers.

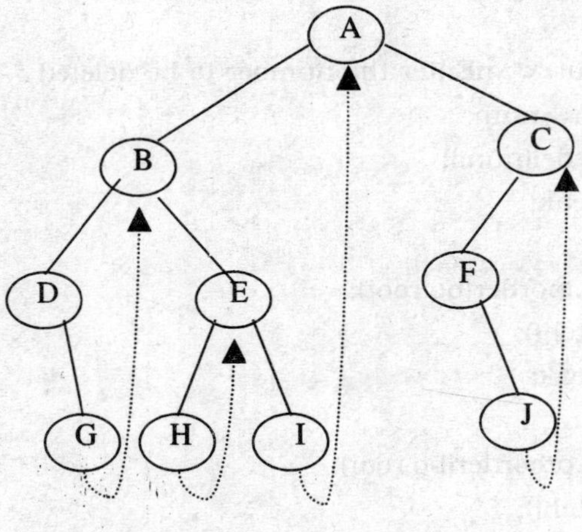

Fig. 8.20. Threaded binary tree

There are many ways to thread a binary tree. Right most nodes in the threaded binary tree have a NULL right pointer (*i.e.*, in-order successor). Such trees are called right in threaded binary trees. A left in threaded binary tree may be defined similarly as one in which each NULL left pointer is altered to contain a thread (*i.e.*, in-order predecessor). An in-threaded binary tree may be defined as a binary tree that is both left-in-threaded and right-in-threaded.

We can implement a right in threaded binary tree using arrays by distinguishing threads from ordinary pointers. Threads are denoted by negative numbers, when ordinary pointers are denoted by positive integers. The array representation of the right in thread binary tree in Fig.8.20 is shown below table (Fig. 8.21)

	Info	*Lchild*	*Rchild*
A[0]	A	1	2
A[1]	B	3	4
A[2]	C	5	
A[3]	D		8
A[4]	E	9	10
A[5]	F		12
A[6]			
A[7]			
A[8]	G		– 1
A[9]	H		– 4
A[10]	I		– 0
A[11]			
A[12]	J		– 2
A[13]			
A[14]			

Fig. 8.21

To implement a right-in-threaded binary tree using dynamic memory allocation, an extra 1 bit logical field, rthread, is used to distinguish threads from ordinary pointers. If a right pointer of a node is threaded, then the rthread = TRUE otherwise FALSE. Following program will construct a right-in-threaded binary tree and will traverse in-order fashion.

8.9. EXPRESSION TREE

An ordered tree may be used to represent a general expressions, is called expression tree. Nodes in one expression tree contain operators and operands.

For example: The expression, f(A,B,C) * (Sin(D) – Log(E * F!)), is represented in Fig. 8.22.

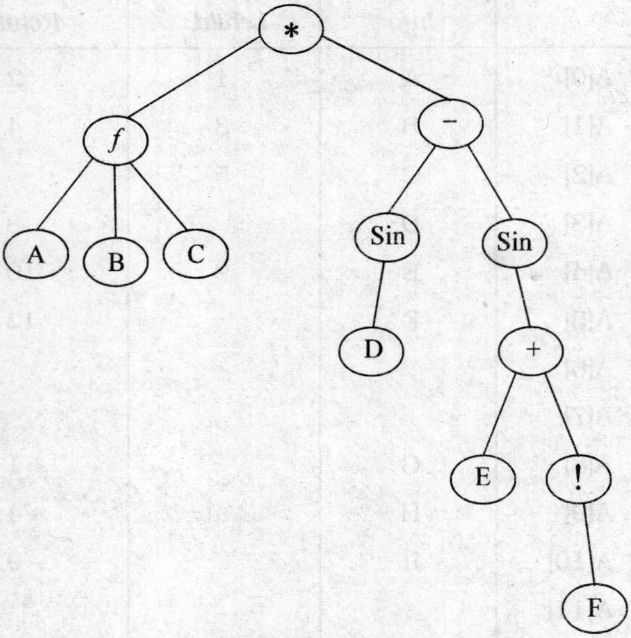

Fig. 8.22

A binary tree is used to represent a binary expression called binary expression tree. Root node of the binary expressions trees contains operator and two children node contain its operand.

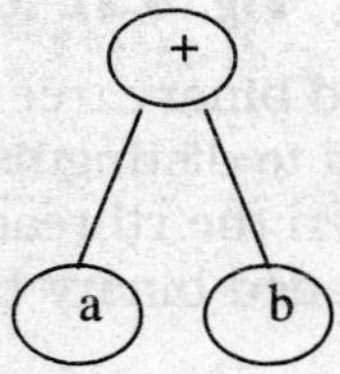

Fig. 8.23

For example, a+b can be represented in Fig. 8.23. And the expression E = (a + b) * (c / (d – e)))with more operators and operands) can be represented in binary expression tree as follows :

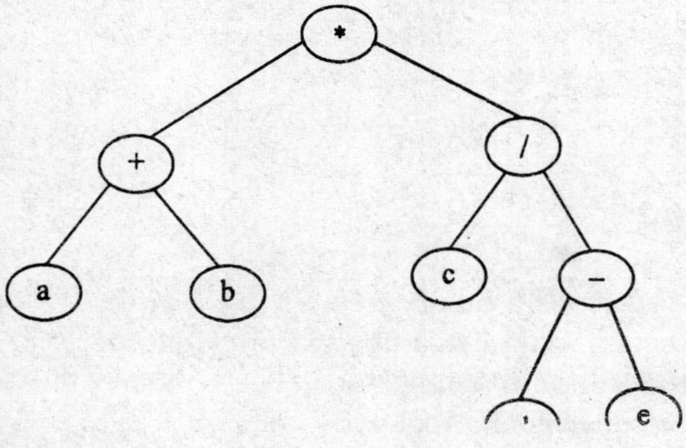

Expression tree can be evaluated, if its operands are numerical constants. Following section will explain a C/C++ program that accepts a pointer of an expression tree and returns the value of the expression represented by the tree.

8.10. DECISION TREE

A decision tree is a binary tree, where sorting of elements is done by only comparisons. That is a decision tree can be applied to any sorting algorithms that sorts by using comparisons. (The sorting techniques were discussed in chapter 6). The external nodes (or leafs) correspond to the $n!$ ways that n items can appear, because we are trying to sort n items $a1$, $a2$, ..., an. And internal nodes correspond to the different comparison that may take place during the execution. The decision tree is Fig. 8.25 represents an algorithm that sorts the tree elements x, y and z. The first comparison prefers at the root node between x and y and goes down.

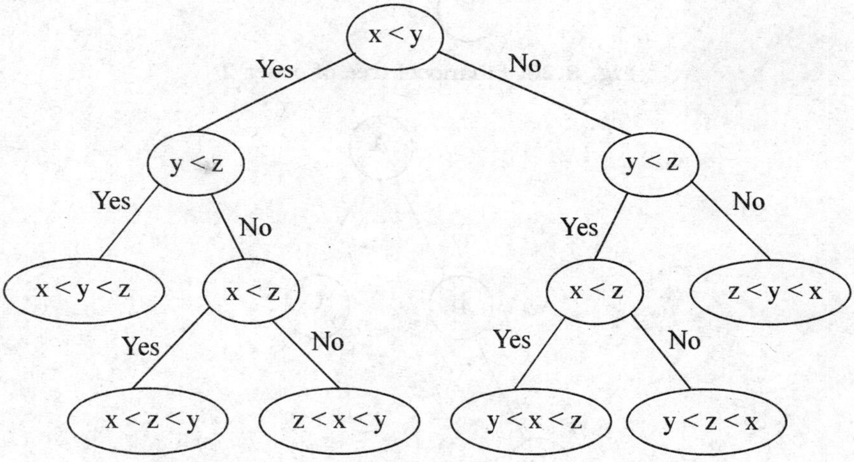

Fig. 8.25

The sorting techniques discussed in chapter 6 takes minimum of O(n log n) to sort an array of n elements. The objective of decision tree is to develop an algorithm, which can sort n items of the order less than O(n Log n).

The decision tree is more suitable when extremely small input size is to be sorted. The number at comparisons in the worst case is equal to the depth of the deepest leaf (*i.e.*, the largest path). In Fig. 8.25, maximum of three comparisons used, which is a worst case *i.e.*, O(n) and it is less than O(n log n). Moreover, in the average case, the average number(s) of comparisons are sufficient to sort the elements, which is equal to the average external path length of the tree (*i.e.*, average depth of the leaves).

8.11. FIBANOCCI TREE

Fibanocci tree of order n is a binary tree, which build by the following restriction :

1. If $n = 0$, then the empty tree is a fibanocci tree of order 0.
2. If $n = 1$, then the tree with a single node is a fibanocci tree of order 1.
3. If $n > 1$, the tree consists of a root with a left subtree of order $n - 1$ and right sub tree of order $n - 2$.

Here are some exmples of fibanocci tree

Fig. 8.26. Fibanocci tree of order 0

Fig. 8.27. Fibanocci tree of order 1

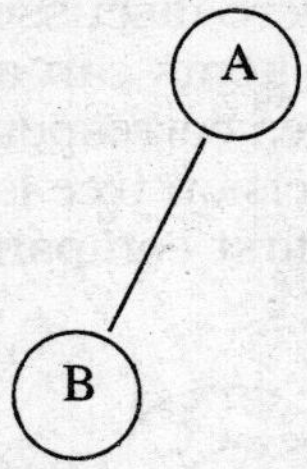

Fig. 8.28. Fibanocci tree of order 2

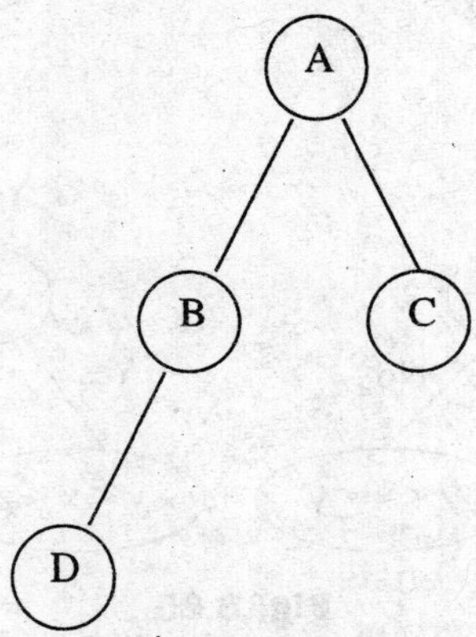

Fig. 8.29. Fibanocci tree of order 3

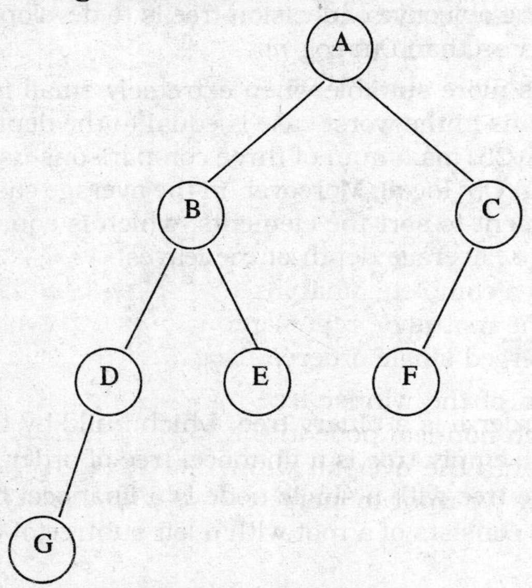

Fig. 8.30. Fibanocci tree of order 4

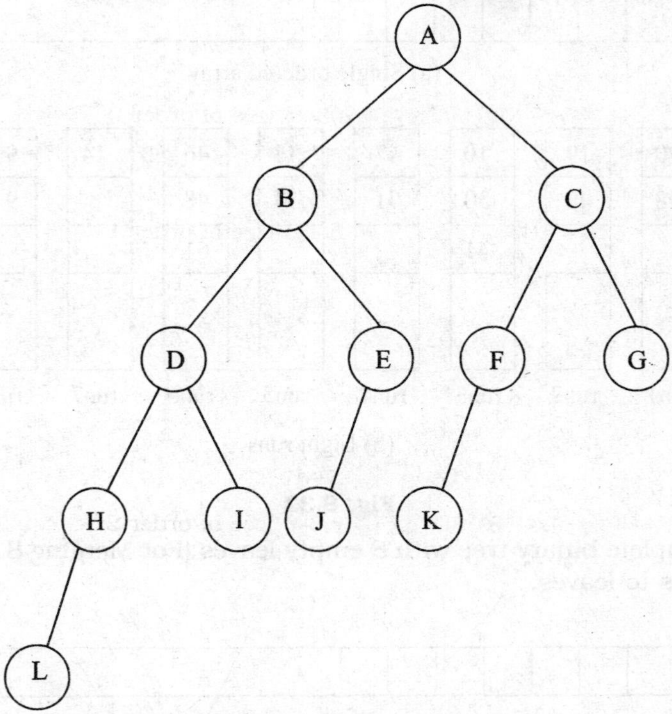

Fig 8.31. Fibanocci tree of order 5

8.12. SELECTION TREES

Suppose we have *k* ordered set of arrays, called runs, which are to be merged into a single ordered array. Each run consists of some elements and is in ascending order. The merging task can be accomplished by repeatedly outputting the smallest element from the *k* runs. The most general way to merge *k* runs is to make (*k* – 1) comparisons to output the smallest element, (from the *k* runs) in every iteration. By using the data structure selection tree, we can reduce the number of comparisons needed to find the next smallest element. There are two kinds of selection trees :

(*a*) Winner trees

(*b*) Loser trees

8.12.1. WINNER TREES

A Winner Tree is a complete binary tree in which each node represents the smallest of its children. Thus the root node represents the smallest node in the tree, which is the next element in the merged single ordered array.

The construction of the winner tree may be compared to the playing of a tennis tournament. Then, each non-leaf node in the tree represents the winner of a tournament and root node represents the over all winner. Winner tree can be illustrated with the following example. Here we want to merge 8 runs into single sorted array..

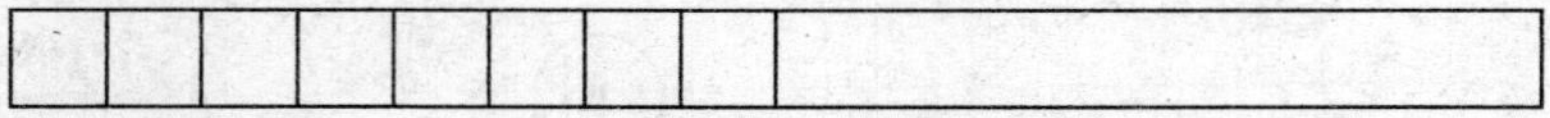

(a) Single ordered array

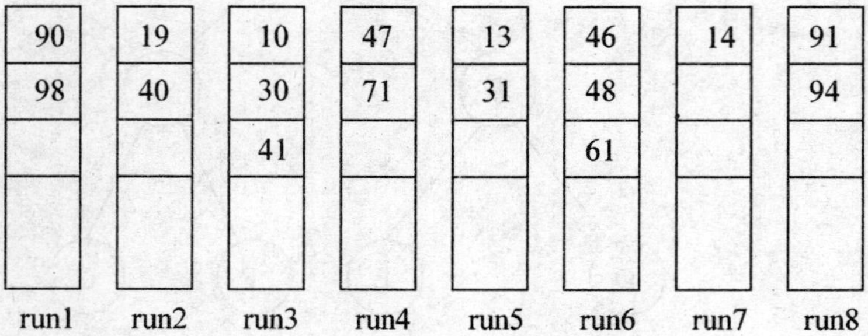

(b) Eight runs

Fig. 8.32

Create a complete binary tree with 8 empty leaves (For Merging 8 run). Place the 1st element in the runs to leaves.

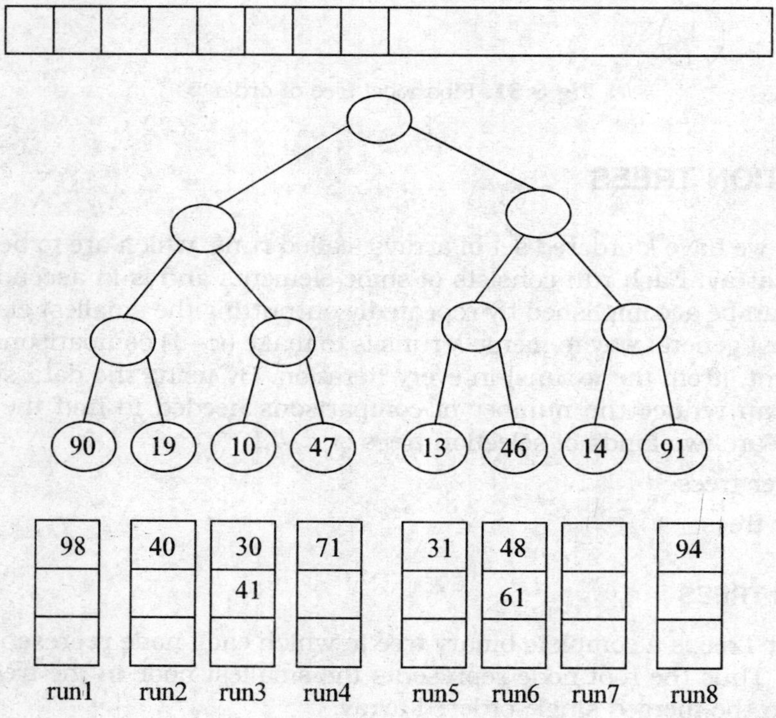

Fig. 8.33

Each of the empty nodes represents the smallest elements of its children. That is, since (19 < 90), place 19 at the father node etc.

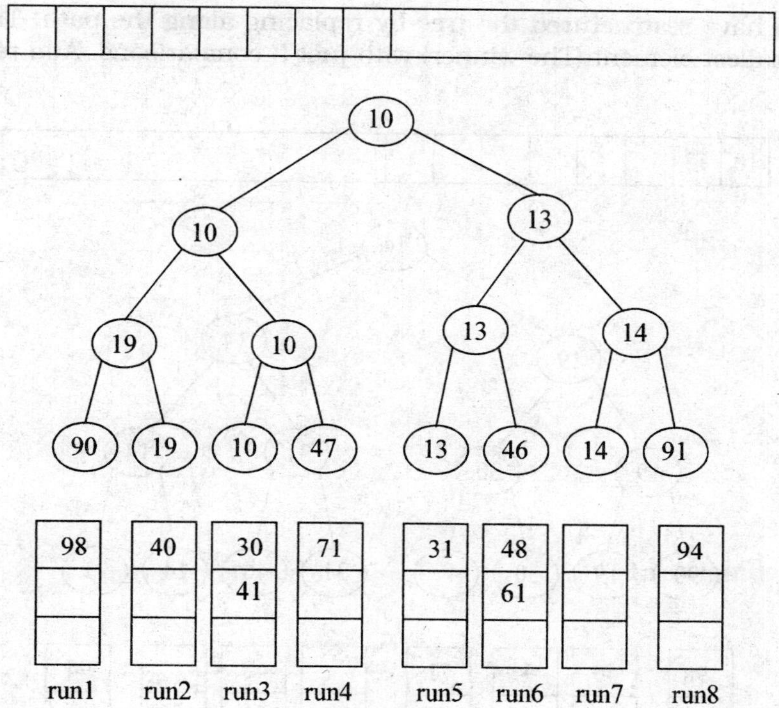

Fig. 8.34

Place 10, the root node, into the single ordered array. And replace the leaf node 10 with the next element in the corresponding run (*i.e.*, 30).

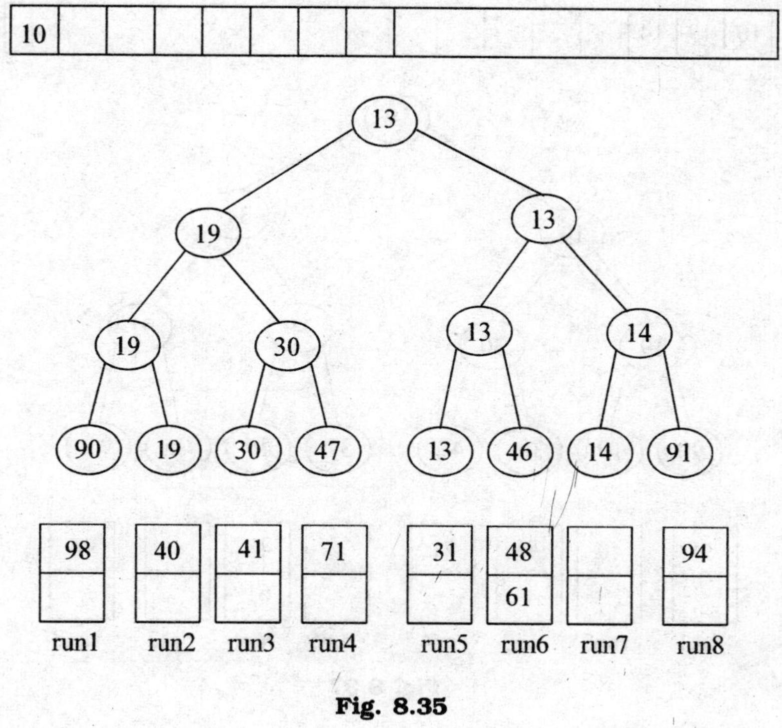

Fig. 8.35

Here we have restructured the tree by replacing along the path. That is we have located the smallest element (The winner) with just 3 comparisons. And repeat the process.

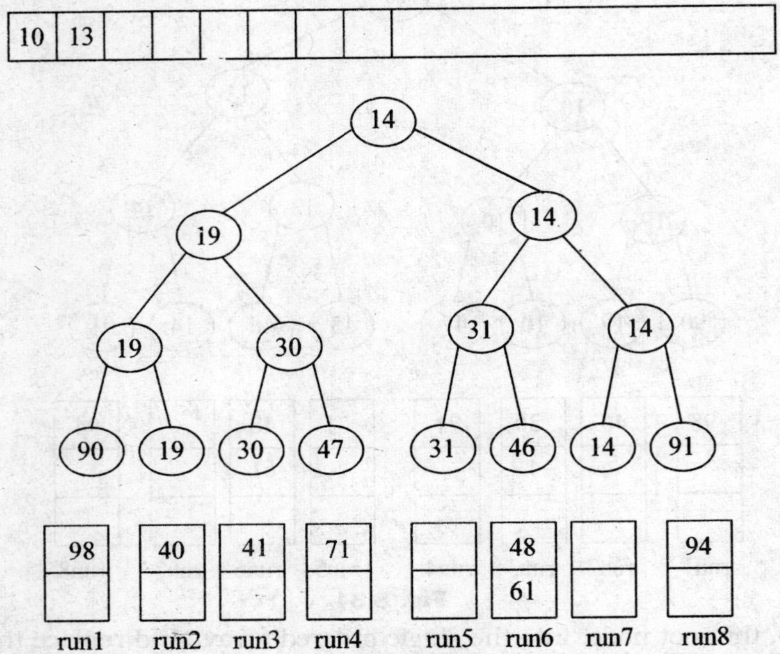

Fig. 8.36

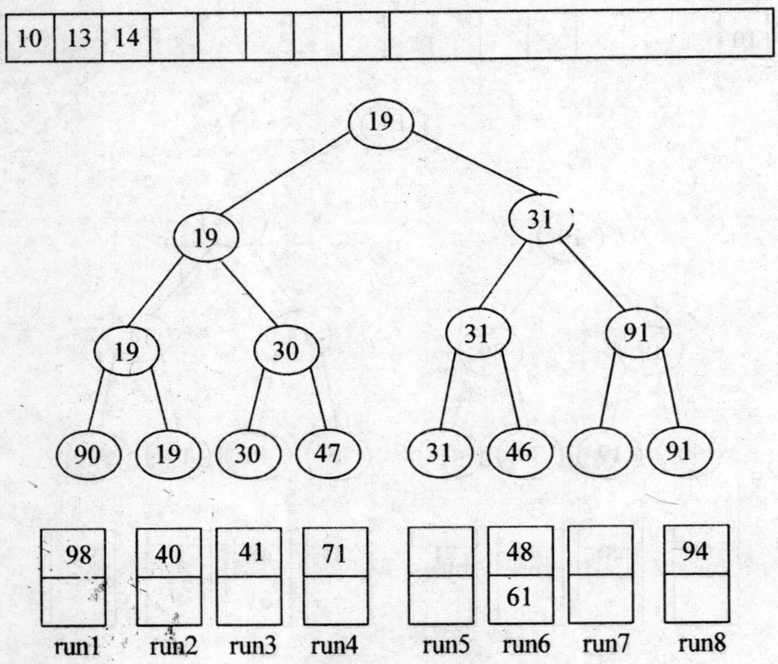

Fig. 8.37

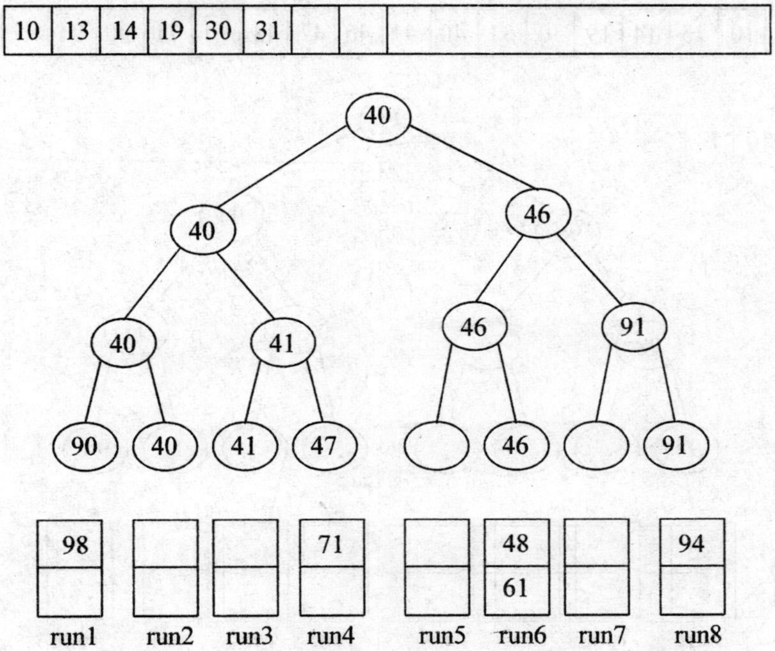

Fig. 8.38

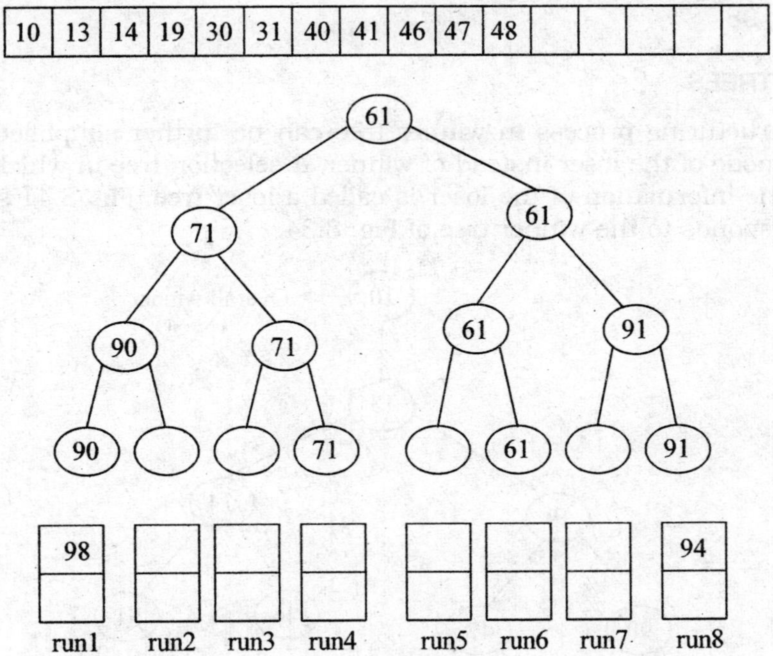

Fig. 8.39

10	13	14	19	30	31	40	41	46	47	48	61	71	90	91	

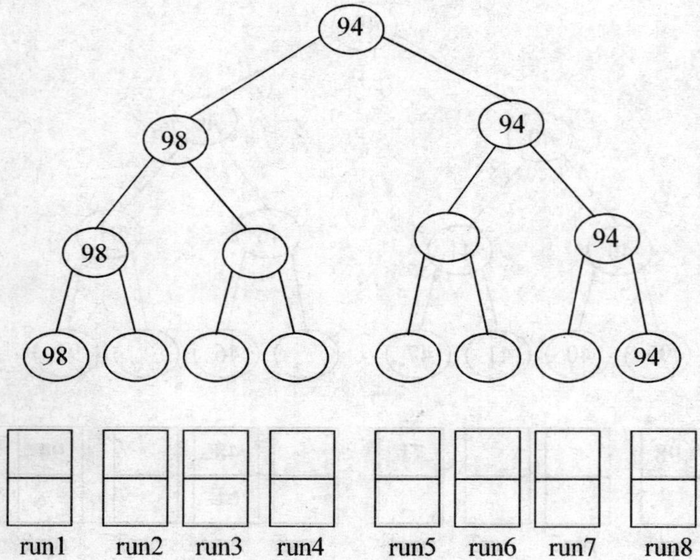

Fig. 8.40

The final merged sorted array of 8 runs is, 10, 13, 14, 19, 30, 31, 40, 41, 46, 47, 48, 61, 71, 90, 94, 98.

8.12.2. LOSER TREES

The restructuring process in winner tree can be further simplified by placing in each non-leaf node of the loser instead of winner. A selection tree in which each non-leaf node retains the information of the loser is called a loser tree. Fig. 8.41 shows the loser tree that corresponds to the winner tree of Fig. 8.34.

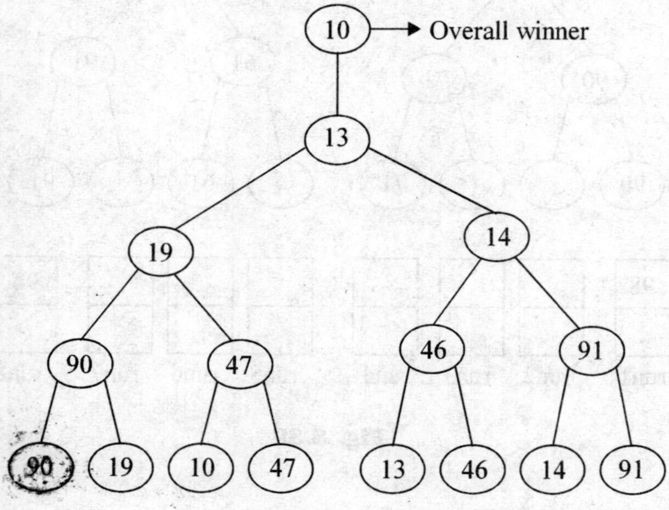

Fig. 8.41

8.13. BALANCED BINARY TREES

A balanced binary tree is one in which the largest path through the left sub tree is the same length as the largest path of the right sub tree, *i.e.*, from root to leaf. Searching time is very less in balanced binary trees compared to unbalanced binary tree. *i.e.*, balanced trees are used to maximize the efficiency of the operations on the tree. There are two types of balanced trees :

1. Height Balanced Trees
2. Weight Balanced Trees

8.13.1. HEIGHT BALANCED TREES

In height balanced trees balancing the height is the important factor. There are two main approaches, which may be used to balance (or decrease) the depth of a binary tree :

(*a*) Insert a number of elements into a binary tree in the usual way, using the algorithm given in the previous section (*i.e.*, Binary search Tree insertion). After inserting the elements, copy the tree into another binary tree in such a way that the tree is balanced. This method is efficient if the data(s) are continually added to the tree.

(*b*) Another popular algorithm for constructing a height balanced binary tree is the AVL tree, which is discussed in the next section.

8.13.2. WEIGHT BALANCED TREE

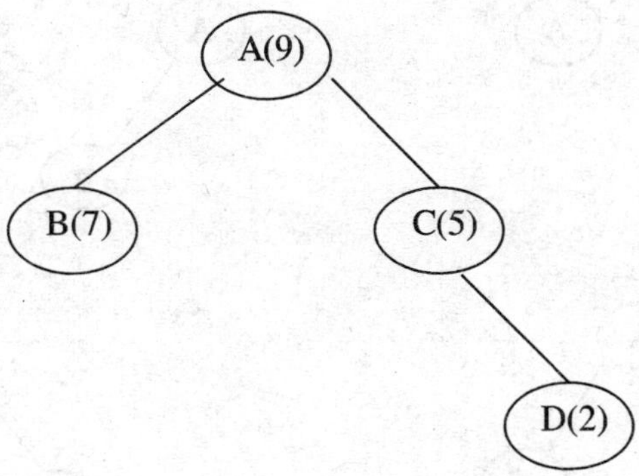

Fig. 8.42

A weight-balanced tree is a balanced binary tree in which additional weight field is also there. The nodes of a weight-balanced tree contain four fields :

(*i*) Data Element

(*ii*) Left Pointer

(*iii*) Right Pointer

(*iv*) A probability or weight field

The data element, left and right pointer fields are save as that in any other tree node. The probability field is a specially added field for a weight-balanced tree. This field holds the probability of the node being accessed again, that is the number of times the node has been previously searched for.

When the tree is created, the nodes with the highest probability of access are placed at the top. That is the nodes that are most likely to be accessed have the lowest search time. And the tree is balanced if the weights in the right and left sub trees are as equal as possible. The average length of search in a weighted tree is equal to the sum of the probability and the depth for every node in the tree.

The root node contain highest weighted node of the tree or sub tree. The left sub tree contains nodes where data values are less than the current root node, and the right sub tree contain the nodes that have data values greater than the current root node.

8.14. AVL TREES

This algorithm was developed in 1962 by two Russian Mathematicians, G.M. Adel'son Vel'sky and E.M. Landis; here the tree is called AVL Tree. An AVL tree is a binary tree in which the left and right sub tree of any node may differ in height by at most 1, and in which both the sub trees are themselves AVL Trees. Each node in the AVL Tree possesses any one of the following properties :

(*a*) A node is called left heavy, if the largest path in its left sub tree is one level larger than the largest path of its right sub tree.

(*b*) A node is called right heavy, if the largest path in its right sub tree is one level larger than the largest path of its left sub tree.

(*c*) The node is called balanced, if the largest paths in both the right and left sub trees are equal. Fig. 8.37 shows some example for AVL trees.

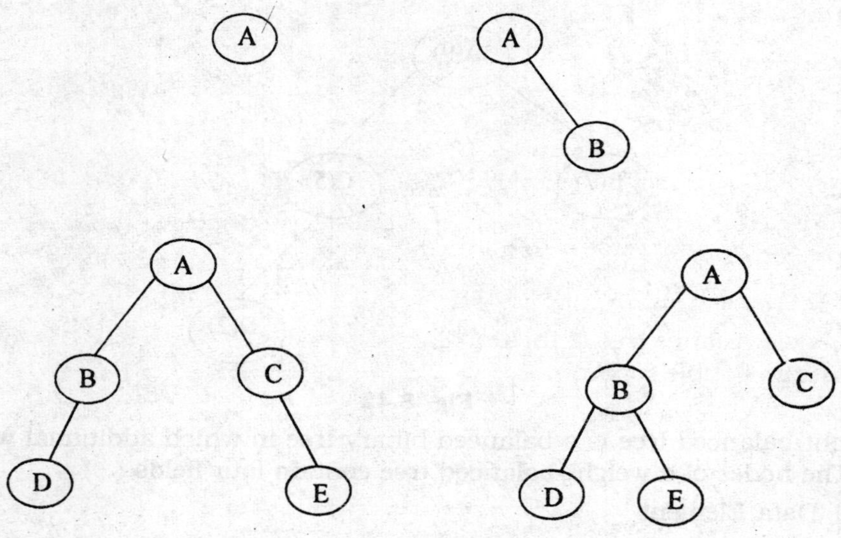

Fig. 8.43. AVL tree

The construction of an AVL Tree is same as that of an ordinary binary tree except that after the addition of each new node, a check must be made to ensure that the AVL balance conditions have not been violated. If the new node causes an imbalance in the tree, some rearrangement of the tree's nodes must be done. Following algorithm will insert a new node in an AVL Tree :

ALGORITHM

1. Insert the node in the same way as in an ordinary binary tree.
2. Trace a path from the new nodes, back towards the root for checking the height difference of the two sub trees of each node along the way.
3. Consider the node with the imbalance and the two nodes on the layers immediately below.
4. If these three nodes lie in a straight line, apply a *single rotation* to correct the imbalance.
5. If these three nodes lie in a dogleg pattern (*i.e.*, there is a bend in the path) apply a *double rotation* to correct the imbalance.
6. Exit.

The above algorithm will be illustrated with an example shown in Fig. 8.44, which is an unbalance tree. We have to apply the rotation to the nodes 40, 50 and 60 so that a balance tree is generated. Since the three nodes are lying in a straight line, single rotation is applied to restore the balance.

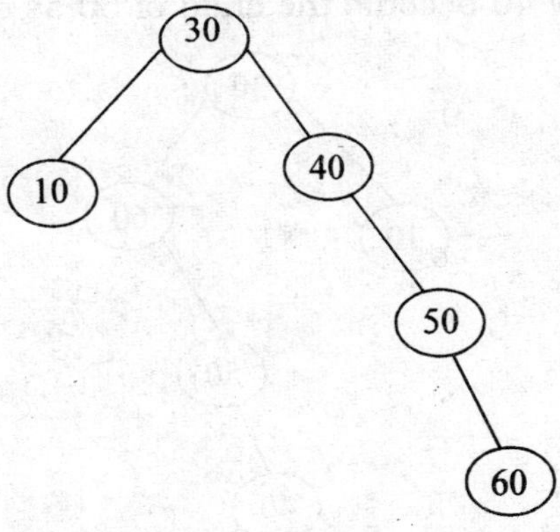

Fig. 8.44

Fig. 8.45 is a balance tree of the unbalanced tree in Fig. 8.44. Consider a tree in Fig 8.46 to explain the double rotation.

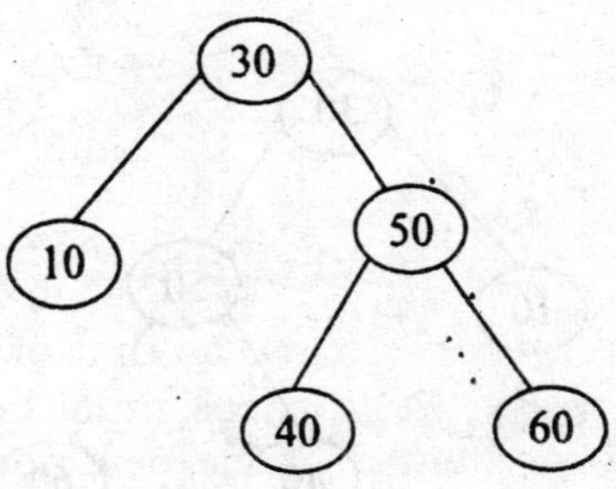

Fig. 8.45

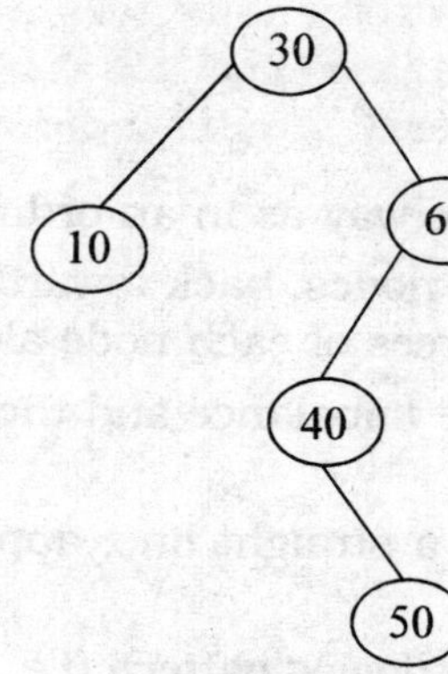

Fig. 8.46

While tracing the path, first imbalance is detected at node 60. We restrict our attention to this node and the two nodes immediately below it (40 and 50). These three nodes form a dogleg pattern. That is there is bend in the path. Therefore we apply double rotation to correct the balance. A double rotation, as its name implies, consists of two single rotations, which are in opposite direction. The first rotation occurs on the two layers (or levels) below the node where the imbalance is found (*i.e.*, 40 and 50). Rotate the node 50 up by replacing 40, and now 40 become the child of 50 as shown in Fig. 8.47.

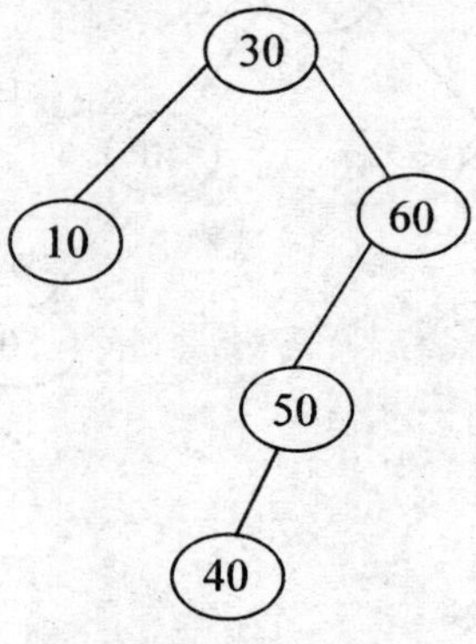

Fig. 8.47

Apply the second rotation, which involves the nodes 60, 50 and 40. Since these three nodes are lying in a straight line, apply the single rotation to restore the balance, by replacing 60 by 50 and placing 60 as the right child of 50 as shown in Fig. 8.48.

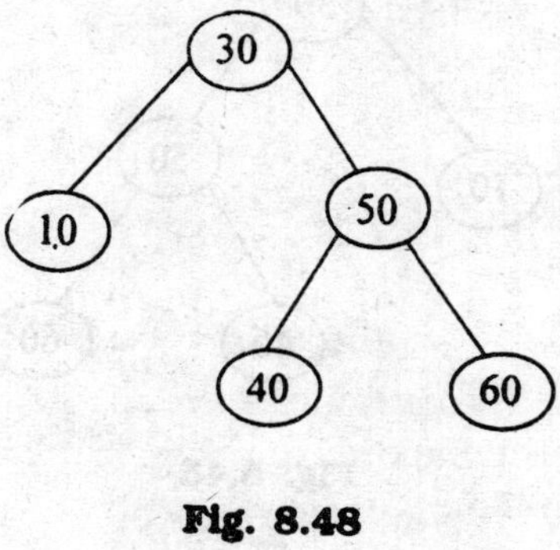

Fig. 8.48

Balanced binary tree is a very useful data structure for searching the element with less time. An unbalanced binary tree takes O(*n*) time to search an element from the tree, in the worst case. But the balanced binary tree takes only O(Log *n*) time complexity in the worst case.

8.15. M-WAY SEARCH TREES

Trees having (m–1) keys and *m* children are called *m*-way search trees. A binary tree is a 2-way tree. It means that it has $m - 1 = 2 - 1 = 1$ key (here $m = 2$) in every node and it can have maximum of two children. A binary tree is also called an *m*-way tree of order 2.

Similarly an *m*-way tree of order 3 is a tree in which key values could be either 1 or 2 (*i.e.*, inside every node and it can have maximum of two children). For example an *m*-way tree at order (degree) 4 is shown in Fig. 8.49.

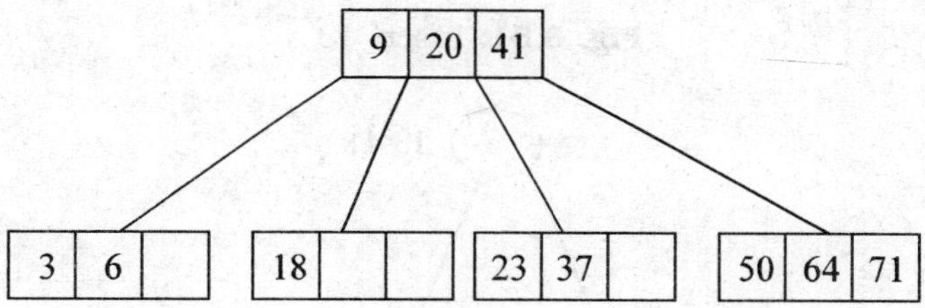

Fig. 8.49

8.16. 2-3 TREES

Every node in the 2-3 trees has two or three children. A 2-3 tree is a tree in which leaf nodes are the only nodes that contains data values. All non-leaf nodes contain two values of the sub trees. All the leaf nodes have the same path length from the root node. Fig. 8.50 show a typical 2-3 tree.

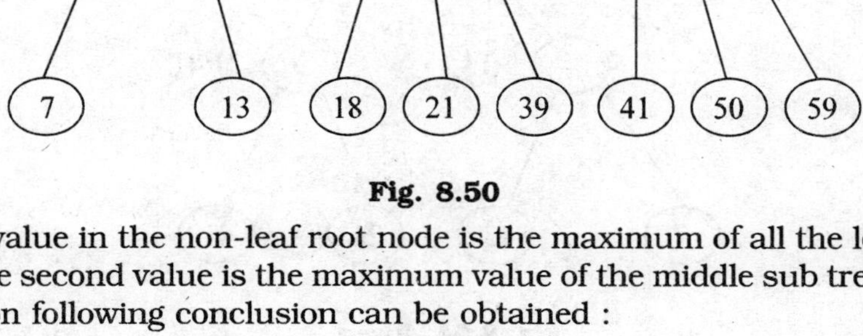

Fig. 8.50

The first value in the non-leaf root node is the maximum of all the leaf values in the left sub tree. The second value is the maximum value of the middle sub tree. With this root node information following conclusion can be obtained :

1. Every leaf node in the left sub tree of any non-leaf node is equal to or less than the first value.

2. Every leaf node in the middle sub tree is less than or equal to the second value and greater than the first value.

3. Every leaf node in the right sub tree is greater than the second value

Following figures will illustrate the construction (or insertion) of the 2-3 trees :

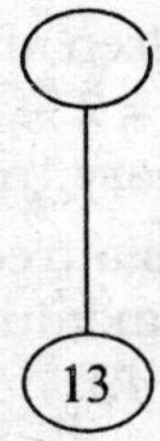

Fig. 8.51. Insert 13

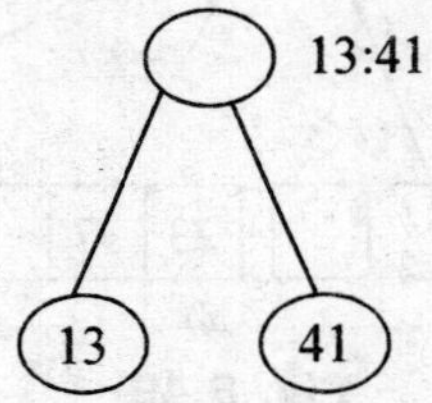

Fig. 8.52. Insert 41

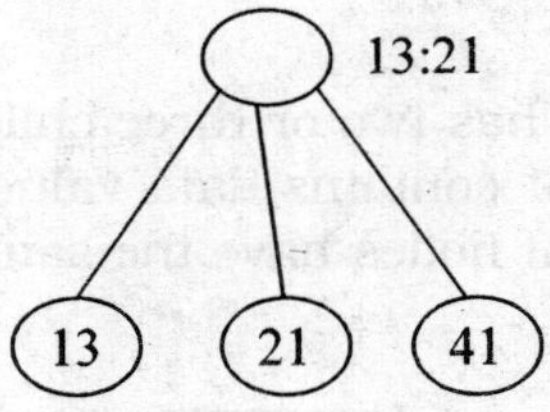

Fig. 8.53. Insert 21

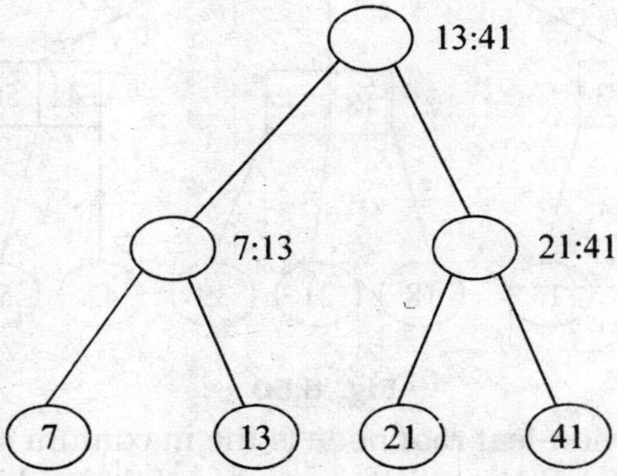

Fig. 8.54. Insert 7

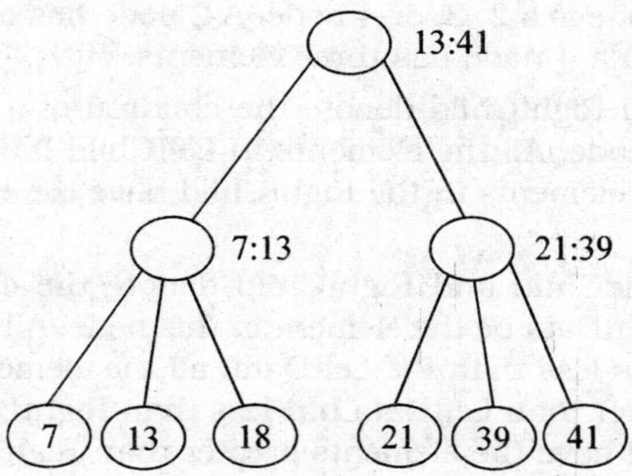

Fig. 8.55. Insert 18, 39

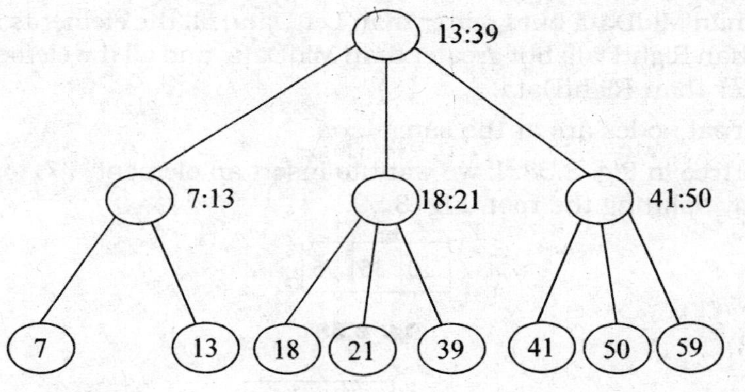

Fig. 8.56. Insert 50, 59

8.17. 2-3-4 TREES

A 2-3-4 tree is an extension of a 2-3 tree. Every node in the 2-3-4 trees can have maximum of 4 children. A typical 2-3-4 tree is shown in Fig. 8.57.

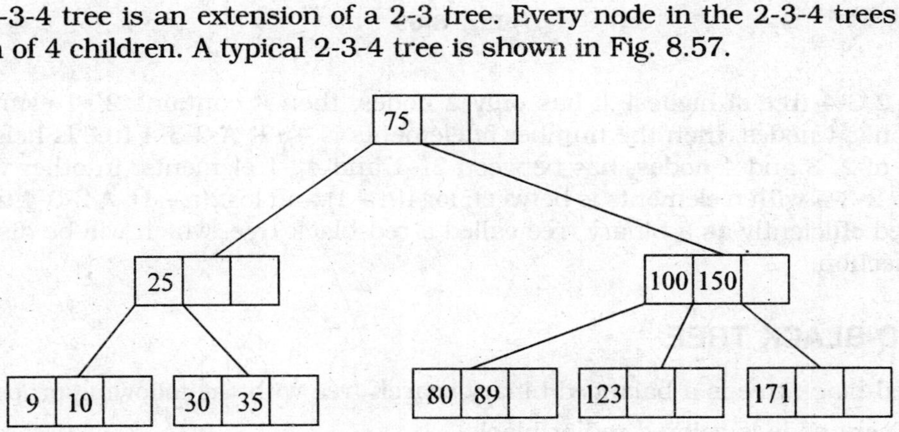

Fig. 8.57

A 2-3-4 tree is a search tree that is either empty or satisfies the following properties.

1. Every internal node is a 2, 3, or 4 node. A 2 node has one element, a 3 node has two elements and a 4 node has three elements.
2. Let LeftChild and RightChild denote the children of a 2 node and Data be the element in this node. All the elements in LeftChild have the elements less than the data, and all elements in the RightChild have the elements greater than the Data.
3. Let LeftChild, MidChild and RightChild denote the children of a 3 node and LeftData and RightData be the element in this node. All the elements in LeftChild have the elements less than the LeftData, all the elements in the MidChild have the element greater than LeftData but less than RightData, and all the elements in the RightChild have the elements greater than Right Data.
4. Let LeftChild, LeftMidChild, RightMidChild, and RightChild denote the children of a 4 node. Let LeftData, MidData and RightData be the three elements in this node. Then LeftData is less than MidData and it is less than RightData. All the elements in the LeftChild is less than LeftData, all the elements in the Left MidChild is less than MidData but greater than LeftData, all the elements in RightMidChild is less than RightData but greater than MidData, and all the elements in RightChild is greater than RightData.
5. All external nodes are at the same level.

Consider a tree in Fig. 8.58. If we want to insert an element, 77, top-down insertion method is used by splitting the root, Fig. 8.59.

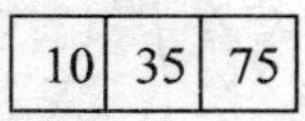

Fig. 8.58

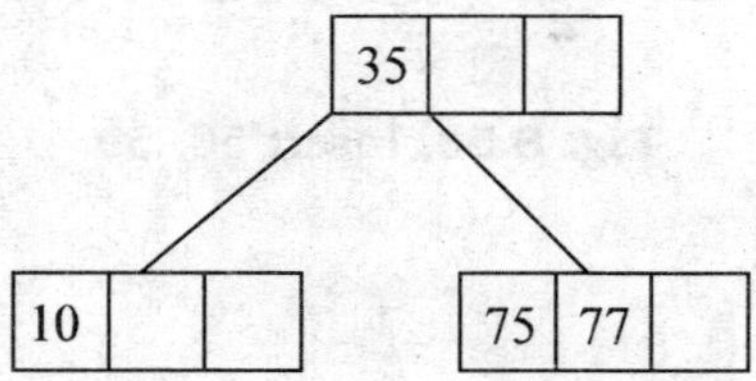

Fig. 8.59

If a 2-3-4 tree of highest h has only 2 nodes, then it contains 2_h-1 elements. If it contains only 4 nodes, then the number of elements is 4_h-1. A 2-3-4 tree is height h with a mixture of 2, 3 and 4 nodes, has between 2_h-1 and 4_h-1 elements. In other words, the height of a 2-3-4 with n elements is between log4(n + 1) and log2(n + 1). A 2-3-4 tree can be represented efficiently as a binary tree called a red-black tree, which will be discussed in the next section.

8.18. RED-BLACK TREE

A red-black tree is a balanced binary search tree with the following properties :

1. Every node is colored red or black.

2. Every leaf is a NULL node, and is colored black.
3. If a node is red, then both its children are black.
4. Every simple path from a node to a descendant leaf contains the same number of black nodes.

The red-black tree algorithm is a method for balancing trees. The name derives from the fact that each node is colored red or black, and the color of the node is instrumental in determining the balance of the tree. During insert and delete operations, nodes may be rotated to maintain tree balance. Both average and worst-case search time is O(log *n*).

We classify red-black trees according to the order *n*, the number of internal nodes. In the Fig. 8.60, *n* = 6. Among all red-black trees of height 4, this is one with the minimum number of nodes. A red-black tree with *n* nodes has height at least O(log *n*) and at most 2O(log *n* + 1).

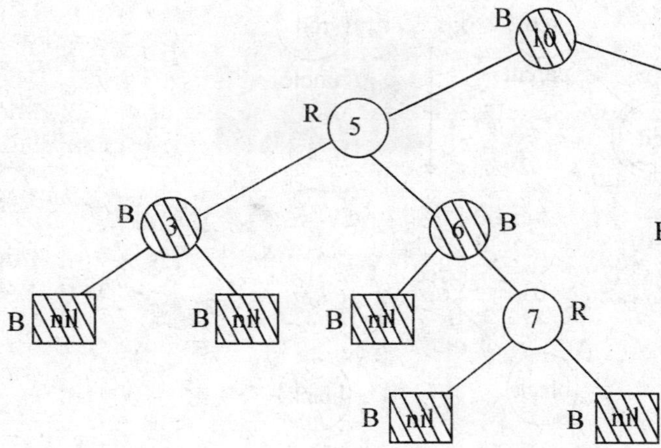

Fig. 8.60

To insert a node, we search the tree for an insertion point, and add the node to the tree. A new node replaces an existing NULL node at the bottom of the tree, and has two NULL nodes as children. In the implementation, a NULL node is simply a pointer to a common *sentinel* node that is colored black. After insertion, the new node is colored red. Then the parent of the node is examined to determine if the red-black tree properties have been violated. If necessary, we recolor the node and do rotations to balance the tree.

By inserting a red node with two NULL children, we have preserved black-height property (property 4). However, property 3 may be violated. This property states that both children of a red node must be black. Although both children of the new node are black (they're NULL), consider the case where the parent of the new node is red. Inserting a red node under a red parent would violate this property. There are two cases to consider:

- *Red parent, red uncle*: Fig. 8.61 illustrates a red-red violation. Node X is the newly inserted node, with both parent and uncle colored red. A simple recoloring removes the red-red violation. After recoloring, the grandparent (node B) must be checked for validity, as its parent may be red. Note that this has the effect of propagating a red node up the tree. On completion, the root of the tree is marked black. If it was originally red, then this has the effect of increasing the black-height of the tree.

- *Red parent, black uncle:* Fig. 8.62 illustrates a red-red violation, where the uncle is colored black. Here the nodes may be rotated, with the subtrees adjusted as shown. At this point the algorithm may terminate as there are no red-red conflicts and the top of the subtree (node A) is colored black. Note that if node X was originally a right child, a left rotation would be done first, making the node a left child.

Each adjustment made while inserting a node causes us to travel up the tree one step. At most 1 rotation (2 if the node is a right child) will be done, as the algorithm terminates in this case. The technique for deletion is similar.

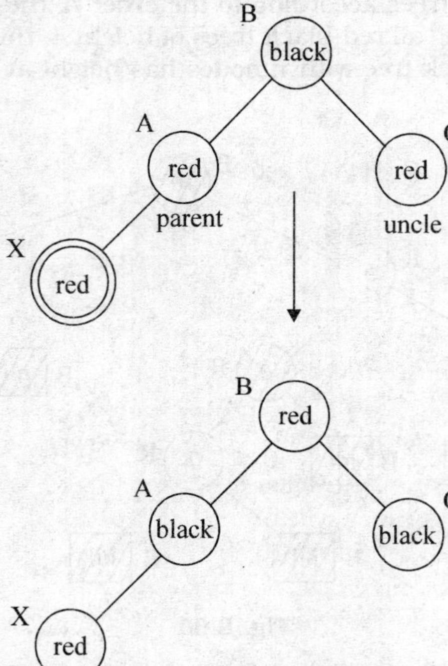

Fig. 8.61

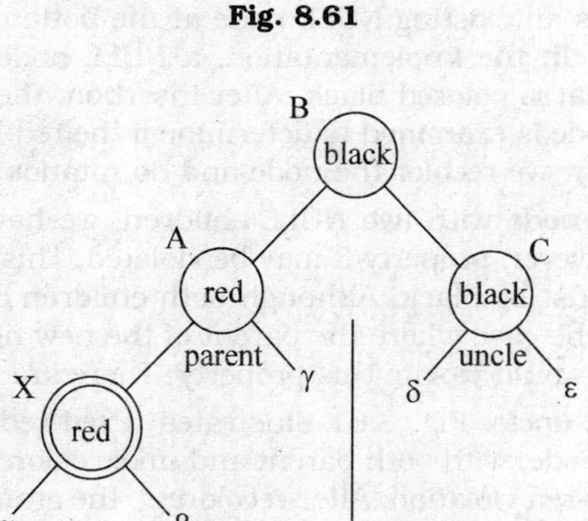

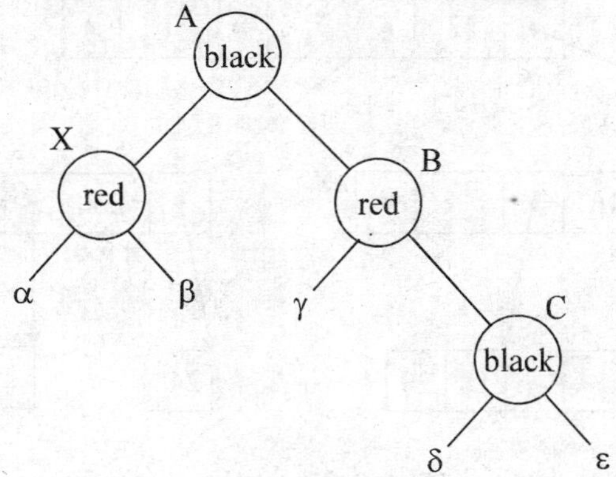

Fig. 8.62

8.19. B-TREE

B-trees are tree data struture that are most commonly found in databases and file systems. B-trees keep data sorted and allow amortized logarithmic time insertions and deletions. B-trees generally grow from the bottom up as elements are inserted, whereas most binary tree grow down.

B-trees have substantial advantages over alternative implementations when node access times far exceed access times within nodes. This usually occurs when most nodes are in secondary storage such as hard drive. By maximizing the number of child nodes within each internal node, the height of the tree decreases, balancing occurs less often, and efficiency increases. Usually this value is set such that each node takes up a full disk block or an analogous size in secondary storage.

The idea behind B-trees is that inner nodes can have a variable number of child nodes within some pre-defined range. Hence, B-trees do not need re-balancing as frequently as other self-balancing binary search trees. The lower and upper bounds on the number of child nodes are fixed for a particular implementation. For example, in a 2-3 B-tree (often simply 2-3 tree), each internal node may have only 2 or 3 child nodes. A node is considered to be in an illegal state if it has an invalid number of child nodes.

The B-tree's creator, Rudolf Bayer, has not explained what the B stands for. The most common belief is that B stands for *balanced*, as all the leaf nodes are at the same level in the tree. B may also stand for *Bayer*, or for *Boeing*, because he was working for *Boeing Scientific Research Labs*.

Fig. 8.63 illustrates a B-tree with 3 keys/node. Keys in internal nodes are surrounded by pointers, or record offsets, to keys that are less than or greater than, the key value. For example, all keys less than 22 are to the left and all keys greater than 22 are to the right.

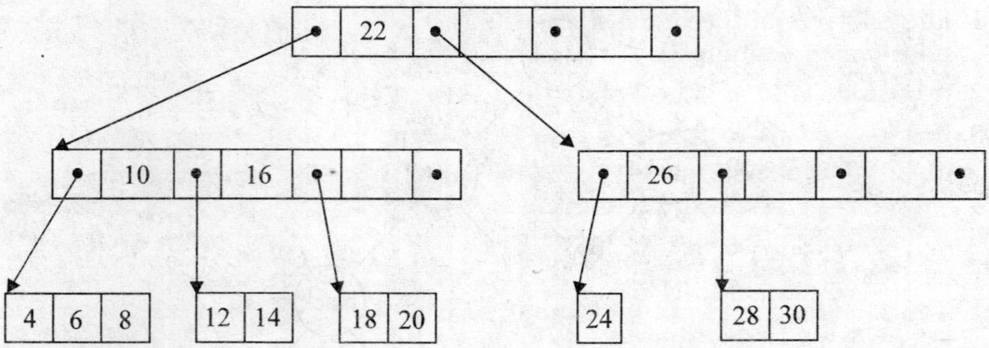

Fig. 8.63. B-tree

Nodes in a B-Tree are usually represented as an ordered set of elements and child pointers. Every node but the root contains a minimum of m elements, a maximum of n elements, and a maximum of $n + 1$ child pointers, for some arbitrary m and n. For all internal nodes, the number of child pointers is always one more than the number of elements. Since all leaf nodes are at the same height, nodes do not generally contain a way of determining whether they are leaf or internal.

Each inner node's elements act as separation values which divide its subtrees. For example, if an inner node has three child nodes (or subtrees) then it must have two separation values or elements a_1 and a_2. All values in the leftmost subtree will be less than a_1 , all values in the middle subtree will be between a_1 and a_2, and all values in the rightmost subtree will be greater than a_2.

ALGORITHMS

SEARCH

Search is performed in the typical manner, analogous to that in a binary search tree. Starting at the root, the tree is traversed top to bottom, choosing the child pointer whose separation values are on either side of the value that is being searched. Binary search is typically used within nodes to determine this location.

INSERTION

For a node to be in an illegal state, it must contain a number of elements which is outside of the acceptable range.

1. First, search for the position into which the node should be inserted. Then, insert the value into that node.
2. If no node is in an illegal state then the process is finished.
3. If some node has too many elements, it is split into two nodes, each with the minimum amount of elements. This process continues recursively up the tree until the root is reached. If the root is split, a new root is created. Typically the minimum and maximum number of elements must be selected such that the minimum is no more than one half the maximum in order for this to work.

DELETION

1. First, search for the value which will be deleted. Then, remove the value from the node which contains it.
2. If no node is in an illegal state then the process is finished.
3. If some node is in an illegal state then there are two possible cases:
   (*a*) Its sibling node, a child of the same parent node, can transfer one or more of its child nodes to the current node and return it to a legal state. If so, after updating the separation values of the parent and the two siblings the process is finished.
   (*b*) Its sibling does not have an extra child because it is on the lower bound. In that case both siblings are merged into a single node and we recurse onto the parent node, since it has had a child node removed. This continues until the current node is in a legal state or the root node is reached, upon which the root's children are merged and the merged node becomes the new root.

Several variants on the B-tree are listed in following table :

	B-Tree	*B*-Tree*	*B′-Tree*	*B″-Tree*
Data stored in	Any node	Any node	Leaf only	Leaf only
On insert, split	$1 \times 1 \rightarrow 2 \times 1/2$	$2 \times 1 \rightarrow 3 \times 2/3$	$1 \times 1 \rightarrow 2 \times 1/2$	$3 \times 1 \rightarrow 4 \times 3/4$
On delete, join	$2 \times 1/2 \rightarrow 1 \times 1$	$3 \times 2/3 \rightarrow 2 \times 1$	$2 \times 1/2 \rightarrow 1 \times 1$	$3 \times 1/2 \rightarrow 2 \times 3/4$

As we have discussed earlier the *standard* B-tree stores keys and data in both internal and leaf nodes. When descending the tree during insertion, a full child node is first redistributed to adjacent nodes. If the adjacent nodes are also full, then a new node is created, and half the keys in the child are moved to the newly created node. During deletion, children that are 1/2 full first attempt to obtain keys from adjacent nodes. If the adjacent nodes are also 1/2 full, then two nodes are joined to form one full node. B*-trees are similar, only the nodes are kept 2/3 full. This results in better utilization of space in the tree, and slightly better performance.

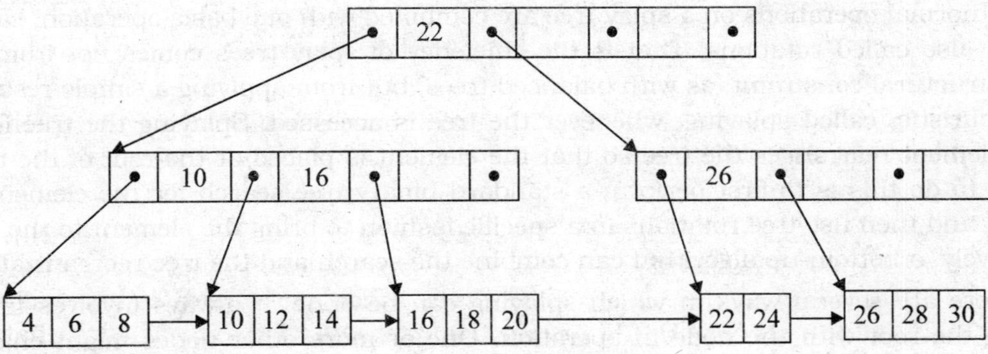

Fig. 8.64. B′-Tree

Fig. 8.64 illustrates a *B^+-tree*. All keys are stored at the leaf level, with their associated data values. Duplicates of the keys appear in internal parent nodes to guide the search. Pointers have a slightly different meaning than in conventional B-trees. The left pointer designates all keys less than the value, while the right pointer designates all keys greater than or equal to the value. For example, all keys less than 22 are on the left pointer, and all keys greater than or equal to 22 are on the right. Notice that key 22 is duplicated in the leaf, where the associated data may be found. During insertion and deletion, care must be taken to properly update parent nodes. When modifying the first key in a leaf, the tree is walked from leaf to root. The last greater than or equal to pointer found while descending the tree will require modification to reflect the new key value. Since all keys are in the leaf nodes, we may link them for sequential access.

The organization of *B^{++}-trees* is similar to B^+-trees, except for the split/join strategy. Assume each node can hold k keys, and the root node holds $3k$ keys. Before we descend to a child node during insertion, we check to see if it is full. If it is, the keys in the child node and two nodes adjacent to the child are all merged and redistributed. If the two adjacent nodes are also full, then another node is added, resulting in four nodes, each 3/4 full. Before we descend to a child node during deletion, we check to see if it is 1/2 full. If it is, the keys in the child node and two nodes adjacent to the child are all merged and redistributed. If the two adjacent nodes are also 1/2 full, then they are merged into two nodes, each 3/4 full. This is halfway between 1/2 full and completely full, allowing for an equal number of insertions or deletions in the future.

Recall that the root node holds $3k$ keys. If the root is full during insertion, we distribute the keys to four new nodes, each 3/4 full. This increases the height of the tree. During deletion, we inspect the child nodes. If there are only three child nodes, and they are all 1/2 full, they are gathered into the root, and the height of the tree decreases.

8.20. SPLAY TREES

A splay tree is a self-balancing binary search tree with the additional unusual property that recently accessed elements are quick to access again. It performs basic operations such as insertion, search and removal in O(log(n)) amortized time. For many non-uniform sequences of operations, splay trees perform better than other search trees, even when the specific pattern of the sequence is unknown. The splay tree was invented by Daniel Sleator and Robert Tarjan.

All normal operations on a splay tree are combined with one basic operation, called splaying, also called rotations. That is the efficiency of splay trees comes not from an explicit structural constraint, as with balanced trees, but from applying a simple restructuring heuristic, called splaying, whenever the tree is accessed. Splaying the tree for a certain element rearranges the tree so that the element is placed at the root of the tree. One way to do this is to first perform a standard binary tree search for the element in question, and then use tree rotations in a specific fashion to bring the element to the top. Alternatively, a bottom-up algorithm can combine the search and the tree reorganization.

There are several ways in which splaying can be done. It always involves interchanging the root with the node in operation. One or more other nodes might change position as well. The purpose of splaying is to minimize the number of (access) operations required to recover desired data records over a period of time.

SPLAY OPERATION

The most important tree operation is splay, also called rotation. If we apply splay rotation to splay(N), which moves an element N to the root of the tree. In case N is not present in the tree, the last element on the search path for N is moved instead.

To do a splay, we carry out a sequence of rotations, each of which moves the target node N closer to the root. Each particular step depends on only two factors:

Whether N is the left or right child of its parent node, P,

Whether P is the left or right child of its parent, G (for grandparent node).

Thus, there are four cases:

Case 1: N is the left child of P and P is the left child of G. In this case we perform a double right rotation, so that P becomes N's right child, and G becomes P's right child.

Case 2: N is the right child of P and P is the right child of G. In this case we perform a double left rotation, so that P becomes N's left child, and G becomes P's left child.

Case 3: N is the left child of P and P is the right child of G. In this case we perform a rotation so that G becomes N's left child, and P becomes N's right child.

Case 4: N is the right child of P and P is the left child of G. In this case we perform a rotation so that P becomes N's left child, and G becomes N's right child.

Finally, if N doesn't have a grandparent node, we simply perform a left or right rotation to move it to the root. By performing a splay on the node of interest after every operation, we keep recently accessed nodes near the root and keep the tree roughly balanced, so that we achieve the desired amortized time bounds.

The run time for a splay(N) operation is proportional to the length of the search path for N: While searching for N we traverse the search path top-down. Let Z be the last node on that path. In a second step, we move Z along that path by applying rotations. There are six different rotations :

1. Zig Rotation (Right Rotation)
2. Zag Rotation (Left Rotation)
3. Zig-Zag (Zig followed by Zag)
4. Zag-Zig (Zag followed by Zig)
5. Zig-Zig
6. Zag-Zag

Consider the path going from the root down to the accessed node. Each time we move left going down this path, we say we "zig" and each time we move right, we say we "zag."

Zig Rotation and Zag Rotation: Note that a zig rotation is the same as a right rotation whereas the zag step is the left rotation. See Fig. 8.65.

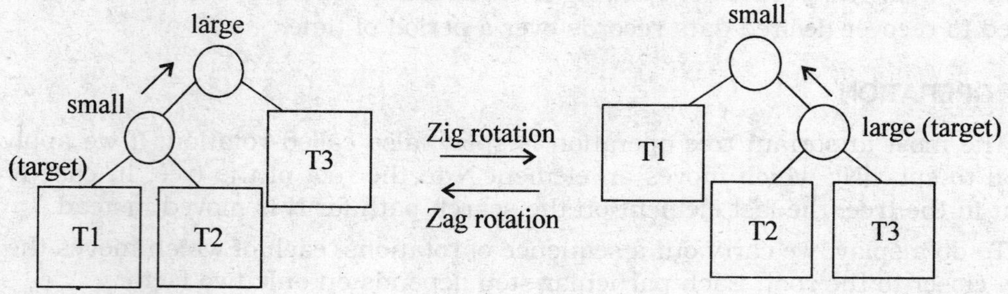

Fig. 8.65. Zig rotation and zag rotation

Zig-Zag: This is the same as a double rotation in an AVL tree. Note that the target element is lifted up by two levels. See Fig. 8.66

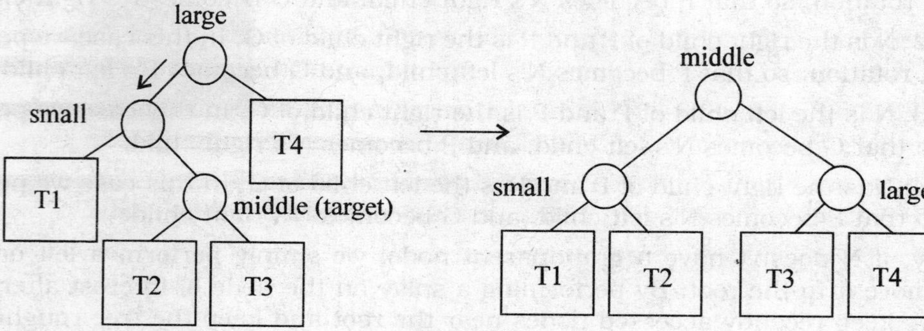

Fig. 8.66. Zig-zag rotation

Zag-Zig: This is also the same as a double rotation in an AVL tree. Here again, the target element is lifted up by two levels. See Fig. 8.67

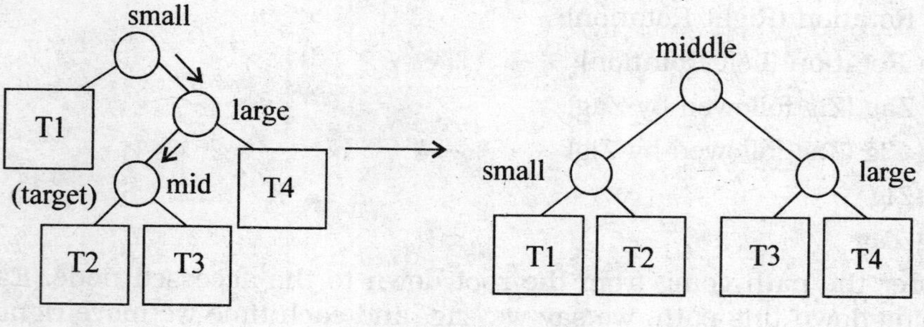

Fig. 8.67. Zag-zig rotation

Zig-Zig and Zag-Zag: The target element is lifted up by two levels in each case. Zig-Zig is different from two successive right rotations; zag-zag is different from two successive left rotations. For example, see Fig. 8.68 and Fig. 8.69.

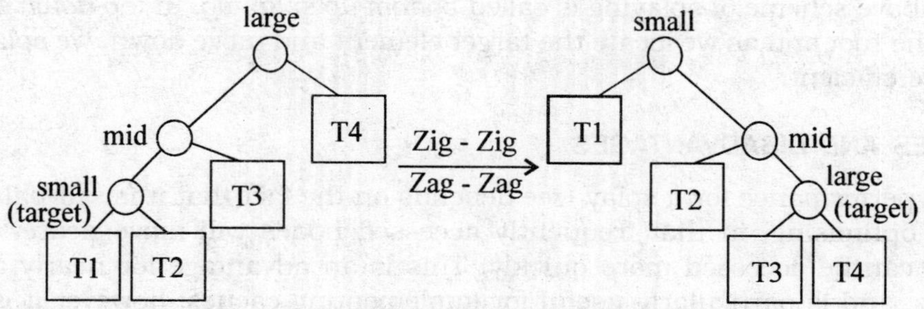

Fig. 8.68. Zig-zig and zag-zag rotations

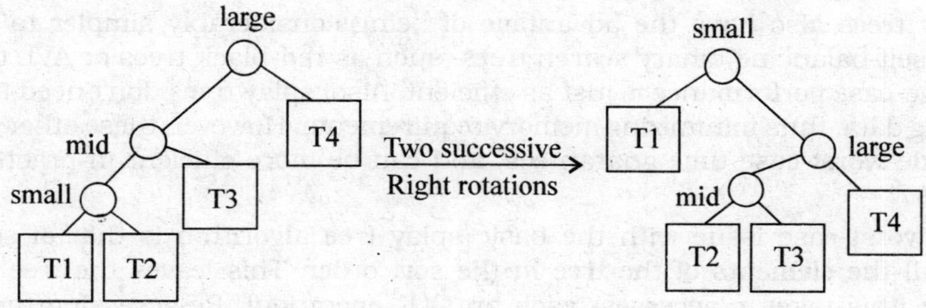

Fig. 8.69. Two successive right rotations

You may see an example in Fig. 8.70

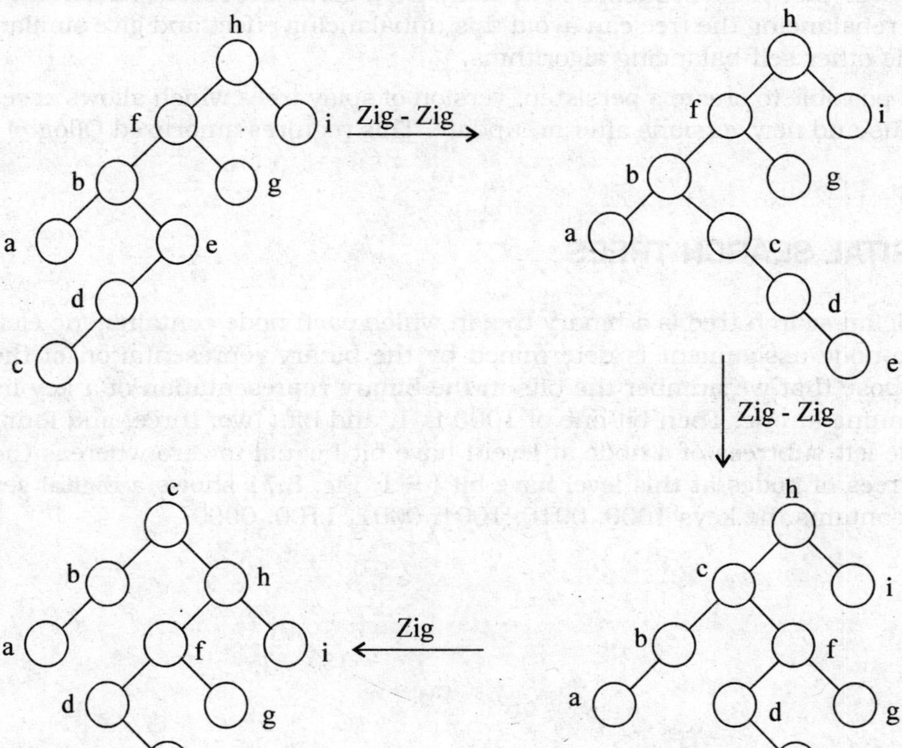

Fig. 8.70. An example of splaying

The above scheme of splaying is called *bottom-up splaying*. In *top-down splaying*, we start from the root and as we locate the target element and move down, we splay as we go. This is more efficient.

ADVANTAGES AND DISADVANTAGES

Good performance for a splay tree depends on the fact that it is self-balancing, and indeed self-optimising, in that frequently accessed nodes will move nearer to the root where they can be accessed more quickly. This is an advantage for nearly all practical applications, and is particularly useful for implementing caches; however it is important to note that for uniform access, a splay tree's performance will be considerably (although not asymptotically) worse than a somewhat balanced simple binary search tree.

Splay trees also have the advantage of being considerably simpler to implement than other self-balancing binary search trees, such as red-black trees or AVL trees, while their average-case performance is just as efficient. Also, splay trees don't need to store any bookkeeping data, thus minimizing memory requirements. However, these other data structures provide worst-case time guarantees, and can be more efficient in practice for uniform access.

One worst-case issue with the basic splay tree algorithm is that of sequentially accessing all the elements of the tree in the sort order. This leaves the tree completely unbalanced (this takes n accesses- each an O(1) operation). Re-accessing the first item triggers an operation that takes O(n) operations to rebalance the tree before returning the first item. This is a significant delay for that final operation, although the amortized performance over the entire sequence is actually O(1). However, recent research shows that randomly rebalancing the tree can avoid this unbalancing effect and give similar performance to the other self-balancing algorithms.

It is possible to create a persistent version of splay trees which allows access to both the previous and new versions after an update. This requires amortized O(log n) space per update.

8.21. DIGITAL SEARCH TREES

A digital search tree is a binary tree in which each node contains one element. The element-to-node assignment is determined by the binary representation of the element keys. Suppose that we number the bits in the binary representation of a key from left to right beginning at one. Then bit one of 1000 is 1, and bits two, three, and four are 0. All keys in the left subtrees of a node at level I have bit I equal to zero whereas those in the right subtrees of nodes at this level have bit I = 1. Fig. 8.71 shows a digital search tree. This tree contains the keys 1000, 0010, 1001, 0001, 1100, 0000.

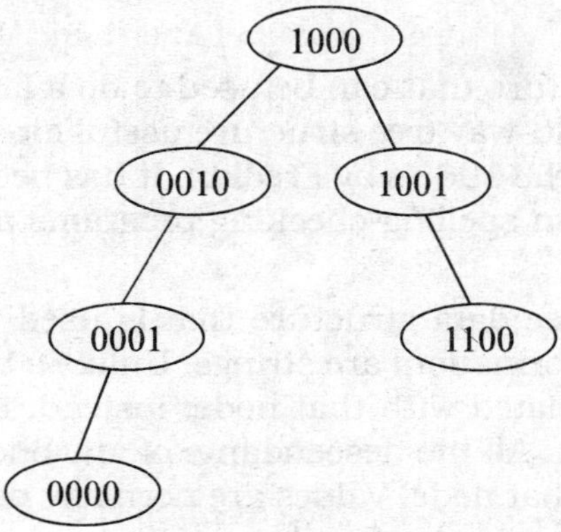

Fig. 8.71

Suppose we are searching for a key $k = 0011$ in the tree (Fig. 8.71). k is first compared with the key in the root. Since k is different from the key in the root, and since bit one of k is 0, we move to the left child (*i.e.*, 0010) of the root. Now, since k is different from the key in node and bit two of k is 0, we move to the left chills (*i.e.*, 0001). Since k is different from the key in node and bit three of k is one, we move to the right child of node 0001, which is NULL. From this we conclude that $k = 0011$ is not in the search tree. If we wish to insert k into the tree, then it is added as the right child of node 0001 as shown in the Fig. 8.72.

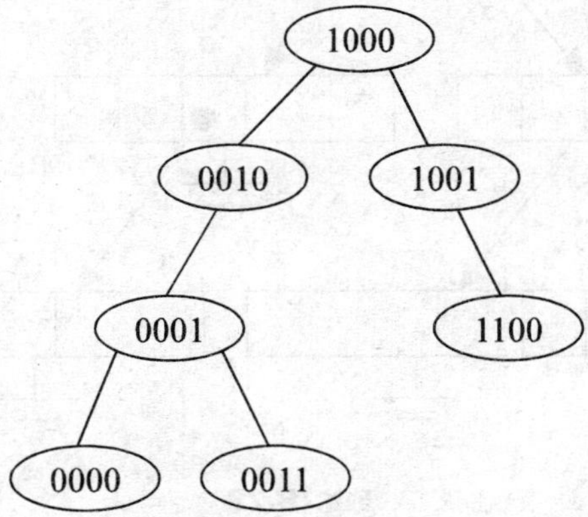

Fig. 8.72

The digital search tree functions to search and insert are quite similar to the corresponding functions for binary search trees. The essential difference is that the subtree to move to is determined by a bit in the search key rather than by the result of the comparison of the search key in the current node. The deletion of an item in a leaf is done by removing the leaf node. To delete from any other node, the deleted item must be replaced by a value from any leaf in its subtree and that leaf removed.

Each of these operations can be performed in $O(h)$ time, where h is the height of the digital search tree. If each key in a search tree has SIZE bits, then the height of the digital search tree is at most SIZE + 1.

8.21. TRIES

The trie is a data structure that can be used to do a fast search in a large text. And a *trie* (from retrieval), is a multi-way tree structure useful for storing strings over an alphabet and it was introduced in the 1960's by Fredkin. It has been used to store large dictionaries of English (say) words in spelling-checking programs and in natural-language "understanding" programs.

A trie is an ordered tree data structure that is used to store an associative array where the datas (or key or information) are strings. Unlike a binary search tree, no node in the tree stores the key associated with that node; instead, its position in the tree shows what key it is associated with. All the descendants of any one node have a common prefix of the string associated with that node. Values are normally not associated with every node, only with leaves and some inner nodes that happen to correspond to keys of interest.

That is no node in the trie contains full characters (or information) of the word (which is a key). But each node will contain associate characters of the word, which may ultimately lead to the full word at the end of a path. For example consider the data: an, ant, cow, the corresponding trie would look like be in Fig. 8.73, which is a non-compact trie.

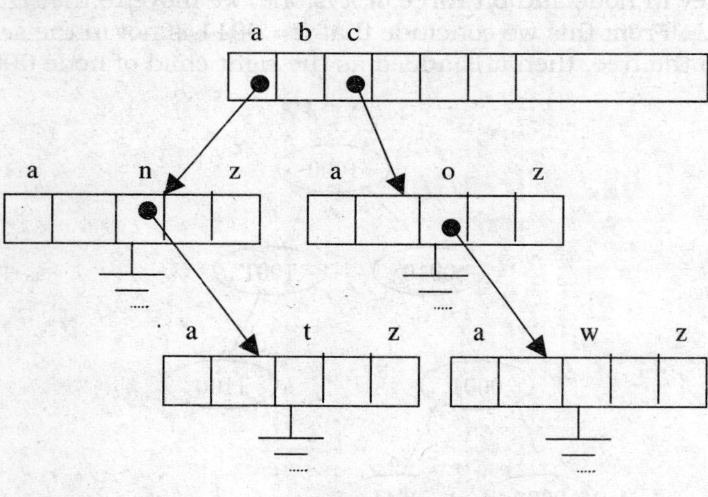

Fig. 8.73

The idea is that all strings sharing a common stem (or character or *prefix*) hang off a common node. When the strings are words over {*a*, *z*}, a node has at most 27 children — one for each letter plus a terminator.

The elements in a string can be recovered in a scan from the root to the leaf that ends a string. All strings in the trie can be recovered by a depth-first scan of the tree. The height of a trie is the length of the longest key in the trie.

ADVANTAGES AND DISADVANTAGES

There are three main advantages of tries over binary search trees (BSTs):

Searching a data is faster in tries. Searching a key (or data) of length *m* takes worst case O(*m*) = O(1) time; where BST takes O(log *n*) time, because initial characters are examined repeatedly during multiple comparisons. Also, the simple operations tries use during search, such as array indexing using a character, are fast on real machines.

Tries require less space. Because the keys are not stored explicitly, only an amortized constant amount of space is needed to store each key.

Tries make efficient longest-prefix matching, where we wish to find the key sharing the longest possible prefix with a given key. They also allow one to associate a value with an entire group of keys that have a common prefix.

Although it seems restrictive to say a trie's key type must be a string, many common data types can be seen as strings; for example, an integer can be seen as a string of bits. Integers with common bit prefixes occur as map keys in many applications such as routing tables and address translation tables.

Tries are most useful when the keys are of varying lengths and we expect some key search to fail, because the key is not present. If we have fixed-length keys, and expect all search to succeed, then we can improve key search by combining every node with a single child (such as "*i*" and "in" above) with its child, producing a patricia trie. That is when we are dealing with very long keys, the cost of a key comparison is high. We can reduce the number of key compariosns to one by using a related structure called patricia (Practical Algorithm To Retrieve Information Coded In Alphanumeric). We shall develop this structure in three steps. First, we introduce a structure called binary tries. Then we transform binary tries into compressed binary tries. Finally from compressed binary tries we obtain patricia. Binary tries and compressed binary tries are introduced only as a means of arriving at patricia.

SELF REVIEW QUESTIONS

1. Define and explain trees and binary trees.
[KERALA - DEC 2004 (BTech), MG - MAY 2004 (BTech)]

2. What is binary search tree? Write an algorithm to insert and delete an item from a binary search tree. *[CUSAT - NOV 2002 (BTech), MG - MAY 2004 (BTech)*
ANNA - MAY 2004 (BE)]

3. What are different methods of binary tree traversal with examples?
[MG - NOV 2004 (BTech), MG - NOV 2003 (BTech)
KERALA - DEC 2003 (BTech)]

4. Write an algorithm for the in-order traversal of a binary tree. *[MG - NOV 2004 (BTech)]*

5. Explain the structure of a threaded tree. What are the conventions of representing threads?
[MG - MAY 2003 (BTech), MG - MAY 2000 (BTech)]

6. Explain a height balanced binary tree.
[CUSAT - MAY 2000 (BTech), MG - MAY 2003 (BTech)
ANNA - MAY 2004 (MCA)]

7. Discuss the improvement in performance of binary trees brought by using threads.
[MG - NOV 2003 (BTech)]

8. Discuss the difference between a general tree and a binary tree. What is a complete binary tree? Give an algorithm for deleting an information value X from a given lexically ordered binary tree. *[MG - NOV 2003 (BTech)]*

9. What is a threaded binary tree? Explain in-order threading. *[MG - NOV 2002 (BTech)]*
10. Given an account of the different classification of trees. *[MG - NOV 2002 (BTech)]*
11. What are common operations performed on binary trees? *[MG - MAY 2002 (BTech)]*
12. Write notes on height balanced and weight balanced trees. *[MG - MAY 2002 (BTech)]*
14. Discuss the linked storage representation for binary trees. *[MG - MAY 2002 (BTech)]*
15. What is a height of a binary tree? *[MG - MAY 2000 (BTech)]*
16. Draw a binary tree for the expression A*B–(C+D)*(P/Q). *[MG - MAY 2000 (BTech)]*
17. Discuss the internal memory representation of a binary tree using sequential and linked representation? *[MG - MAY 2000 (BTech)]*
18. How to insert a node to the right of a given node in a threaded binary tree? *[Calicut - APR 1995 (BTech)]*
19. Give a non-recursive algorithm for post order traversal of a binary tree. *[Calicut - APR 1995 (BTech)]*
20. What are the applications of tree data structure? *[Calicut - APR 1997 (BTech), Calicut - APR 1995 (BTech)]*
21. Explain preorder, Inorder and Post order traversals. *[CUSAT - MAY 2000 (BTech)]*
22. Explain binary tree traversals. Write an iterative function for inorder traversal. Explain the advantages of threaded binary tree over ordinary binary tree. *[CUSAT - JUL 2002 (MCA), CUSAT - MAY 2000 (BTech) ANNA - MAY 2004 (MCA)]*
23. Explain the techniques for balancing heights of a binary tree. *[CUSAT - NOV 2002 (BTech)]*
24. What is a threaded binary tree? Write algorithm for adding an element to a threaded binary tree. *[CUSAT - DEC 2003 (MCA)]*
25. Define Binary search tree and its operations. *[ANNA - DEC 2003 (BE)]*
26. Define various tree traversal methods. Write non-recursive algorithm for in-order tree traversal. *[ANNA - DEC 2004 (BE), ANNA - DEC 2003 (BE) ANNA - MAY 2003 (BE)]*
27. What is Weight balanced tree? *[ANNA - MAY 2004 (MCA)]*
28. Write an algorithm to convert a general tree to binary tree. *[ANNA - MAY 2004 (BE), ANNA - MAY 2003 (BE)]*
29. Define single rotation on AVL tree. *[ANNA - MAY 2003 (BE)]*
30. What is the difference between binary tree and binary search tree? *[ANNA - MAY 2003 (BE)]*
31. Write iterative procedure for preorder tree traversal. *[KERALA - DEC 2004 (BTech)]*
32. Write an algorithm to traverse a binary tree in port order. *[KERALA - MAY 2003 (BTech)]*
33. What are the uses of tree traversals? *[KERALA - DEC 2002 (BTech)]*
34. Give the binary tree representation. *[KERALA - MAY 2001 (BTech)]*
35. Write an iterative procedure for post-order tree traversal. *[KERALA - MAY 2001 (BTech)]*
36. Draw a binary tree for the following expression A * B - (C - D) * (P / Q). *[KERALA - MAY 2002 (BTech)]*
37. Write an algorithm to count the leaf nodes in a binary tree. *[KERALA - MAY 2002 (BTech)]*

9 Graphs

This chapter discusses another nonlinear data structures, graphs. Graphs representations have found application in almost all subjects like geography, engineering and solving games and puzzles.

A graph G consist of

1. Set of vertices V (called nodes), (V = $\{v_1, v_2, v_3, v_4......\}$) and
2. Set of edges E (*i.e.*, E $\{e_1, e_2, e_3......$cm$\}$

A graph can be represents as G = (V, E), where V is a finite and non empty set at vertices and E is a set of pairs of vertices called edges. Each edge '*e*' in E is identified with a unique pair (*a*, *b*) of nodes in V, denoted by *e* = [*a*, *b*].

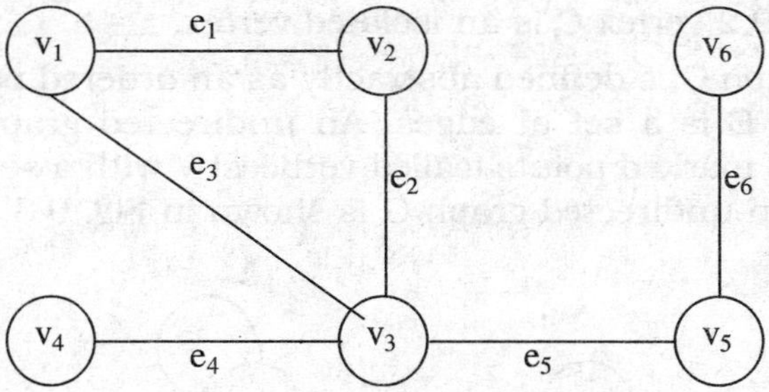

Fig. 9.1

Consider a graph, G in Fig. 9.1. Then the vertex V and edge E can be represented as: V = $\{v_1, v_2, v_3, v_4, v_5, v_6\}$ and E = $\{e_1, e_2, e_3, e_4, e_5, e_6\}$ E = $\{(v_1, v_2)\ (v_2, v_3)\ (v_1, v_3)\ (v_3, v_4), (v_3, v_5)\ (v_5, v_6)\}$. There are six edges and vertex in the graph

9.1. BASIC TERMINOLOGIES

A *directed graph* G is defined as an ordered pair (V, E) where, V is a set of vertices and the ordered pairs in E are called edges on V. A directed graph can be represented geometrically as a set of marked points (called vertices) V with a set of arrows (called edges) E between pairs of points (or vertex or nodes) so that there is at most one arrow from one vertex to another vertex. For example, Fig 9.2 shows a directed graph, where G = $\{a, b, c, d\}$, $\{(a, b), (a, d), (d, b), (d, d), (c, c)\}$

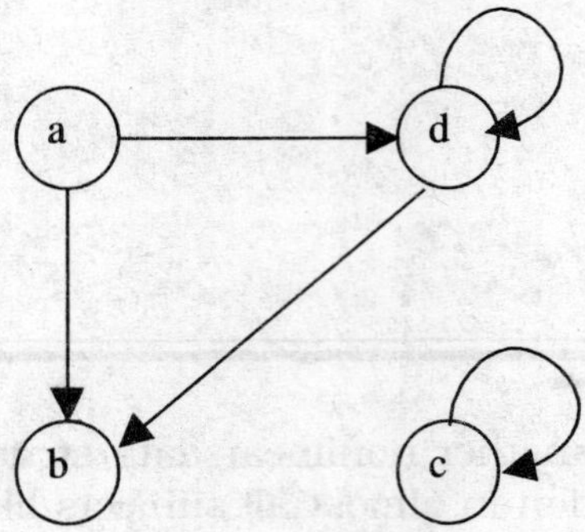

Fig. 9.2

An edge (*a*, *b*), in said to the incident with the vertices it joints, *i.e.*, *a*, *b*. We can also say that the edge (*a*, *b*) is incident from *a* to *b*. The vertex a is called the *initial vertex* and the vertex *b* is called the *terminal vertex* of the edge (*a*, *b*). If an edge that is incident from and into the same vertex, say (*d*, *d*) of (*c*, *c*) in Fig. 9.2, is called a *loop*.

Two vertices are said to be adjacent if they are joined by an edge. Consider edge (*a*, *b*), the vertex *a* is said to be adjacent to the vertex *b*, and the vertex *b* is said to be adjacent from the vertex *a*. A vertex is said to be an *isolated vertex* if there is no edge incident with it. In Fig. 9.2 vertex C is an isolated vertex.

An *undirected graph* G is defined abstractly as an ordered pair (V, E), where V is a set of vertices and the E is a set at edges. An undirected graph can be represented geometrically as a set of marked points (called vertices) V with a set at lines (called edges) E between the points. An undirected graph G is shown in Fig. 9.3.

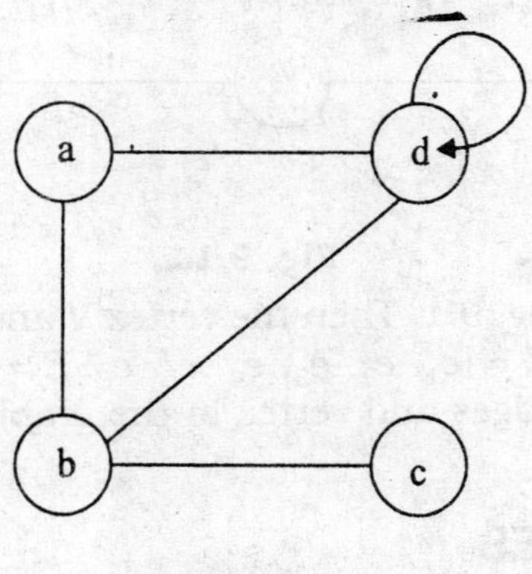

Fig. 9.3

Two graphs are said to be *isomorphic* if there is a one-to-one correspondence between their vertices and between their edges such that incidence are prevented. Fig. 9.4 show an isomorphic undirected graph.

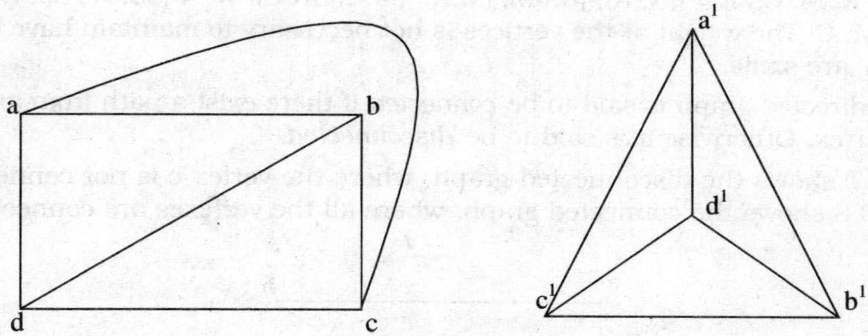

Fig. 9.4

Let G = (V, E) be a graph. A graph $G^1 = (V^1, E^1)$ is said to be a *sub-graph* of G if E^1 is a subset at E and V^1 is a subset at V such that the edges in E^1 are incident only with the vertices in V^1. For example Fig 9.5 (*b*) is a sub-graph at Fig. 9.5(*a*). A sub-graph of G is said to be a *spanning sub-graph* if it contains all the vertices of G. For example Fig. 9.5(*c*) shows a spanning sub-graph at Fig. 9.5(*a*).

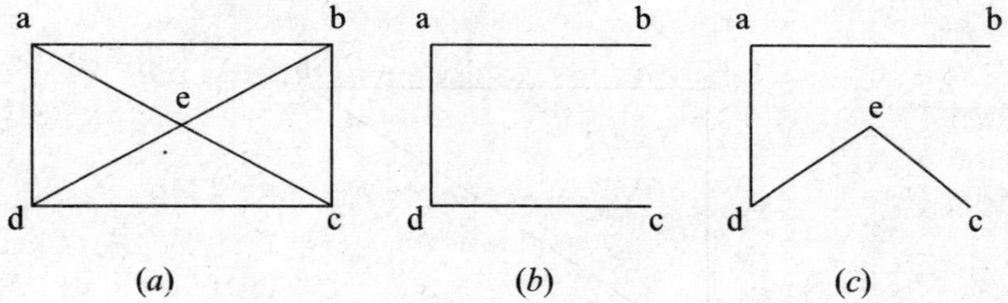

Fig. 9.5

The number of edges incident on a vertex is its *degree*. The degree of vertex *a*, is written as degree (*a*). If the degree of vertex a is zero, then vertex *a* is called isolated vertex. For example the degree of the vertex *a* in Fig. 9.5 is 3.

A graph G is said to be *weighted graph* if every edge and/or vertices in the graph is assigned with some weight or value. A weighted graph can be defined as $G = (V, E, W_e, W_v)$ where V is the set of vertices, E is the set at edges and W_e is a weights of the edges whose domain is E and W_v is a weight to the vertices whose domain is V. Consider a graph.

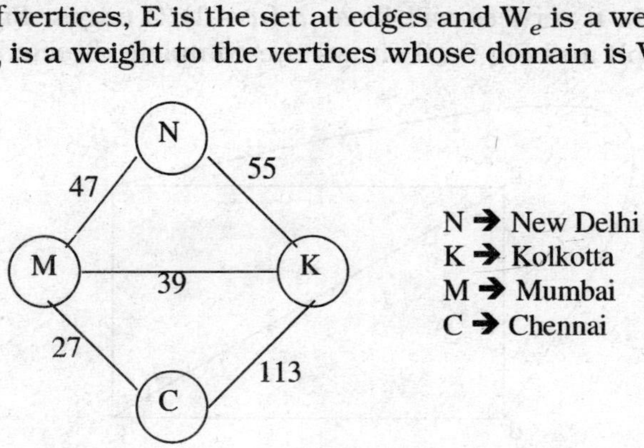

Fig. 9:6

In Fig 9:6 which shows the distance in km between four metropolitan cities in India. Here V = {N, K, M, C,} E = {(N, K), (N,M,), (M,K), (M,C), (K,C)} W_e = {55,47, 39, 27, 113} and W_v = {N, K, M, C} The weight at the vertices is not necessary to maintain have become the set W_v and V are same.

An undirected graph is said to be *connected* if there exist a path from any vertex to any other vertex. Otherwise it is said to be *disconnected*.

Fig. 9.7 shows the disconnected graph, where the vertex c is not connected to the graph. Fig. 9.8 shows the connected graph, where all the vertexes are connected.

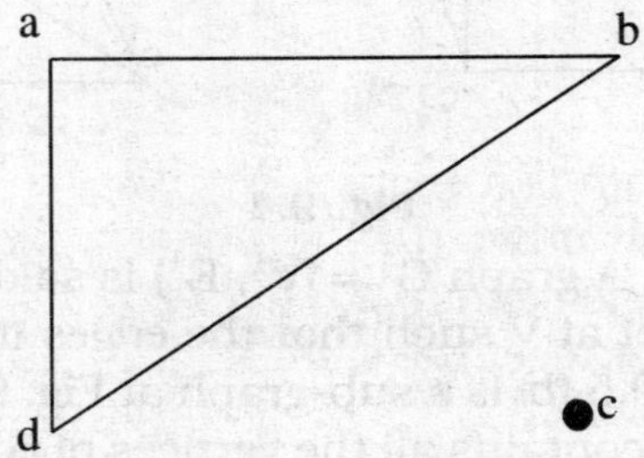

Fig. 9.7

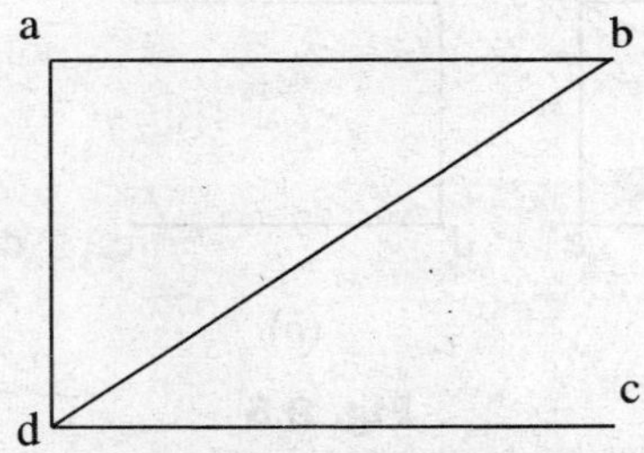

Fig. 9.8

A graph G is said to complete (or fully connected or strongly connected) if there is a path from every vertex to every other vertex. Let *a* and *b* are two vertices in the directed graph, then it is a complete graph if there is a path from *a* to *b* as well as a path from *b* to *a*. A complete graph with *n* vertices will have *n* (*n* – 1)/2 edges. Fig 9.9 illustrates the complete undirected graph and Fig 9.10 shows the complete directed graph.

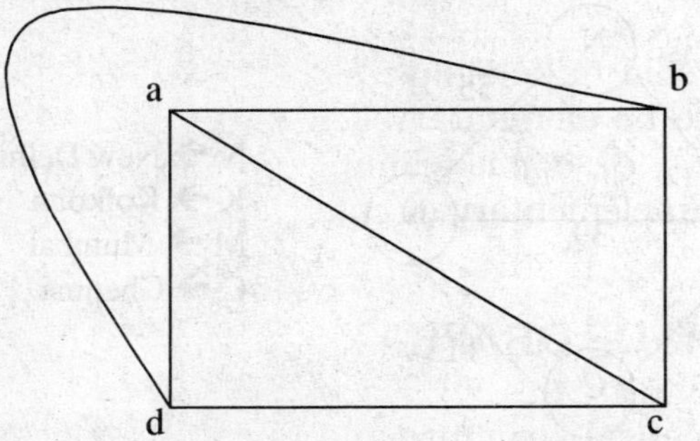

Fig. 9.9

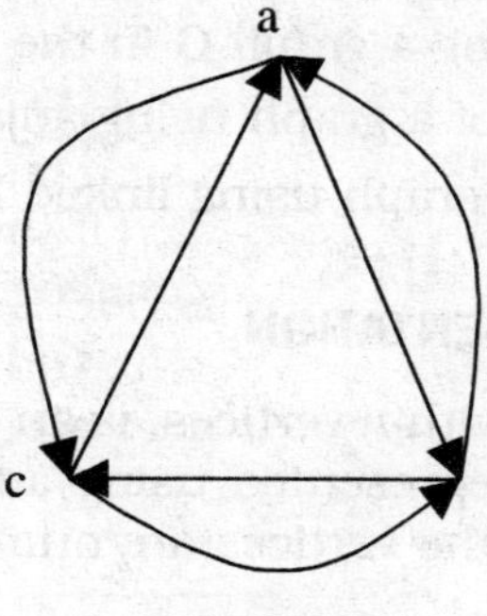

Fig 9:10

In a directed graph, a *path* is a sequence of edges (e_1, e_2, e_3, ... e_n) such that the edges are connected with each other (*i.e.*, terminal vertex e_n coincides with the initial vertex e_1). A path is said to be *elementary* if it does not meet the same vertex twice. A path is said to be *simple* if it does not meet the same edges twice. Consider a graph in Fig. 9.11

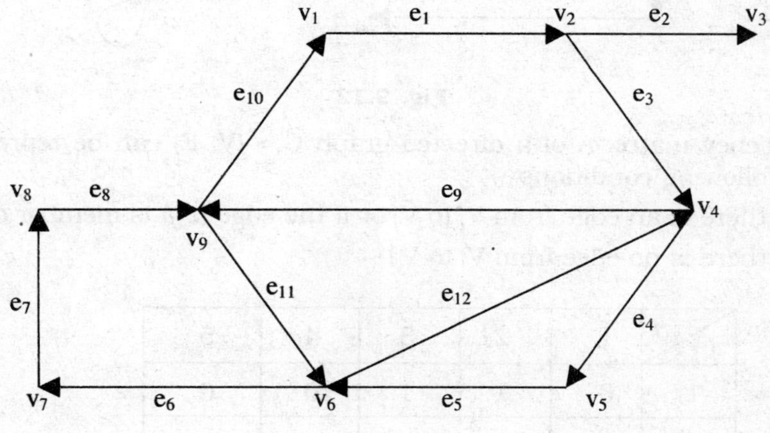

Fig. 9.11

Where (e_1, e_2, d_3, e_4, e_5) is a path; (e_1, e_3, e_4, e_5, e_{12}, e_9, e_{11}, e_6, e_7, e_8, e_{11}) is a path but not a simple one; (e_1, e_3, e_4, e_5, e_6, e_7, e_8, e_{11}, e_{12}) is a simple path but not elementary one; (e_1, e_3, e_4, e_5, e_6, e_7, e_8) is an elementary path.

A circuit is a path (e_1, e_2, ... e_n) in which terminal vertex of en coincides with initial vertex of e1. A circuit is said to be simple if it does not include (or visit) the same edge twice. A circuit is said to be elementary if it does not visit the same vertex twice. In Fig. 9:11 (e_1, e_3, e_4, e_5, e_{12}, e_9, e_{10}) is a simple circuit but not a elementary one; (e_1, e_3, e_4, e_5, e_6, e_7, e_8, e_{10}) is an elementary circuit.

9.2. REPRESENTATION OF GRAPH

Graph is a mathematical structure and finds its application is many areas, where the problem is to be solved by computers. The problems related to graph G must be represented in computer memory using any suitable data structure to solve the same. There are two standard ways of maintaining a graph G in the memory of a computer.

1. Sequential representation of a graph using adjacent
2. Linked representation of a graph using linked list

9.2.1. ADJACENCY MATRIX REPRESENTATION

The s A of a graph G = (V, E) with *n* vertices, is an $n \times n$ matrix. In this section let us see how a directed graph can be represented using adjacency matrix. Considered a directed graph in Fig. 9.12 where all the vertices are numbered, (1, 2, 3, 4...... etc.)

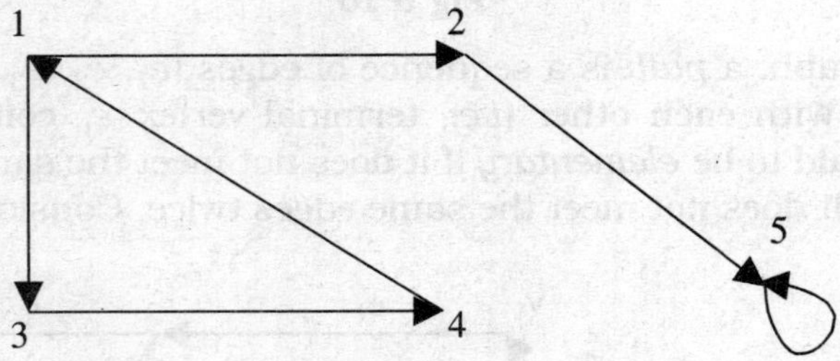

Fig. 9.12

The adjacency matrix A of a directed graph G = (V, E) can be represented (in Fig 9.13) with the following conditions

A_{ij} = 1 {if there is an edge from V_i to V_j or if the edge (*i*, *j*) is member of E.}

A_{ij} = 0 {if there is no edge from V_i to V_j}

i \ *j*	1	2	3	4	5
1	0	1	1	0	0
2	0	0	0	0	1
3	0	0	0	1	0
4	1	0	0	0	0
5	0	0	0	0	1

Fig. 9.13

We have seen how a directed graph can be represented in adjacency matrix. Now let us discuss how an undirected graph can be represented using adjacency matrix. Considered an undirected graph in Fig. 9.14

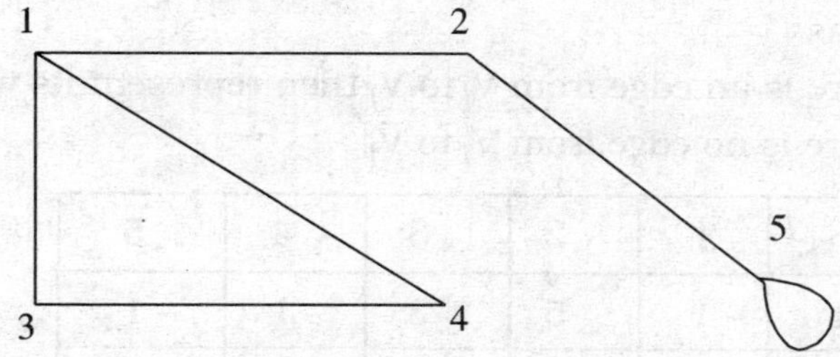

Fig. 9.14

The adjacency matrix A of an undirected graph G = (V, E) can be represented (in Fig 9.15) with the following conditions

$A_{ij} = 1$ {if there is an edge from V_i to V_j or if the edge (i, j) is member of E}

$A_{ij} = 0$ {if there is no edge from V_i to V_j or the edge $i, j,$ is not a member of E}

i \ j	1	2	3	4	5
1	0	1	1	1	0
2	1	0	0	0	1
3	1	0	0	1	0
4	1	0	1	0	0
5	0	1	0	0	1

Fig. 9.15

To represent a weighted graph using adjacency matrix, weight of the edge (i, j) is simply stored as the entry in ith row and jth column of the adjacency matrix. There are some cases where zero can also be the possible weight of the edge, then we have to store some sentinel value for non-existent edge, which can be a negative value; since the weight of the edge is always a positive number. Consider a weighted graph, Fig. 9.16

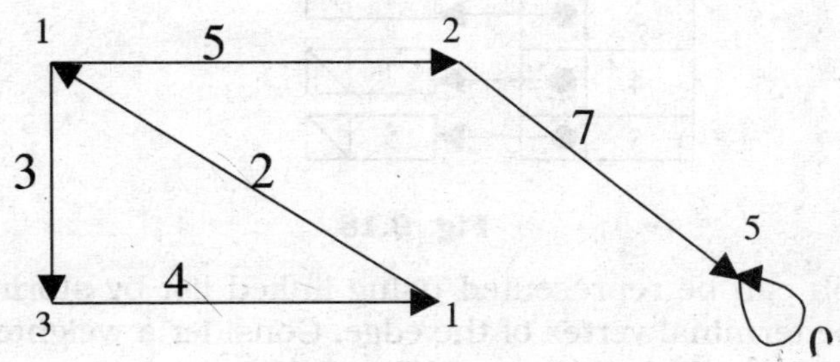

Fig. 9.16

The adjacency matrix A for a directed weighted graph G = (V, E, W_e) can be represented (in Fig. 9.17) as

$A_{ij} = W_{ij}$ { if there is an edge from V_i to V_j then represent its weight W_{ij}.}

$A_{ij} = -1$ { if there is no edge from V_i to V_j}

i \ *j*	1	2	3	4	5
1	– 1	5	3	– 1	– 1
2	– 1	– 1	– 1	– 1	7
3	– 1	– 1	– 1	4	– 1
4	2	– 1	– 1	– 1	– 1
5	– 1	– 1	– 1	– 1	0

Fig. 9.17

In this representation, n^2 memory location is required to represent a graph with *n* vertices. The adjacency matrix is a simple way to represent a graph, but it has two disadvantages.

1. It takes n^2 space to represent a graph with *n* vertices, even for a spars graph and
2. It takes $O(n^2)$ time to solve the graph problem

9.2.2. LINKED LIST REPRESENTATION

In this representation (also called adjacency list representation), we store a graph as a linked structure. First we store all the vertices of the graph in a list and then each adjacent vertices will be represented using linked list node. Here terminal vertex of an edge is stored in a structure node and linked to a corresponding initial vertex in the list. Consider a directed graph in Fig. 9.12, it can be represented using linked list as Fig. 9.18.

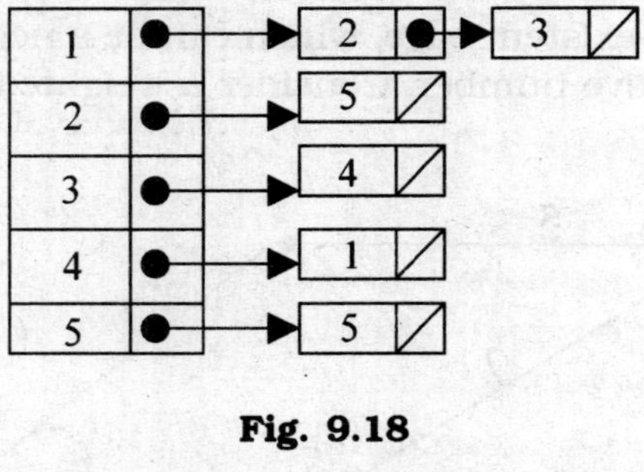

Fig. 9.18

Weighted graph can be represented using linked list by storing the corresponding weight along with the terminal vertex of the edge. Consider a weighted graph in Fig. 9.16, it can be represented using linked list as in Fig. 9.19.

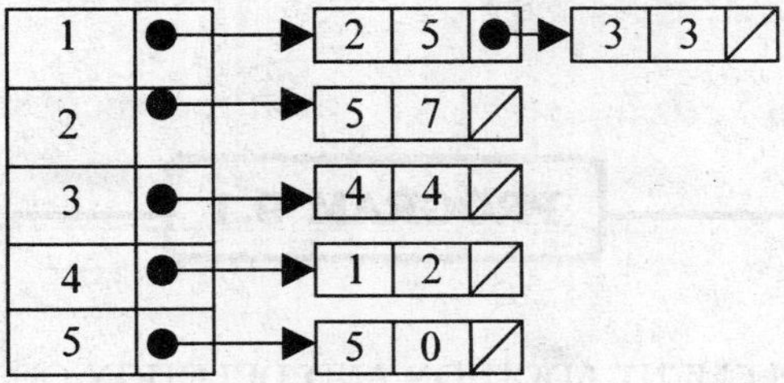

Fig. 9.19

Although the linked list representation requires very less memory as compared to the adjacency matrix, the simplicity of adjacency matrix makes it preferable when graph are reasonably small.

9.3. OPERATIONS ON GRAPH

Suppose a graph G is maintained in memory by the linked list representation. This section discuss the different operations such as creating a graph, searching, deleting a vertices or edges.

9.3.1. CREATING A GRAPH

To create a graph, first adjacency list array is created to store the vertices name, dynamically at the run time. Then the node is created and linked to the list array if an edge is there to the vertex.

Step 1: Input the total number of vertices in the graph, say *n*.

Step 2: Allocate the memory dynamically for the vertices to store in list array.

Step 3: Input the first vertex and the vertices through which it has edge(s) by linking the node from list array through nodes.

Step 4: Repeat the process by incrementing the list array to add other vertices and edges.

Step 5: Exit.

9.3.2. SEARCHING AND DELETING FROM A GRAPH

Suppose an edge (1, 2) is to be deleted from the graph G. First we will search through the list array whether the initial vertex of the edge is in list array or not by incrementing the list array index. Once the initial vertex is found in the list array, the corresponding link list will be search for the terminal vertex.

Step 1: Input an edge to be searched

Step 2: Search for an initial vertex of edge in list arrays by incrementing the array index.

Step 3: Once it is found, search through the link list for the terminal vertex of the edge.

Step 4: If found display "the edge is present in the graph".

Step 5: Then delete the node where the terminal vertex is found and rearrange the link list.

Step 6: Exit

PROGRAM 9.1

```
//PROGRAM TO IMPLEMENT ADDITION AND DELETION OF NODES
//AND EDGES IN A GRAPH USING ADJACENCY MATRIX
//CODED AND COMPILED IN TURBO C

#include<conio.h>
#include<stdio.h>
#include<process.h>

#define max 20

int adj[max][max];
int n;

void create_graph()
{
	int i,max_edges,origin,destin;
	clrscr();
	printf ("\nEnter number of nodes:");
	scanf("%d",&n);
	max_edges=n*(n-1); /* Taking directed graph */

	for(i=1;i<=max_edges;i++)
	{
		printf ("\nEnter edge %d( 0 0 ) to quit:",i);
		scanf ("%d %d",&origin,&destin);
		if ((origin==0) && (destin==0))
			break;
		if ( origin > n || destin > n || origin<=0 || destin<=0)
		{
			printf ("\nInvalid edge!\n");
			i--;
		}
		else
			adj[origin][destin]=1;
	}/*End of for*/
```

```
}/*End of create_graph()*/

void display()
{
        int i,j;
        for(i=1;i<=n;i++)
        {
                for(j=1;j<=n;j++)
                printf("%4d",adj[i][j]);
                printf("\n");
        }
}/*End of display()*/

void insert_node()
{
        int i;
        n++;    /*Increase number of nodes in the graph*/
        printf ("\nThe inserted node is %d \n",n);
        for(i=1;i<=n;i++)
        {
                adj[i][n]=0;
                adj[n][i]=0;
        }
}/*End of insert_node()*/
void delete_node(char u)
{
        int i,j;
        if(n==0)
        {
                printf ("\nGraph is empty\n");
                return;
        }
        if ( u>n )
        {
                printf ("\nThis node is not present in the graph\n");
                return;
        }
        for(i=u;i<=n-1;i++)
           for(j=1;j<=n;j++)
           {
                adj[j][i]=adj[j][i+1];  /* Shift columns left */
                adj[i][j]=adj[i+1][j];  /* Shift rows up */
```

```
        }
        n--; /*Decrease the number of nodes in the graph */
}/*End of delete_node*/
void insert_edge(char u,char v)
{
        if (u > n)
        {
                printf ("\nSource node does not exist\n");
                return;
        }
        if(v > n)
        {
                printf("\nDestination node does not exist\n");
                return;
        }
        adj[u][v]=1;
}/*End of insert_edge()*/

void del_edge(char u,char v)
{
     if (u>n || v>n || adj[u][v]==0)
     {
        printf("\nThis edge does not exist\n");
        return;
     }
     adj[u][v]=0;
}/*End of del_edge()*/
void main()
{
        int choice;
        int node,origin,destin;

        create_graph();
        while(1)
        {
                clrscr();
                printf ("\n1.Insert a node\n");
                printf ("2.Insert an edge\n");
                printf ("3.Delete a node\n");
                printf ("4.Delete an edge\n");
                printf ("5.Dispaly\n");
                printf ("6.Exit\n");
```

```
printf ({\nEnter your choice:");
scanf ("%d",&choice);

switch(choice)
{
case 1:
        insert_node();
        break;
case 2:
        printf("\nEnter an edge to be inserted:");
        fflush(stdin);
        scanf("%d %d",&origin,&destin);
        insert_edge(origin,destin);
        break;
case 3:
        printf ("\nEnter a node to be deleted:");
        fflush(stdin);
        scanf ("%d",&node);
        delete_node(node);
        break;
case 4:
        printf ("\nEnter an edge to be deleted:");
        fflush(stdin);
        scanf ("%d %d",&origin,&destin);
        del_edge(origin,destin);
        break;
case 5:
        display();
        break;
case 6:
        exit(0);
default:
        printf("\nWrong choice\n");
        break;
}/*End of switch*/
}/*End of while*/
}/*End of main()*/
```

9.3.3. TRAVERSING A GRAPH

Many application of graph requires a structured system to examine the vertices and edges of a graph G. That is a graph traversal, which means visiting all the nodes of the graph. There are two graph traversal methods.

(*a*) Breadth First Search (BFS)

(*b*) Depth First Search (DFS)

9.4. BREADTH FIRST SEARCH

Given an input graph G = (V, E) and a source vertex S, from where the searching starts. The breadth first search systematically traverse the edges of G to explore every vertex that is reachable from S. Then we examine all the vertices neighbor to source vertex S. Then we traverse all the neighbors of the neighbors of source vertex S and so on. A queue is used to keep track of the progress of traversing the neighbor nodes.

BFS can be further discussed with an example. Considering the graph G in Fig. 9.20

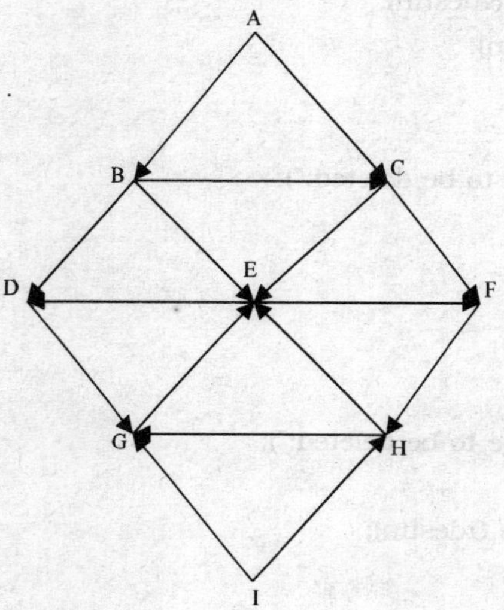

Vertex	*Adjacency list*
A	B, C
B	C, D, E
C	E, F
D	G
E	D, F
F	H
G	E
H	E, G
I	G, H

Fig. 9.20

The linked list (or adjacency list) representation of the graph Fig. 9.20 is also shown. Suppose the source vertex is A. Then following steps will illustrate the BFS.

Step 1: Initially push A (the source vertex) to the queue.

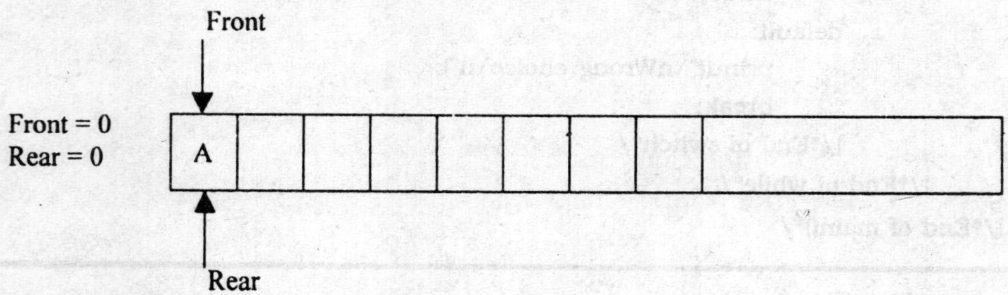

Step 2: Pop (or remove) the front element A from the queue (by incrementing front = front +1) and display it. Then push (or add) the neighboring vertices of A to the queue, (by incrementing Rear = Rear +1) if it is not in queue.

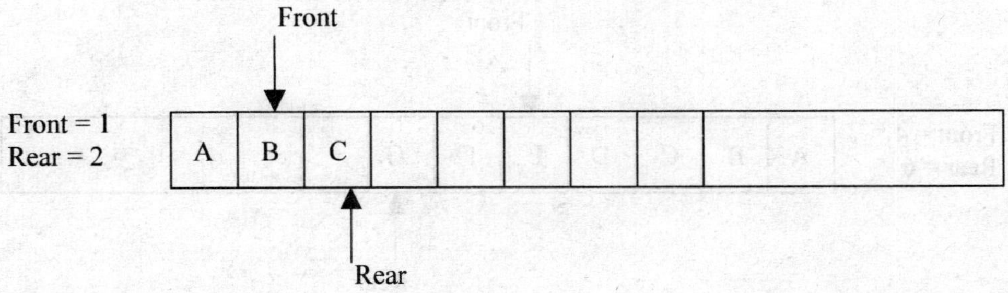

Step 3: Pop the front element B from the queue and display it. Then add the neighboring vertices of B to the queue, if it is not in queue.

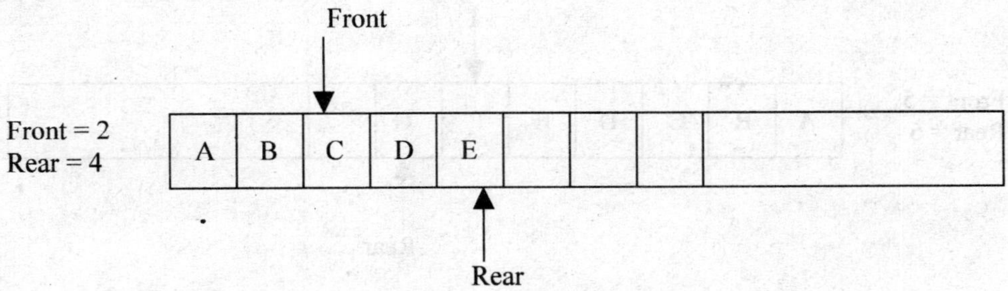

One of the neighboring element C of B is preset in the queue, So C is not added to queue.

Step 4: Remove the front element C and display it. Add the neighboring vertices of C, if it is not present in queue.

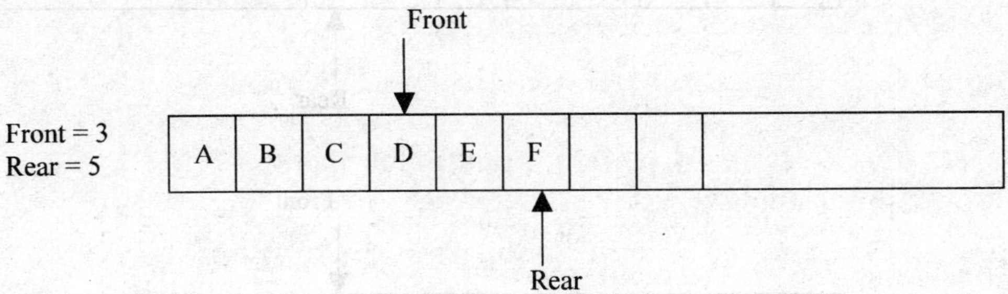

One of the neighboring elements E of C is present in the queue. So E is not added.

Step 5: Remove the front element D, and add the neighboring vertex if it is not present in queue.

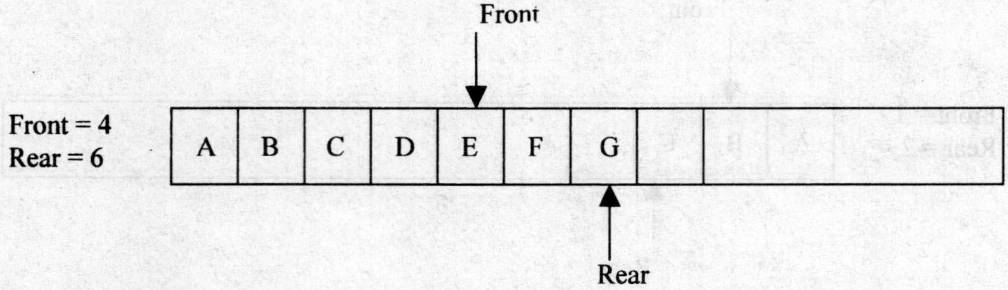

Step 6: Again the process is repeated (Until front > Rear). That is remove the front element E of the queue and add the neighboring vertex if it is not present in queue.

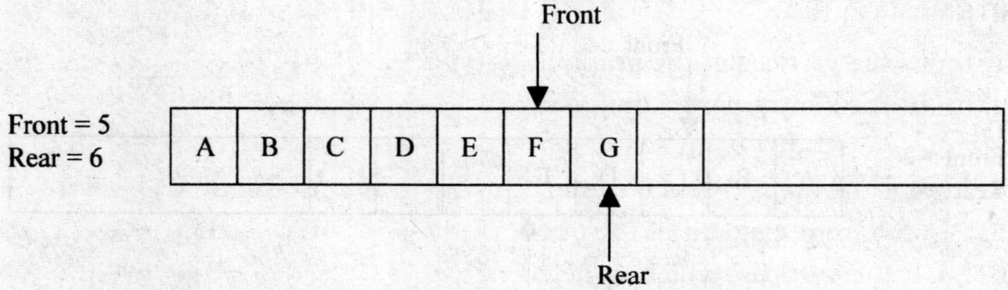

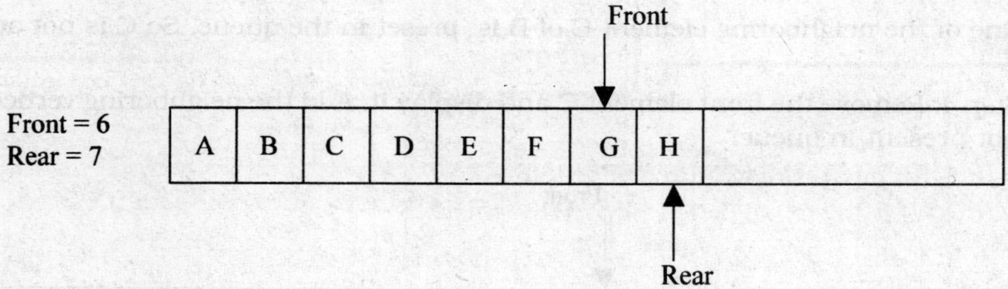

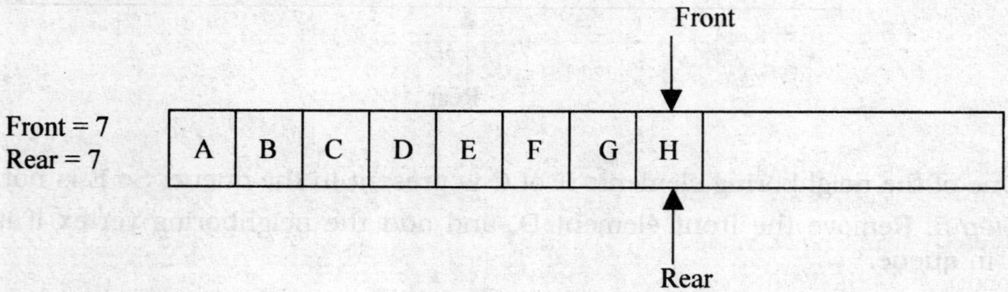

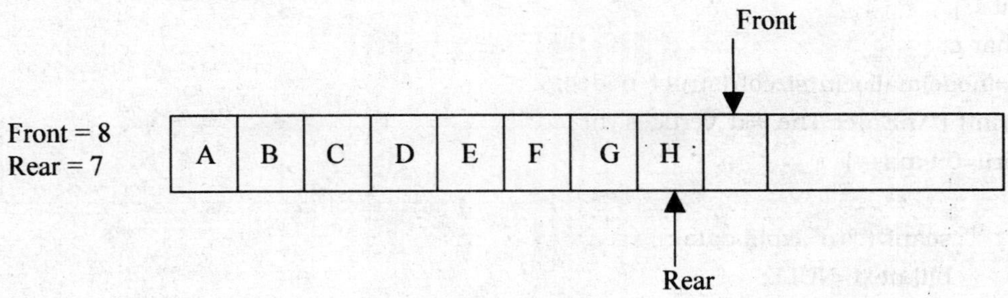

So A, B, C, D, E, F, G, H is the BFS traversal of the graph in Fig. 9.20

ALGORITHM

1. Input the vertices of the graph and its edges G = (V, E)
2. Input the source vertex and assign it to the variable S.
3. Add or push the source vertex to the queue.
4. Repeat the steps 5 and 6 until the queue is empty (*i.e.*, front > rear)
5. Pop the front element of the queue and display it as visited.
6. Push the vertices, which is neighbor to just, popped element, if it is not in the queue and displayed (*i.e.*, not visited).
7. Exit.

PROGRAM 9.2

```
//PROGRAM TO IMPLEMENT BFS USING LINKED LIST
//CODED AND COMPILED USING TURBO C

#include<conio.h>
#include<stdio.h>

struct node
{
int data;
struct node *next;
};
typedef struct node *node;
node bpush(node,int);

node create(int n)
{
node b,t;
```

```
int i, j;
char c;
b=(node)malloc(n*sizeof (struct node));
printf ("\nEnter The %d Vertices",n);
for(i=0;i<n;i++)
{
        scanf ("%d",&b[i].data);
        b[i].next=NULL;
}
for(i=0;i<n;i++)
        for(j=0;j<n;j++)
        {
        do
        {
printf ("\nThe vertice %d have any edge to %d (y/n)....:",b[i].data,b[j].data);
                        c=getche();
                }while(c!='n'&&c!='N'&&c!='y'&&c!='N');
                if(c=='y' | | c=='Y')
                {
                        t=&b[i];
                        while(t->next!=NULL)
                        t=t->next;

                        t->next=(node)malloc(sizeof(struct node));
                        t=t->next;
                        t->next=NULL;
                        t->data=b[j].data;
                }
        }
return b;
}

void bfs(node b,int n)
{
        node h=NULL,f,t,m=NULL;
        int s,j=-1,i;
        printf ("\nEnter the Starting Vetice:");
        scanf ("%d",&s);
        do
        {
                j++;
}while(b[j].data!=s && j<n);
```

```
printf ("\n\tBFS Traversal:");
if(j >= n)
{
        printf ("\n%d is Not Present in the Graph",s);
        bfs(b,n);
        return;
}
h=bpush(h,b[j].data);
m=h;
while(h!=NULL)
{
    t=&b[j];
    while(t!=NULL)
    {
            t=t->next;
            if(t->data!=0)
            bpush(m,t->data);
}
    i=bpop(h);
    h=h->next;
    j=-1;
    do
    {
            j++;
    }while(b[j].data!=i && j<n );
}
getch();
return;
}

node bpush(node s,int i)
{
    int fla=1;
    node f=s,n=s;
    if(s==NULL)
{
        s=(node)malloc(sizeof(struct node));
        f=s;
        s->next=NULL;
        s->data=i;
}
else
```

```
{
        while(n!=NULL)
        {
            if(n->data==i)
            fla=0;
            n=n->next;
        }
        if(fla==1)
        {
            while(s->next!=NULL)
                s=s->next;
            s->next=(node)malloc(sizeof(struct node));
            s=s->next;
            s->next=NULL;
            s->data=i;
        }
}
return f;
}

int bpop(node f)
{
    int i=f->data;
    f=f->next;
    printf("\t%d",i);
    return i;
    }

void main()
{

    node b;
    int n;
    clrscr();
    printf("\nEnter The Number Of Vertices     :");
    scanf("%d",&n);
    b=create(n);
    bfs(b,n);
    return;
```

9.5. DEPTH FIRST SEARCH

The depth first search (DFS), as its name suggest, is to search deeper in the graph, when ever possible. Given an input graph G = (V, E) and a source vertex S, from where the searching starts. First we visit the starting node. Then we travel through each node along a path, which begins at S. That is we visit a neighbor vertex of S and again a neighbor of a neighbor of S, and so on. The implementation of BFS is almost same except a stack is used instead of the queue. DFS can be further discussed with an example. Consider the graph in Fig. 9.20 and its linked list representation. Suppose the source vertex is I.

The following steps will illustrate the DFS

Step 1: Initially push I on to the stack.

STACK: I

DISPLAY:

Step 2: Pop and display the top element, and then push all the neighbors of popped element (*i.e.*, I) onto the stack, if it is not visited (or displayed or not in the stack.

STACK: G, H

DISPLAY: I

Step 3: Pop and display the top element and then push all the neighbors of popped the element (*i.e.*, H) onto top of the stack, if it is not visited.

STACK: G, E

DISPLAY: I, H

The popped element H has two neighbors E and G. G is already visited, means G is either in the stack or displayed. Here G is in the stack. So only E is pushed onto the top of the stack.

Step 4: Pop and display the top element of the stack. Push all the neighbors of the popped element on to the stack, if it is not visited.

STACK: G, D, F

DISPLAY: I, H, E

Step 5: Pop and display the top element of the stack. Push all the neighbors of the popped element onto the stack, if it is not visited.

STACK: G, D

DISPLAY: I, H, E, F

The popped element (or vertex) F has neighbor(s) H, which is already visited. Then H is displayed, and will not be pushed again on to the stack.

Step 6: The process is repeated as follows.

STACK: G

DISPLAY: I, H, E, F, D

STACK: //now the stack is empty

DISPLAY: I, H, E, F, D, G

So I, H, E, F, D, G is the DFS traversal of graph Fig 9:20 from the source vertex I.

Algorithm

1. Input the vertices and edges of the graph G = (V, E).
2. Input the source vertex and assign it to the variable S.
3. Push the source vertex to the stack.
4. Repeat the steps 5 and 6 until the stack is empty.
5. Pop the top element of the stack and display it.
6. Push the vertices which is neighbor to just popped element, if it is not in the queue and displayed (ie; not visited).
7. Exit.

PROGRAM 9.3

```
//PROGRAM TO IMPLEMENT DFS USING ADJACENCY MATRIX
//CODED AND COMPILED IN TURBO C

#include<conio.h>
#include<stdio.h>
#define max 10
/* a function to build adjacency matrix of a graph */
void buildadjm(int adj[][max], int n)
{
    int i,j;
    for(i=0;i<n;i++)
        for(j=0;j<n;j++)
        {
            printf("\nEnter 1 if there is an edge from %d to %d, otherwise enter 0 \n",i,j);
            scanf("%d",&adj[i][j]);
        }
}

/* a function to visit the nodes in a depth first order */
void dfs(int x,int visited[],int adj[][max],int n)
{
    int j;
    visited[x] = 1;
    printf("\nThe node visited id %d\n",x);
    for(j=0;j<n;j++)
        if (adj[x][j] ==1 && visited[j] ==0)
            dfs(j,visited,adj,n);
}
void main()
{
    int adj[max][max],node,n;
```

```
    int i, visited[max];
    printf("\nEnter the number of nodes in graph maximum = %d\n",max);
    scanf("%d",&n);
    buildadjm(adj,n);
    for(i=0; i<n; i++)
    visited[i] =0;
    for(i=0; i<n; i++)
       if(visited[i] ==0)
            dfs(i,visited,adj,n);
}
```

9.6. MINIMUM SPANNING TREE

A minimum spanning tree (MST) for a graph G = (V, E) is a sub graph $G^1 = (V^1, E^1)$ of G contains all the vertices of G.

1. The vertex set V^1 is same as that at graph G.
2. The edge set E^1 is a subset of G.
3. And there is no cycle.

If a graph G is not a connected graph, then it cannot have any spanning tree. In this case, it will have a spanning forest. Suppose a graph G with *n* vertices then the MST will have (*n* – 1) edges, assuming that the graph is connected.

A minimum spanning tree (MST) for a weighted graph is a spanning tree with minimum weight. That is all the vertices in the weighted graph will be connected with minimum edge with minimum weights. Fig. 9.22 shows the minimum spanning tree of the weighted graph in Fig. 9.21.

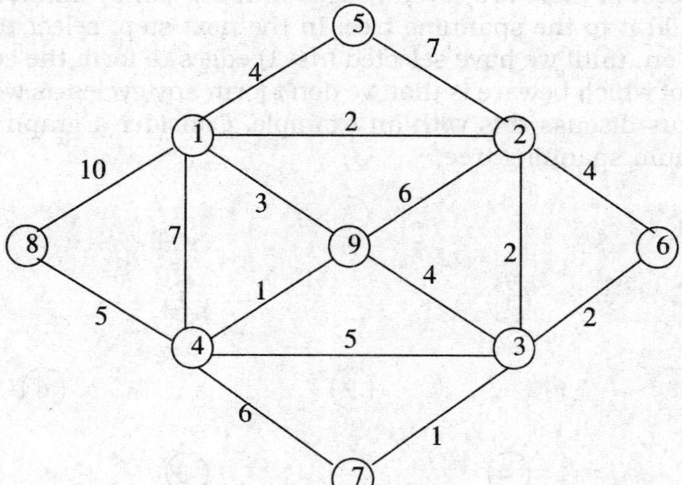

Fig. 9.21

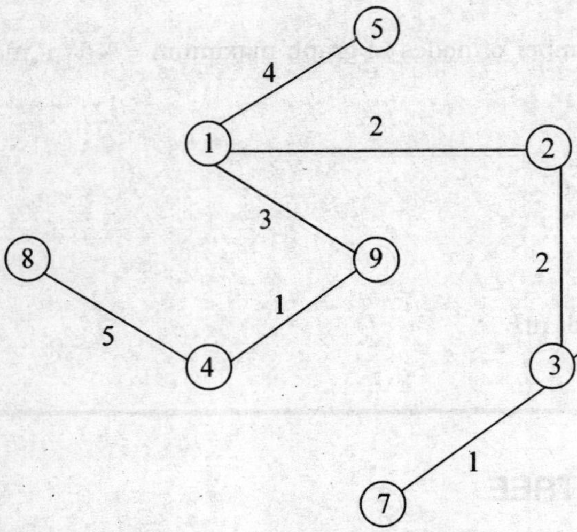

Fig. 9.22

Three different famous algorithms can be used to obtain a minimum spanning tree of a connected weighted and undirected graph.

1. Kruskal's Algorithm
2. Prim's Algorithm
3. Sollin's Algorithm

All three algorithms are using a design strategy called the greedy methods that is one which seeks maximum gain at each step.

9.6.1. KRUSKAL'S ALGORITHM

This is a one of the popular algorithm and was developed by Joseph Kruskal. To create a minimum cost spanning trees, using Kruskalls, we begin by choosing the edge with the minimum cost (if there are several edges with the same minimum cost, select any one of them) and add it to the spanning tree. In the next step, select the edge with next lowest cost, and so on, until we have selected $(n-1)$ edges to form the complete spanning tee. The only thing of which beware is that we don't form any cycles as we add edges to the spanning tree. Let us discuss this with an example. Consider a graph G in Fig. 9.21 to generate the minimum spanning tree.

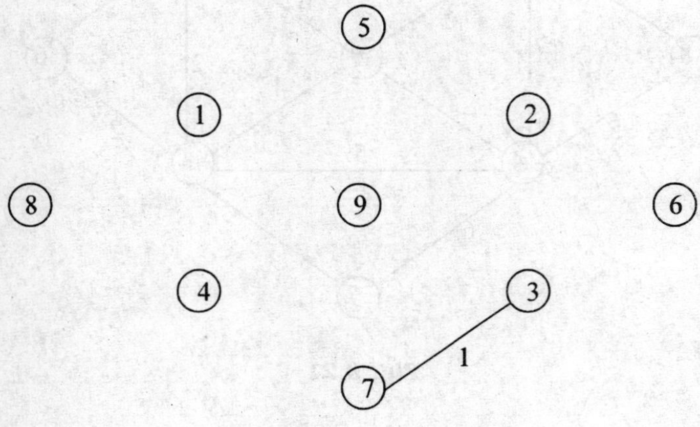

The minimum cost edge in the graph G in Fig. 9.21 is 1. If you analyze closely there are two edges (*i.e.*, (7, 3), (4, 9)) with the minimum cost 1. As the algorithm says select any one of them. Here we select the edge (7, 3) as shown in Fig. 9.23. Again we select minimum cost edge (*i.e.*, 1), which is (4, 9) as shown in Fig. 9.24.

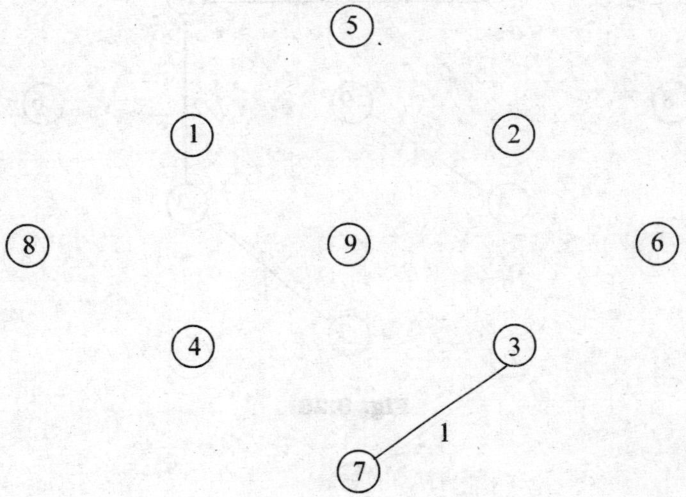

Fig 9:24

Next we select minimum cost edge (*i.e.*, 2). If you analyze closely there are two edges (*i.e.*, (1, 2), (2, 3), (3, 6)) with the minimum cost 2. As the algorithm says select any one of them. Here we select the edge (1, 2) as shown in the above Fig. 9.25. Again we select minimum cost edge (*i.e.*, 2), which is (2, 3) as shown in Fig. 9.26. Next we select minimum cost edge (*i.e.*, 2), which is (3, 6) as shown in Fig. 9.27.

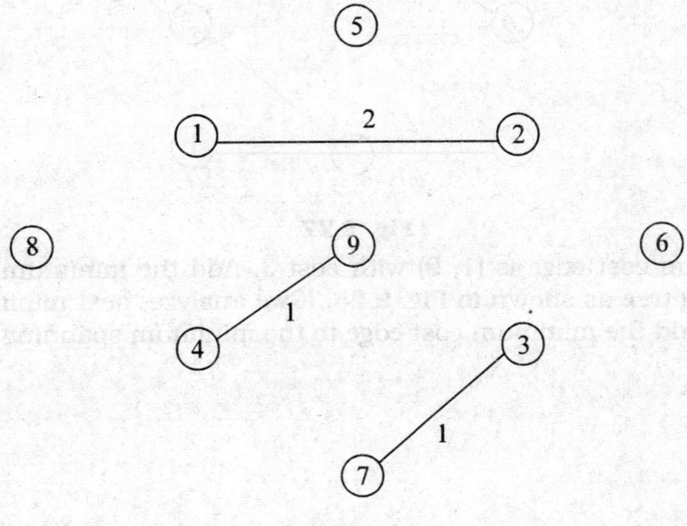

Fig. 9.25

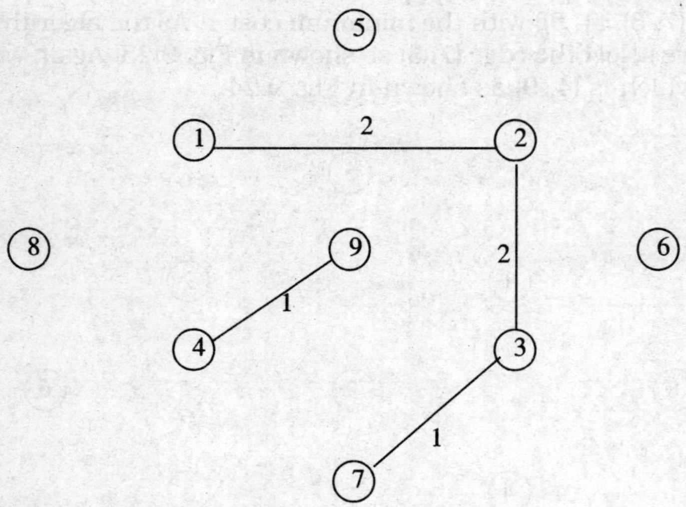

Fig. 9.26

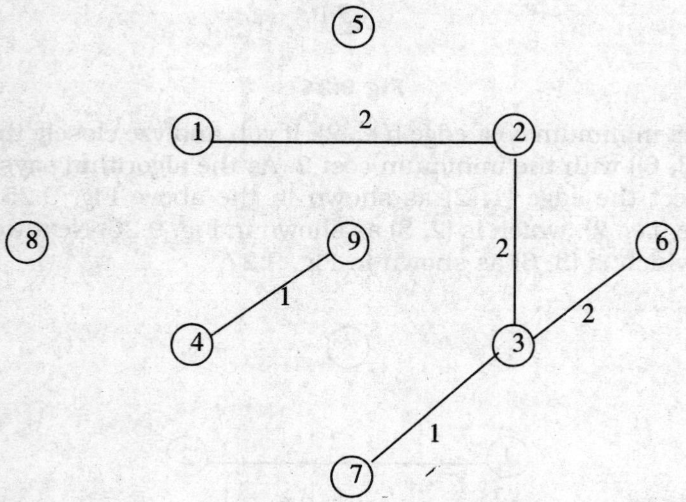

Fig. 9.27

Next minimum cost edge is (1, 9) with cost 3. Add the minimum cost edge to the minimum spanning tree as shown in Fig. 9.28. If we analyze, next minimum cost edge is (1, 5) with cost 4. Add the minimum cost edge to the minimum spanning tree as shown in Fig. 9.29.

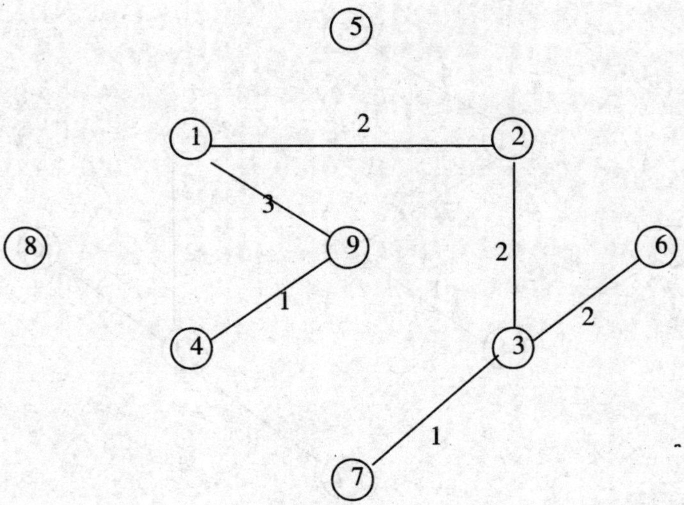

Fig. 9.28

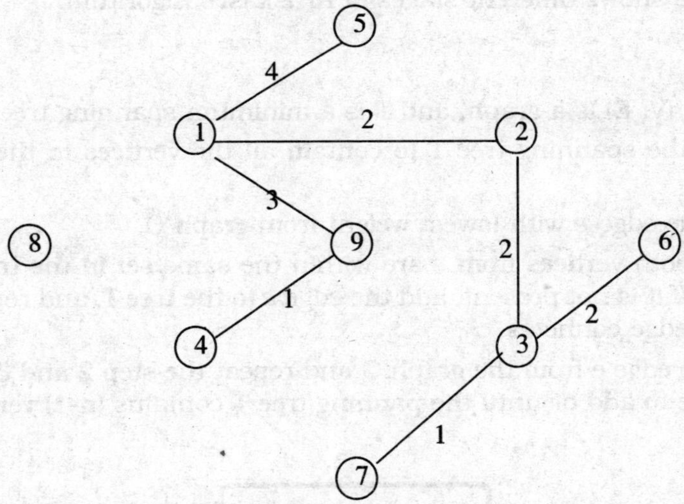

Fig. 9.29

Next minimum cost edge is (4, 8) with cost 5. Add the minimum cost edge to the minimum spanning tree as shown in Fig 9.30.

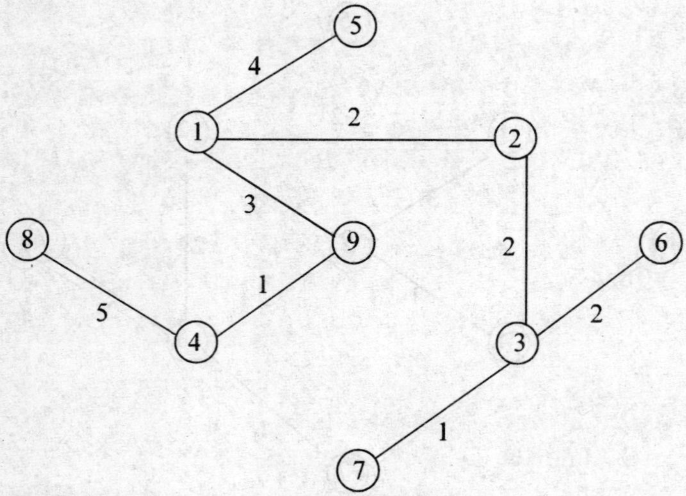

Fig. 9.30

Above figures shows different stages of Kruskasl's Algorithm.

ALGORITHM

Suppose G = (V, E) is a graph, and T is a minimum spanning tree of graph G.

1. Initialize the spanning tree T to contain all the vertices in the graph G but no edges.
2. Choose the edge *e* with lowest weight from graph G.
3. Check if both vertices from *e* are within the same set in the tree T, for all such sets of T. If it is not present, add the edge *e* to the tree T, and replace the two sets that this edge connects.
4. Delete the edge e from the graph G and repeat the step 2 and 3 until there is no more edge to add or until the panning tree T contains (n-1) vertices.
5. Exit

PROGRAM 9.4

```
//PROGRAM TO CREATING A MINIMUM SPANNING TREE
//USING KRUSKAL'S ALGORITHM
//CODED AND COMPILED IN TURBO C

#include<stdio.h>
#include<conio.h>
#include<malloc.h>
#include<process.h>
```

```
#define MAX 20

struct edge
{
        int u;
        int v;
        int weight;
        struct edge *link;
}*front = NULL;

int father[MAX]; /*Holds father of each node */
struct edge tree[MAX]; /* Will contain the edges of spanning tree */
int n;   /*Denotes total number of nodes in the graph */
int wt_tree=0; /*Weight of the spanning tree */
int count=0;    /* Denotes number of edges included in the tree */

/* Functions */
void make_tree();
void insert_tree(int i,int j,int wt);
void insert_pque(int i,int j,int wt);
struct edge *del_pque();

void create_graph()
{
        int i,wt,max_edges,origin,destin;

        printf ("Enter number of nodes:");
        scanf ("%d",&n);
        max_edges=n*(n-1)/2;
        for(i=1;i<=max_edges;i++)
        {
                printf ("Enter edge %d(0 0 to quit):",i);
                scanf ("%d %d",&origin,&destin);
                if ((origin==0) && (destin==0))
                        break;
                printf("Enter weight for this edge:");
                scanf("%d",&wt);
                if( origin > n || destin > n || origin<=0 || destin<=0)
                {
                        printf ("Invalid edge!\n");
                        i--;
                }
```

```
			else
				insert_pque(origin,destin,wt);
		}/*End of for*/
		if(i<n-1)
		{
			printf("Spanning tree is not possible\n");
			exit(1);
		}
}/*End of create_graph()*/

void main()
{
		int i;
		clrscr();
		create_graph();
		make_tree();
		printf("\nEdges to be included in spanning tree are :\n");
		for(i=1;i<=count;i++)
		{
			printf("%d->",tree[i].u);
			printf("%d\n",tree[i].v);
		}
		printf("\nWeight of this minimum spanning tree is : %d\n", wt_tree);
}/*End of main()*/

void make_tree()
{
		struct edge *tmp;
		int node1,node2,root_n1,root_n2;

		while( count < n-1) /*Loop till n-1 edges included in the tree*/
		{
			tmp=del_pque();
			node1=tmp->u;
			node2=tmp->v;

			printf ("n1=%d  ",node1);
			printf ("n2=%d  ",node2);

			while( node1 > 0)
			{
				root_n1=node1;
```

```
                node1=father[node1];
            }
            while( node2 >0 )
            {
                root_n2=node2;
                node2=father[node2];
            }
            printf ("rootn1=%d  ",root_n1);
            printf ("rootn2=%d\n",root_n2);

            if(root_n1!=root_n2)
            {
                insert_tree(tmp->u,tmp->v,tmp->weight);
                wt_tree=wt_tree+tmp->weight;
                father[root_n2]=root_n1;
            }
        }/*End of while*/
}/*End of make_tree()*/

/*Inserting an edge in the tree */
void insert_tree(int i,int j,int wt)
{
        printf("This edge inserted in the spanning tree\n");
        count++;
        tree[count].u=i;
        tree[count].v=j;
        tree[count].weight=wt;
}/*End of insert_tree()*/
/*Inserting edges in the priority queue */
void insert_pque(int i,int j,int wt)
{
        struct edge *tmp,*q;

        tmp = (struct edge *)malloc(sizeof(struct edge));
        tmp->u=i;
        tmp->v=j;
        tmp->weight = wt;

        /*Queue is empty or edge to be added has weight less than first edge*/
        if(front == NULL || tmp->weight < front->weight )
        {
```

```
            tmp->link = front;
            front = tmp;
      }
      else
      {
            q = front;
            while( q->link != NULL && q->link->weight <= tmp->weight )
                  q=q->link;
            tmp->link = q->link;
            q->link = tmp;
            if(q->link == NULL)/*Edge to be added at the end*/
                  tmp->link = NULL;
      }/*End of else*/
}/*End of insert_pque()*/

/*Deleting an edge from the priority queue*/
struct edge *del_pque()
{
      struct edge *tmp;
      tmp = front;
      printf("Edge processed is %d->%d  %d\n",tmp->u,tmp->v,tmp->weight);
      front = front->link;
      return tmp;
}/*End of del_pque()*/
```

9.6.2. JARNIK-PRIM'S ALGORITHM

This algorithm was discovered by Vojtech Jarnik in 1936 and later rediscovered by Robert Prim. Prim's algorithm also constructs the minimum-cost spanning tree, edge by edge. Prim's algorithm begin with a tree T that contain a single vertex (This vertex can be of any vertices in the original graph), generally it is selected as lower most cost edge in the tree. Then we add a least cost edge (u, v) to T such that T U { (u, v) } is also a tree. Repeat this edge-addition step until T contains $n - 1$ edges.

Construction of the minimum-cost spanning tree using Prim's algorithm can be explained with an example. Consider a graph G in Fig. 9.21.

The minimum cost edge in the graph G in Fig. 9:21 is 1. If you analyze closely there are two edges (*i.e.*, (4, 9), (7, 3)) with the minimum cost 1. As the Prim's algorithm says select any one of them. Here we select the edge (4, 9) as shown in Fig. 9.31.

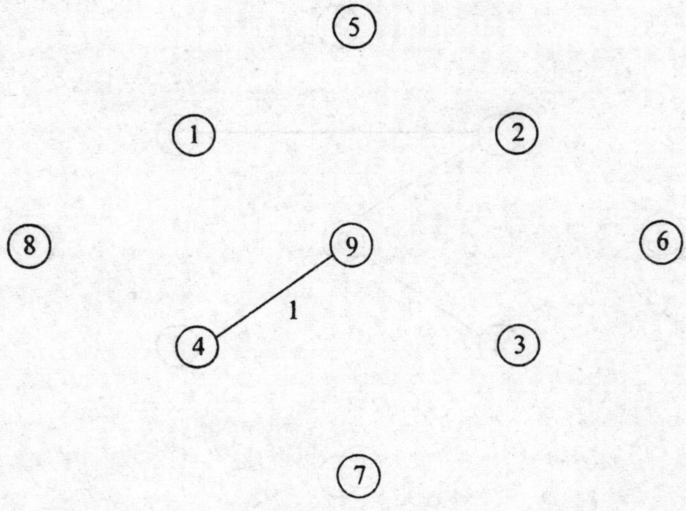

Fig. 9.31

Consider all the edges adjacent to the vertices of the recently selected edge (here recently selected edge is (4, 9)). And find the minimum cost edge that connects from recently selected edge. Here it is (9, 1) as shown in Fig. 9.32.

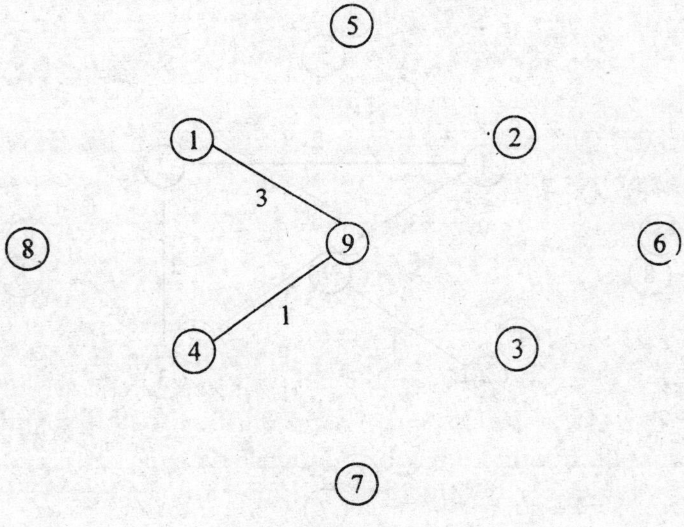

Fig. 9.32

Again consider all the edges adjacent to the vertices of the recently selected edge (here recently selected edge is (9, 1)). And find the minimum cost edge that connects from reçently selected edge. Here it is (1, 2) as shown in Fig. 9.33.

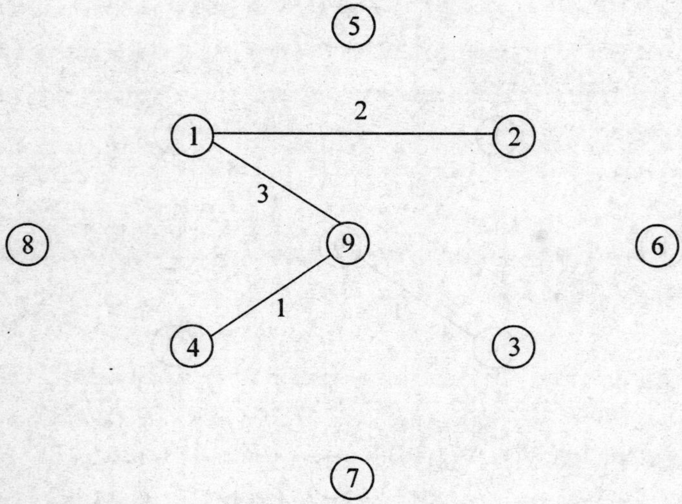

Fig. 9.33

Consider all the edges adjacent to the vertices of the recently selected edge (here recently selected edge is (1, 2)). And find the minimum cost edge that connects from recently selected edge. Here it is (2, 3) as shown in Fig 9:34. And repeat the process of finding the minimum cost edge that connects from recently selected edge.

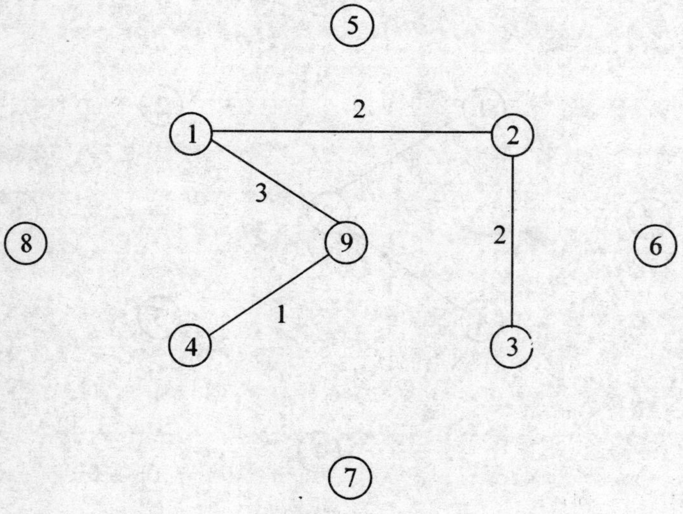

Fig. 9.34

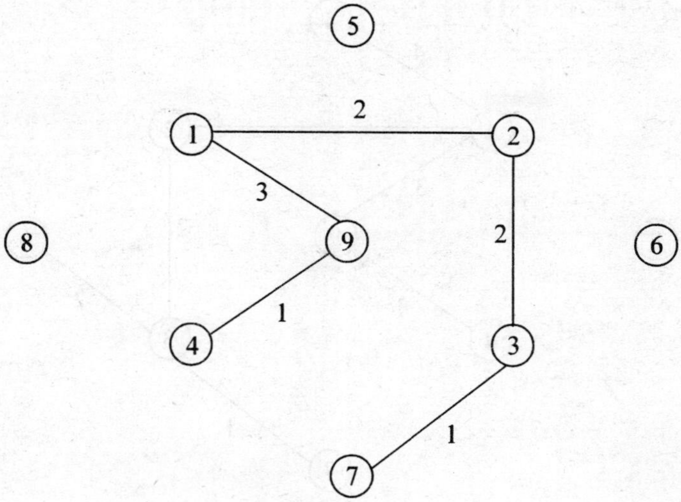

Fig. 9.35

Since all the vertices in the adjacent edges that can be reached from the recently selected edge (*i.e.*, (2, 3)) are visited, backtrack (or go back) to the path so as any other minimum cost adjacent edges is there to connect the vertices which are not connected yet. Thus we find the adjacent edge (3, 6) as shown in the Fig. 9.36.

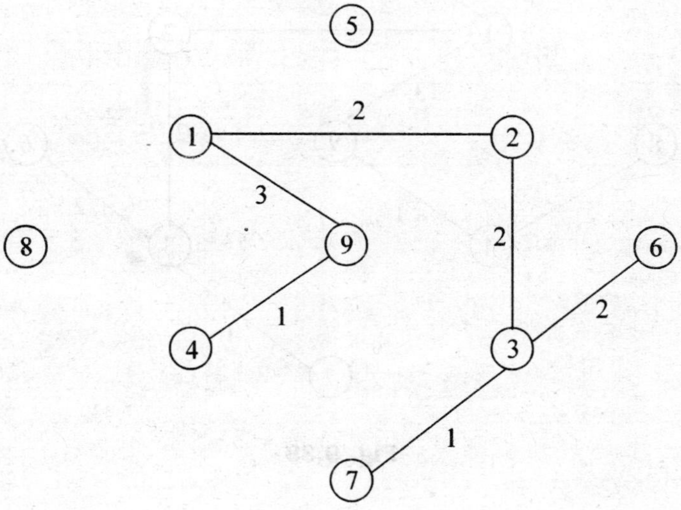

Fig. 9.36

Again since all the vertices in the adjacent edges that can be reached from the recently selected edge (*i.e.*, (3, 6)) are visited, backtrack (or go back) to the path so as any other minimum cost adjacent edges is there to connect the vertices which are not connected yet. Thus we find the adjacent edge (1, 5) as shown in the Fig. 9.37.

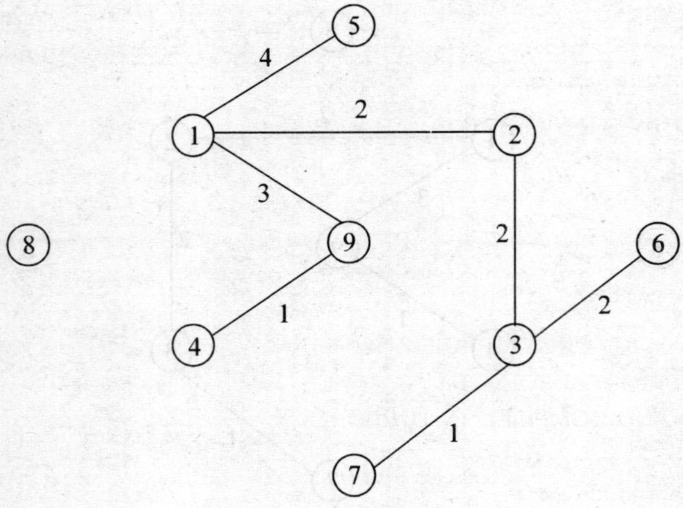

Fig. 9.37

Next we find the minimum cost adjacent edges (4, 8) as shown in the Fig. 9.38.

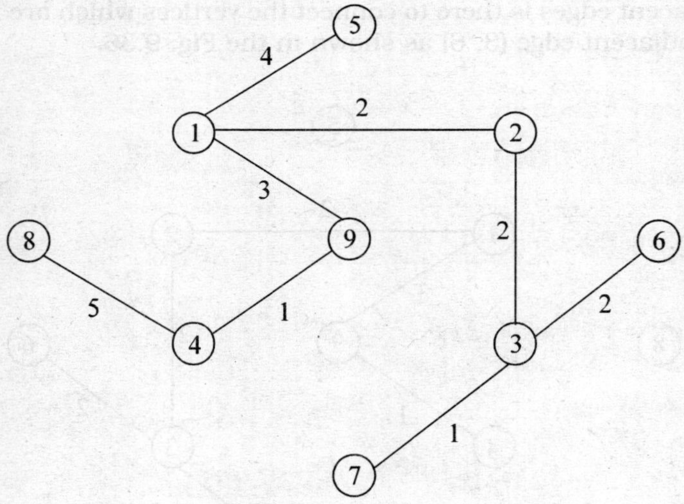

Fig. 9.38

ALGORITHM

Suppose G = (V,E) is a graph and T is a minimum spanning tree of grph G.

1. Initialize the spanning tree T to contain a vertex v_1.
2. Choose an edge $e = (v_1, v_2)$ of G such that v_2 not equal to v_1 and e has smallest weight among the edges of G incident with v_1.
3. Select an edge $e = (v_2, v_3)$ of G such that v_2 is not equal to v_3 and e has smallest weight among the edge of G incident with v_2.

4. Suppose the edge e_1, e_2, e_3, ... e_i Then select an edge $e_i + 1 = (V_j, V_k)$ such that
   (a) $V_j \in \{v_1, v_2, v_3, \ldots\ldots v_i, v_i + 1\}$ and
   (b) $V_k \notin \{v_1, v_2, v_3, \ldots\ldots v_i, v_i + 1\}$ such that ei+1 has smallest weight among the edge of G
5. Repeat the step 4 until $(n - 1)$ edges have been chosen
6. Exit

PROGRAM 9.5

```
//PROGRAM TO CREATE MINIMUM SPANNING TREE
//USING PRIM'S ALGORITHM
//CODED AND COMPILED IN TURBO C

#include<conio.h>
#include<stdio.h>
#include<process.h>

#define MAX 10
#define TEMP 0
#define PERM 1
#define FALSE 0
#define TRUE 1
#define infinity 9999

struct node
{
	int predecessor;
	int dist; /*Distance from predecessor */
	int status;
};

struct edge
{
	int u;
	int v;
};

int adj[MAX][MAX];
int n;

void create_graph()
{
	int i,max_edges,origin,destin, wt;
```

```
        printf ("Enter number of vertices:");
        scanf ("%d",&n);
        max_edges=n*(n-1)/2;

        for(i=1;i<=max_edges;i++)
        {
                printf ("Enter edge %d(0 0 to quit):",i);
                scanf ("%d %d",&origin,&destin);
                if((origin==0) && (destin==0))
                        break;
                printf ("Enter weight for this edge:");
                scanf ("%d",&wt);
                if( origin > n || destin > n || origin<=0 || destin<=0)
                {
                        printf ("Invalid edge!\n");
                        i--;
                }
                else
                {
                        adj[origin][destin]=wt;
                        adj[destin][origin]=wt;
                }
        }/*End of for*/
        if(i<n-1)
        {
                printf ("Spanning tree is not possible\n");
                exit(1);
        }
}/*End of create_graph()*/

void display()
{
        int i,j;
        for(i=1;i<=n;i++)
        {
                for(j=1;j<=n;j++)
                        printf ("%3d",adj[i][j]);
                printf ("\n");
        }
}/*End of display()*/
```

```
/*This function returns TRUE if all nodes are permanent*/
int all_perm(struct node state[MAX] )
{
	int i;
	for (i=1;i<=n;i++)
	   if( state[i].status == TEMP )
	       return FALSE;
	return TRUE;
}/*End of all_perm()*/

int maketree(struct edge tree[MAX],int *weight)
{
	struct node state[MAX];
	int i, k, min, count, current, newdist;
	int m;
	int u1,v1;
	*weight=0;
	/*Make all nodes temporary*/
	for(i=1;i<=n;i++)
	{
		state[i].predecessor=0;
		state[i].dist = infinity;
		state[i].status = TEMP;
	}
	/*Make first node permanent*/
	state[1].predecessor=0;
	state[1].dist = 0;
	state[1].status = PERM;

	/*Start from first node*/
	current = 1;
	count = 0; /*count represents number of nodes in tree */
	while( all_perm(state) != TRUE ) /*Loop till all the nodes become PERM*/
	{
		for(i=1;i<=n;i++)
		{
			if(adj[current][i] > 0 && state[i].status == TEMP)
			{
				if(adj[current][i] < state[i].dist)
				{
					state[i].predecessor = current;
					state[i].dist = adj[current][i];
```

```
                }
            }
        }/*End of for*/

        /*Search for temporary node with minimum distance
        and  make it current node*/
        min=infinity;
        for(i=1;i<=n;i++)
        {
            if (state[i].status == TEMP && state[i].dist < min)
            {
                min = state[i].dist;
                current=i;
            }
        }/*End of for*/

        state[current].status=PERM;

        /*Insert this edge(u1,v1) into the tree */
        u1=state[current].predecessor;
        v1=current;
        count++;
        tree[count].u=u1;
        tree[count].v=v1;
        /*Add wt on this edge to weight of tree */
        *weight=*weight+adj[u1][v1];
    }/*End of while*/
    return (count);
}/*End of maketree()*/
void main()
{
    int i, j;
    int path[MAX];
    int wt_tree,count;
    struct edge tree[MAX];
    clrscr();
    create_graph();
    printf("\nAdjacency matrix is:\n");
    display();

    count = maketree(tree,&wt_tree);
```

```
printf("\nWeight of spanning tree is:%d\n", wt_tree);
printf("\nEdges to be included in spanning tree are:\n");
for(i=1;i<=count;i++)
{
        printf ("%d->",tree[i].u);
        printf ("%d\n",tree[i].v);
}
getch();
}/*End of main()*/
```

9.6.3. SOLLIN'S ALGORITHM

Sollin's Algorithm construct the minimum cost spanning tree by selecting several edge at each stage. Select few edges of lowest weight, to form a spanning forest. If more than one edge exists with minimum cost, select all the edges. Next stage, we select one edge of minimum weight for each tree in this forest. It is possible for two trees in the forest to select the same edge. So multiple copies of the same edge is eliminated. Also, when the graph has several edges with the same cost, it is possible to select two different edges that connect them together. Repeat the steps until there is only one three or when no edges remain to be selected.

Construction of the minimum-cost spanning tree using Prim's algorithm can be explained with an example. Consider a graph G in Fig. 9.21. Following figures shows different stages in Sollin's Algorithm.

The minimum cost edge in the graph G in Fig. 9.21 is 1. If you analyze closely there are two edges (*i.e.*, (7, 3), (4, 9)) with the minimum cost 1. As the algorithm says select all minimum cost edges as the edges in the minimum-cost spanning tree as shown in Fig. 9.39.

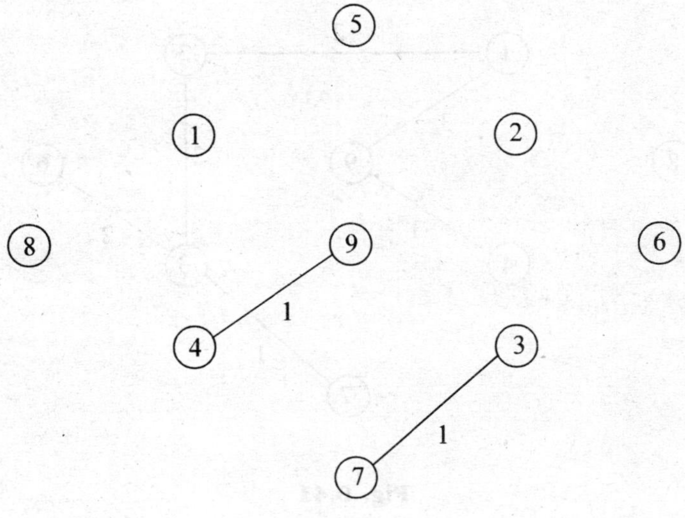

Fig. 9.39

Next select minimum weight edge incident to recently selected edge(s). Here (4,9), (7, 3) are the recently selected edges. Minimum cost edges incident to this edges are (9, 1) and (3, 6) respectively. As the algorithm says select these minimum cost edges as the edges in the minimum-cost spanning tree as shown in Fig. 9.40. And repeat the same process.

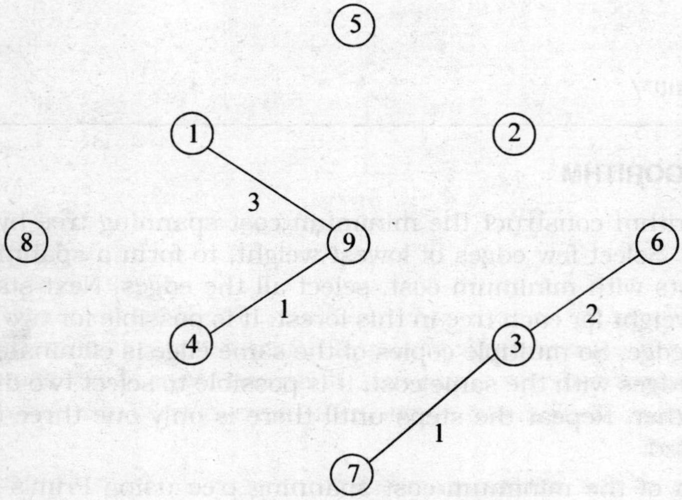

Fig. 9.40

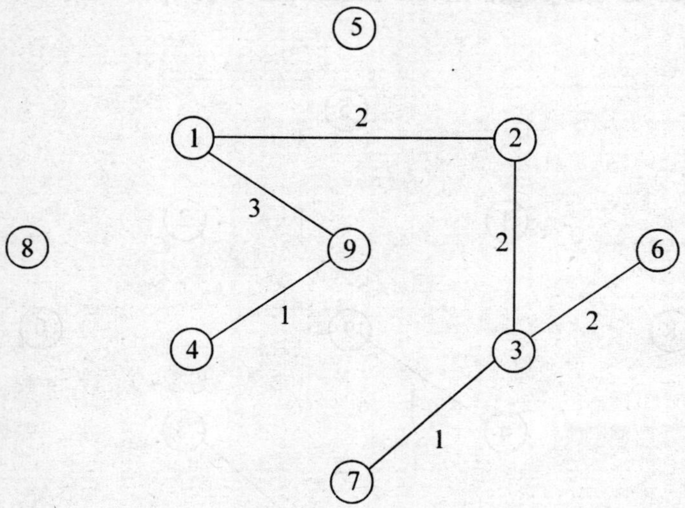

Fig. 9.41

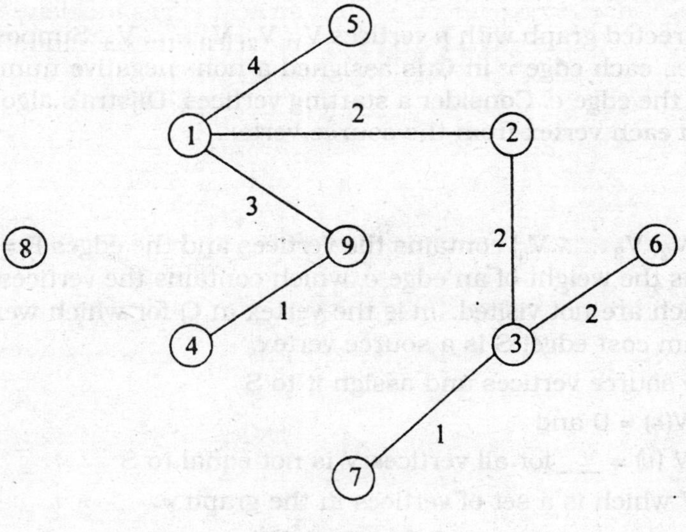

Fig. 9.42

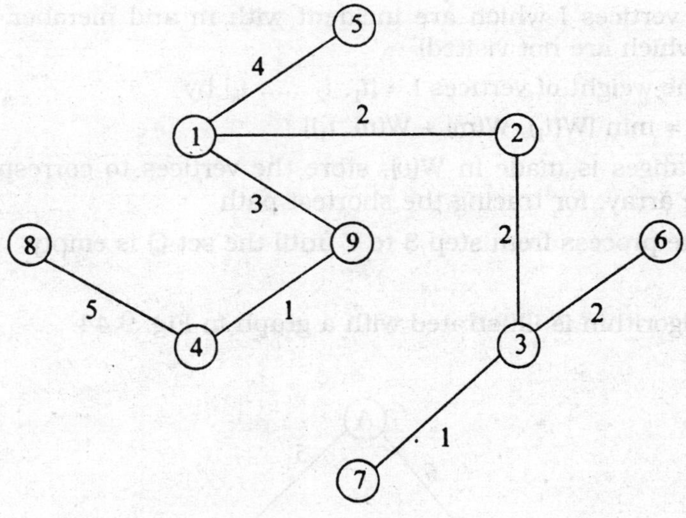

Fig. 9.43

9.7. SHORTEST PATH

A path from a source vertex *a* to *b* is said to be shortest path if there is no other path from *a* to *b* with lower weights. There are many instances, to find the shortest path for traveling from one place to another. That is to find which route can reach as quick as possible or a route for which the traveling cost in minimum. Dijkstra's Algorithm is used find shortest path.

9.7.1. DIJKSTRA'S ALGORITHM

Let G be a directed graph with n vertices V_1, V_2, V_3 ...... V_n. Suppose G = (V, E, W_e) is weighted graph. *i.e.*, each edge *e* in G is assigned a non- negative number, we called the weight or length of the edge *e*. Consider a starting vertices. Dijstra's algorithm will find the weight or length to each vertex from the source vertex.

ALGORITHM

Set V = {V_1, V_2, V_3 ...... V_n} contains the vertices and the edges E = {e_1, e_2, ... e_m} of the graph G. W(e) is the weight of an edge *e*, which contains the vertices V_1 and V_2. Q is a set of vertices, which are not visited. *m* is the vertex in Q for which weight W(*m*) is minimum, *i.e.*, minimum cost edge. S is a source vertex.

1. Input the source vertices and assign it to S
   (*a*) Set W(*s*) = 0 and
   (*b*) Set W (*v*) = ___ for all vertices V is not equal to S
2. Set Q = V which is a set of vertices in the graph
3. Suppose *m* be a vertices in Q for which W(*m*) is minimum
4. Make the vertices *m* as visited and delete it from the set Q
5. Find the vertices I which are incident with m and member of Q (That is the vertices which are not visited)
6. Update the weight of vertices I = {i_1, i_2 ...... i_k} by
   (*a*) W(i_1) = min [W(i_1), W(*m*) + W(*m*, i_1)]
7. If any changes is made in W(*v*), store the vertices to corresponding vertices *i*, using the array, for tracing the shortest path
8. Repeat the process from step 3 to 7 until the set Q is empty
9. Exit

The above algorithm is illustrated with a graph in Fig. 9.44

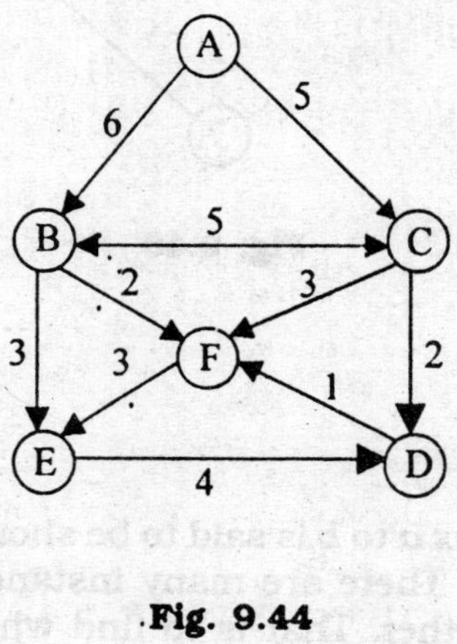

Fig. 9.44

Source vertices is = A   W (A) = 0

V = {A, B, C, D, E, F) = Q

V	A	B	C	D	E	F
W(V)	0					
Q	A	B	C	D	E	F

A	
B	
C	
D	
E	
F	

ITERATION 1:

m = A

W(A, A) = 0 (Distance from A to A)

Now the Q = { B, C, D, E, F}

Two edges are incident with m

i.e., I = { B, C}

W(B) = min (W(B), W (A) + W (A, B)]

= Min (_, 0 + 6)

= 6

W(C) = min (w(c), W (A) + W (A,C)]

= min (–, 0 + 5) = 5

V	A	B	C	D	E	F
W(V)	0	6	5			
Q		B	C	D	E	F

A	/
B	A
C	A
D	
E	
F	

ITERATION 2:

m = C (Because W(v) in minimum vertex and is also a member of Q)

Now the Q become (B, D, E, F)

Two edge are incident with C = {D, F} = I

W(D) = min (W(D), [W(C) + W(C, D)])

= min (_, [5+2]) =7

W(F) = min (W(F), [W(C) + W (C, F)])

= min (_, [5+3]) =8

V	A	B	C	D	E	F
W(V)	0	6	5	7		8
Q		B		D	E	F

A	/
B	A
C	A
D	C
E	
F	C

ITERATION 3:

m = B (Because *w* (V) in minimum in vertices B and is also a member of Q)

Now the Q become (D, E, F)

Three edge are incident with B = { C, E, F}

Since C is not a member of Q so I = {E, F}

W(E) = min (_ , 6 + 3) =9

W(F) = min (8, 6 + 2) =8

V	A	B	C	D	E	F
W(V)	0	6	5	7	9	8
Q				D	E	F

A	
B	A
C	A
D	C
E	B
F	C

ITERATION 4:

m = D

Q = {E, F)

Incident vertices of D = { F } = I

W(F) = min (W(F) , [W(D) + W(D,F))

W(F) = min (8 , 7 + 1) =8

V	A	B	C	D	E	F
W(V)	0	6	5	7	9	8
Q					E	F

A	
B	A
C	A
D	C
E	B
F	C

ITERATION 5:

s = F

Q = { F)

Incident vertices of F = { E }

W(E) = min (W(F) , [W(E) + W(F,E))

W(E) = min (9 , 9 + 3) = 9

V	A	B	C	D	E	F
W(V)	0	6	5	7	9	8
Q					E	

A	
B	A
C	A
D	C
E	B
F	C

now E is the only chain, hence we stop the iteration and the final table is

V	A	B	C	D	E	F
W(V)	0	6	5	7	9	8

A	
B	A
C	A
D	C
E	B
F	C

If the source vertex is A and the destination vertex is D then the weight is 7 and the shortest path can be traced from table at the right side as follows.

Start finding the shortest path from destination vertex to its shortest vertex. For example we want to find the shortest path from A to D. Then find the shortest vertex from D, which is C. Check the shortest vertex, is equal to source vertex. Otherwise assign the shortest vertex as new destination vertex to find its shortest vertex as new destination vertex to find its shortest vertex. This process continued until we reach to source vertex from destination vertex.

D → C

C → A

A, C, D is the shortest path

The efficiency of the Dijskras's algorithm is analyzed by the iteration of the loop structures. The while loop iteration $n - 1$ times to visit the minimum weighted edge. Potentially loop must be repeated n times to examine every vertices in the graph. So the time complexity is $O(n^2)$.

PROGRAM 9.6

```
//PROGRAM OF SHORTEST PATH BETWEEN TWO NODE IN
//GRAPH USING DJIKSTRA ALGORITHM
//CODED AND COMPILED IN TURBO C

#include<conio.h>
#include<stdio.h>
#include<process.h>

#define MAX 10
#define TEMP 0
#define PERM 1
#define infinity 9999

struct node
{
```

```
        int predecessor;
        int dist; /*minimum distance of node from source*/
        int status;
};

int adj[MAX][MAX];
int n;

void create_graph()
{
        int i,max_edges,origin,destin,wt;

        printf ("\nEnter number of vertices:");
        scanf ("%d",&n);
        max_edges=n*(n-1);

        for(i=1;i<=max_edges;i++)
        {
                printf ("\nEnter edge %d(0 0 to quit):",i);
                scanf("%d %d",&origin,&destin);
                if((origin==0) && (destin==0))
                        break;
                printf ("\nEnter weight for this edge:");
                scanf ("%d",&wt);
                if ( origin > n || destin > n || origin<=0 || destin<=0)
                {
                        printf("\nInvalid edge!\n");
                        i--;
                }
                else
                        adj[origin][destin]=wt;
        }/*End of for*/
}/*End of create_graph()*/

void display()
{
        int i,j;
        for(i=1;i<=n;i++)
        {
                for(j=1;j<=n;j++)
                        printf("%3d",adj[i][j]);
                printf ("\n");
```

```
        }

}/*End of display()*/

int findpath(int s,int d,int path[MAX],int *sdist)
{
        struct node state[MAX];
        int i,min,count=0,current,newdist,u,v;
        *sdist=0;
        /* Make all nodes temporary */
        for(i=1;i<=n;i++)
        {
                state[i].predecessor=0;
                state[i].dist = infinity;
                state[i].status = TEMP;
        }

        /*Source node should be permanent*/
        state[s].predecessor=0;
        state[s].dist = 0;
        state[s].status = PERM;

        /*Starting from source node until destination is found*/
        current=s;
        while(current!=d)
        {
                for(i=1;i<=n;i++)
                {
                        /*Checks for adjacent temporary nodes */
                        if (adj[current][i] > 0 && state[i].status == TEMP)
                        {
                                newdist=state[current].dist + adj[current][i];
                                /*Checks for Relabeling*/
                                if ( newdist < state[i].dist )
                                {
                                        state[i].predecessor = current;
                                        state[i].dist = newdist;
                                }
                        }
                }/*End of for*/

                /*Search for temporary node with minimum distand make it current node*/
```

```
            min=infinity;
            current=0;
            for(i=1;i<=n;i++)
            {
                  if(state[i].status == TEMP && state[i].dist < min)
                  {
                        min = state[i].dist;
                        current=i;
                  }
            }/*End of for*/

            if(current==0) /*If Source or Sink node is isolated*/
                  return 0;
            state[current].status=PERM;
      }/*End of while*/

      /* Getting full path in array from destination to source*/
      while( current!=0 )
      {
            count++;
            path[count]=current;
            current=state[current].predecessor;
      }

      /*Getting distance from source to destination*/
      for(i=count;i>1;i—)
      {
            u=path[i];
            v=path[i-1];
            *sdist+= adj[u][v];
      }
      return (count);
}/*End of findpath()*/

void main()
{
      int i,j;
      int source,dest;
      int path[MAX];
      int shortdist,count;
      clrscr();
      create_graph();
```

```
    printf("\nThe adjacency matrix is:\n");
    display();
    getch();

    while(1)
    {
        clrscr();
        printf("\nEnter source node(0 to quit):");
        scanf("%d",&source);
        printf("\nEnter destination node(0 to quit):");
        scanf("%d",&dest);

        if(source==0 || dest==0)
            exit(1);

        count = findpath(source,dest,path,&shortdist);
        if(shortdist!=0)
        {
            printf("\nShortest distance is:%d\n", shortdist);
            printf("\nShortest Path is:");
            for(i=count;i>1;i—)
                printf("%d->",path[i]);
            printf("%d",path[i]);
            printf("\n");
        }
        else
        printf("\nThere is no path from source to destination node\n");
    }/*End of while*/
}/*End of main()*/
```

SELF REVIEW QUESTIONS

1. Define a graph. Explain depth first search of traversing ? [*MG - MAY 2004* (*BTech*)]
2. Write an algorithm for the depth first search of a graph? State its advantages and disadvantages? [*MG - MAY 2004* (*BTech*), *MG - NOV 2004* (*BTech*), *MG - MAY 2003* (*BTech*)]
3. Distinguish between adjacency matrix and adjacency list? [*MG - NOV 2004* (*BTech*)]
4. Explain the method of representing graphs by using matrices? [*MG - NOV 2002* (*BTech*)]
5. Explain the use of graph in data structures? [*MG - MAY 2000* (*BTech*)]
6. Explain the two methods of graph traversing? [*MG - MAY 2000* (*BTech*)]

7. Write an algorithm to find the shortest path between any two nodes of a given graph. Illustrate with an example. *[Calicut - APR 1995 (BTech), CUSAT - JUL 2002 (MCA)]*
8. Give the various representations of a graph.

   [ANNA - DEC 2004 (BE), Calicut - APR 1997 (BTech)

   ANNA - MAY 2004 (MCA)]
9. What is a spanning tree? Present algorithms to obtain the spanning trees for a graph. Illustrate them with examples. *[ANNA - MAY 2004 (BE), Calicut - APR 1997 (BTech)]*
10. Discuss the implementation of dfs and bfs graph traversals with suitable example.

    [ANNA - DEC 2004 (BE), CUSAT - NOV 2002 (BTech)

    KERALA - MAY 2002 (BTech), ANNA - DEC 2004 (BE)]
11. Explain the Dijkstra's algorithm for shortest path in a graph with suitable example.

    [CUSAT - NOV 2002 (BTech)]
12. Explain the following:

    (*a*) Graph (*b*) Multigraph (*c*) Digraph (*d*) Spanning tree.

    (*e*) Give anyone representations for a graph structure.

    (*f*) Explain what is a minimum spanning tree.

    (*g*) Explain Kruskal's algorithm. *[CUSAT - JUL 2002 (MCA)]*
13. Explain the Prim's algorithm to find minimal spanning tree for a graph.

    [ANNA - MAY 2004 (BE)]
14. Explain various application of the graph

    [KERALA - JUN 2004 (BTech), KERALA - DEC 2004 (BTech) ;]

    KERALA - DEC 2003 (BTech)]
15. Distinguish between DFS and BFS

    [KERALA - DEC 2002 (BTech), KERALA - DEC 2004 (BTech)
16. Explain complete Graph. *KERALA - DEC 2004 (BTech)]*
17. What are graphs? Give various representation of graphs?

    [KERALA - MAY 2003 (BTech)]
18. Define Directed graph and Undirected graph. *[KERALA - DEC 2002 (BTech)]*
19. What is the time required to determine the total number of edges in G ?

    [KERALA - DEC 2002 (BTech)]
20. Explain the various procedure for finding the shortest path in a network.

    [KERALA - DEC 2002 (BTech)]
21. What are graphs? Explain the applications of graphs. *[KERALA - MAY 2001 (BTech)]*

BIBLIOGRAPHY

1. Tremblay, Sorenson: "*An Introduction to Data Structures with Applications*," Second Edition, Tata McGraw-Hill.
2. R. S. Salaria: "*Data Structures and Algorithm*," Khanna Book Pub tions.
3. Drozdek: "*Data Structures and Algorithms in C++*," Vikas Publishing House.
4. "*Data Structures and Algorithms in 24 Hours*" SAMS teach yourself, Techmedia.
5. Lipschutz, "Data Structures," Tata McGraw-Hill.
6. Kruse, Tondo, Leung, "*Data Structures and programming Design in C*," Seciond Edition, Low Price Edition, Person Education Asia.
7. Aho, Hopcraft, Ullman, "*Data Structures and Algorithm*," Low Price Edition, Person Education Asia.
8. Lengsan, Augenstein, Tanenbaun, "*Data Structures Uisng C and C++*," Low Price Edition, Person Education Asia.
9. Ellis Horowitz, Sartaj Sahini, Dinesh Mehtha, "*Fundamentals of Data Structures in C++*," Galgotia Publications.
10. Glenn W. Rowe, "*Introduction to Data Structures and Algorithms with C++*," Pentice-Hall of Inida.
11. P.S. Deeshpande, O.G. Kakde, "*C & Data Structures*," Dreamtech Press.
12. Maria Litvin, Gary Litvin, "*Programming with C++ and Data Structures*," Vikas Publishing House.
13. E. BalaGurusmy, "*Programming in ANSI C*," Edition 2.1, Tata McGraw-Hill.
14. Ajay Kumar, "*Data structures for C programming*," Firewall Media.
15. Mark Allen Weiss, "*Data Structures and Algorithm analysis in C++*," Low Price Edition, Person Education Asia.
16. Sanjeev Safat, "*Data Structures with C and C++*," Khanna Book Publications.
17. R.B. Patel, M.M.S. Rautham, "*Expert Data Structures with C++*," Khanna Book Publications.
18. D. Knuth, "*The Art of Computer Programming: Sorting and Searching*", Second Edition, Addison-Wesley.

Index